THE BATTLE FOR THE MIND

THE
BATTLE
FOR THE
MIND

War and Peace in the
Era of Mass Communication

Gary S. Messinger

University of Massachusetts Press

Amherst and Boston

LC 2010045185
ISBN 978-1-55849-853-2 (paper); 852-5 (library cloth)

Designed by Dennis Anderson
Set in Janson Text with Gill Sans display by Westchester Book
Printed and bound by Thomson-Shore, Inc.

Library of Congress Cataloging-in-Publication Data

Messinger, Gary S., 1943–
The battle for the mind : war and peace in the era of mass communication /
Gary S. Messinger.
        p. cm.
Includes bibliographical references and index.
ISBN 978-1-55849-853-2 (paper : alk. paper)—
ISBN 978-1-55849-852-5 (library cloth : alk. paper)
1. Mass media and war—History.   2. Communication—Social aspects—History.
3. Communication—Political aspects—History.   4. Mass media and propaganda—History.
5. War and society—History.   6. Peace-building—History.
7. United States—History, Military.   8. Europe—History, Military.
9. International relations—History.
I. Title.
P96.W35M47 2011
303.6'6—dc22
        2010045185

British Library Cataloguing in Publication data are available.

To Eric
With Love

Contents

Preface

A Change in the Landscape

IMAGINE A war that involves no physical violence. The stakes are the ones typically addressed: territory, economic resources, control over an enemy population, defense of one's own population, and intangibles like honor, glory, freedom, adventure, fear, greed, revenge, and justice. There is pain. There are serious injuries. But not a single drop of blood is spilled. No one loses an arm or a leg. No bodies need to be buried. The war has a physical dimension, but only with regard to the equipment being used.

Now imagine a movement to end war permanently. It is successful. Like all efforts at peacemaking, it emphasizes nonphysical strategies such as bargaining, reminders of the consequences of war, and appeals to love, kindness, international order, fairness, and dignity. And yet this effort relies on the very same physical tools that the makers of war employ, and even persuades them to stop using those tools.

Neither of these scenarios is at present a reality. But in the early twenty-first century the two are closer to being realized than at any previous time in human history. In both cases the reason is the same: mass communication. For more than a century it has been remaking war and efforts to end war, and we are only just beginning to understand the full scope of the change.

Consider some of the things that have been happening around us in recent years. On the television screen we see images of war that affect us deeply and that seem to confront us in an almost endless stream, as planes crash into two towers in New York City, a political leader struts on the deck of an aircraft carrier in a pilot's jumpsuit, soldiers with dogs compel prisoners to perform obscene acts, and newscasters interview totemic dignitaries about "late-breaking developments" in long-running military conflicts. Other media affect us just as deeply. For example, at an Academy Awards ceremony in Hollywood, many of the films being honored are about war, even including one that is about a photograph, in this case an image of six marines and a flag that was once raised during a battle. The military itself uses media as a weapon, both for persuasion and for combat. Thus in the sky over a battlefield, an airplane drops a hundred thousand leaflets urging one side in the conflict to surrender to the other, and at a military press conference, a briefing officer awes reporters with the latest videotape of a laser-guided bombing mission shot by a camera mounted in the nose of a plane. Meanwhile, on the wall of a building on a university campus, a carefully designed poster seeks to persuade students to enlist in the military.

The enemy also exploits mass communication. On the screen of a laptop computer, a patron in a coffee bar views a clandestinely produced videotape of a bearded man who employs fear as a weapon by saying he intends to make war against all unbelievers. The public participates as, on a home computer, a boy enthusiastically plays a war game that was given to him by his father as a birthday present. We are reminded of the emotional scars that can be left by wars as a newspaper editorial urges necessary improvements in medical care for troops and asks why the predictable need to treat their psychological wounds was not adequately addressed before they were sent into battle. Peacemakers play their roles. In the mailbox of a house in a wealthy suburban neighborhood, a letter waits to be opened, asking for a cash donation to relieve the sufferings of refugees caught in a war on another continent. On a radio talk show, an interviewer converses with the head of a human rights group about a proposed peace conference. Even reputation becomes an element in the calculus of war and peace as, in an academic journal, an article about opinion polling shows how the most powerful nation in the world is losing the trust of other nations, not only because of that nation's conduct in a certain war in progress but also because of the country's failure to use mass communication effectively as a tool for garnering allies.

In these and numerous similar instances we are reminded of the remarkable degree to which war and efforts to end war have become intertwined with large-scale communication, and we can sense the growing importance of intangibles in matters that used to be determined more physically. We think of war as something fought with swords and guns and gas and bombs and planes and missiles, but gradually it has evolved to include propaganda campaigns and television at the battlefront and strategic use of the Internet. Peace initiatives are exhibiting similar changes. By their very nature they have always emphasized matters of the mind and spirit. But because of access to mass communication, they are now more able to circumvent and counter the material elements of armed conflict that have overwhelmed them in the past. War continues to create bloodshed and bodily injury and death. But more and more it is becoming a battle for the mind, with thoughts being employed to defeat other thoughts, and raising the possibility of spiritual rather than physical annihilation. Efforts to end war are changing as well. Almost as if in a contest with those who pursue war, peacemakers are becoming increasingly ingenious in using the tools of mass dissemination for persuasion.

If we wish to know where these long-term changes in the nature of war and peacemaking are likely to take us next, it is essential that we know where they came from and what seeds of the future are now being planted. The purpose of this book is to provide a cogent exploration of those matters, one that is useful as an introduction for general readers and as a framework for specialists.

I approach the problem historically. By going back to the years 1850–1914, we can see the roots of our present-day situation, as war began to be deeply affected by the industrialization of communication and the emergence of the phenomenon we have come to call mass society. The story then moves to 1914–1918 and the First World War, when mass communication officially became a weapon of military conflict. After that war, peacemakers and liberal constitutional states tried to use mass communication to prevent future conflicts. But nations ruled by dictators took control of their media and began another world war, in which every person's experience was even more deeply affected by the increasing power of mass communication. Then in the cold war that followed, from 1945 until 1991, mass communication became so important that for the first time in history, one could speak of a war that, despite episodes of physical violence, was fought primarily through symbols. The intermingling of physical and nonphysical warfare has continued since 1991, with a growing number of nation-states as well as nongovernmental groups throughout the world becoming involved. During these same years, often with a surprising degree of success, peacemakers have used mass communication to keep alive the possibility that at some point war in any form might no longer exist. We cannot say with certainty what will happen next. But it is clear that important clues to the future of war and peace lie in understanding how they have already been shaped by technologically amplified communication directed at billions of people.

Acknowledgments

THIS BOOK began as an article, "Truth Under Fire: War and the Media," in the Winter 2005 issue of the *New England Journal of Public Policy* (19, no. 2). I would like to thank the editor of the *Journal*, Padraig O'Malley, for inviting me to write the article, and Patricia Peterson, the managing editor, for her very helpful guidance.

At University of Massachusetts Press, Paul Wright invited me to submit a proposal, based on the article, for a full-length book. He capably managed the peer review of the proposal and provided me with the comments of the anonymous readers, who provided highly useful criticisms. Bruce Wilcox offered additional advice and guidance as the project proceeded.

I am grateful to my son, Eric, for his encouragement while this book was being written and for many instructive observations over the years regarding film and the ever-increasing role of the Internet.

I would also like to record my gratitude to my wife, Cleo. She has played a vital role in the creation of this book as editor, researcher, critic, loving companion, and fascinating conversationalist.

THE BATTLE FOR THE MIND

I WAR ENCOUNTERS MASS COMMUNICATION
1850–1914

IN JANUARY 1815 in southern Louisiana, an army of four thousand Americans defeated a British force of eight thousand at the Battle of New Orleans. This encounter effectively ended the War of 1812. Both sides displayed gallantry and strategic brilliance, and the battle helped to set an American general, Andrew Jackson, on the road to becoming president of his country. But the Battle of New Orleans is perhaps most significant because of its redundancy. Across the Atlantic, on December 24, 1814, British and American diplomats had already agreed on terms of peace. News of the treaty did not arrive in America until February.

In the early nineteenth century, delays in vital information were typical of warfare. Battlefield communication was extensive and energetic but dependent on a limited range of techniques, such as oratory, individual conversation, pennants, and notes transmitted by runners, horses, and ships. Some of the methods of communication were ingenious. Armies used carrier pigeons and, by the late eighteenth century, balloons. Even more resourceful was the military network of towers six to ten miles apart between Strasbourg and Paris that the French built in the 1790s. Men with telescopes sat on top of each structure ready to send and receive messages. Provided the weather was clear, soldiers sent messages in code based on the manipulation of semaphores consisting of three sections of wood alternately painted black and white. At night, messages were sent by lanterns. The towers were first used in 1794 to carry the official report of the French victory over Austria at Condé. By 1812 the semaphores had expanded to 220 stations serving most of France. In the 1830s similar networks were operating in Russia, England, and other European countries. But even in these cases, military communication failed to keep pace with military action.[1]

The ability to provide the general population with the latest information about warfare was also limited. London papers did not publish news of the great British naval victory at the Battle of Trafalgar, fought off the Atlantic coast of Spain on October 21, 1805, until November 7. News of the Duke of Wellington's decisive victory over Napoleon on June 18, 1815, at the Battle of Waterloo in Belgium was not published in London until June 24. Nor did generals typically consider the potential role of the press as a tool for persuading mass audiences. Realizing that popular appeal was essential if he wished to retain power, Napoleon vigorously used and controlled the press to serve his ends, anticipating the expanded role that journalism was to play later in the nineteenth century. But Napoleon was an exception. Most commanders were more like Wellington. He was somewhat sensitive to the importance of communication to promote mass appeal. He was capable of projecting great compassion for his troops, who in most cases were from the lower levels of society. And he regularly published reports on his campaigns in London's official newspaper, the *Gazette*. But Wellington did not extensively explore the use of strategic communication with the public, and he kept journalists away from his camp and the battlefield for fear that they would disclose secret information.[2]

Soon, however, indications began to appear of a revolution in communication that would greatly alter the conduct of war, the provision of news about war, and efforts to prevent war.

The Press Expands Its Reach

News sheets—that is, small leaflets containing fragmentary information—were a common feature of mass communication in the sixteenth century. Newspapers did not emerge until the seventeenth century. During the Thirty Years' War (1618–1648), printers turned a profit by selling broadsheets that offered the latest information on troop movements and battles won and lost in continental Europe. The *London Gazette*, possibly the world's first printed periodical, appeared in 1666. By the 1700s, newspapers proliferated in every Western country, offering not only news but also strongly worded opinions. The first daily newspaper in London was the *Daily Courant* (1702). A colonial imitator, the *New England Daily Courant*, appeared in Boston in 1721. The first daily newspaper in France was the *Journal de Paris*, founded in 1777. By the late 1700s, the power of newspapers was widely recognized. Governments sought to control printers and the circulation of ideas they made possible. The press became known as "the fourth estate," a power in society that expressed the voice of the people and was on a par with monarchs, parliaments, and organized religion.

During the nineteenth century, the press gradually extended its reach, propelled by broad transformations affecting all of society. In the 1830s the first railroads appeared. Soon thereafter machine-powered ships became more common. These improvements made it easier for people to engage in face-to-face exchange of information, and to transport recorded information such as books, magazines, and newspapers. Correspondence proliferated as well. The British invented the adhesive postage stamp in 1840, and expansion of the postal services followed, making it easier for reporters to transmit foreign news to their home offices and for readers with the necessary financial means to subscribe to papers printed in locales far from their home towns and cities.

Important transformations resulted from improved scientific understanding of the fundamental natural force of electromagnetism. In 1837 an American, Samuel F. B. Morse, invented the electrical telegraph. The first commercial telegraph in the United States—between Washington, D.C., and Baltimore—appeared in 1844. The British established the first commercial telegraph link in 1838, and they had a public telegraph service by 1851. Telegraphy not only increased the speed of communication but also made possible the founding of wire services, nation-based syndicates that operated on several continents to gather news and transmit it to papers in the home country and elsewhere. Wire services supplied foreign news to papers that could not afford their own international correspondents, and often provided a low-cost supplement to larger papers that could. Charles Havas led the way, establishing the world's first wire service, in France, in 1835. By 1850, through aggressive marketing, polished writing and editing, translation services, personal connections, use of carrier pigeons when telegraph lines were not available, and bribery of editors and government officials, Havas gained a near monopoly over distributing foreign news in France. Imitators quickly appeared in other countries, including the Associated Press in the United States (founded in 1848), Reuters in Britain (1849), and the Wolff agency in Germany (1849).

By far the most consequential transformations involved the use of printing presses. At the beginning of the nineteenth century, the Koenig steam press made possible the printing of a thousand newspapers per hour. The speed increased to ten thousand per hour by 1848 with the introduction of cylinders instead of flat beds. The linotype was invented in 1886; it made possible the mechanized, rapid setting of type for printing—a development as important as the invention of movable type by Gutenberg in 1453 to produce the first printed edition of the Bible in 1455. In 1880 the *New York Graphic* printed the first halftone photographs.

By the late nineteenth century, every industrialized nation had its powerful newspapers, like the *Morning Chronicle* (1789) and *The Times* in

Britain (founded in London as the *Daily Universal Register* in 1785), and the *New York Times* (founded in 1851) in the United States. Many of the papers served a combination of audiences. For example, in England the *Manchester Guardian* (founded in 1821) and the London *Financial Times* (founded in 1888), and in the United States the *Wall Street Journal* (founded in 1889), served business audiences but also provided articles for middle-class readers generally. The "confessional" press, made up of religiously oriented papers such as the *Christian Science Monitor* in the United States and *L'Osservatore Romano*, published by the Vatican, followed a similar strategy of building outward from a core constituency. There were also papers explicitly designed as the organs of mass political parties, such as *Vorwärts* (Forward), founded in 1884 as the organ of the German Socialist Party. These papers included serious opinion and reportage, although they were extremely slanted and written in highly dramatic prose to appeal to their politicized audiences.

Through most of the early and mid-nineteenth century, the press directed its reportage and commentary to upper- and upper-middle-class audiences. These were the groups that had the greatest power within governments, the greatest ability to buy printed matter, the highest levels of formal education, and the most extensive social connections with rulers and opinion leaders. But as the century progressed, the focus changed to include wider segments of the population. Because of industrialization, large numbers of people moved to cities, where they increased their earning power and gained greater access to education as well as participation in the political process, through voting and other means such as public demonstrations. City dwellers lived close together but did not always know one another personally. They sometimes came together in crowds focused on a fleeting interest they shared in common. They were the "masses."[3] The term began to supplant the older terms "the mob" and "the crowd." In its new uses the word evoked scientific descriptions of the packing together of elements in molecules as well as images of factory workers brought close together in their workplaces.

The large populations of cities had to develop ways of coming and going that preserved public order. They needed information to deal with the urban environment and to find meaning and reassurance in it. Some needs could be met by non-print means: parades, political canvassing, hand-painted announcements and illustrations on walls, or rabblerousing oratory in squares and at local assembly halls. But the most effective tool for providing information and meaning proved to be the press. Supplementing the elite press, newspapers, magazines, and other forms of print began to appear to serve middle- and working-class audiences. Publications of this kind, designed for very large sales, had almost nothing to say about culture and politics but instead concentrated on police news, sports, health, gossip, scandals, family matters, games, jobs, and neighborhoods. The first mass-circulation newspaper was probably the *New York Sun*, established in 1833, which sold for a penny. The first cheap newspaper in Britain was the *Daily Telegraph*, established in 1855.

In Britain the leader in popular journalism was Alfred Harmsworth, who later became Lord Northcliffe. Not well educated, but possessing a keen awareness of the average person's tastes, he undertook freelance writing of mass-market books in the 1880s, publishing titles such as *One Thousand Ways to Earn a Living* and *All about Our Railways*. In London in 1887, using his life savings, he founded *Answers*, a popular weekly that served up gossip, very simple summaries of the news, and urban trivia. Within five years the publication netted sales of more than 1 million copies a week. In 1896 he founded the *Daily Mail*, a half-penny morning newspaper that announced its purpose as providing "all the news in the smallest space." The paper gave great attention to news of the empire, while adopting a condescending or belligerent attitude toward other powers. Exciting articles reported on new fads like motoring and flying. The *Daily Mail* financed overseas expeditions to exotic lands. Special articles appealed to women. The paper gave prizes for skill in gardening and household management. Northcliffe's riches, combined with his purchase of *The Times* in 1908, confirmed his place in the establishment and symbolized the ever-growing reach of the popular press.[4]

The two most powerful mass-audience papers in the United States were Joseph Pulitzer's *World* in New York City (1883) and William Randolph Hearst's *New York Journal* (1895). Both published material of interest to educated readers but depended on sensationalism for their large sales. Crime stories were a staple. Pulitzer employed headlines like "Was He a Suicide?" and "Screaming for Mercy." He also exploited the device of the urban crusade, simultaneously battling for improvements in the lives of the working class and feeding the public appetite for titillating detail. In a heat wave in 1883 the *World* reported on the sufferings of immigrants in tenements in stories that carried headlines like "How Babies Are Baked" and "Burning Babies Fall from the Roof." Hearst began in California as publisher of the *San Francisco Examiner*, which he inherited from his father. Its marketing of crime and scandal earned him the money to buy the *Journal* in New York City. He and Pulitzer were soon conducting circulation wars as they drove the price of their papers ever lower, stole each other's reporters, and sought new ways of grabbing attention, from attacking each other's integrity to enlarging their Sunday supplements. In 1897 editors at other papers began calling the approach of the two press magnates "yellow kid journalism," noting the coincidence that both Pulitzer and Hearst published an eye-catching comic strip called "The Yellow Kid," which exploited the newly invented technique of color printing. Commentators quickly shortened this to "yellow journalism." The term became a synonym for sensationalism.[5]

Continental publishers repeated the British and American pattern of mass journalism. In 1890 the French popular newspaper *Le Petit Journal* attained a circulation of a million copies. It epitomized "the boulevard press," as observers collectively termed the sensational papers in France. In Paris, by 1913, total newspaper circulation reached 6 million copies daily; with a few popular papers such as *Le Petit Journal*, *Le Matin*, and *l'Echo de Paris* accounting for 5 million of the copies. In Germany, in the capital city of Berlin, between 1885 and 1913 total newspaper circulation doubled from approximately 8 million to 16 million. The *Berliner Lokal-Anzeiger* and the *Berliner Morgenpost* each sold over 200,000 copies a day after 1900. By the turn of the century, in greater Berlin, which by then had a population of 3.5 million, there were more than 1 million newspaper subscribers. Even a small country like Hungary had more than five hundred daily and weekly papers. The influence of journalism on such a vast scale was not merely cultural; it was also physically apparent. Every large city had its newsstands, kiosks, and railway shops where books, magazines, and newspapers were sold, and passers-by were attracted by the cries of newsboys and the sight of large-print headlines. In addition, nearly every large city had its own press district, like Fleet Street in London and the Zeitungsviertel (newspaper quarter) in Berlin, where one found the large clusters of buildings that housed the editorial and business offices and the massive machinery needed to produce the printed matter. Many newspapers had special addresses, for example, Printing House Square for *The Times* in London and Herald Square and Times Square in New York City. More than in any previous era, the "fourth estate" profoundly influenced the perceptions of every member of society.[6]

The Press Sells War

For all the publications, both middle class and lower class, war, the coming of war, and the aftermath of war were important topics. During the nineteenth century, newspaper editors and publishers increasingly realized that they could affect the way the state conducted war, because the press controlled many kinds of information and was able to persuade the citizenry of the desirability of one form of state conduct over another. Governments had their own sources of information and ways of communicating, but increasingly they turned to the privately owned press for assistance. Gradually assuming the role of the old royal court circulars, the press became the source of announcements about day-to-day government functions, such as appearances of the monarch, meeting times of legislatures, and opportunities to bid on contracts. The press provided daily information on the economy, and listed arrivals and departures of ships. All of these matters were useful to the state. The press also gathered foreign news that states found valuable, supplementing and sometimes even factually contradicting the information obtained by governments through their own channels, embassies, and military reconnaissance. These developments gave the press an ever-increasing presence in matters related to war and peace.[7]

By the time of the Crimean War (1854–1856), the press was transforming the way that audiences received their information about military conflict. William Howard Russell, the foreign correspondent for *The Times* of London, exemplified the process. An adventurer who had made his reputation covering British difficulties in Ireland, Russell went to the Crimea on assignment from the great mid-Victorian editor in chief of *The Times*, William Delane, who had a prescient understanding of the market value of war news. In his telegraph dispatches home, Russell immortalized the story of the gallant but foolhardy Charge of the Light Brigade, disclosed shocking inefficiencies in British supply operations, and called attention to the cruelly inadequate treatment of the wounded, inspiring Florence Nightingale to organize her celebrated expedition of nurses.

Russell also covered the American Civil War (1861–1865). By that time he and his paper were such a presence in foreign news reporting that, upon meeting him, President Abraham Lincoln commented: "Mr. Russell, I am very glad to make your acquaintance and to see you in this country. The London *Times* is one of the greatest powers in the world—in fact, I don't know anything which has much more power—except the Mississippi. I am glad to know you as its Minister."[8] In the North, however, Russell soon found himself unwelcome because he and his paper had adopted the side of the Confederacy. In any case, Russell was not part of a large international contingent. Only a few other foreign journals, including the *Daily Telegraph* and *Daily News* of London, sent correspondents to the United States. Most European papers simply lifted stories from the many American papers that were covering the conflict in detail.

American journalism during the Civil War proved to be of great international importance. More than ever before, the telegraph became a factor, not only militarily but also in terms of reportage, as the North cut lines to the South to paralyze Confederate communication and censor news. By the 1860s, the United States had fifty thousand miles of telegraph line in the eastern states. The cost of transmission was high, but newspapers discovered that they could profitably carry two or three pages of the latest information about battles, giving the public a growing sense of participation. Military censorship was extensive, the quality of analysis in most dispatches was poor, and factual errors were frequent, especially when papers relied on thousands of part-time amateur correspondents recruited to fill the burgeoning demand for news. This was nevertheless war reportage on a larger scale than ever before. Visual journalism supplemented print. Illustrated journals like *Harper's* and *Frank Leslie's Illustrated Weekly* followed the war closely. *Leslie's* had a staff of eighty artists and published over three thousand sketches and drawings of battles and other war scenes over the four years of the conflict. Photography, invented in 1827, also advanced coverage of war news. Newspapers did not yet have the capacity to print halftone blocks, so no photographs appeared there. But exhibitions brought the powerful visual work of Matthew Brady and other Civil War photographers to large audiences. Indirectly, the camera even altered the process of grieving. In newspapers and magazines, military authorities placed pen-and-ink sketches drawn from photographs of soldiers who had died in battle in the effort to locate survivors, as people attempted to learn the fate of friends and relatives by every available means.[9]

In succeeding years the relationship between the conduct of war and the reporting of war became ever more intense. Newspapers and magazines reported on military buildups, economic matters such as railway construction that might affect the war, battles and their aftermath, and the administration of territory won or lost in battle. When at liberty to do so, the press also published well-argued, often eloquent analysis and opinion about decision making related to war and peace. These reflections were sometimes at odds with government policies. For example, in France in 1898, in the Paris literary newspaper *L'Aurore* (The Dawn), the journalist Émile Zola published *J'Accuse*, a series of dramatic disclosures written in the form of an open letter to the president of France about the wrongful conviction and imprisonment of Alfred Dreyfus, a Jew who was a captain in the French army. The articles sparked sensational trials and a long-running debate about anti-Semitism, bribery, and inefficiency in the French military, and brought international embarrassment to France before Dreyfus was reinstated with full military honors in 1906. Similarly, in 1908, when the *Daily Telegraph* of London reported intemperate, belligerent remarks made by

Kaiser William II about the possibility of war, the information caused an escalation of international tensions and led to strong criticism of the emperor in German papers, even though official censorship was part of the German scene.[10]

Because it spoke to so many basic human appetites and needs, news of war generated large sales. Cheering for one's side in a war or a run-up to war offered the vicarious pleasures of sport and provided a sense of belonging and participation that helped to counter feelings of alienation experienced by city dwellers who found the urban environment puzzling or frustrating. News of war offered escape and adventure, and helped readers to determine whether armed conflicts far and near would affect their daily routines. Newspaper readers wanted maps of city life. The detailed and instantaneous information they received about the urban environment also created expectations for information about activity in the nation as a whole, and in the world beyond state borders, in so far as it impinged on local life—as war increasingly did. Newspapers published war-related maps, illustrations, detailed statistics, and eyewitness accounts. The people who controlled such information could exert great influence. In the United States, William Randolph Hearst helped to precipitate the Spanish-American War (1898) by publishing stories implicating Spain in the sabotage of the battleship USS *Maine*. Hearst's star correspondent Richard Harding Davis became famous for his reports on the war, such as his elegiac account "The Death of Rodriguez" and his stirring description of the charge of the "Rough Riders" volunteer cavalry up San Juan Hill (originally known as Kettle Hill), which helped the rising political star Theodore Roosevelt gain national fame.

In the Anglo-Boer War (1899–1902), battle reportage reached a new scale. The war was Britain's attempt to drive out or at least control Dutch farmers within its colonial territory and in neighboring areas, and to lessen the influence of Germans who supported the Boers. At one point there were some two hundred full-time journalists covering the conflict, a historic high. *The Times* alone had twenty. Throughout the war, the British populace eagerly bought up editions reporting the news from South Africa; men wearing sandwich boards displaying the latest headlines walked through city streets hawking the papers. By now readers believed that a paper's point of view could affect the outcome of a war. When the *Manchester Guardian* took a position against the conflict, police had to guard the building for several months to protect the staff from mobs gathered outside.[11] The young Winston Churchill greatly advanced his career through the exciting eyewitness accounts of action that he wrote for the British

Morning Post while serving as a lieutenant in the South African Light Horse.[12]

Tensions between military authorities and journalists covering the war, echoing the preceding century and heralding a theme of the century ahead, were much in evidence. Correspondents wore military-style uniforms and in other ways had links to the military. But most senior officers manifested the view that reporters were merely members of the lower class who deserved disdain. Access to telegraph lines and postal services was poor. The papers often treated rumors as fact, rushing to print any information that might beat the competition.[13] In spite of the large number of publications in Britain at the time and the vast resources at their disposal, the press performed poorly. British readers were used to accounts of easy victories in colonial wars against badly equipped native tribes. They could not accept the fact that the Boers were a skilled, well-equipped fighting force using guerrilla warfare. Instead of recording the facts they witnessed, which would have challenged British perceptions, reporters and newspaper proprietors pandered to readers' desires for reassurance. In 1900, when the Boers surrounded British troops in the small town of Mafeking and laid siege to it for 217 days, the press turned the engagement into an epic struggle. The Boers, usually skillful, did not manage the siege well. They allowed mail service and telegraph lines to stay open. Their bombardments of the town were ineffective and frequently off target, and many of their shells proved to be duds. The Boers mounted attacks but never with decisive force. The British general, Robert Baden-Powell, sent messages back to Britain that usually expressed the literal truth, but in a style and tone that conveyed stiff-upper-lip, plucky British demeanor. "One or two small field guns shelling the town. Nobody cares," he wrote in a typical dispatch. Readers at home chose to believe that the army was in a struggle to rival great imperial battles of the past. Five British war correspondents were in Mafeking during the siege. Their stories exploited the myth. On May 18, 1900, when news reached London that the Boers had lifted their siege, the population went crazy. Five days of street celebrations followed, involving larger crowds than the reactions to news of victory at the end of the First and Second World Wars.

At the same time, throughout the Boer War, British papers did almost nothing to make known the extent of the slaughter in battle: the British dead piled three deep in the trenches at the Battle of Spion Koop, or the decapitations of Boer fighters by British troops. They also neglected to report the mutiny of some three hundred Australian soldiers in reaction to British abuse, and the poor sanitation and medical care in British soldiers' camps. A British M.P., William Burdett-Coutts, learned of the conditions on his own while on a trip to South Africa. Of the 22,000 men lost by the British in the war, some 14,000 of the deaths were from sickness. British correspondents also neglected to report on the British "concentration camps" used by General Horatio Kitchener to control Boer women and children left homeless by the war, where heat, crowding, and disease produced astounding death rates: at Bloemfontein, for example, 383 deaths per thousand adults and 50 per thousand children. Instead, the British public first learned of mismanagement in the camps through a Quaker woman, Emily Hobhouse, who made a dramatic report to Parliament. The British papers did, however, frequently reprint stories of purported Boer atrocities, such as the massacres of pro-British civilians and the killing Boers who wanted to surrender.

Correspondents also failed to raise larger issues about the war. Only one, the American Richard Harding Davis, appears to have noticed that the tactic of guerrilla war used by the Boers called into question the longstanding assumption on the part of the British army that trenches and flanking movements were a reliable way to fight wars. He recalled the history of the American Revolution, when George Washington's troops had used surprise and small-group tactics to pick off British soldiers, who fought in large, slow-moving, rigid formations. In the peace settlement codified by the Treaty of Vereeniging in 1902, the British had to accept highly unfavorable terms. This left the public confused and distressed. The press had not kept the people well informed.[14]

Communication Becomes Cause

Even when no war was officially in progress, the press in the late nineteenth and early twentieth centuries played a large role in increasing tensions. In England, France, and Germany in the decade preceding the First World War, newspapers, magazines, and mass-circulation books were full of stories about the construction of new battleships, along with serialized, fictional, often frantic accounts of events. The various kinds of publications reinforced one another. For example, a newspaper story about disputes among diplomats might inspire an author to write a stage play or a short story or adventure novel, which in turn would be serialized in a magazine. Examples of this phenomenon in Britain were *The Battle of Dorking* by Sir George Tomkyns Chesney, first published in *Blackwood's Magazine* in 1871, in which a German invasion force takes over Britain; *A Conning Tower* by Hugh Arnold-Fraser, which appeared in *Murray's Magazine* in 1888; *The Great War in England in 1897* by William Le Queux, which first appeared as a serial in the periodical *Answers* during the war scare of 1893, going through five editions in its first four weeks in book form in 1894; *The Riddle of the Sands* by Erskine Childers, published in 1903, in which a secret fleet of armed tugboats built by the Germans and preparing to invade England is discovered in Holland; and *Danger!* by Sir Arthur Conan Doyle, which appeared in the *Strand Magazine* in July 1914. Other countries countered with their own "invasion" stories, like *Wehrlos zur See* (1910), in which the English and other enemies invade Germany; *La fin de la Prusse et le démembrement de l'Allemagne*, in which the French invade Germany; *Der Weltkrieg* (1904), by a German writer, in which Germany conquers most of western Europe; and *La guerra del 190–*, in which the French are thwarted in an attempt to invade Italy.[15]

It was now also easier to transfer anxiety from one person to another because of continuing expansion in the realm of communications technology. Telegraphy, which dated from the 1830s, became increasingly important by the end of the century, when cables laid on ocean floors transmitted strategic information as Western armies and navies fought for control of overseas colonies.[16] In 1897 Guglielmo Marconi patented the wireless telegraph. In 1901 the first wireless transatlantic telegraph transmission occurred, from England to Canada. The first wireless transmission of the human voice took place in 1902, after the invention of the telephone, patented in the United States in 1876 by Alexander Graham Bell. In 1878 the United States constructed the first telephone lines. In 1887 the first international telephone call was placed, between Paris and Brussels, via underwater phone cables. Another innovation in the realm of sound occurred in 1878 with invention of the phonograph. The typewriter was a factor in communication by 1873, when the Remington Acme Company massproduced the Sholes and Glidden mechanical typewriter. It gradually altered the way people corresponded, improved communication within and among large organizations, and enabled journalists to write their stories with greater speed and accuracy.

The many advances in technology had the capacity to bring people together constructively. But they were also becoming dysfunctional influences on decisions about going to war. This became fatefully clear in the summer of 1914. From the moment of the assassination of Archduke Franz Ferdinand of Austria by Serbian terrorists on June 28, 1914, to the last declarations of war on August 4, 1914, newly available structures of communication deeply affected the run-up to the Great War. Traditionally, diplomats and heads of state had assumed that except in the case of surprise attacks, time would be available, during periods of tension, to exchange offers and counteroffers and perhaps defuse crises instead of automatically going to war over a dispute. Deliberation, private conversation, and contemplation were vital elements of traditional diplomacy. During the several "war scares" of the early twentieth century, averting conflict by this approach had still been possible. But the thirty-seven days of the "July Crisis" did not have such an outcome. There were many reasons why war broke out in 1914, including nationalistic hatreds, lack of vision among political and military leaders, economic interests that hoped to profit from selling armaments and acquiring territory, and an increased belief that war would be the best way to resolve long-standing international disputes while diverting the attention of populations from domestic problems such as inequalities in the distribution of wealth and the exclusion of many groups from political power. Not the least important cause of the war, however, was the rapid pace of communication.

During the crisis, letters and personal emissaries played lesser roles than they had in past war scares. Telegrams, telephone calls, and press releases were the dominant means of official communication. During the final period of the crisis, from July 23 to August 4, the key negotiators exchanged five ultimatums by telegraph, each demanding an immediate reply. The French premier and the minister of foreign affairs, who was at sea, stayed in touch by radiogram. Tsar Nicholas and Kaiser Wilhelm II personally exchanged telegrams, but it did not occur to the Kaiser to use the telephone, which was available to him to keep in contact with his ministers. Meanwhile, all the generals exchanged communiqués, mobilizing their armies according to precise timetables set years before. Gradually the generals ordered troops into place and prepared to move them forward to battle positions by means of railroads, which operated according to minute-by-minute schedules, further increasing momentum and the sense of inevitability. Newspapers added to the tension. Whenever they received press releases or were able to penetrate the curtain of official negotiations, they published breathless stories and belligerent editorials, inflaming the population in ways that made it more difficult for political leaders to back down.

Events in the Russian capital, St. Petersburg, illustrate the large role of new communications technologies in the European nations. On July 29, under pressure from the chief of his general staff, the tsar gave an order for full mobilization of troops. The general in charge of mobilization secured the necessary signatures from the ministers of war, marine, and the interior, and then proceeded to the central telegraph office in St. Petersburg to send the tsar's order to all of the empire. While the operator was typing the communiqué in preparation for transmission, a messenger arrived in person and advised that the tsar wanted to change the order to one of partial mobilization. The tsar had had second thoughts in response to a personal telegram from the Kaiser, who hoped that Russia would not get involved in the dispute between Austria and Serbia. Then, later in the day, after deciding that he did not want to lose the offensive, the tsar reinstated the order for full mobilization and commanded that it be relayed by telephone to the telegraph office. As the general in charge of mobilization later recalled: "Every operator was sitting by his instrument waiting for the copy of the telegram in order to send to all the ends of the Russian Empire the momentous news of the calling up of the Russian people. A few minutes after six, while absolute stillness reigned in the room, all the instruments began at once to click. That was the beginning moment of the great epoch." In the next few hours, additional telegraph installations relayed the orders to regional and local military centers. The result was the mobilization of some 2 million men—the greatest simultaneous mobilization of military forces in history up to that time.[17]

2 MASS COMMUNICATION ENLISTS

1914–1918

In August 1914, when the conflict that we have come to call the First World War broke out, alert observers began to notice its strangeness. Compared to earlier military encounters among nations, the war was shocking in its level and scope of violence. And it was not the quick, limited war of movement that had been predicted, but an inconclusive, wearing struggle between armies dug into ditches, in which hundreds of thousands of lives might be lost in a matter of weeks to conquer a few miles of territory.

Most of the characteristics that made the war startling were physical: the piles of dead bodies, the enormous mobilizations of troops and supplies, the columns of refugees and wounded who straggled along the roadsides, and as time passed, the ever greater use of frightening weapons like the machine gun, poison gas, the tank, the submarine, the airplane, and the dirigible.

But one of the elements that made the war different was the spread of information through mass communication. It had by no means been absent in earlier conflicts. Now, however, it began to take on much more importance. In villages and small towns, to be sure, news of the war could be slow in arriving, and the major channel of communication might be a mayor's announcement in the public square. In every large city, however, crowds collected in front of telegraph offices and waited for the latest details about battles won and lost. At newsstands, on an almost hourly basis, fresh headlines conveyed up-to-the minute drama and suspense, and the photographs that could now be printed in newspapers and magazines brought an increased sense of reality and immediacy. Other visual media, such as posters, added to the psychological impact.

Analysts pondered the growing importance of these developments. In Vienna, for example, the prominent essayist and coffeehouse wit Karl Kraus declared that the most significant element in the new war was the mass press. "Through decades of practice," he asserted, "the newspaper reporter has brought to us that degree of impoverishment of the imagination which makes it possible for us to fight a war of annihilation against ourselves. . . . [He] can now implant in us the courage in the face of death which we need in order to rush off into battle." The chief cause of the war, Kraus opined, was "the mental self-mutilation of mankind through its press." This was because "acts not only produce reports, [but] reports are also responsible for actions."[1]

An English observer who held similar opinions was the prominent science fiction novelist and political essayist H. G. Wells. In September 1914, in a widely read pamphlet, Wells declared that the world was now involved in a conflict that was not caused primarily by material factors. People needed to understand that "all the realities of this War are things of the mind." The war resulted from thoughts, particularly those circulated by "idea mongers" who had used society's increasingly powerful resources of communication to persuade many Germans that their civilization was superior and should be imposed on others. Thus "the real task before mankind" was "quite beyond the business of the fighting line" and involved putting "better sense into the heads of these Germans, and therewith and thereby into the heads of humanity generally, and to end not simply a war, but the idea of war," wrote Wells, adding: "What printing and writing and talking have done, printing and writing and talking can undo. Let no man be fooled by bulk and matter. Rifles do but kill men, and fresh men are born to follow them. Our business is to kill ideas."[2]

In reaction to this kind of analysis, many contemporaries were skeptical. In 1914, when told that publicity and arguments directed at broad audiences might play a large role in the war, the British general Sir Henry Wilson countered, "The thing was to kill Germans."[3] Moreover, many intellectuals of the era, including George Bernard Shaw and Bertrand Russell, argued that the war was merely a struggle among selfish interests and should either be pursued frankly as such through the usual physical means or brought to an end by peace overtures and compromise regarding matters such as economic influence and control of weaponry. They had a point. But so did Wells.

Communication Becomes a Weapon

The developments noticed by Wells, Kraus, and others who thought along similar lines were traceable to many causes, including the continuing increase in sales of news publications that had started well before the war, and expansions in networks involving powerful tools of communication like the telegraph and the telephone. But there was also a highly significant new factor: a major expansion in the relationship between mass communication and government.

Prior to 1914, governments subsidized private groups to disseminate favorable national publicity to their imperial possessions. In addition, during the same period, in election campaigns political parties tried to influence the press. But government seldom became involved directly. Occasionally a government leader might provide information to the press in order to affect public opinion, as, for example, Lord Palmerston did in the mid-nineteenth century when he cleverly managed gossip and newspaper stories to whip up mass support for the Crimean War. All such instances were, however, on a relatively small scale—tied closely to a single figure and focused on specific tasks carried out by small staffs for small amounts of money, without much thought to long-term or massive involvement by government in similar tasks. Thus, in the decade before the First World War, the British Foreign Office still employed only a small group of people to deal with the press, and high-level diplomats, who were drawn mostly from the aristocracy, usually remained aloof from reporters, whom they saw as members of a lower class.[4] As the First World War progressed, however, officials became increasingly aware that control of information could mean the difference between victory and defeat. This had long been recognized, but now people began to see that if all the elements of persuasion were managed and coordinated, as only government was large enough to do, then a new and powerful tool—official propaganda—might take its place in a nation's arsenal.[5]

The term "propaganda" became widespread during the war but was never easy to define. It dated from the year 1622, when the Roman Catholic Church under Pope Gregory XV established a committee of cardinals known as Congregatio de Propaganda Fide, or College for the Propagation of the Faith, to assist and monitor missionary activity against Protestants during the Counter-Reformation. The word had primarily religious connotations until the time of the First World War. Many people also understood it simply as the process of disseminating or publicizing, which could be a morally neutral or benign activity, for example, in the circulation of a scientific report. Contemporaries used the term at times in its broad sense, as a synonym for "persuasion" of any kind, whether by legitimate or nefarious means—and usually referring to the attempt to win over a group rather than an individual. But with the development of mass communication as a weapon in the Great War, most observers came to view "propaganda" as the sinister manipulation of public opinion by official elites.

Many people also thought of private-sector forms of mass persuasion, like advertising or writing a newspaper editorial, as "propaganda." But increasingly the word evoked images of government activity.

Germany Hammers Its Message

Germany manifested an interest in the governmental manipulation of opinion very early. There was a strong belief among German military leaders, particularly in the army, in the doctrines of Karl von Clausewitz, who had argued, earlier in the nineteenth century as he observed the rise of the nation-state, that the morale of troops and civilian populations was becoming an important variable in the calculus of war. By the end of the nineteenth century, *Schrecklichkeit*—the calculated use of terror as part of a lightning-like disabling of the enemy designed to win quick victory and minimize casualties on both sides—was the concept that tied German military propaganda activities together. Mental disorientation was a means to this end. Almost from the first day of the Great War, the German army was circulating propaganda among enemy troops and civilian populations encountered as the army advanced. In Belgium, for example, in the early months of the war, the Germans airdropped leaflets, directed at enemy troops and civilians, claiming that resistance was futile. Soon the Germans were also printing and circulating attractive, well-written illustrated magazines directed at foreign audiences, such as the *Gazette des Ardennes*, the *Antwerpsche Tydingen*, and the *Gazet van Brussell* in Belgium and France and the *Glos Stolicy* in Warsaw. These publications reported on German victories and sought to sow dissent, for example, by claiming that the English were not paying their allies a fair share of finances for the war.[6]

The civil government's entry into propaganda also began well before the war. In the 1880s, to help gain greater control over German public opinion, Bismarck had set up a small press office (*Presseamt*) to monitor news coverage and release information favorable to the government. Such activities were expanded by Bismarck's successors. Upon the outbreak of hostilities in 1914, the civilian government was able quickly to issue pamphlets, brochures, doctored news stories, and other forms of propaganda that supplemented the military's efforts. The material was circulated throughout Europe, as well as in the United States, Latin America, and elsewhere. German civilian propaganda was greatly aided by the willingness of large numbers of writers and academic figures to endorse armed conflict. For example, ninety-three prominent thinkers, ranging from the playwright Gerhart Hauptmann to scientists such as Max Planck and Wilhelm Roentgen, issued a manifesto during the earliest days of the war to support their country's attack on Belgium, and the great novelist Thomas Mann also wrote in support of his country's actions.

But German efforts to manipulate opinion suffered from organizational confusion. The various offices responsible for propaganda production argued with one another over control, competed in the Reichstag for budgetary appropriations, and frequently conveyed contradictory messages to the public regarding such vital matters as how captured enemy soldiers would be treated, the extent of Germany's territorial aims, and the terms on which peace might be acceptable. An especially serious problem for the Germans was their failure to understand foreign audiences. There was a blustering quality to much of the German rhetoric—an overcompensation for the nation's recent arrival as an international power, as well as the consequence of life in an autocratic culture where debate was not always allowed, practice in listening to opposing points of view was limited, and the process of motivating audiences by persuasion rather than blunt assertion was not well understood.

This lack of subtlety led to numerous errors and lost opportunities. An example was the famous case of the English nurse Edith Cavell. In 1915 the German occupying army in Belgium executed her on charges of spying and aiding prisoners to escape. She may not have been directly engaged in espionage, but she did help some 250 men make their way out of enemy territory. Nevertheless, Allied governments scored a propaganda coup by orchestrating a worldwide campaign of condemnation against her execution. A short time later the French executed two German nurses in very similar circumstances, but nothing was said about this act in German newspapers or in propaganda directed to other nations. An American reporter in Berlin pointed out the discrepancy to the Prussian director of propaganda for the general staff, asking him why the Germans did not make propagandistic use of the event. The Prussian officer replied: "What? Protest? The French had a perfect right to shoot them."[7] This may have been true, but his response revealed an inability to understand how civilian audiences in other countries might be influenced by the use of such information.

The Germans were equally clumsy in their management of the propaganda office they set up in the United States. America did not initially enter the war. All the combatants sought to win its support. Germans at that time were the largest ethnic group in the United States. In Washington, D.C., the German ambassador, Count Bernstorff, was in regular discussions with Congress and the White House. At the same time, the Germans set up a secret office in New York City with a staff of twelve. The office was successful in circulating pamphlets favorable to the German cause and supplying newspapers with informative stories. But too much of what was produced was bombastic and showed no awareness of how to package messages so that they would be picked up by editors looking for human interest stories about weeping women and suffering children, portrayals of British villains, and sagas of German heroes with whom the large German populations in cities such as Milwaukee and St. Louis might identify. The German tendency to adopt a frontal posture when indirection would have been more effective is epitomized by one of the pamphlets financed by the New York office, which carried the title *Facts—War or no war, you have to face the facts either now or later.*[8]

The Germans, dimly sensing that they were not particularly good at propaganda addressed to other nations, ultimately came to believe that the superior persuasive strategies of enemy countries, especially Britain, were contributing to a crisis of morale at home, even more than other factors such as Germany's enormous loss of men in battle and the economic block-ade by the Allies, which helped bring about starvation, supply shortages, and eventually revolution against the Kaiser. In their postwar memoirs the two greatest German generals, Ludendorff and Hindenburg, voiced regret that they had not paid more attention to the new weapon. "Today words have become battles," Ludendorff declared. "The right words, battles won; the wrong words, battles lost." The generals ascribed almost magical power to propaganda. "We were hypnotized . . . as a rabbit by a snake," Luden-dorff stated. "In the neutral countries we were subject to a sort of moral blockade."[9]

Similarly, Chancellor Theobald von Bethmann Hollweg spoke of a "blockade of minds," although he thought it was the result of Germany's failure to offer a vision of a future world as inspiring as that of Britain, France, and America. He concluded that his country's characterizations of its policy as conveyed through propaganda were unconvincing. Germany claimed that it had a natural destiny to be the controlling power in central Europe, and that such an arrangement would lead to harmony and prosper-ity. This was a debatable proposition at best. In German propaganda it came across as a crude announcement to foreign audiences that German domination would be good for them. This message could not penetrate the enemy's wall of claims, which emphasized rescue, not domination.[10] Such a vision of liberation was ironic. Britain, France, Russia, and the United States all had sought for more than a century preceding the war to domi-nate weaker nations through imperialism. And yet there was some truth to the idea that they were seeking to protect the countries being attacked by the Central Powers and to create a postwar world of liberal constitutional states in which people could determine their own destinies. Germany's perplexity regarding the new weapon of propaganda would have very negative consequences after the war, when right-wing politicians, including Hitler, claimed that Germany had not been beaten in a fair fight and, in the next war, would need to outdo other nations in the use of mendacity.[11]

Some Fight from the Edge

The French experience with wartime propaganda was in some ways similar to that of the Germans. The late-nineteenth-century dictator Napoleon III was a demagogue who censored and bribed the press. Moreover, when the Great War began, French officials frequently squabbled among themselves over who would control press relations. A central office to work with reporters, the Maison de la Presse, was not established until early 1916. Nevertheless, the French were able to use media effectively because of centuries of experience coordinating the national bureaucracy, a patriotic willingness to cooperate for the protection of the nation they loved, and a cultural heritage that equipped them to understand diverse audiences and the art of motivating people by methods other than command. The result was strong loyalty to the war effort at home and considerable sympathy for the French cause in other nations. The French coordinated their official propaganda activity with the work of their intelligence agencies, and produced books, news dispatches, and pamphlets for distribution to neutral countries. To reach areas of France conquered by the Germans, the French government developed elaborate methods of distributing propaganda through the army and secret agents. German-speaking Alsatians loyal to France were particularly helpful. One result was *Die Feldpost*, a German-language newspaper produced by the French, which was circulated in Alsace and behind German lines. It catalogued German atrocities in Belgium and declared that the German use of submarines was barbaric.

One weakness in the French propaganda program was the relatively limited effort to develop mass persuasion for use against enemy troops. This probably resulted from skepticism among French generals. They gradually came to appreciate the importance of favorable newspaper coverage, which led them, for example, to craft more carefully the bulletins they provided to reporters during the siege of Verdun in 1916. But for the most part, the generals viewed tools such as propaganda leaflets as of marginal value and preferred to husband their limited resources while leaving the task of producing propaganda for the enemy to others.

Belgium, which had been almost completely overrun by the Germans in the first few days of the war, was a conquered nation that could not conduct propaganda from home except in a small part of its territory. The Belgians therefore relied on France and Britain for propaganda assistance. Italy was another example of a peripheral participant. Given the many factions jockeying for governmental power and the country's frequent switches in policy, it never crafted a coherent propaganda strategy, although it had some success, such as the respect it gained after publishing stunning photographic accounts of Italy's Alpine campaigns. Italy also played an important role in the campaign against Austria-Hungary, particularly in designing the highly effective propaganda leaflets in multiple languages directed at the Hapsburg monarchy's frontline troops.[12]

Britain Emphasizes Subtlety

By far the most sophisticated users of mass persuasion during the Great War were the British. Nongovernmental organs of communication quickly assumed much of the work of justifying the British cause, through newspaper editorials, magazine articles, books, pamphlets, and other material issued voluntarily by publishers. Even comic publications like *Punch*, the famous political humor magazine, were part of the conversation. Given Britain's great literary tradition and its longtime familiarity with political debate, discourse in support of the war often rose to high levels of eloquence. But newspapers and magazines also circulated hate speech and stories of atrocities committed by the enemy—for example, articles describing German factories that turned human bodies into glue—whether these could be documented or not.

Even in the face of such excesses, most public opinion leaders in Britain were eager to support the cause. In the first months of war, among the authors who expressed their willingness to assist the government were Arthur Conan Doyle, Arnold Bennett, J. M. Barrie, G. K. Chesterton, John Galsworthy, John Masefield, and Gilbert Murray. Owners of *The Times*, the *Daily News*, the *Pall Mall Gazette*, and the *Spectator*, among other publications, were equally willing to help. As the war went on, an increasing number of prominent writers and press lords served as directors of offices related to government publicity. Arnold Bennett was in charge of British official propaganda in France; H. G. Wells directed civilian propaganda against Germany late in the war; the press barons Lord Northcliffe and Lord Beaverbrook were each for a time involved in overseeing large governmental offices of propaganda; and the head of official propaganda midway through the war was the novelist John Buchan. The government co-opted the talents of these men but also wisely gave them latitude in directing official propaganda, and all were allowed to continue their private careers without being required to curtail their activities or sign special secrecy agreements. There was a gentlemanly aspect to it all, a chivalric quality in press-government relations that was not to be seen in later wars.[13]

Because so much propaganda was being produced voluntarily, the government decided to limit its role in media manipulation. This strategy was partly the reflection of the long-held idealistic British belief that government should exemplify civility. But the calculation also relieved political leaders of the need to decide how far to go in manipulating opinion. The state did go too far in censorship, particularly when it issued the Defence of the Realm Acts (1914 and later), which prohibited statements "by word of mouth or in writing or in any newspaper, periodical . . . or other printed publication" that were "intended or likely" to undermine loyalty to the king, troop recruitment, or confidence in the currency.[14] Such sweeping language made it easy to imprison highly vocal pacifists and radicals. The government imprisoned the great philosopher and mathematician Bertrand Russell for voicing objections to the war, and the police cruelly harassed the novelist D. H. Lawrence because of his antiwar comments. The government also exhibited highly dishonorable lapses in rhetorical restraint from time to time. For example, early in the war, Prime Minister Herbert Asquith persuaded the distinguished jurist James Bryce to issue an internationally publicized report that greatly exaggerated the extent of atrocities committed by the Germans and diverted attention from cruelties practiced by the British in Ireland.[15] Similarly, later in the war, the government paid large sums of money to reprint and disseminate vicious cartoons drawn by the famous Dutch artist Louis Raemakers that purported to be true records of German violence toward civilians.[16]

The British experienced great success in the use of propaganda scattered behind enemy lines by airplanes or timed-release balloons. Generals on both sides were so perplexed and frightened by this new weapon of war that they frequently ordered their men to refrain from reading the propaganda or face execution. The Germans were the first to make use of airdropped material when they scattered leaflets over Belgium and France in September 1914. British military leaders, mired in concepts of strategy inherited from previous wars, were slow to see the potential of this new weapon. But by 1915, after urgings from Lord Northcliffe and powerful officers in military intelligence, British distributions by air became extensive, involving not only leaflets but also newssheets such as *Le Courrier de l'Aire*, which was written by officers of the military intelligence office M.I.7.B and translated for audiences in Belgium and France. Airdrops expanded even further when the United States entered the war in 1918 and assisted with the operation. In

June and July 1918, for example, the British dropped over 3 million leaflets behind German lines.

The most common type of airdropped propaganda used by the Allies, and the most successful, was the leaflet designated as a safe-conduct pass for enemy soldiers, which described recent enemy defeats in battle, catalogued sufferings on the home front, and encouraged its reader to desert, with a promise of fair treatment including repatriation after the war. Many leaflets sought to exploit controversies in the enemy's home society, for example, the discontent among subject nationalities in places like Ukraine and Hungary, and the anger among low-paid soldiers at rich industrialists who were not in combat. As the war dragged on and supply shortages in Germany and Austria became a major problem, propaganda leaflets told soldiers that they could avoid starvation and get adequate medical care by laying down their arms.

Another form of mass communication exploited by the British, in this case on the home front, was advertising. By the time of the Great War, commercial advertising was a centuries-old element of society, sufficiently extensive to give rise to professional agencies. Wartime advertising was simultaneously a sincere attempt to serve a patriotic cause, a form of war profiteering, and a debasing simplification of the concept of citizenship. In addition, advertising increased the tendency already visible in political campaigns to reduce discussion of issues to slogans, and it promoted an assumption that participation in the political process was merely a matter of purchasing something. Wartime advertising was ubiquitous. In Britain there were advertisements for "Lifebuoy Soap: the Royal Disinfectant," showing it in use in a military hospital; for the kitchen cleanser Vim, portrayed as a motorized gun; and for Gibbs dentifrice, which was used, so the ad claimed, by an airman who found it to be "as fragrant as the lofty air." The Michelin company placed an ad in 1915 in the *Illustrated London News* showing one of its tires, described as "The Rib of Life," being supplied to a disabled military ambulance.[17]

Advertising was soon mobilized for official purposes. Before the war, governmental use of advertising focused on functional matters, like announcing new bond issues or opportunities to bid on contracts. This was probably because of the high rates charged by newspapers, which found the government's ads so boring as to risk lowering their readership. With the coming of war, however, advertising became a tool for stimulating military recruitment without resort to conscription, which did not begin until 1916. The War Office took out quarter-page and full-page recruitment ads, especially in the colder months, when, it was reasoned, unemployed men would be most concerned about finding a paying job. Concluding that the ads were a major cause of increased enlistments, the War Office took out more ads and established an advisory committee of advertising agents. For their assistance during the war, several of the agents received knighthoods.

The British made extensive efforts to recruit the United States to the Allied cause. Such support could not be taken for granted. Britain had invaded America in the War of 1812 and sided with the South in the American Civil War, and there were boundary and trade disputes between the two countries in the years thereafter. There were large German populations in America, and in sectors such as science and higher education there was high respect among Americans for German achievements. Britain countered such factors through high-level diplomatic conversations in London and Washington, D.C., and with speaking tours and the circulation of articles, pamphlets, and books by authors well known in America, such as the novelist and poet John Masefield and the historian G. M. Trevelyan.

Within a few months of the outbreak of war in 1914, the British established a secret office in London to coordinate propaganda in the United States. It was directed by a Canadian, Sir Gilbert Parker, who had become rich as the author of best-selling novels about the Canadian frontier. He was loyal to the British cause and knew America well. Parker undertook regular detailed analyses of the American press and put together a list of several thousand influential Americans, to whom he regularly sent published materials with cloying, prestigiously printed enclosure cards that played on the American desire for status by association with the English aristocracy. Sometimes the cards carried Parker's name; sometimes they were from a prominent person such as a member of the House of Lords or a British author well known in elite circles in America, like the novelists Rudyard Kipling, John Galsworthy, and John Buchan (whose thriller *The 39 Steps* had appeared in 1915) or the classicist Gilbert Murray. In spite of some setbacks, including the inability to blunt outrage against the Allied blockade of neutral and enemy shipping, which Americans saw as starving noncombatants, Parker was enormously successful. He did not even feel the need to journey to the United States until January 1917, when he went there to intensify efforts to bring the Americans into the war. His reward came in April 1917, when the United States finally entered the conflict as an "associated power" on the side of the Allies. Parker's work became public after the war and was the subject of irritated commentary in the American press. In 1938 the memory of Parker's activities was one of the factors leading to passage in the United States of the Foreign Agents Registration Act, in response to the presence by then of a large, clandestine Nazi movement in America.[18]

An important example of the role of mass communication in the Great War involves the clever use by the British of an incident known as the Zimmerman telegram. After the Germans resumed unrestricted submarine attacks in February 1917, the United States broke off diplomatic relations with Germany. Soon after, British code breakers intercepted a telegram from German foreign minister Arthur Zimmerman to the government of Mexico, urging Mexico to ally with Germany and offering the return of Texas, New Mexico, and Arizona if the United States was defeated. The British unofficially leaked the text of the telegram to the Associated Press, and the resulting tidal wave of news reports and public outrage pushed the Americans much more strongly in the direction of armed conflict. In March 1917 the sinking of three American ships by German U-boats further aroused public opinion, moving President Woodrow Wilson to go to Congress for the declaration of war made on April 6.[19]

America Democratizes Propaganda

Even before U.S. entry, the Great War was a subject of major news coverage in the United States. By 1915 some five hundred American correspondents were in Europe representing newspapers, magazines, press associations and syndicates. Americans felt a common anxiety about the possibility of Europe being dominated by one nation. Major crises, such as the German sinking of the English Cunard passenger liner *Lusitania*, heightened the perceived threat.[20]

Before 1917 the United States was not generating propaganda. It was, instead, a theater for the propaganda struggle among nations already engaged in the war. A week after war was declared, President Wilson created a euphemistically named Committee on Public Information (CPI), drawing from British and French models for a central coordinating agency, and responsible for providing factual information about the war, guiding government propaganda, and working with the press. Wilson appointed George Creel, a prominent, hardworking newspaper reporter with liberal political sympathies and experience in New York, Kansas City, and Denver, to direct the CPI. By war's end, Creel was able to involve more than 150,000 Americans directly in the committee's work, some for pay but most as volunteers. In May 1917 Creel began publishing an *Official Bulletin* that provided government news releases in newspaper format; daily circulation of the *Bulletin* eventually reached 118,000. The CPI also circulated a weekly digest of war news for rural papers and provided all publishers with still photographs, copper photographic plates, and paper mats to aid printing preparation.

Beyond mere dissemination and the resources of his own staff, Creel also involved publicists, advertising agents, painters, sculptors, illustrators, cartoonists, photographers, writers, and moviemakers in causes like promoting military enlistment, ensuring the cooperation of industrial leaders, and conserving food. The CPI assisted the Red Cross in fund-raising campaigns and produced inspirational posters created by prominent artists of the time such as Charles Dana Gibson and James Montgomery Flagg. Hollywood stars like Douglas Fairbanks and Mary Pickford appeared at Liberty Bond sales events organized through Creel's efforts. Creel established a national bureau of talented speakers, dubbed "Four Minute Men," who eventually numbered 75,000. They toured the nation delivering fiery presentations. The CPI mobilized college and university professors through a special division of pamphleteering headed by the historian Guy Stanton Ford of the University of Minnesota. The division produced a *War Cyclopedia* and 75 million pieces of printed materials that were distributed not only in the United States but also in Europe, even behind enemy lines. To assist him in planning, Creel established a Psychological Strategy Board, an early step toward involving the social sciences in mass persuasion, even though most members of the board were historians and did not extensively represent other branches of the discipline.

While the CPI concentrated most of its work on the United States, the committee also was active in Europe. Its Foreign Section, established in the fall of 1917, operated a Wireless and Cables Service, which circulated news about American activities; a Foreign Press Bureau, which produced longer stories and magazine-style articles distributed by mail; and a Foreign Film Service which distributed American productions in European countries, including Norway, Sweden, and Holland, as channels became available. In battlefield areas the CPI worked with the U.S. Military Intelligence Branch on leaflet drops, analysis of civilian opinion, and the smuggling of books and pamphlets into Germany, among other activities.

Journals for American soldiers emerged, on the model of the "trench newspapers" which had appeared among military forces of the other belligerent nations. An eight-page American paper, *Stars and Stripes*, began publication in Paris in February 1918 and met with great approval among fighting forces. The chief editor was Harold Ross, who later attained fame as editor of the *New Yorker*. Other outstanding journalists, including Grantland Rice and Alexander Woollcott, also wrote for the paper.

The CPI quickly realized that one of its most effective weapons of persuasion was the oratory of President Wilson, who declared that the war was about idealistic objectives such as securing freedom for subjugated nationalities, ensuring openness in the making of treaties, and establishing a fair and merciful peace. One of Creel's assistants, the newsman Edgar G. Sisson, suggested that the president's speeches be condensed into a summary for newspapers abroad. The suggestion prompted Wilson to compose his "Fourteen Points," which greatly added to his fame and the frenzied mass approval with which he was welcomed in Europe after the war. The initiative radiated idealism. It was also a masterly use of the latest techniques of large-scale communication. Wilson packaged his pronouncements as a series of "points" to accord with the belief of advertisers that brief, arresting statements were most likely to capture the attention of modern audiences.

In spite of his idealistic rhetoric, Wilson showed very little tolerance for views opposed to his during the war. Congress was equally suspicious of dissent. The Espionage Act of June 15, 1917, specified fines and imprisonment for anyone convicted of willfully making false statements or issuing false reports intended to interfere with the war effort, promote disloyalty, or obstruct military recruitment. The act gave the postmaster general greatly increased powers to screen the mails, much reducing the expression of dissenting opinion in the American press.

Enforcement was particularly harsh against socialist publications owing to fears in capitalist countries after the 1917 Bolshevik takeover in Russia, which raised the possibility of violent worldwide revolution by workers and the abolition of all private ownership of property. Few Americans understood the difference between communism on the Bolshevik model and more moderate socialism, which concentrated on recognition of labor unions, increased public works, and ownership of only a few basic industries by the government. The government banned the journal *American Socialist* from the mails immediately, and soon thereafter *Solidarity*, the magazine of the International Workers of the World labor union. The moderate socialist publication *The Masses*, edited by the widely respected Max Eastman, was suppressed for publishing four antiwar cartoons and a poem defending radical politics. (The courts dismissed charges against the magazine in 1919.) Some seventy-five periodicals either lost their mailing privileges during the first year the Espionage Act was in effect or had to agree to avoid nearly all discussion of the war. Public intimidation was also widespread. Many groups boycotted William Randolph Hearst's newspapers, which remained skeptical of U.S. participation in the war; Hearst was often hanged in effigy. Oswald Garrison Villard, who defended civil liberties and argued against involvement in the war, had to sell his paper, the *New York Evening Post*, in 1918 because of declining sales.

Two additional laws further stifled public discourse. The Trading with the Enemy Act of October 1917 gave the government power to censor all communications going in or out of the United States and to demand translations of foreign-language publications. The intent was to handicap activities of the German-language press in the United States. The Sedition Act of May 1918 increased the reach of the earlier Espionage Act by forbidding publication of any statement that was "disloyal, profane, scurrilous or abusive" regarding the United States, the Constitution, the flag, or the armed forces. This wording was so vague as to give President Wilson nearly unlimited powers over public opinion. Mindful of the political problems that President John Adams had created for himself by clumsy use of the Sedition Act of 1798, which had banned as treason all criticism of the president or Congress, resulting in the arrest of several newspaper editors, Wilson was careful and measured in the way he used his powers of censorship. But he was draconian in his treatment of pro-German minorities and left-wing groups. Former president Theodore Roosevelt and Senator Robert La Follette of Wisconsin were among the mainstream politicians who could, in theory, have been prosecuted under the provisions of all the censorship laws in effect during the war. But Wilson directed his efforts elsewhere. A notorious case involved Eugene V. Debs, the four-time Socialist Party candidate for president. In June 1918, at a Socialist Party meeting, Debs declared that the Allies were "out for plunder" and defended the Bolshevik Revolution in Russia. The authorities jailed him for violating the Espionage and Sedition Acts, and the Supreme Court upheld his sentence unanimously. (Debs campaigned for president in 1920 from federal prison. President Harding pardoned him that same year.)[21]

As in Britain, commercial advertising quickly became entwined with official wartime propaganda. George Creel, the director of the Committee on Public Information, titled his postwar memoir *How We Advertised America*. He described his job as "a plain publicity proposition, a vast enterprise in salesmanship, the world's greatest adventure in advertising." One would have hoped for deeper reflection from the head of the nation's chief agency of public communication. The U.S. military cooperated with business to advertise products deemed important for morale. General "Black Jack" Pershing gave permission for the tobacco industry to quote him as saying: "You ask me what we need to win this war. I answer tobacco as much as bullets." On the sides of the boxcars that shipped their cigarettes to American seaports, tobacco companies painted slogans like "Roll Your Own into Berlin" and "When Our Boys Light Up the Huns Will Light Out." Other products also benefited from government cooperation. To encourage hygiene and personal pride, the War Department purchased 3.5 million razors and 32 million blades from the Gillette Company for free distribution to the troops. Both the War Department and Gillette knew that such publicity would stimulate consumer demand for Gillette products after the war.[22]

Images Supplement Words

Throughout the First World War the printed word was the most important medium of communication in the battle to win loyalties and affect morale. But the war also stimulated limited use of other media. For example, the Allies used hand-operated gramophones in battles against the Austro-Hungarian armies. Loudly playing recordings of the national anthems of the many discontented ethnic groups under Hapsburg rule, they frequently prompted soldiers from these nationalities to desert.[23]

Image-oriented media were the most powerful supplements to the word. Especially important was the growing role of motion pictures. In 1896 in France the Lumière brothers launched the motion picture camera, which began to play a limited part in war publicity soon thereafter. In 1898, in the Spanish-American War, the Vitagraph company made a four-minute film that included scenes of a Spanish flag being replaced by an American flag and burial of the dead from the battleship USS *Maine* in Arlington National Cemetery. Thomas Edison made a short film depicting fictional reenactments of war scenes, which was screened to an accompaniment of live patriotic music.[24] During the Anglo-Boer War the new medium of motion pictures added to the misrepresentation already widespread in the press. A film produced and circulated by the British—one of the first newsreels ever made—showed Boers firing on a Red Cross hospital tent at the front while British medical personnel courageously tried to treat a wounded soldier. Unknown to the audiences, the film was a dramatization produced in a London suburb—with informal encouragement, one suspects, from the military.

In 1907 the French newsreel production company Pathé began operations. In 1911 the first film studio opened in Hollywood, followed in 1912 by two U.S. film companies, Fox and Universal. By the time of the Great War, because of the rapid growth of the motion picture industry, all the powers were experimenting with the use of films. On the Allied side, the first official production was *Britain Prepared* (1915), which showed soldiers in training and home front scenes emphasizing loyalty and spirit. Several scenes featured the Royal Navy. These unfailingly brought British audiences to their feet in wild cheering, and made contemporaries very interested in the potential of the moving image to touch the deepest chords of a nation's sensibility. A later production, *The Battle of the Somme* (1916), included actual footage of British fighting men in battle, although the public was unaware at the time that some of the scenes had been staged. *The Battle of the Somme* was the first instance of a war movie showing images of the dead. At a time when popular sensibilities were still largely Victorian, these scenes ignited a national debate on whether it was proper to film such things.[25]

After viewing British productions, German generals vigorously supported the making of their own films, strongly believing in their value as tools to build morale among fighting men. The Germans produced documentaries that made their case powerfully, foreshadowing that country's postwar prominence in cinema. These included *Behind the Fighting Lines of the German Army* (1915), *Germany on the Firing Line* (1916), *Germany and Its Armies of Today* (1917), and *On the Austro-German Battlefronts* (1917).[26]

Even before the United States entered the war in 1917, the American film industry had already discovered the business potential of the conflict. Examples of early documentary productions by American commercial producers include *European Armies in Action* (1915) and *History of the World's Greatest War in Motion Pictures* (1915), produced by William Randolph Hearst and his General Film Company. Once the United States entered the war, production increased greatly in response to audience demand and the urgings of the Committee on Public Information. Examples of the many documentary titles include *Our Fighting Forces* (1917), *America's Merchant Marine* (1917), *Saving the Food of a Nation* (1917), *The Salvation Army on the Job* (1918), and *Rebuilding Broken Bodies* (1919). Along with these commercial films, the CPI directly produced many documentary titles on topics such as troop training, ambulance work, and shipbuilding, most of which were uneven in quality and did not interest audiences. Soon the committee turned to producing feature-length documentary films like *Pershing's Crusaders* (1918) and *Under Four Flags* (1918), which were more successful.[27]

Hollywood, meanwhile, was discovering the potential of feature-length fictional films with wartime settings. In 1917 the new Paramount studio produced *The Secret Game* (1917), which starred Sessue Hayakawa as a Japanese agent helping the United States foil German spies in the Pacific. D. W. Griffith took his production crew to France in 1917 to make *Hearts of the World*, starring Lillian Gish as a civilian mistreated by evil Germans. It was credited with greatly increasing military enlistment in the United States. Another film that drew large audiences was *Shoulder Arms* (1918), starring Charlie Chaplin, which was released a month before the end of the war.[28]

Still photographs, paintings, and drawings proved to be highly effective propaganda during the war, particularly in traveling exhibitions or prestigiously printed publications that appealed to upper-class audiences.[29] The quantity and quality of still photographs were remarkable, given the obstacles of censorship at and near the front and the difficulty of carrying photographic equipment, which was large and cumbersome. For reaching broad audiences, the most powerful visual medium by far was the poster. Even today, many decades later, the first image that comes to mind for many people upon mention of the First World War is the military recruiting poster that showed Kitchener (or Uncle Sam in the United States) soberly staring out and pointing at the viewer, with the words "I want you" below. Another famous example is the poster that shows a young father sitting comfortably at home in civilian clothes with his daughter next to him asking, "What did you do in the war, Daddy?"

A striking example of the adaptation of visual communication was the picture postcard. Printing companies had been manufacturing postcards for several decades before 1914, usually with drawings and photographs of interest to tourists. Once the war began, the companies used new themes to motivate purchasers. For example, one postcard showed a photograph of four uniformed men from the Allied nations, posed in the "living tableau" style popular at the time, each with his flag, exhorting all to fight for victory. A German postcard carried the color illustration of a wife at home in her parlor dreaming of her man at the front. In France, where social codes were less Victorian, the postcards were often sexual. For example, one carried the photograph of a man and woman in bed, mostly covered by sheets and blankets, smiling affectionately at each other, with a caption reading, "Tender moments . . . that I shall remember always." The theme of another French postcard was that German artillery could not rise to the challenge.[30]

Myth Dominates Content

In the realm of civilian propaganda, the Great War may have been the last in which Victorian-style rhetoric played a very large role. Many—perhaps most—of the highly articulate people involved in directing the war were the products of an educational system that emphasized grounding in literature and practice in platform oratory as the keys to effective communication.[31] The growth of mass communication had begun to chip away at this tradition. Newspaper reporters were beginning to write in ways that catered to the more rapid pace of city life and the short attention spans of many readers, and nonverbal forms of discourse, such as film and the poster, were undermining the primacy of the word. Nevertheless, a strong emphasis on chains of logic and citation of evidence and example was still widespread. Hence the war stimulated an outpouring of hundreds of thousands of books, pamphlets, and articles in newspapers and magazines that almost seemed to be derived from a legalistic, declamatory template, with titles like *Why* _____ (insert name of country) *Is at War*, _____*'s* (insert country) *Case for War*, and *The Crimes of* _____ (insert country). Examples of actual titles (in this case British pamphlets) included *What Europe Owes to Belgium* (1914), by the academic H. W. C. Davis; *The Truth about German Atrocities* (1915), issued by the Parliamentary Recruiting Committee; and *The Purpose of War: An Address Delivered for the Fight for Right Movement* (1916), by the novelist John Buchan. In 1914, in the same vein, all the combatants assembled hefty collections of official prewar diplomatic communiqués and treaties, published under titles like the *German White Book*, the *Russian Orange Book*, and the *Belgian Grey Book*, to support each nation's case for going to war. These approaches to the challenges of wartime communication were effective within the limited circles to which they were addressed.

Throughout the Great War, however, most of the large-scale initiatives in official propaganda, private-sector communication, and news reportage departed radically from nineteenth-century styles. Discourse still relied on literary traditions and other aspects of prewar culture like those in painting and opera. But mass persuasion now focused more aggressively on, and almost isolated for attention, the *symbols* that united the citizens of each nation, exploiting touchstones that propagandists knew were important. The United States emphasized the theme of American innocence: its finest young men were making the journey "over there" to rescue a sinful Europe and defend the goddess who was enshrined in the nation's most famous statue. The French emphasized protection of their superior civilization and "la belle France." Dominant themes in French public discourse were the religious significance of the war, the need to avenge the German victory over France in 1871, and the call to high and rather abstract ideals such as justice and freedom from tyranny, as articulated in the world's most powerful national anthem. Germany portrayed itself as the victim of all the nations that were conspiring against it, the bringer of its superior *Kultur*—particularly its great science, literature, music, and philosophy—and exploited stereotypes of sinful French and unscrupulous English commercial travelers that were already widespread. Propagandists elaborated age-old proven techniques of wartime inspiration, keying off great national epics and sagas to justify wartime conduct as the acting out of the latest chapter in an ancient, primal drama of survival and morality. Wartime discourse of this kind is perhaps best described as mythic. That does not necessarily mean it was untrue. Myths can embody a nation's most admirable values. But when they descend to the level of negative stereotypes, myths do great long-term psychological harm.

The use of myths is especially evident in posters from the war years. These came from a variety of sources, including private charities, corporate advertisers, quasi-governmental organizations like the Parliamentary Recruiting Committee in Britain, and governments themselves. One striking fact, however, is the very frequent reliance, regardless of which organization produced the poster, on allusions to familiar myth-related symbols. For example, a U.S. poster of 1917–18 showed a beautiful young woman in medieval armor holding a sword, with the words "Joan of Arc Saved France. Women of America Save Your Country. Buy War Savings Stamps." Another American poster, issued in 1918, carried the caption "The Greatest Mother in the World." Exploiting visual allusions to Mary the Mother of Jesus, it showed a woman in biblical dress, with a cross on her headband, holding a wounded soldier in her arms. The poster called for donations in response to the "Red Cross Christmas Roll Call." In contrast to these relatively high-minded appeals, many posters trafficked in hate and stereotypes. A relatively mild example was a German poster issued in 1915 that showed the goddess Germania carrying a triumphal banner with the words "Einigkeit Macht Stark" (Unity Brings Strength) and a placard proclaiming "Gott mit Uns" (God with Us) as she stands on top of a vanquished Russian bear, a selfish British pig, and a crowing French cock. An American poster of 1918, issued to stimulate sales of war bonds, carried the heading "Remember Belgium" above a menacing silhouette of a pike-helmeted German soldier dragging a small girl away to an unspecified but easily imaginable fate. A British poster issued in 1914 was captioned "Once a German Always a German." It showed a German soldier shooting a nurse and bayoneting a baby, and then the same soldier after the war, dressed in a business suit, cordially touring factories. It warned against dealing with "this Man, who has shelled Churches, Hospitals and Open Boats at Sea . . . who after the War will want to sell you his German Goods."[32] Such shabby uses of myth added to the very high spiritual cost of the war.

Reporters Struggle

Tensions between truth and falsehood also challenged journalists. In the First World War, as in the Anglo-Boer War of 1899–1902, limitations in the process of news gathering were evident. An example was the way British news organizations came to learn of the German attack on Belgium. An American freelance reporter, Granville Fortescue, was living in Belgium near the German border in 1914. In early August, after hearing rumors of war, he sent a telegram to the *Daily Telegraph* in London inviting the paper to hire him. There was no reply. Fortescue went to Brussels hoping to learn what was happening from the American embassy. There he overheard a conversation between the Flemish doorman and his brother, who was saying that German troops on motorcycles were already crossing the eastern border. Fortescue telephoned the *Daily Telegraph* and filed a story. In its August 3 edition the *Telegraph* carried a large headline: "COUNTRY INVADED BY GERMAN TROOPS." None of the other papers carried the story; the *Telegraph* appeared to have a major scoop. But then, within hours, the *Telegraph* phoned Fortescue and angrily informed him that the Foreign Office had denied the story. In another twenty-four hours, however, the *Telegraph* again phoned Fortescue to offer embarrassed apologies and a contract. Britain had just declared war on Germany for violation of Belgian neutrality.[33]

Other examples followed. For instance, in August 1914, newspapers failed completely to report the Battle of the Frontiers near Paris, where some 300,000 French troops died in a period of ten days; the information remained unreported throughout the entire war. The press in Allied nations also failed to report the impressive success that year of German troops at the Battle of Tannenberg, where the Russians suffered massive losses and the German generals Ludendorff and Hindenburg attained national fame.

Failures of this kind were due in part to the censorship policies of all the governments involved in the war. In Germany and Russia there was almost no freedom of the press throughout the conflict. But even in Allied countries censorship was a major obstacle. At the start of the war this was due in part to governmental clumsiness. But even after clear policies and practices were in place, restrictions were severe. All news stories from the front had to be cleared by a tiny board composed of censors, all of whom erred on the extreme side of caution. Only five English and two American reporters, acting on behalf of one or more newspapers and the wire services, had clearance to go to the front. A censor almost always accompanied them. Most generals and admirals mistrusted reporters and were out of date in their understanding of the growing importance of public opinion. The war also presented publishers with complex challenges of self-regulation: whether to make unauthorized visits to the front to cover battles, for example, and how to balance the desire of readers for complete information against the need to censor coverage that might provide advantage to an enemy. These problems were not new, but they now appeared on a vast scale and with very large consequences.[34]

The most able journalists managed to write excellent reports. For example, the Australian reporter Keith Murdoch wrote a detailed and eloquent exposé of British bungling during the Gallipoli campaign against Turkey in 1915. Newspapers and the government at first suppressed the account, but the editors of *The Times* eventually decided to run it, and it helped to precipitate a parliamentary investigation. American journalism, too, at times attained distinction. Among the more famous American reports before the nation joined the war were the coverage by Richard Harding Davis of the German troops' entry into Brussels and Will Irwin's reports on the Battle of Ypres and the first use of poison gas by the Germans. An example of distinguished reporting after the United States entered the war was Heywood Broun's exposé, in 1917 for the *New York World*, of major deficiencies in the supply operation for U.S. troops. The number of American reporters in Europe increased after U.S. entry, with about forty stationed at or near the front lines of battle with American forces.[35]

Fear that openness would negatively affect home front populations was a much larger factor than in earlier conflicts. The war effort required energy, discipline, and sacrifice from the civilian populace who built the weapons and bought the war bonds and were to refrain from rioting. Civilian and military leaders believed that news of losses and disorder at the front could increase the risk of defeat. This was especially true during the early years of the conflict, when there was no conscription. Governments assumed, probably correctly, that men and women would not voluntarily enlist for military service if they were told the full extent of the slaughter. Even with the strict censorship, however, reporters could have done more to disclose important information while still protecting military secrecy. And as in the Anglo-Boer War, they failed to provide extensive analysis of the larger issues of military strategy, diplomatic alternatives, and planning that the war presented.

After the war, in memoirs and retroactively published collections of their writings, both censors and reporters admitted that they had failed in many ways to uphold their responsibilities for adequate candor, and they told many of the stories they had not revealed earlier. Their confessions were one cause of a the shock that occurred during the 1920s, when the people learned many more details about the conflict and realized that they had not been told the full truth.[36]

One of the memoirs published and widely read after the war was *Disenchantment* (1922), by Charles Montague. A highly respected editor before the war for the *Manchester Guardian*, Montague was an army officer who, during the conflict, oversaw the five English and two American correspondents who were allowed to cover activities on the Western Front. His experience as a censor left him with deep misgivings. He acknowledged the need for information control and propaganda in modern warfare, but he wondered whether, now that nations had unleashed their powers of lying, they could ever get back to the habits of peace. The potential for manipulating public opinion had scarcely begun to be realized during the war, Montague asserted, asking, "What would be left by a war in which Propaganda had come of age and the state had used the press, as camouflaging material, for all it was worth?" Montague challenged readers to recall ancient Athens in the time of the Peloponnesian War and the accompanying plague, as described by Thucydides, when (quoting Thucydides), "the meaning of words had no longer the same relation to things, but was changed by men as they thought proper." Montague was frightened by the thought that war had worked that way on the soul of ancient Greece, when armed conflict was tamer than in the twentieth century. Moral recuperation would take time, like building up devastated French towns brick by brick. But it would be possible, particularly if veterans took the lead. "There must still be five or six million ex-soldiers," wrote Montague. "They are the most determined peace party that ever existed."[37]

3 THE DEMOCRACIES TRY TO DEMOBILIZE
1919–1939

For two decades after the Great War, all the democratic nations struggled to reorient their use of mass communication toward peaceful ends. But larger, menacing developments gradually pulled the democracies into the vortex of another world conflict.

Peacemakers Utilize the Media

In the years immediately following the war, it did not seem at first that the democracies would be making much official use of mass communication. By mid-1919 Britain had abolished nearly all of its government offices related to propaganda. The United States acted even earlier, closing down George Creel's Committee on Public Information two weeks *before* the war ended. The French and the new Weimar Republic in Germany also reconfigured their propaganda operations, focusing on foreign ministries. Why was this so? One hypothesis is that many people, especially members of the elite working in government, still did not fully appreciate the importance of public opinion in mass society, let alone the techniques by which it could be affected. The wartime experience with media, though intense, may have been too brief and too confined to certain groups for everyone to sense its ramifications. An important point is that the exhaustion of war led many people to want to eliminate all weapons of destruction—not only tanks and battleships but also the tools of propaganda. Expense was another consideration, especially in France and Germany, where the economic burdens of the war were very heavy.

The arm's-length pattern continued at the Paris Peace Conference, convened in January 1919 to draw up the final terms of settlement for the Great War. Premier Georges Clemenceau of France and his deputies spoke directly with only a few of the more influential French reporters, particularly André Tardieu, the foreign editor of *Le Temps*, and André Géraud ("Pertinax") of *L'Echo de Paris*. The British established an official press center at one of the downtown hotels, led by Sir George Riddell, publisher of the *News of the World* and a friend of Prime Minister David Lloyd George. The staff at the center was helpful and assisted correspondents from many countries. But British leaders were very selective in their contacts with the press. They had reason to be cautious. For example, at one point in the conference Lloyd George had to go back to Britain on short notice to address the House of Commons regarding charges made by the Northcliffe papers that he was being too lenient toward Germany.

The American relationship with reporters was similarly mixed. The U.S. delegation established a press department in one of the downtown hotels, led by Ray Stannard Baker, the distinguished Progressive Era journalist and White House press aide to Wilson. But its information tended to be general, and Wilson kept many details to himself. The "Big Four" heads of state—Clemenceau, Lloyd George, Wilson, and Italian prime minister Vittorio Orlando—were all experienced practitioners of mass politics, but at the conference they showed little taste for public discourse. They held most discussions privately, then emerged to provide reporters with cryptic summaries. Journalists found out much of their information by talking indirectly or off the record with deputies or staff members of the official press offices.

Reporters took lodgings in Paris at various large hotels, and the French government established a service center on the Champs-Élysées in the mansion of a recently deceased manufacturer. Although government publicity staffs were small, the presence of journalists was conspicuous. Some six hundred reporters attended—mostly print writers, but also photographers, artists, and others. This was by far the largest group of journalists ever to cover an international diplomatic conference. The American delegation was the largest, including some 250 reporters. The British press representatives numbered about a hundred. The victors did not allow journalists representing the Central Powers to attend the conference until April, when the treaties had been nearly completed. Premier Clemenceau, himself a newspaper owner and former journalist, wanted to keep reporters under his control. He was successful in controlling the French press.[1]

The journalists at the conference faced a challenge almost as great as the one the war had presented, for millions of people saw the daily news reports on the peace negotiations as the key to their future. Although most of the journalists from major countries had centrist views, some of the papers from those countries represented specific groups, such as socialist journals from the United States and the *Guardian* from England, which reflected the interests of labor. In addition to news organizations from major countries, there were press representatives from smaller countries. The Balkan nations seeking independence sent representatives. Unofficial delegations, including one from Vietnam led by Ho Chi Minh, who held odd jobs in Paris to support himself, reported on the conference and expressed bitterness about their lack of access.

The final ceremonial signing of the Treaty of Versailles, in the Hall of Mirrors, was a major event in the history of mass communication. Reporters joined other observers in craning their necks for views of the proceedings. Within minutes typewriters began to clatter, and stories made their way by telegraph around the world.

This excitement masked underlying misgivings. In Germany most of all, the treaty was an object of widespread disapproval. Symbolic of the German attitude was the fate of Matthias Erzberger, a Catholic Centrist Party leader and cabinet member who had been minister of civilian propaganda during the war. The Germans had sent him as one of their representatives to sign the Armistice agreement of November 1918. Shortly after Germany signed the Treaty of Versailles, right-wing groups made him a scapegoat. They attempted to assassinate him in 1919 and 1920 and succeeded in 1921.

Many observers at the time believed that a major weakness of the conference was its underutilization of the potential of communication. The economist John Maynard Keynes held that Wilson's failure to exploit his popularity, evident in large parades and in numerous favorable stories in the papers from the moment he arrived in France, was a colossal mistake. The British diplomat Harold Nicolson noted the way newspapers in the victor nations spewed out hate—notably the many papers in France controlled by Clemenceau, who detested the Germans, and in England the papers controlled by Lord Northcliffe, who had a racist contempt for all things Hunnish. This climate of opinion, in Nicolson's view, was a key reason for the inadequacy of the treaties.[2]

The conference at Paris was nevertheless a major landmark in efforts to use mass persuasion for purposes of promoting peace. By creating the League of Nations, the peace settlement provided, almost inadvertently, the first extensive opportunity in history to use a major institution of government for large-scale publicity against war. The League possessed only limited official authority, and the states that brought it into being were by no means pacifistic. But they did allow the League to explore strategies supplementing private-sector approaches to mass communication that had been emphasizing alternatives to war for some time.

In the years before the Great War, the press sometimes played an important role in advocating peace. Major newspapers covered the peace

conferences held at The Hague in 1899 and 1907, two gatherings that produced significant agreements to promote arms limitations and respect for
international law.[3] In at least one case, in 1895, the press played the key role
in preventing an international conflict when Joseph Pulitzer, who would
later stridently support the Spanish-American War, published a strongly
worded editorial in *The World* opposing President Grover Cleveland's attempts to push the United States into war against Britain in the wake of
British attempts to dominate disputed territory in Venezuela, in violation
of the United States' long-standing Monroe Doctrine, opposing incursion
into the Americas by outside nations.

During the Great War there were extensive, organized private-sector
efforts to use mass communication as a tool for hastening peace. Labor and
socialist groups mobilized their newspapers to advocate a quick end to the
conflict through negotiation and compromise. For them the war was an
out-of-date nationalistic struggle that undermined worldwide solidarity
among workers. Religious groups, especially the Quakers, used their publications to promote pacifism. There were also significant attempts by individuals, such as the widely reported efforts in Britain in 1916 by a prominent Conservative politician, Lord Lansdowne, who advocated negotiating
an end to hostilities through compromise with the enemy.

But all such efforts had to struggle against widespread public support for
the war; and groups seeking an early brokered peace did not have the vast
publicity resources of governments and the mainstream press. Moreover,
governments often crushed the peace initiatives. That was the fate in Britain, for example, of E. D. Morel. In 1914 he helped to establish an organization called the Union of Democratic Control (UDC), which sought to
broaden public access to processes of official decision making, especially
those involving secret negotiations among aristocratic diplomats, who did
not represent the common people who had to do the actual fighting, as a
way of bringing an early end to the war. The UDC enjoyed the support of
trusted figures like Charles Trevelyan, the Liberal member of Parliament,
and Ramsay MacDonald, the labor leader who was to become prime minister in the 1920s. But the authorities remembered the trouble Morel had
caused ten years earlier when he had organized the Congo Reform Association to publicize the atrocities committed in Africa by Belgian colonial
administrators and business interests on behalf of King Leopold. In 1917,
alarmed by the growing influence of the UDC, the government arrested
Morel on charges that he was violating the Defence of the Realm Acts by
conducting overseas correspondence with pacifists. After a sham trial
Morel spent six months in prison. Nevertheless, he and others like him

inspired many people to think creatively in the period immediately after the war about using the press and other tools of publicity to prevent future conflicts.[4]

When the League of Nations began operations in 1920 with its head-quarters in Geneva, it sought a candid, productive relationship with jour-nalists. The League established a well-staffed Information Section within the permanent Secretariat. Its first director was the distinguished French journalist Pierre Comert, and the second was Arthur Sweetser, an Ameri-can journalist with foreign experience, who believed in the League even though his country was not a member. The Information Section supplied reporters with comfortable facilities, transmission services, copies of docu-ments, and up-to-the-minute information on League meetings. The League also organized international conferences on the future of journalism. True to the purpose of the organization, its headquarters provided a forum where not only diplomats but also journalists from many countries could meet face-to-face and form productive relationships. The press activity of the League contributed to an increased appreciation worldwide of the impor-tance of news reportage in foreign relations.[5]

Effective promotion of mass communication to advance world peace was difficult because of the general reluctance among the great powers to oper-ate through the organization. For example, at the Geneva Disarmament Conference of 1932–1934, the League made elaborate, impressive arrange-ments to assist journalists and facilitate international dialogue. But the at-tending diplomats and heads of state undercut this effort. They reverted to earlier patterns of conferring with reporters infrequently and only in con-trolled circumstances.[6] Useful work nevertheless took place. For example, in 1936 the League brokered an international agreement, which had some constructive effects even in the climate of the times, to prevent the use of radio for propaganda purposes.[7]

In 1922 the League convened a meeting of fifty-eight influential think-ers drawn, remarkably, not only from Western nations but also from coun-tries such as India and Colombia, to discuss the potential of cultural ex-change as a force for world peace. The outcome was the International Committee on Intellectual Cooperation, based in Geneva, and, in 1926, a closely allied International Institute for Cultural Cooperation, based in Paris. By the end of the 1930s some thirty countries had established affili-ated national committees. In Britain the committee members included the classicists Gilbert Murray and Alfred Zimmern (who was then on the staff of the Foreign Office), several historians, and the director of the British Museum. The United States also cooperated with the League in intellectual exchanges even though it was not a member. The League's initiative was elitist. It did not extensively explore the use of mass communication. But it did establish a precedent for official dialogue that transcended nationalism, and important projects resulted, for example, the effort begun in 1926 by French and German teachers to eliminate inflammatory nationalistic references from schoolbooks (unfortunately not successful), and famous instances of exchanges of letters, such as the public correspondence regarding war and peace between Albert Einstein and Sigmund Freud in 1932.[8]

Fatigue Complicates the Task

Efforts to use the media for promoting peace ran up against the general sense of disillusionment that became widespread after the Great War. For the most part, media discourse during the conflict had been mature and responsible, even in the more autocratic countries like Germany and Austria-Hungary. But excesses did much long-term emotional harm. The tendency on all sides to portray the war as a great crusade of right against wrong resulted in deep cynicism afterwards, as people learned about secret treaties, war profiteering, errors made by political and military leaders, the true extent of casualties, and the barbaric methods of killing practiced by all the belligerents. In works such as *The Sun Also Rises* (1926) by Ernest Hemingway, *Goodbye to All That* (1929) by Robert Graves, and *The Road Back* (1931) by Erich Maria Remarque, authors struggled to come to terms with the sorrow, anger, irony, and cynicism that the combination of death, censorship, and media-fueled hatred had produced. This pessimism spilled over into diplomatic negotiations, along with lingering stereotypes of barbarous Huns, sly Frenchmen, and devious Englishmen, making it harder for negotiators to trust one another.

Postwar journalism exacerbated the problem. Audiences received a significant amount of news about foreign affairs and issues of war and peace, but coverage tended to be disjointed and discontinuous and was merely one element of a larger informational environment that emphasized whatever was personal, trivial, comforting, or amusing. American reportage paid more attention to things like Charleston dance contests, rescues of lost children from coal mines, ocean liner disasters, high society scandals, and bank robberies than it did to foreign affairs. So extensive was the sensationalism in American news reporting that in the 1920s it had a name: "ballyhoo." In Britain, similarly, the media reflected and also helped to produce the trancelike mood of the interwar years which has been described as a "long weekend." Leading British newspapers such as the *Daily Mail* and the *Daily*

Telegraph put the emphasis on escapist pursuits: roller-skating, boxing, cricket, motorcycle racing, detective novels, hiking, nudism, the private lives of entertainers, gardening, jitterbugging, psychics, religious evangelism, rumors of a talking mongoose, and visits to London by exotic monarchs such as the king and queen of Afghanistan.[9]

Other media-related developments also undermined efforts to promote a sense of international responsibility. When President Wilson returned from the Paris Peace Conference to the United States, he began an extended effort to win over the Senate and the general population to the possibility of joining the League of Nations. He was ultimately unsuccessful. This was due in part to his wartime treatment of the American press, which had been draconian. Many of the liberal and socialist journalists who would have been most willing to help Wilson win the battle of public opinion were in prison because, in his haste to silence them, he had used his wartime powers to put them there.[10]

America's general turning inward after the Great War was also due to fear of international communism. This anxiety had many causes, including nativist worries about foreign influence and fear of the loss of private property. But the media intensified the concern. In an article in the February 1920 *Forum* magazine titled "The Case against the Reds," Attorney General A. Mitchell Palmer invoked the image of a "prairie fire" of communist revolution "sweeping over every American institution of law and order." Palmer and J. Edgar Hoover, general intelligence director of the Bureau of Investigation, sent informers into labor unions, ethnic organizations, and left-wing political groups. They established a Justice Department publicity bureau that issued daily press releases asserting the existence of a Moscow-based conspiracy to overthrow the United States and warning Americans not to be duped by communist propaganda. On November 7, 1919, a date chosen because it marked the second anniversary of the Bolshevik Revolution, Palmer initiated raids and arrests throughout the United States. Newspapers added to the hysteria. On January 3, 1920, the *New York World* asserted the existence of a "vast working plot to overthrow the government." A headline in the *New York Times* proclaimed, "REDS PLOTTED COUNTRY-WIDE STRIKE—ARRESTS EXCEED 5,000." A minority of publications did protest against Palmer's conduct. The editor of the *Nation*, Oswald Garrison Villard, even called for impeaching the attorney general.[11]

It was in this fear-ridden climate of opinion that commercial advertising expanded, catering to mass impulses to pursue individual and family concerns. In newspapers, magazines, shop and department store windows, and other venues, advertisements attempted, often with great success, to persuade consumers to purchase not only necessary articles such as soap and clothing but less necessary objects like cigarettes and fashionable jewelry as well. Ads catered to considerations of the basic standard of living, but also to emotional matters such as attractiveness, the desire to impress friends and neighbors, and the wish to escape from everyday concerns through travel, whether on the highways of America or to exotic places. Topics like foreign affairs and the duties of citizenship were seldom part of the advertiser's world in the 1920s and 1930s—although, ironically, growing communication skills meant that, in ways no one could anticipate at the time, advertising was becoming an increasingly powerful weapon. It exuded an air of influence and glamour, as reflected, for example, by the British mystery writers Dorothy L. Sayers in *Murder Must Advertise* (1933) and Agatha Christie, whose novel *The Secret Adversary* (1922) featured the characters Tuppence and Tommy Beresford, two young London residents, an ex-nurse and an intelligence agent, who advertise in the newspapers as "two young adventurers for hire."

A related spillover into the commercial world after the war was the new profession of public relations. The pioneer was an American, Ivy Lee. Before the war, imitating in more gentlemanly form the tactics of carnival barkers and theater publicists, he had helped the Rockefellers gain favorable press coverage that counterbalanced suspicion of the family's great wealth. The most influential professional practitioner of public relations in the postwar years was an American, Edward Bernays (1891–1995), a nephew of Sigmund Freud. During the war Bernays had worked for the Committee on Public Information. Afterwards he combined insights gained from that experience with concepts from psychology and journalism and applied them to consulting work for political and corporate clients, including Presidents Calvin Coolidge and Herbert Hoover, Procter & Gamble, the new Columbia Broadcasting System (CBS), the American Tobacco Company, and General Electric. Public relations sought to obtain publicity—and its corollaries public approval and participation—without paying for it directly, through techniques such as using personal networks, writing news stories and offering them to busy journalists at no cost, and staging events that would attract decision makers or create word-of-mouth attention.

Bernays frequently described public relations as the "engineering of consent." In *Propaganda*, published in 1928, he offered what was perhaps his most articulate defense of the possibilities for benign commercial use of his techniques. He avoided utopian perceptions of the public, but he had faith in the average person's capacity to make intelligent decisions, especially regarding concrete matters such as whether to buy a specific product.

Bernays unapologetically emphasized forms of persuasion that would not be readily apparent. For example, in 1929, while working as a consultant for the American tobacco industry, he devised a strategy to promote smoking among women, which was still seen by many as a symbol of prostitution. For the Easter Parade held that year in New York City, Bernays hired glamorous models who marched while holding lit cigarettes and a banner proclaiming that each cigarette was a "torch of liberty." Sales of cigarettes to women soared.[12] In such cases, Bernays knew, the average person would not be aware of the chain of events leading to a decision; but as long as the engineers of consent were ethical, Bernays believed, collective good would be the result.[13] Increasingly, as the years passed, the government began to use public relations tactics, for example, by expanding its recruitment of celebrities to endorse official policies, supplying prewritten stories to over-worked newspaper editors, and asking radio networks to insert calls for patriotic behavior into the dialogue of popular dramas and comedy shows. Public relations later played a sizable role in wartime, adding yet another temptation to reduce public discourse about citizenship and national pur-pose to the level of slogans and unexamined, undisclosed suggestion.

The Media Expand Their Influence

In the 1920s and 1930s, continuing the pattern that had begun in the nine-teenth century, mass communication developed ways of reaching ever larger audiences, not only through print but also by other means, and this expansion had important consequences for war and peace. *Reader's Digest*, founded in 1922 as a response to the fast pace and short attention span of urban life, was the first magazine devoted to excerpts and condensed ver-sions of articles from other publications. *Time*, the world's first "news mag-azine," which emphasized condensation and summary, appeared in 1923. These publications covered foreign affairs in snippets, offering readers al-most no background analysis or continuity. *Life*, the first illustrated news magazine based almost exclusively on still photography, appeared in 1936. Its powerful images brought a new immediacy to foreign affairs, although most readers did not understand the effects of the visual compositions that manipulated their perceptions.

Book publishing now took on some of the reach and timeliness of news-papers and magazines with the development in the 1930s of cheap paper-backs. The British publisher Penguin Books led what many observers even-tually called a "revolution" in publishing and in reading habits. Paperbacks could not supplant newspapers as a source of up-to-the-minute informa-tion about war and peace; even when produced in a few weeks, they took longer to reach an audience. But publishers could produce paperbacks more quickly than other kinds of books, and because of their low price, they reached many more purchasers. This led to an increase in the amount of analytic and commemorative material about issues related to international affairs, and to wider circulation of fiction on the subject, involving literary writers as well as the more sensationalistic. Like other expansions of the media, the paperback revolution was double-edged. It increased the power of those who controlled communication and offered yet another tool to groups that might want to abuse that power.

In the newspaper world, in both the United States and continental Europe, the technology of printing improved, making it possible to produce papers at less cost. Commercial use of advertising increased greatly. The price of a newspaper fell as a result of these two developments, leading to increases in sales as well as publishers' profit margins. This led newspapers to place greater emphasis on "objectivity"—a word that became popular at the time—as publishers realized they could win the largest possible audiences by offering neutral, fact-based, but still interesting stories about foreign affairs and other matters instead of slanting reportage to please a specific political or economic interest group, as papers had tended to do earlier. Layout also changed significantly. Editors made greater use of white space. To give busy readers a summary of a story and help them quickly decide whether it would be of interest, headlines became much more hierarchized in form and in the case of very important stories now traversed several columns of print. Editors used large typeface to direct the reader to the stories they judged to be the most important of the day. In slightly smaller typeface under the main headline, subheads provided a capsule summary for busy readers or offered enticing details to draw them into reading the full story. Protocols emerged; for example, the story judged by editors to be the most important would be placed in the far right-hand column on page one, with the second most important story in the far left-hand column on the same page. Developments of this kind increased even further the power of editors to decide what constituted news and how it ought to be presented— for example, whether a story about politics in Europe ought to have more prominence than one about domestic politics, or one about business or entertainment.

The most consequential development for print during the interwar years was the emergence of a powerful new competitor that would soon exert enormous influence on reporting about war and peace. In the late nineteenth century, scientists and engineers discovered ways to transmit electrical signals through the atmosphere without having to rely on wires as the telegraph did. The leader in this work was the Italian Guglielmo Marconi. In 1897 he patented the wireless telegraph. The first wireless transatlantic telegraph transmission occurred in 1903, from England to Canada. The first wireless transmission of the human voice occurred in 1902. In 1918 those with the necessary receiving equipment were able to hear President Wilson broadcast his "Fourteen Points" speech and his plans for peace. Wilson also used the U.S. government radio station (call letters NFF) for propaganda abroad, urging the German people to overthrow the Kaiser. In the closing months of the First World War, the United States and the Soviet Union broadcast propagandistic messages by Morse code to encourage international acceptance of their preferred peace terms. Radio news broadcasting began in the United States in 1920 with special coverage of election returns. In 1922 the first regular radio broadcasts and the first radio commercials went on the air in New York City. By 1928 there were an estimated 9.6 million radio receivers in the United States used by an audience of 40 million listeners.

Radio developed via commercial means in the United States, relying on income from advertisers, licensing fees to listeners, and profits from the sale of receiving sets. There were many local broadcasting stations. Intense competition took place regarding patents related to technology, copyright of on-air content, and control of markets. Gradually a few business organizations began to dominate. The most powerful was the National Broadcasting Company (NBC), developed by General Electric (GE) and the Radio Corporation of America (RCA), with Westinghouse Corporation as an additional shareholder. The original purpose was to increase sales of radio receivers, for which the three companies held important patents. In 1926 NBC began network broadcasting, linking twenty-five stations in twenty-one U.S. cities.

The major rival to NBC was the Columbia Broadcasting System, established in 1928. It held no patents and survived by sale of advertising. Like NBC, it emphasized popular entertainment and initially did not assign a large role to news broadcasting. But CBS gradually discovered that radio news could attract large audiences. Radio often brought listeners the latest information more quickly than the newspaper. It conveyed a feeling of heightened realism by capturing the sounds of an event. Politicians increasingly sensed the power of the medium, making it easier for the networks to report on the activities of governments and the results of elections. Broadcasters exploited the intimacy of radio through such devices as the on-air interview and regular broadcasts by sonorous, cultivated announcers, who were called "newscasters" and "radio correspondents." By

1930 CBS was the dominant news broadcaster in the United States, though NBC and other networks also played major roles. By the late 1930s, listening to brief broadcasts of news about foreign affairs had become a regular part of daily life in industrialized countries. Nevertheless, American radio continued to be primarily a source of personally oriented entertainment that reinforced the habit of escapism from larger world events.

Radio broadcasting also expanded after the First World War in Britain. A British Broadcasting Company began operations in 1922 as a private entity. But the medium did not grow through commercial means. In 1925 Parliament held hearings on the ideal future of radio, and in 1927 the government officially chartered the British Broadcasting Corporation. The British believed that direction by the government allowed for more planning and helped emphasize the connection between mass communication and civic life. Eloquent, farsighted debates accompanied the founding of the BBC. Much of the discourse focused on the internal life of Britain and to some extent its colonies. Major themes were the importance of creating a deeper and more literate culture for the masses and an asserted duty to nourish English civilization overseas. This included giving attention to news reporting so as to provide listeners in Britain with extensive information about both domestic and foreign matters. During its early years, however, the BBC made no provision for broadcasting to the empire or to foreign countries.[14]

War Co-opts Analysis

Propelled by the experience of the Great War, rigorous investigation of the role of the media emerged in the 1920s and 1930s. Some of the analysts put the emphasis on citizenship, part of the long tradition of teaching by reference to rhetoric. In *Falsehood in War-Time*, published in Britain and the United States in 1928, the Englishman Arthur Ponsonby caused a sensation by rigorously documenting the duplicity practiced by all the belligerent powers during the Great War, including secret agreements for the turnover of territory, censorship far beyond what was necessary, and deliberate circulation of atrocity stories, most though not all of which was untrue.[15]

Many of the new students of mass communication were working journalists. Probably the most influential in this category was Walter Lippmann, already a respected, nationally known reporter before the Great War. After the United States entered the conflict, he served in London as an army captain assigned to the propaganda unit that was working independently of Creel's committee but on a parallel track. After the war, Lippmann was a member of Wilson's research staff at the Paris Peace Conference. Then he returned to journalism in the United States. Observing American politics, and the potential for future wars as a result of the breakdown of attempts to establish democracy in parts of Europe, Lippmann became concerned about the need of citizens in modern mass society for a reliable means of getting the information essential to making intelligent decisions about voting and civic participation.

The absence of such means, and what to do about it, was the subject of his book *Public Opinion* (1922). Lippmann pointed out that the framers of the U.S. Constitution were members of a relatively small, agrarian, preindustrial elite who assumed that the people who really mattered in terms of governing their society could obtain all the information they needed through the methods available at the time: from face-to-face contact and long-distance communication through personal letters, as well as newspapers printed on hand-operated presses and transported by horse-drawn wagon or ship. The framers did not anticipate a vast mass society in which most of the population would have the right to vote, and governing would require detailed knowledge about many specific matters. In the twentieth century, Lippmann noted, members of the elite still talked to one another, but most citizens, including to some extent the elites, were dependent for their information on new categories of agents such as journalists, propagandists, advertisers, and political party organizers. These classes of people often skewed information for their own purposes at the expense of others. Moreover, a large number of citizens were vulnerable to manipulation, whether because of lack of education or the large role emotion plays in all human decision making. Nor could the press solve this problem. Journalism was a business that marketed itself by emphasizing whatever was most dramatic: news defined as "episodes, incidents, and eruptions." The press provided very little analysis, certainly not enough to counteract other forces affecting mass opinion. It would be politically unwise, however, to deprive the average person of the fiction that he or she was participating intelligently in the political process or had any real influence over it. Ironic democracy would have to continue. But the truth was that most citizens were destined to be "outsiders." Actual governing would have to be restricted to "insiders," an exclusive class of educated, talented people able to develop expertise on specific issues and competent to form serious opinions. Specially created "intelligence bureaus" separate from the press would have to be created to assist the insiders.[16]

Lippmann's book became an almost instant classic. But, critics asked, if all human beings are born with a propensity to surrender to selfish emotions, why would centralization of power and the feeding of mass illusions necessarily produce better government?[17] Foremost among those who disagreed with Lippmann was John Dewey, at that time America's greatest philosopher, known particularly for his belief in the educability of the common man. First in a magazine article in the *New Republic* (1922), then in his book *The Public and Its Problems* (1927), Dewey agreed that modern democracy needed insiders, such as leaders of industry and enlightened public administrators with specialized knowledge and skills. He also granted that national leaders could not share all the information necessary for the running of society with the broad public; at least initially, some facts might have to be kept secret, and in any case, the average person could not even understand all the available news. Simply distributing facts to the broad population would not be effective. The key was the strategic, well-intentioned sharing of information. To prevent civil chaos and the emergence of violent dictatorships, leaders of mass democracies had a profound obligation to make information available in ways that would maximize comprehension, outline options for collective decision making, and help the average person understand the importance of active citizenship and the long-term consequences of actions. Dewey believed that, somewhat like members of the public empanelled to serve on juries in court cases, average men and women had the inborn capacities for reason and feeling needed to make sound judgments about common concerns. Furthermore, he maintained, these capacities would increase over the decades as nations more effectively pursued universal education. Dewey granted Lippmann's point that the press was not doing a good job of informing the public. But he felt that on this and other issues, Lippmann focused too much on aspects of the democratic system that were technical—for example, the mechanics, forms of social organization, and economics of distributing information—rather than intrinsic to human nature. Dewey did not, however, have much to say about specific actions to remedy the technical deficiencies.

Dewey bridged the world of working journalists, like Lippmann, who were interested in mass communication, and the world of academia, where extensive analysis was also in progress after the First World War. For example, historians began to look more closely at the origins of the popular press and the influence of the media on diplomacy. Probably the most influential analyst in this mode was the Harvard professor Sidney B. Fay. In his widely respected, highly detailed study *The Origins of the World War* (1928–1930), he declared emphatically that one of the major underlying causes of the conflict was "the poisoning of public opinion by the newspaper press in all the great countries."[18]

Many analysts of mass communication emerged after the Great War as part of the enormous development of the social sciences. In the 1920s and

1930s, new insights about human nature, based on the emerging branch of the social sciences called psychology, were making their way into the cultures of all the industrialized countries, through the work of thinkers like Freud, Jung, and Pavlov. These principles helped people understand the vast influence of trauma, reflexive behavior, and subconscious motivations; and they often resulted in great good, as, for example, in the emergence of psychoanalysis as a new tool of medicine. The principles also contributed to important findings about mass persuasion. The leader in this movement was the political scientist Harold Lasswell. First at the University of Chicago, then at Yale, he inspired an ever larger group of colleagues who together brought about fundamental changes in the way analysts viewed the media and society. Lasswell's pathbreaking book *Propaganda Technique in the Great War*, which appeared in 1927, was filled with interesting stories and references to archival documents of the kind that a historian might have produced. But for the most part it was a schematic analysis intended to provide conceptual tools for the scientific understanding of opinion manipulation that were applicable to all cultural circumstances. Lasswell and his colleagues hoped that their research would lead to more enlightened use of mass communication for peaceful purposes and prevent another outbreak of fear and hatred like the one that had fueled the Great War. By the 1930s, however, they were very worried about the growing power of dictatorships. In 1937 they founded the influential journal *Public Opinion Quarterly* to provide a forum for organized counterresponse to events in dictator-dominated countries and to educate the American public on the nature of political persuasion.

Work of this kind made social science–based analysis of mass communication highly visible. When the Second World War began, Lasswell and hundreds of other social scientists joined the war effort. The result was a propaganda operation very different from that of the First World War. Newly available tools included statistically based opinion polls, which built on academic research and on the experience of commercial polling firms such as those established by George Gallup and Elmo Roper in the United States, and in Britain the more impressionistic Mass Observation; content analysis, that is, counting the frequency of word usage in public interchanges and analyzing the patterns; studies of foreign cultures by those trained in expanding branches of the social sciences such as anthropology and sociology; and construction of psychological profiles of political leaders. There had been some use of the social sciences for media-related purposes during the Great War; for instance, in the United States, George Creel's Committee on Public Information included a Psychological Strategy

Board composed mostly of historians. But use of the social sciences in official information strategies was much more extensive by the late 1930s.[19]

Mass Communication Joins the Stampede

By the early 1930s a severe economic depression was evident in much of the world. In some countries, such as Germany, it had its roots in the 1920s. In the United States, the Great Depression began to exert devastating effects after the Wall Street stock market crash of 1929. The inability to meet economic challenges was a major factor in the replacement of Herbert Hoover as president in March 1933 by Franklin Roosevelt, who immediately began pursuing government programs of many kinds, often experimentally, to ward off potential class warfare and societal dissolution.

Roosevelt's response to the depression included a domestic media strategy of great sophistication. Some observers, including Lippmann, were urging the president to assume emergency powers and become, at least temporarily, a virtual dictator. Instead Roosevelt chose to use his powers aggressively but to emphasize persuasion.[20] He had always been intensely interested in the media. In 1931, in an interview for the advertising trade publication *Printer's Ink*, he declared, probably with only slight exaggeration, "If I were starting life over again, I am inclined to think that I would go into the advertising business in preference to almost any other."[21] One of Roosevelt's tools was oratory. He was one of the most skillful public speakers ever to serve as president. In a steady, patrician, but benevolent style, he and his immensely talented speechwriters coined utterances like "The only thing we have to fear is fear itself" that became part of the culture and attracted international respect. Roosevelt was also masterly in his dialogues with reporters. Woodrow Wilson had pioneered the press conference as a feature of White House practice, but Roosevelt was brilliant in his use of the venue. In addition, he made highly effective use of radio, which was beginning to rival print as a medium gathering and disseminating news. Roosevelt broadcast all of his major addresses over the radio. He and his speechwriters often crafted phrasing to take particular account of the new medium, in addition to accounting, as they always had, for the requirements of platform oratory. Alert to the intimacy of radio, and to the fact that so many citizens listened to it in their homes, Roosevelt developed the new format of the "fireside chat." By the end of the 1930s, the president was using the medium not only to communicate about domestic politics but also to instruct and reassure audiences with regard to the increasingly ominous wars in Europe and Asia.

Although George Creel's propaganda agency had been abolished after the First World War, and no other such agency emerged during the 1930s, a new governmental propaganda effort did arise during Roosevelt's time in office. To build support domestically for his "New Deal" and its many programs to lift the United States out of the depression, Roosevelt created a vast publicity apparatus. The federal government published pamphlets and sponsored the production of hundreds of documentary films on subjects ranging from building dams to fighting counterfeit currency to being on the alert for foreign agents. The government also produced thousands of posters. Photography exerted immense power through artists such as Walker Evans and Dorothea Lange working for agencies like the Works Progress Administration. Theater also became a tool of mobilization. It was simultaneously personal and far-reaching in its effects, having face-to-face impact on audiences but also using publicity surrounding the play to advertise the performance and criticize it afterward. One category of subsidized drama combined genres; it was called "living newspapers." While all these uses of publicity addressed domestic audiences, they also conveyed an implicit awareness of conditions in other countries where the failure to meet the challenges of the global depression was leading to internal violence and the external spread of war.

In the 1930s Americans also had to cope with effects spilling over from foreign dictatorships. The United States had its own indigenous Communist Party, which received support and advice from the Soviet Union. There was an American Nazi Party as well. Hitler and his advisers regarded it as rather silly, but it did cause social unrest. On radio, the Roman Catholic priest Father Charles Coughlin gave seductive speeches in favor of fascism, and in his best-selling novel *It Can't Happen Here* (1935), Sinclair Lewis imagined a fascist takeover of America. To increase the sale of newspapers, the press exaggerated the possibility of subversion by external forces, as did Roosevelt's director of the Federal Bureau of Investigation, J. Edgar Hoover, who was eager to expand his power. The dangers were nevertheless real, and the news reportage of Roosevelt's effort to cope with foreign threats at home was an important element in the psychological adjustment of Americans to the possibility of U.S. involvement in another foreign war.

Private-sector entertainment media—particularly the American film industry in Hollywood and radio drama based in New York and Hollywood—also reflected and fed the run-up to war. In 1938 American radio programming happened to include an on-air dramatization of the old H. G. Wells novel *War of the Worlds*, brilliantly produced by Orson Welles as a series of news broadcasts gone wrong, as announcers in many cities gradually realize that Martians are taking over the country. The all too realistic on-air drama led to a national panic, an apology from Welles, and fame that included a picture of the drama's author on the cover of *Time* magazine. In 1939 Welles continued to explore the power of mass communication through his film *Citizen Kane*, a commentary on the life and influence of William Randolph Hearst.

Throughout the 1930s American newsreels covered the rise of Mussolini and Hitler. The exposure of the details of Nazi rule was becoming quite explicit by the closing years of the decade, when the long-running newsreel series *The March of Time* produced *Inside Nazi Germany* (1938), based on actual news footage combined with staged scenes.

The motion picture industry also reflected Americans' anxieties about falling under foreign influence. In many of its productions, Hollywood sought to reaffirm the nation's long-standing belief in Manifest Destiny, the doctrine that the United States is a special nation created by God to save the world, a nation that would therefore endure even amidst great trials. Productions of this kind included John Ford's classic *Stagecoach* (1939), in which the stagecoach symbolizes the advance of civilization against its enemies, and which virtually defined the genre of the western; Cecil B. DeMille's *Union Pacific* (1939), in which the railroad opens the continent to settlement and civilization; *Gone With the Wind* (1939), which reaffirmed the nation's capacity to survive civil war; and even the many B-grade westerns of the 1930s made by Republic Studios, starring John Wayne and other cowboy heroes who vanquish mysterious interlopers such as munitions traders and help to cleanse society.

Another category of Hollywood films featured portrayals of dangerous foreigners associated with warlike nations. Some of the productions emphasized atmosphere and general anxiety. For example, in the *Mr. Moto* films (1937–1939), starring Peter Lorre, a morally ambiguous Japanese nobleman draws American travelers to the Far East into intrigue, though no possibility of war against Japan is raised overtly. But in other films, allusions to possible U.S. involvement in war were more direct. This was due in part to the large number of émigré artists and intellectuals from Europe who were residing in Hollywood by the late 1930s. There were so many British actors and actresses, producers, and directors that their community in Los Angeles came to be called the Hollywood Raj. Representatives of democratic, non-Hitlerian Germany included the actor Peter Lorre (Hungarian by birth, but a product of the German studio system) and the directors Ernst Lubitsch and Billy Wilder. Even before the United States entered the conflict in 1941, Hollywood was already producing films sympathetic to democracies at war. One sensational example was *Confessions of a Nazi Spy* (1939), starring Edward G. Robinson, the first American feature film to mention Hitler explicitly by name. Like Lorre, Robinson was an immigrant from Hungary. After emigrating to the United States from England, director Alfred Hitchcock made *Foreign Correspondent* (1940), the first film of his Hollywood career. Another refugee was the Hungarian-born director Michael Curtiz. At Warner Brothers, a studio very sympathetic to the British and interested in European themes, he directed *Captain Blood* (1935), *The Charge of the Light Brigade* (1936), *The Adventures of Robin Hood* (1938), *Elizabeth and Essex* (1939), and *The Sea Hawk* (1940). All used the swashbuckling magnetism of the Australian Errol Flynn to glorify British courage or, more generally, the battle of a brave individual against tyranny. Curtiz was later the director of the Warner Brothers classic *Casablanca* (1942). In the summer of 1941 Warner Brothers released *International Squadron*, to honor the RAF, and *Sergeant York*, starring Gary Cooper, about one man's decision to fight in the First World War. The studio used the latter production in its long-running campaign against the famous aviator Charles Lindbergh and the isolationist groups for which he garnered favorable publicity.

Other studios followed suit. Twentieth Century–Fox produced *The Man I Married* (1940), originally titled *I Married a Nazi*. In 1940 Charlie Chaplin completed *The Great Dictator*. The small American film company PRC produced *Beasts of Berlin* (1939), originally titled *Hitler, Beast of Berlin*, and later released as *Goose Step* and *Hell's Devils*.

Two U.S. senators, Gerald Nye of North Dakota and Bennett Champ Clark of Missouri, recalling how the British had drawn America into the First World War, became increasingly upset by Hollywood's potential influence in pushing America toward war. In August 1941 they began an official investigation of pro-Allied activity in Hollywood, then held hearings in September 1941. The senators had not viewed most of the films they criticized, however, and the hearings proved embarrassing to them in many circles.

Although the United States did not have much in the way of an official foreign propaganda agency before the war, there was some activity. From 1932 on, shortwave radio broadcasts from Italy, Germany, and Japan directed increasingly hostile commentary against Great Britain, France, and the United States in several foreign languages in an attempt to affect public opinion in the Middle East, Asia, and Latin America. In the mid-1930s Britain and France began their own foreign-language broadcasts to counter this propaganda. The U.S. response to Axis broadcasts focused on Latin America, which was closer to U.S. borders, and where President Roosevelt had been pursuing his "Good Neighbor" policy to stimulate the American economy via trade and to ward off communist and fascist influence in the Western Hemisphere. With British help, the United States established "listening posts" to monitor broadcasts. In 1938 a Division of Cultural Relations was formed within the Department of State. The federal government also subsidized private broadcasters and supported monitoring services at Princeton University and Stanford University. After the German attack on Poland in 1939 and intensification of German propaganda in Latin America, a Council of National Defense was founded in August 1940, and the publicity and broadcast functions of the State Department were gradually upgraded and reorganized under the direction of a young Nelson A. Rockefeller.

In Europe, too, liberal constitutional states gradually realized the need to adapt communication to the atmosphere of international instability. In Britain in the 1920s, Prime Minister Lloyd George decided to be his own director of propaganda. Because he was a powerful orator with many contacts in the newspaper world, he did reasonably well in matters of publicity. There were other successes too. For example, at the Washington Naval Conference in 1921, the prime minister and his foreign secretary, Lord Balfour, were impressive in their relations with reporters; they answered questions in detail, persuaded journalists that some matters had to be kept confidential, and used news channels as a way to stimulate international dialogue. In this and other situations the prime minister and foreign secretary had the assistance of a small department at the Foreign Office that was responsible for press matters, but the arrangement was not to the liking of some civil servants there. Individuals such as Rex Leeper, Stephen Tallents, and Arthur Willert began a long-term effort to make the government more aware of the need for organized attention to international publicity. During the 1920s Britain did not have much to show for it. One exception to the pattern was the Empire Marketing Board, established in 1926, a joint effort of business and government. But efforts to deal with the publicity aspects of colonial relations were generally piecemeal. For example, in the 1920s, when world press coverage dwelt on the brutality of British responses to the Irish independence movement, Britain's reputation suffered for lack of a sophisticated media strategy. And in India in the 1920s and 1930s the British proved to be no match for Gandhi, who brilliantly utilized the media to garner international respect for his campaign of civil disobedience.[22]

France also made piecemeal use of international publicity. The French had led the world in such activity in the period 1880–1914, when all the great powers used cultural propaganda to consolidate and expand empires. And, like the British, the French retained a press section at their foreign ministry after the war. But the French were generally less effective than the British in using mass communication as a tool of foreign policy. The problem proceeded in the first instance from the nature of journalism in France. The French press was vigorous: in Paris in 1929 more newspapers were published daily than in any other city in the world.[23] But French newspapers tended to be journals of opinion. Editorials and long philosophical essays occupied much of the space. There was great diversity of opinion but not much emphasis on empirical, "objective" reporting—getting out into the streets and going to sources. Many French journalists were authors with literary goals, while an equal number preferred to expound political philosophy, reflecting the multiplicity and fragmentation in viewpoints among the nation's numerous parties. The papers carried advertising but less than in Britain or the United States. Most depended on subsidies from interest groups, which often involved bribery. A journalistic environment of this kind had its strengths, for example, eloquence and literary quality. But it did not condition French diplomats and heads of state to make ingenious use of mass communication directed at very broad audiences of newspaper readers, including foreign audiences. Thus, at the same Washington Naval Conference of 1921 where the British were communicating effectively, the French were clumsy in their relations with journalists, and their international prestige suffered as a result.[24] This happened again at the negotiations leading to the London Naval Treaty of 1930.[25]

The French also had to cope with the barrage of German newspaper publicity circulated from 1919 until 1933 by the Weimar Republic in protest against such actions as the stationing of French troops in the Ruhr Valley in 1923 and the insistence of France that the Germans pay the reparations imposed by the Treaty of Versailles. Overcoming the problem of adverse press coverage was especially challenging because of the many changeovers in government in France and the consequent difficulty of pursuing any strategy of publicity consistently. In any case, there was a broad consensus among all the major French political leaders during the interwar period that mass publicity was not the best tool of discourse for the country to use in foreign affairs. The French preferred to focus on elites. Language was one consideration. Theirs was still the lingua franca of diplomacy. Most French leaders knew a fair amount of English or other languages. But they did not believe they knew enough to create publicity materials or craft quotable remarks that would adeptly manipulate the cultural symbols of the masses outside their own country. The French focused instead on direct, usually private conversations with opinion makers in the countries they wanted to influence, and on favorable support among the many cultural organizations formed by admirers of the nation of Descartes, Molière, Hugo, and Cézanne. For example, French representatives in London and Washington, D.C., were very effective in winning adherents among high-level Francophile members of the business, journalistic, and diplomatic communities, who in turn spread the French message through cultural societies such as the Alliance Française (founded in Paris in 1882 to promote "French civilization") and broader channels of communication. Along with private conversation, the French made strategic use of elite cultural events like museum exhibitions, concerts, and banquets. The cultural resources the French could bring to bear by this means were impressive. For instance, Jules Jusserand, who served as French ambassador to the United States from 1902 to 1925, was the winner of the first Pulitzer Prize in History and was later elected president of the American Historical Association.[26]

In Britain in the interwar years, one enormous exception to the deemphasis on mass communication for international purposes occurred in 1932, when the government reluctantly authorized creation of a BBC Empire Service. Another important development came in 1934 with the creation of the British Council to improve cooperation with overseas groups interested in cultural exchange. This was a tardy effort to match the international effectiveness of French cultural propaganda supported by elite clubs and societies in friendly countries. It also evidenced increased awareness among the British of the need to counter the explicitly political propaganda coming from the dictatorships in Italy, Germany, and Russia.

Another indicator of growing—if limited—awareness was the effort begun in 1935 to plan for creation of a Ministry of Information, on the model of the First World War agency, in case war broke out. In the late 1930s the government set up several small, semi-secret organizations, with offices in London, to sketch out plans for subversive propaganda operations. And there were a few private-sector efforts. For example, in 1935, the government coordinated with Gaumont British News to produce newsreels making the case for rearmament. The various efforts were not centralized, and they worked at cross purposes until 1940, well after war had begun, when management became more effective.

In a speech he delivered to political leaders and opinion makers in London in 1938, Sir Arthur Willert, one of the respected diplomats who had been struggling for many years to improve Britain's overseas publicity, described a recent visit to Italy to conduct official business. In Rome he hailed a taxi and asked the driver to take him to the propaganda ministry. When they reached their destination, the driver asked for more specific directions. Willert had not known that the ministry occupied four large buildings over an area of several blocks. The British Foreign Office at that time still needed only a few small spaces to house its publicity functions.[27]

If governmental inattention to publicity was a factor in increasing international tension during the interwar years, so also was the private-sector failure of the press in the democracies to meet the challenge fully. A striking example of this contradiction was the tendency of interwar journalism to minimize the dangers inherent in the growth of the armaments industry. Large economic interests found it easy to identify their own business success with patriotism and worked to distort the emphasis in news reportage. In France, leading newspapers received subsidies from French armaments manufacturers to run stories portraying ever larger arms buildups as the surest guarantees of peace. In the fledgling republic of Czechoslovakia, the Skoda armaments firm subsidized several newspapers. In 1927, at the Geneva Naval Conference, American arms manufacturers engaged in behind-the-scenes attempts to influence press coverage. By 1934, in the United States, lobbying and manipulation of public opinion by international arms traffickers was of such concern that Congress undertook a special eighteen-month committee investigation, which was widely reported in the press. The hearings disclosed the many questionable activities of arms companies and offered a platform for isolationists who hoped to avoid involvement in another world conflict.[28]

4 DICTATORS CONQUER THEIR MEDIA

1919–1939

FROM THE EARLY 1920s on, there was a growing divergence in attitudes toward media manipulation between the democracies and those countries where dictatorships were taking root: in Mussolini's Italy; in the new Soviet Union; in Germany, where Hitler became chancellor in 1933 and then, in 1934, führer; and in the autocratic regimes of China and Japan. While the democracies were ambivalent about the use of media in foreign affairs, the dictatorships were all too willing to continue exploring the relation between war and mass communication.[1]

Russia Becomes a Propaganda State

As industrialization came slowly to Russia in the late nineteenth century, the apparatus of mass communication also developed. In addition to a growing number of rail and telegraph links, there were, by 1913, 1,158 newspapers, several with a circulation of over 100,000. Most of the papers had readerships only in the largest cities, including Moscow and St. Petersburg, although even in these cases the suburbs were not well served. Tsarist bureaucrats censored all the publications, though less so after concessions to liberal reformers in the Revolution of 1905. By that time even the Bolsheviks had sufficient press freedom to publish their party newspaper, *Pravda* (Truth), at least from 1912 to 1914.

Lenin viewed mass communication as an essential tool of revolution. In *What Is to Be Done?* (1902) and other early writings, he described the establishment of a national newspaper as imperative, and he laid great emphasis on coordinating reportage closely with reinforcing action by the party organization.

After the Bolshevik Revolution of 1917 and the communist takeover of Russia, Lenin and the Communist Party enjoyed complete control of all communications media. Russia after 1917 has been called "the first propaganda state."[2] The term emphasizes the degree to which the Soviet rulers exerted a mastery of information, and to which indoctrination became an integral instrument of their rule.

By the time of the Bolshevik Revolution, Lenin had come to view propaganda in multiple ways. At times he saw it as synonymous with all types of controlled dissemination of information, as, for example, in the design of the educational system. At other times he viewed it as part of the discourse on all subjects that took place among educated people. With regard to the masses, however, he tended to speak of "agitation propaganda" (*agitprop*), which was the focused marshaling of carefully assembled information— backed up by party action—to get people to do specific things. In all this there was a paradox. As a true believer, one of the many Marxists who were convinced that communism would gradually spread to the whole world through the power of historical determinism, Lenin was rather smug in his attitude toward propaganda. In some ways his thinking could be said to resemble that of the Roman Catholic Church during the Counter-Reformation. If one simply disseminated the already revealed, undeniable truth, then, in Lenin's view, all people would be persuaded by its self-evident power. In this attitude Lenin was different from Hitler and Stalin, whose use of information had a nervous, insecure quality. In action, however, Lenin was just as vigorous in his employment of propaganda as they were. Through agitation, he believed, the inevitable coming of the classless society could be hastened.

Cinema received a great deal of attention. Because of tsarist censorship and the fear of new forms of communication, early-twentieth-century Russia had only an embryonic film industry, and hardly exploited the propaganda potential of the new medium even during the First World War. Tsarist rule emphasized command, not persuasion. The role of loyal subjects was to obey. Lenin proceeded to woo the few private filmmakers who were in operation, offering them much-needed supplies and cash, and then in 1919 nationalized the film industry and began its slow expansion. Most early Soviet efforts were newsreels. Soviet filmmakers also produced propaganda films, five to thirty minutes long, such as *Proletarians of the World Unite*, which had no plot and emphasized posed scenes evoking the French Revolution; *Frightened Burzhui*, about a capitalist who becomes an insomniac; and *For the Red Flag*, in which a father joins the Red Army to atone for his son's lack of communist zeal. The films were shown in cities and taken by specially equipped *agit*-trains to thousands of villages in the countryside, providing many peasants with the first motion picture experience of their lives, and reaching large illiterate audiences in a way that print could not. Party-endorsed speakers, or agitators, reinforced the messages of the films. Lenin also made extensive use of posters, mobilizing the greatest Russian artists of the time. Some of them had to be forced to do the work. Others worked willingly, because they believed in the cause or saw it as their only way of earning a living and gaining an audience. Works of great creativity resulted, like the world-famous poster by D. S. Moor of a peasant enduring famine during the difficult early years of Bolshevism, and the graphically startling posters produced by various famous artists for display in the windows of Russian telegraph shops (one, for example, showing the revolutionaries of the Paris Commune of 1871 rising from the dead and marching under the red flag of the Soviets).

Although the communist takeover of Russia was a historically momentous event, observers in western Europe and the United States had great difficulty understanding it. Much of the perplexity was traceable to deficiencies in journalism. Western reporters were indeed present during the revolution. But the American freelance journalist John Reed and the *Manchester Guardian* correspondent Morgan Philips Price were the only two Western reporters who manifested a deep understanding of events. Reed was a young, Harvard-educated bohemian socialist with a poetic sensibility. As correspondent for *The Masses*, a socialist journal published in the United States, Reed was in Petrograd in 1917 when Lenin returned from abroad and assumed control of the revolution. As he listened to the speeches, he realized that the communists truly did believe they could remake the world, and he was able to convey this awareness in his dramatic yet factual reports. Philips Price was able to capture the significance of the revolution not only because of his personal insight but also because his paper, the *Manchester Guardian*, had almost a century of experience in reporting on labor-owner relations in the industrial north of England.[3]

A more typical reaction to the Bolshevik Revolution was that of the *New York Times*. In March 1918, when the new Soviet government made peace with Germany through the Brest-Litovsk Treaty, American news media reflected the widespread shock and dismay among Western capitalist nations. Walter Lippmann and his friend and fellow journalist Charles Merz documented this perplexity in an article of August 4, 1920, in the *New Republic* magazine in which the two reporters analyzed news stories and editorials in the *Times* from March 1917 to March 1920. The survey revealed that up to the time of the Bolshevik Revolution, the coverage was optimistic to the point of distortion and reinforced an assumption that Russia would continue to fight against Germany. After March 1918, however, the *Times* coverage was so skewed against the Soviets as to amount, in the words of Lippmann and Merz, to "organized propaganda for intervention" against the Bolsheviks. For example, during the first two years of the new Soviet state, the *Times* reported the collapse of the government ninety-one times, and throughout the period covered by the article the *Times* repeatedly editorialized about the need for vigilance against the Soviet drive for worldwide revolution. "The news about Russia is a case of seeing not what was, but what men wished to see," Lippmann and Merz commented. They saw no reason to believe that other American newspapers were any more accurate in their coverage. The American people were being deprived of information that could have helped them make intelligent judgments about an important aspect of their country's place in the world.[4]

Upon Lenin's death in 1924, Stalin immediately began consolidating his power and soon became head of the party and the government. Stalin had personally witnessed the effects of propaganda during the Russian Revolution and Lenin's coming to power. He had also gained experience as a journalist early in his life. Stalin intensified the censorship that had been common under the tsars and then the Bolsheviks.

He developed additional means of manipulating opinion, such as the "show trials" of the 1930s, in which his opponents blurted out engineered confessions before juries and the foreign press. Stalin's purges, in which he periodically reconfigured the ruling elite around him by murder or exile, were also made to serve propagandistic purposes. Those purged became nonpersons. Their names no longer appeared in the press. Censors doctored photographs of past events to eliminate images of those who had been purged, while in photographs showing Lenin they superimposed images of Stalin to create the impression that he and Lenin had always worked closely together. Stalin also increased his control over the educational system, for example, by ordering history books to be rewritten to exaggerate the importance of Russian and world communism. Perhaps the greatest change in propaganda from Lenin's years was Stalin's strategy of making himself the focus of national attention. Lenin had reluctantly allowed the revolution to depict him in heroic terms. But Stalin purposefully took the process to extremes, not just permitting but consciously using the party publicity apparatus to craft a cult of personality that put him at the center of all things and conditioned the Soviet people to depend on him emotionally as the father without whom all would be lost.

Mussolini Invents the Fascist Model

After the end of the Great War, Italy became an arena for a wide range of conflicting political groups that sought to exploit widespread discontent and reshape the nation according to their views. Benito Mussolini, the leader of the major right-wing group, developed a movement called Fascism (an allusion to the *fasces*, the rods that were the symbol of ancient Roman authority), which advocated government by dictatorship, territorial expansion, domination over inferior races, and emphasis on youthfulness and vigor in daily life. To aid him in his rise to power, Mussolini recruited armed thugs drawn from the ranks of the unemployed, including demobilized veterans who still had their weapons and were inured to brutality. These paramilitary supporters identified themselves by wearing insignia and shirts and hats of specific colors, and they built morale through devices such as secret initiations, rousing songs, and rallies. The Fascist model was soon dominant in Italy and also began to attract the attention of right-wing groups in other countries, most notably Germany. Mussolini established a Fascist government in Italy in 1922. His entry into Rome to take over the government was chaotic but was quickly turned into a propagandistic event that became part of Fascist legend as the "March on Rome" which strategically inaugurated a new era.

Like Stalin, Mussolini had been a journalist and knew the importance of controlling the press. In December 1926 he issued decrees stating that Italian reporters could be put in jail for publishing stories hostile to the government. In May 1932 he amended existing laws to require that the editor or owner of every newspaper and magazine apply annually for a license to publish, which had to be approved by the local judiciary, the press office of the Ministry of the Interior, and the Fascist Syndicate of Journalists.

In August 1933 Mussolini appointed his son-in-law Count Galeazzo Ciano to direct the press office. In September 1934 he put the office in the Ministry of Foreign Affairs and under the control of the undersecretary of state for press and propaganda; later the same year he added control of the cinema to already existing press oversight. The functions of tourism, theater, and face-to-face cultural exchange were taken on by the same office soon after. In June 1935 Mussolini gave these functions full cabinet status with the creation of a Ministry of Press and Propaganda (Ministero per la Stampa e la Propaganda). Its offices on the Via Veneto in Rome became a place of congregation for journalists. Ciano soon resigned to go off to the Ethiopian campaign, and Dino Alfieri assumed his position. In June 1937 the ministry took on the new name Ministry of Popular Culture (Ministero della Cultura Populare).

Mussolini's governmental structure for press relations was as strict in most ways as that of other dictatorships. An important exception, at least at first, was that foreign newspapers could be published and circulated, and news stories by foreign journalists were not officially censored until

December 1934. By these actions Mussolini hoped to create an illusion of press freedom and lull journalists into overlooking Italy's preparations for going to war in Ethiopia. There was also less direct control. All foreign news reports had to be sent via government communications offices, where they were routed by pneumatic tubes to censors. The censors did not revise dispatches, but they did delay reports they found objectionable, without telling the reporters, who in those days had no quick way of knowing whether their stories made it to the home office promptly and were published. Fascist bureaucrats also monitored stories transmitted by telephone. Reporters knew how this system worked. When timing was not urgent, they often asked friends or fellow citizens heading home to carry information with them. In addition, the post office was available, since the mails were not censored.

The Italian Fascists' treatment of foreign news and the foreign press was clumsy and contradictory even on its own terms. In May 1937 Italy forbade its correspondents and diplomats to report on the coronation of King George VI in London. The following May, when Hitler came to Rome for a meeting with Mussolini, Fascist officials warned the editor of the prominent French daily *Paris Soir* not to attend the event because he was on record as opposing the Rome-Berlin Axis pact and Germany's annexation of Austria. In 1938, when Italy instituted anti-Jewish policies similar to those in Germany, officials compelled five foreign journalists to leave the country. One, Paul Cremona, representing the *Christian Science Monitor*, was not Jewish; in fact he was related to a Catholic family that had been in Italy for three hundred years, but the Italian government refused to admit its mistake. All told, Mussolini ordered some twenty-four foreign correspondents to leave Italy during the years 1936–1939. In December 1938 the government published regulations forbidding Italian citizens to work for foreign news organizations. All of these actions prompted bitter commentary against Italy in the world press.[5]

Unlike other dictators, Mussolini failed to see the potential of the new medium of radio. He seldom entered a radio studio and confined his use of the medium mostly to placing a microphone in front of himself on the balcony of the palace in Rome from which he gave his many bombastic speeches. His assistants were more alert. They exploited radio for purposes such as broadcasting slanted accounts of the news, reminding people to exercise in the morning as part of the national duty to maintain good health, and praising Fascist public works projects like the draining of the Pontine marshes. From 1937 on, Fascist-oriented radio broadcasts were heard weekly in all school classrooms by means of loudspeakers attached to radio receivers.

Mussolini was more imaginative in his use of the visual media. He funded statues and new buildings, encouraged poster art, and posed heroically for thousands of photographs. He made extensive use of the motion picture. Throughout most of the 1920s American imports dominated the Italian film market, but this gradually changed. The regime established a modern film production studio on the outskirts of Rome. It began producing silent film newsreels in 1928, adding sound by 1932. Mussolini himself previewed most of the films before their release and provided a list of his preferences: for example, his favorite image was of the ice skater Sonja Henie, and he did not want coverage of political assassinations. All the newsreels included heavy emphasis on Fascist activities such as peasant festivals, army marches, and contests of strength at Italian beaches. The government also produced documentary films, covering topics like construction of Fascist works of architecture and the elaborate planning for the Ethiopian war.

By the early 1930s the regime was also subsidizing feature films, though more to protect the economy from American domination than because of any rigorous pursuit of propaganda potential. One explicitly Fascist feature film was *Vecchia guardia* (1934), which glorified the formation of youth groups and paramilitary units in small towns to guard against the communist menace. Another typical Fascist film was *La tavola dei poveri* (1932), which praised the heroism of the poor and showed their gratitude when given free food at an outdoor banquet. Many of the subsidized films might be better described as social realism, like the masterpiece *Gli uomini, che mascalzoni!* (1932), starring Vittorio De Sica, which deals with a working-class romance in a big city.[6]

Italian Fascists sought to export their methods. Their efforts were never as extensive as those of the Germans or the Soviets, but there was a presence. The Italians undertook propaganda in Balkan countries, where they had natural ties resulting from centuries of contact across the Adriatic and the presence of Italian businesses and communities in that region. They also established a foreign-language radio broadcast service in the Middle East.

Ethiopia Offers a Preview

Italy invaded Ethiopia in October 1935 and achieved victory seven months later in the spring of 1936. Around the world, newsreel audiences witnessed the pleas of Emperor Haile Selassie in his speech to the League of Nations. The League failed to come to the aid of the emperor, and media coverage magnified its disgrace. In terms of mass communication, the war was a bridge. In the way it was conducted and reported, it often resembled imperial exploits like the South African war of 1899–1902. But it also foreshadowed, in limited ways, the communications environment of later conflicts.

The war in Ethiopia attracted journalists from many nations. This was one of the first times that reporters used airplanes to get to the front to describe combat firsthand. Conditions for reporters, as for combatants, were harsh because of the difficulties of food shipment, heat and dust, dysentery, malaria, and the heavy rain and mud. Gaining access to radio transmitters was also difficult, and the costs of outfitting and transportation made coverage of the war expensive. Addis Ababa, where most reporters were stationed, was a boring town, and bickering developed among journalists as a result.

The war nevertheless attracted celebrated writers. One of the better-known Fascist supporters was Luigi Barzini, whose father had been a prominent journalist in the First World War. Barzini the younger reported for the *Corriere della Sera* of Milan, writing approvingly, even grandiosely, of Italian success in the conflict. Evelyn Waugh represented the *Daily Mail* of London. The quality of his reporting was uneven, but he did attain fame for several novels he wrote about his time in Africa. The most celebrated was *Scoop*, published in 1938, which narrated the saga of a gardening correspondent for a prominent London newspaper, the *Daily Brute*, who is accidentally sent to cover the war and writes dispatches of stunning verbosity. The novel uses comedy and mockery to question the obsessive efforts to feed the public's appetite for sensation.[7]

Not surprisingly, the tone of Fascist propaganda during the Ethiopian conflict was imperialist and racist. For example, an Italian poster justifying the war showed an image of a Roman-style arch emerging from a map of North Africa, and next to it a cartoon depicting an Italian "hygiene" worker hosing down an African child to clean away filth. A caption read, "When England was still barbarous, Rome ruled in Africa."[8]

Germany Moves toward Thought Control

In 1919 German political leaders of liberal constitutional persuasion met in the city of Weimar (a symbol of liberal tradition because of its association with figures such as Goethe and Schiller) and established a republic. The new German state was unstable. Many political groups were dissatisfied with the postwar peace settlement, particularly the requirements that Germany pay large reparations, dismantle most of its military, cede parts of the industrial Rhineland to France, and accept sole guilt for having started the war. Severe economic problems, caused in part by the nation's debts, created additional distress. Splinter groups multiplied. These included right-wing parties that wanted to restore the empire and rebuild the army and navy, as well as left-wing groups including communists with ties to the Bolsheviks in Russia. As in Italy, the groups attracted discontented veterans, the unemployed, and ordinary thugs, who reinforced their identities by wearing shirts of a designated color and pseudo-military insignia. The postwar mood among the right-wing groups included a widespread belief that Germany had not actually been defeated, an interpretation that was assisted by the fact that the war had ended with an armistice and no fighting had occurred within German borders. A legend arose that Germany had lost the war because of a "stab in the back" (*Dolchstoss*), that is, a conspiracy from within. It was never clear whether the perpetrators had directed the "stab" at the entire nation, the monarchy and its supporters, the military as a whole, or the highly venerated officer class. Neither was there agreement as to who had done the deed. All the splinter groups accused one another.

Gradually during the 1920s the extremist group that became the most powerful was the National Socialist German Workers' Party (Nazional Sozialistiche Deutsche Arbeiter Partei, or Nazi for short). It borrowed many of its ideas from Mussolini's Fascist Party in Italy, including extreme nationalism and racism, glorification of youthfulness and vigor, a large role for militarism, and the subsuming of differences of opinion within an unquestioning loyalty to an almost superhuman leader (*Führer* in German, borrowed from Mussolini's use of the title "il Duce," which evoked ties to ancient Rome and Italian glory during the Renaissance). The Nazi Party attracted support from many sources, including former generals, race-baiting intellectuals, and rich owners of large businesses. Although Adolf Hitler did not found the party, he was soon the major figure because of his tremendous energy, mysterious personal magnetism, and ability to rouse crowds through heated speeches based on unoriginal, logically undeveloped ideas that nevertheless sounded profound when he uttered them. Hitler's hyper-intense manner could seem comical to outsiders. But it was dangerous to underestimate him.

In 1920 and again in 1923 Hitler took part in failed attempts to overthrow the government of the Weimar Republic. In prison in 1924, he wrote a self-pitying but perceptive autobiography, *Mein Kampf* (My Battle), published in 1925. The book included a highly detailed plan to take over the German state and restore its international stature. In his strategy for gaining power, both within Germany and beyond, Hitler assigned a very large role to propaganda. He had first realized the importance of publicity and appeals to the mob while, as a down-and-out member of the underclass in -prewar Vienna, he had observed that city's strident politics. He was also impressed by the importance of propaganda as a new weapon in the Great War, and followed its uses in the Russian Revolution and in Mussolini's rise.

In *Mein Kampf,* Hitler divided all members of audiences into three groups. One is the great mass of people. Creatures of emotion, they have a limited capacity for logic, are not thoughtful, are afraid to develop opinions on their own, and need to be given their overarching ideas by others. Their situation is not regrettable as long as they are guided by upright, competent people who love the truth. But societal chaos will be the result if they are not wisely guided. Second, a small group of people have the capacity for leadership but have lost that capacity. For whatever reasons, they have become disillusioned and emotionally exhausted, and are cynical about everything they hear and read. They no longer have positive potential and must be managed carefully. The third group consists of a very small number of people who are capable of rigorous thinking and wise judgment. They read and listen with care and are not taken in by journalists, most of whom are unethical and manipulative. By whatever means necessary, the state must ensure that control goes to this third, elite group. This group, in turn, must aggressively utilize the educational system and the press to direct the energies of the other two groups into serving the state and the nation. The state must not be misled by the "prattle of so-called 'freedom of the press,'" which is dangerous. But the press is still of huge importance. The press plays the major role in the shaping of "public opinion," which is produced for the most part by "what is told to people through the presentation of a continuous penetrating and persistent kind of so-called 'enlightenment.'" This is Hitler's conception of propaganda: a machinelike, relentless education of the populace throughout their lives, not to stimulate freedom of thought but to ensure support for the activities of the state as determined by its leader.[9]

Hitler's chief assistant in the manipulation of information was Paul Josef Goebbels. He received a Ph.D. in 1920 from the University of Heidelberg, then joined the Nazi Party in 1922 and became a member of the national parliament (Reichstag) in 1930. Goebbels was a vain, insecure, bitter individual. He enjoyed controlling others but also seems to have needed a strong-willed person like Hitler for inspiration and a sense of certainty. Goebbels agreed with most of Hitler's ideas about mass persuasion but differed in one important respect. Hitler believed in the power of something that Goebbels came to call the "big lie." Hitler saw almost no limits to the credulity of the masses. They could be mesmerized by the sheer enormity of a claim, especially if it was continually repeated and widely spread through mass communication. Goebbels was equally cynical with regard to the credulity of the masses, and was not above deploying large untruths when he regarded them as useful. But he believed that selective use of fact was the most effective form of propaganda. In his view, the persuader's intentions should be cloaked in the truth whenever possible. By means of careful arrangement of facts and suppression of certain information when necessary, the propagandist could lead an audience to the desired conclusion.

Through vicious, ingenious, relentless mobilization of his mass-based party and maneuvering within the Weimar political system, Hitler became chancellor of Germany in 1933. Then in 1934, after the death of President Paul von Hindenburg, he received the title of führer along with virtually unlimited dictatorial power. Goebbels became head of the Ministry for Propaganda and Enlightenment (Reichsministerium für Volksaufklärung und Propaganda, or RMVP) when it was created in March 1933. He immediately began preparing the German people for war. The RMVP had twelve departments dealing with communications sectors from film, the theater, press, and radio to culture and education. The authority of Goebbels over the government's relations with the media was never complete, however. Joachim Ribbentrop, the erratic diplomat who eventually became foreign secretary, dabbled in media relations and after 1939 persuaded Hitler to enlarge his authority in this area. Hitler also created the position of Reich press chief, held by Otto Dietrich, who was housed in Hitler's office. The Ministry of Propaganda instituted the procedure of daily briefings for members of the press in Berlin, with instructions by telephone to journalists in other cities. This followed the practice begun in Italy in 1926 and also pursued by the Japanese beginning in 1937. Briefing officers frequently answered questions from reporters with the phrase "Hier ist nicht bekannt," in other words, "no comment." Increasingly, foreign correspondents chose not to attend.

An important prewar propaganda device of the Nazis was the *Parteitag* (party day, or party rally). In *Mein Kampf*, Hitler had assigned great importance to the use of mass meetings. The Nazis held a large rally annually in Nuremberg and repeated the format in similar gatherings throughout Germany. Albert Speer, Hitler's chief architect (and later minister for arms production), created impressive stage settings. Over 500,000 party members came to Nuremberg from all parts of Germany to have their banners blessed by the führer, pay homage to party members who, like Horst Wessel,

had died for the cause, hear stirring music, and listen to the führer's ora-
tions. The rallies took place at night, with the haunting canopy of black sky
above. Searchlights pointed upwards, forming a pattern like the arches of
a cathedral. Mass meetings of this kind combined old and new forms of
communication: torches, drums, banners, the sky above, primitive theater,
along with microphones, spotlights, loudspeakers, electricity, and multipli-
cation of on-the-scene effects by radio, film, and the printed word.

Control of the press presented special problems for the Nazis. Radio and
the cinema were state-owned industries in the Weimar Republic, so Hitler
gained control them as soon as he assumed power. The press, however, was
privately owned. The Nazis had to conquer it by stealth. They gradually
created a huge press monopoly.[10] In the early 1920s Germany had one of
the most active newspaper cultures in the world, composed of seven thousand periodicals serving hundreds of audiences, four thousand daily and
weekly newspapers, and a publishing industry that produced thirty thousand
books a year. Gradually the principle of freedom of the press lost strength
because of the political and economic chaos. In 1922, with the promulgation
of a law for the defense of the republic, the Weimar government obtained
power to penalize newspapers for actions judged to be revolutionary or opposed to the state. Controls became tighter in 1931–32 with the issuance of
Article 48, establishing emergency decrees in reaction to increasing chaos;
henceforth the police controlled approval for all public placards and handbills with political content. There were also penalties for intemperate language directed against public officials and organizations; the authorities
could close newspapers for eight weeks and other periodicals for up to six
months. In a separate law of July 1931 the government gained the authority
to require editors and publishers to print apologies for language disruptive
of the social order.

Such actions originated not so much from a philosophical opposition to
freedom of the press as from the need to defend a beleaguered regime. In
addition to the paramilitary violence of the Weimar era and the economic
depression that began immediately after the Great War, the regime also
had to contend with hate-filled attacks in the press. Communists were active in journalism; they founded the *Rote Fahne* (Red Flag) immediately after the Great War. Extreme right-wing journalism appeared in several
newspapers funded by Alfred Hugenberg, former president of the Krupp
armaments concern in the Ruhr area. The leader in capturing the press for
the Nazis was Max Amann, who had been Hitler's sergeant during the
Great War. He used behind-the-scenes legal and business maneuvers, combined with force when necessary. Amann was vulgar and had little formal

education or respect for intellect, but he had a cunning in business that Hitler appreciated. He began by acquiring the Eher Verlag publishing group in Munich and its newspaper, the *Völkischer Beobachter* (People's Observer). Next he directed party officials to develop local newspapers. As the power of the party increased, Amann gradually took over socialist and communist publishing concerns, sometimes by purchase but more often by verbal intimidation and selective use of violence. In the 1930s he gained control of the newspaper publishers' association and engineered special laws and regulations that put hundreds of privately owned newspapers under Nazi Party control. Additional takeovers occurred after the outbreak of war in 1939. In order to claim that capitalism was being preserved, some two thousand newspapers were allowed to remain in private ownership, but regimentation of the press was uniformly strict. Not surprisingly, the accuracy of information in German newspapers declined greatly after 1933.

Spain Becomes a Laboratory

Though not a major power in twentieth-century Europe, Spain took on great importance in the 1930s when its civil war drew the great powers into its vortex. In April 1931 a left-wing movement formed the Second Spanish Republic. It angered rightists by abolishing the titles of the nobility, curtailing the power of the military, challenging the authority of the Catholic Church, and confiscating large landholdings. Leftists were disappointed when the republic dissolved many public meetings, censored newspapers, and suspended many constitutional rights. Communists and extreme socialists attempted to push the republic further to the left. In 1934 the right-wing Falangist Party emerged as the leader of the forces attempting to bring back the older arrangements of power. Frequent street fighting took place in Madrid, Barcelona, and other localities. In July 1936 the right-wing forces supported an army mutiny led by General Francisco Franco. Within only forty-eight hours, all of Spain found itself in a civil war that lasted until 1939, when Franco defeated the Republicans and became dictator.

Great Britain, France, the United States, and the League of Nations all tried to broker an end to the conflict. Foreign intervention in the form of actual combat began in July 1936, when both Hitler and Mussolini provided troops, air support, and equipment to Franco. The Soviet Union sent a small force to help the Republicans. The United States, Great Britain, and other countries provided volunteers for an international brigade made up mostly of idealistic young men, including many artists and writers. Their participation throws into high relief a tendency that was presenting ever greater problems in the era of modern mass communication: the use of literary and artistic portrayal as a tool in its own right, to some extent regardless of actual fact, for purposes beyond depicting the events at hand. The artists and writers who joined the international brigade saw the Spanish civil war as a powerful symbol, larger than the war itself, of struggles between authoritarians and democrats, fascists and communists, intellectual freedom and religious bigotry, the rich and the poor. George Orwell wrote about the war in *Homage to Catalonia* (1938), his bitter description of the takeover of Republican forces by the Stalinist wing of the Communist Party and the failure of his fellow journalists to write honestly about the dangers of totalitarianism. Ernest Hemingway's novel about the war, *For Whom the Bell Tolls* (1940), was a best-selling tribute to the heroism of fighters on the Republican side, but it lapsed into glorification of the Stalinist values that had troubled Orwell. Hemingway also narrated the film documentary *The Spanish Earth*.[11]

A striking example of the tendency of outsiders to see what they wanted to see in the war was a famous photograph by Robert Capa, first published in the French magazine *Vu* on September 23, 1936, and then in *Life* magazine on July 12, 1937. It carried a caption identifying the subject as a soldier "the instant he is dropped by a bullet through the head in front of Cordoba." It was actually a photo of a soldier stumbling during training.[12] The pain and evil of the war were captured on canvas in Pablo Picasso's portrayal, completed in 1937, of the German air attack on the small town of Guernica (approximately six thousand inhabitants at the time). This, too, was an example of outsiders projecting their own concerns onto the war. The painting was a faithful depiction of events, but Picasso also regarded it as an opportunity to express his anger related to developments in his personal life at the time. The image nevertheless exerted worldwide influence almost immediately through its circulation in newspapers and periodicals in many countries.

Although the environment was a dangerous one, reporters were able to cover the civil war extensively, and more easily, for example, than conflicts in Asia. Print journalism was widespread and often eloquent. Radio reports gave a sense of immediacy and conveyed the drama of events through the dimension of sound. Still photography attained a new level of power, as witnessed in the photograph by Capa. Newsreel coverage was also extensive. Not just in Spain but in many other countries, audiences had to come to terms with disturbing information. The media brought news of the first bombardments of cities anywhere in Europe by fleets of airplanes. (There had been a few dirigible attacks on London in the First World War, and German pilots, singly or in small groups, occasionally dropped bombs, but the Spanish civil war marked the first use of concerted air attacks.) The scale of brutality practiced by both sides in the conflict aroused memories of atrocities, actual and fictitious, from the First World War.

Government news networks did not play much of a role in the civil war. Spain's networks were in too much disarray as a result of the violence and also the makeshift nature of the warring regimes. Germany, Italy, and the Soviet Union chose to use their press resources for other purposes. As neutrals, the governments of the United States, Britain, and France did not involve their official media resources. Freelance and news agency correspondents from those three countries dominated the reporting. Some were novices; others were veterans of earlier war coverage and the recent warfare in Ethiopia.

By the time the war ended with Franco's victory in March 1939, over 1 million soldiers and civilians had been killed. As part of his new government, Franco established a publicity organization on the fascist model that already existed in Italy and Germany, with its own official news agency based in Madrid and a network of radio stations in Spain's larger cities. At the outbreak of the Second World War, the Allies justifiably did not trust Franco's declarations that Spain would remain neutral. Nearby Portugal, since 1933 also a dictatorship, came closer to filling that role. It was not so much a producer of newspaper, periodical, and broadcast reports as it was a crossroads for their physical exchange, and a place to trade gossip and the products of espionage.[13]

Asia Regiments Its Media

In the early twentieth century, an important story of war, peace, and the media was unfolding in East Asia. In the late nineteenth century, to avoid being overrun by Western imperialists as the Chinese had been, Japan undertook a radical restructuring of its society which included adopting Western methods of economic and military organization, along with its own increasingly intense program of imperialistic expansion. Japan saw China as a source of raw materials and a vast market for its growing industries. Using its new steam-powered navy, and its military equipped with arms manufactured at Western-style factories, Japan defeated China in the Sino-Japanese War of 1894–95, expanded its influence by victory in the Russo-Japanese War of 1904–5, and annexed Korea in 1910.

There was a Chinese Republic based at Peking, founded in 1912 by Sun Yat-sen. The Kuomintang (National People's Party) established a government at Nanking in 1928, led by Chiang Kai-shek, who had been military adviser to Sun Yat-sen and who gained the reins of power after Sun's death.

Western nations gave Chiang's government diplomatic recognition in 1928. The year before, a radical wing of the Kuomintang, led by Mao Tse-tung, had established a communist organization based at Hankow. It harassed Chiang until 1934, when the communists, increasingly in fear of being overwhelmed by Chiang's forces, made a "Long March" west to Shensi province and established a capital in the mountains at Yenan.

When he proclaimed the Republic of China in 1912, Sun Yat-sen was already aware of the importance of propaganda. He had learned from centuries-old Chinese traditions like the use of imperial edicts to proclaim the ruler's will to the population; and he also understood how, in his own era, local groups of students, business organizations, and his party followers were strengthening their efforts by adapting Western-style techniques of publicity. Sun used newspapers, pamphlets, posters, songs, and cartoons to motivate revolutionaries, along with mass mobilization drives based on trades groups, political clubs, student associations, and other entities. Then in the 1920s, Sun was approached by representatives from the Soviet Union who wanted to move the revolution along. They pointed out to him that Lenin had institutionalized the concept of propaganda as something that ought to function on two tracks: the propagation of ideas, especially to elites and the educated; and agitation, both to reinforce ideas transmitted to the elites and also to motivate the masses through simple messages and reinforcement by techniques such as repetition and the use of party representatives who worked face-to-face with them at the local level. In response, Sun enlarged his concept of propaganda to a certain extent, involving his political party apparatus in more active direction of publicity, and including some efforts at agitation. But he did not follow through. He put his greatest faith in a military solution to the challenge of consolidating the republic, even though the Soviet advisers counseled that such a strategy was premature without adequate advance work to make the common people receptive. Increasingly Sun limited his propaganda to urban elites, the educated, and a few select groups such as secret societies. He assumed that the masses would simply follow along.

After Sun's death in 1925, Chiang Kai-shek continued Sun's pattern and even extended it somewhat, for example, by including mass persuasion as one of the skills taught at his military academy, where, ironically, Mao Tse-tung was initially one of the directors of propaganda.[14] But Chiang's approach was in conspicuous contrast to that of the communists, who did follow through on the Leninist model. From the late 1920s on, after Mao and Chiang split, the communists not only directed propaganda at urban populations but also worked increasingly to win over China's vast rural areas by the use of tools appropriate to an illiterate population, such as illustrated handbills, visually arresting posters, rousing songs, and village speeches and discussions organized by party agitators. To bring home their message further, the communists evolved an elaborate strategy of indoctrination. Recruits to the army and the party underwent a process of reorientation that emphasized self-examination, shame, public expression of remorse for past errors, learning the new way of thinking of the party, and participation in the larger program of proselytizing.[15]

In 1929 Chiang Kai-shek's Nationalist government accused Moscow of violating agreements; the Soviets stationed Red Army troops on the Manchurian border, and four months of frontier battle followed. Japan sent troops into Shantung province in 1929. In 1930 the Nationalists decided that they did not have sufficient resources to force Japan out of China and chose instead to live with the Japanese presence. Squabbles over trade followed until the summer of 1931, when Japan attacked Manchuria, gaining control by the end of the year.

The Japanese drove the Chinese Nationalist government out of Nanking in 1937 and forced it to reestablish its capital far to the west in Chunking in 1938. The Chinese communist government, based to the north in Yenan since 1934, was by this time cooperating with the Nationalists in the effort to drive out the Japanese, although the Japanese military had defeated the combined Chinese forces near Shanghai in 1937.

Western nations were not well equipped to understand these developments. In the West during the 1920s and 1930s, the average person's view of "the Far East" and "the Orient" was a mixture of fragmentary information and stereotypes. The Far East was the source of tea, beautiful art and fashions, amusements like Ping-Pong and mah-jongg, and the sturdy peasants in Pearl S. Buck's novel *The Good Earth* (1931), which helped her win the Nobel Prize for literature the following year. But just as frequently, the images evoked a world of strangeness and evil that led Western audiences to see the region as a place where war was endemic and efforts to broker peace were pointless. Some of the imagery went back to the nineteenth century: Western wars of imperialism, the association of the East with opium, and literary characters like the villains in the wildly successful Sherlock Holmes stories and the *Fu Manchu* novels of Sax Rohmer (born Arthur Henry Ward in Birmingham). Most of the images reinforced fears of a "Yellow Peril" that influenced parties as diverse as Kaiser Wilhelm in Germany and nativists who rioted against Chinese residents in the western United States. The negative imagery persisted and expanded in the 1920s, for example, as an influence on conceptions of noir in popular literature, and the precursors to film noir in Hollywood productions like *Shanghai Express* (1932) starring Marlene Dietrich, *The Mask of Fu Manchu* (1932) with Boris Karloff, and the detective movies of the 1930s featuring Mr. Moto and Charlie Chan.

Western diplomatic staffs assigned to East Asia were small in comparison to the resources focused on the West. And the same was true of news organizations. Institutions of higher education did not produce a large number of graduates with expertise in this part of the world. The hiring pool for the media was also small. Few reporters were stationed in East Asia long enough to develop knowledge in depth.

Newspapers on the Western model came to China in the late nineteenth century, first to provide business news related to international trade in the port cities. Sun Yat-sen developed a party press organized around the *Chung-kuo Jih-pao* (Chinese Daily Paper), begun in 1899. After the Revolution of 1911, some five hundred papers appeared. Most were developed by Chinese who had learned Western journalism overseas. Many were soon suppressed, however, because the regime feared free speech. Those that remained focused on economic development and daily business matters. This pattern continued under Chiang Kai-shek. The Nationalists had an official press agency (Chung Yang Sheh, the Central News Agency), established in 1924, the first significant news agency in China; it also published a newspaper, *Chung Yang Jih Pao* (Central Daily News), at Nanking. The Nationalists also had a Central Publicity Board in the Kuomintang Party, a Department of Intelligence and Publicity in the Ministry of Foreign Affairs, and a separate Ministry of Communications. But Japanese military activity disrupted these functions. Nationalist censorship was mostly unofficial before 1931, but in May of that year the Nationalists announced more stringent policies, for example, censoring the foreign communications organizations based in the International Settlement in Shanghai. Foreign reporters never knew if their dispatches got through to the West or were secretly edited by the Nationalists. Starting in May 1933 the Nationalist government required international correspondents to apply for official accreditation.[16]

Meanwhile, Japan was greatly expanding its mass communications. The first newspapers in Japan on the Western model dated from 1861, when an Englishman founded the *Nagasaki Shipping List and Advertiser*. Readership grew rapidly, more so than in China as a result of the drive for literacy that accompanied the general push for Westernization. After institution of the Meiji Constitution in 1890, papers serving both political and commercial functions emerged, including the *Asahi Shimbun* (Morning

Sun), which received much of its overseas news from Reuters, and its competitor the *Mainichi Shimbun* (Daily Paper), which created its own overseas service.

By 1910 Japan had 250 newspapers. They were a major force leading to the establishment of universal voting rights for men in 1925. There was also a small radio network, the Japan Broadcasting Network (Nippon Hoso Kyokai, or NHK), established in 1925. Two Japanese news agencies, Rengo and Dentsu, supported correspondents in major cities throughout the world. One of Japan's daily newspapers, *Asahi*, producing editions in Tokyo and Osaka, was said to have the largest circulation of any paper in the world. Other major papers were *Mainichi*, which served Osaka and Kyoto, and *Nichi Nichi* in Tokyo.

Even though it was fragmentary, the information about East Asia received in the West was sufficient to engender great fascination and a hunger for more. Western publications such as the *Saturday Evening Post* and *Collier's* were in the market for interesting stories, and they subsidized reporters willing to journey to the region. Thus a Western journalistic presence gradually emerged. Two American journalists, William and Rayna Prohme, were among the earliest. Like John Reed and his wife, Louise Bryant, who had gone to Russia, they were young bohemian idealists eager to visit exotic nations where new forms of society seemed to be in the process of creation. William Prohme was a German American, originally from Brooklyn, who found work with the *San Francisco Examiner* in the 1920s and became fascinated by the Pacific region. Rayna Prohme was from an upper-class Jewish family in Chicago. Defying cultural categories, she moved west and met Prohme in Berkeley. The two made their way to China, where they worked as reporters for Western news outlets and also served as propagandists for Sun Yat-sen. After Chiang Kai-shek came to power, they sided with the communists. American reporters who joined with them to write stories supportive of the communists included Vincent Sheehan, Anna Louise Strong, and Edgar Snow. Snow, in particular, went on to exert enormous influence over Western perceptions of China through newspaper reportage and best-selling books like *Red Star over China* (1937). Although he was a credulous observer, his writings enjoyed huge sales throughout the West and gave readers their first detailed reports about Mao Tse-tung and the kind of society he was trying to create. Two other influential American journalists, slightly younger, were Theodore H. White and Annalee Jacoby. The brilliant reporting they did in the 1930s and 1940s attracted large audiences; it is epitomized in their book *Thunder Out of China* (1946), which recapitulates the experiences of their earlier years there.[17]

For Westerners, covering Japan was more difficult. The Japanese government did not at first exploit the interest of foreign journalists in their country. The famous American writer Jack London, who had journeyed across the Pacific to cover the Russo-Japanese War of 1904–5, was forced to remain in his hotel in Tokyo in the early stages of hostilities and to get information as best he could. The Japanese secret police harassed him at first but eventually gave him permission to go to Korea and witness Japanese troop movements there, enabling him to send exciting reports back to the Hearst newspapers in the United States. But when London got in a fistfight with a Japanese soldier, he was imprisoned and threatened with execution. His fellow correspondent Richard Harding Davis and President Theodore Roosevelt had to intervene to secure London's safe return to America.[18]

A growing community of Western correspondents operated out of Tokyo from the early 1920s on, often traveling to cover stories in Peking and Shanghai. In 1932, when the Japanese invaded Shanghai, correspondents filed some thirty thousand words each day to New York at the cost of $4,000 per day, also providing still photographs and newsreel films that shocked Western audiences.

A small number of Western journalists sought to continue reporting events in Japan under difficult circumstances. Reuters offered facilities. A Danish-owned telegraph provided transmission through Siberia to Copenhagen. But censorship in Japan was a major problem. There was a "Dangerous Thought Act" in effect, dating from 1925, and in 1932 Japan established a Bureau of Thought Supervision in the Ministry of Education. News coverage soon became even more subject to official control. When the Manchurian campaign began in 1931, the chief of the Japanese Information Bureau in the Foreign Ministry tried to be open with reporters, but he was replaced in 1933 by a more rigid official, who was in the habit of responding to all questions, "We have no report." The assassinations of two of Japan's prime ministers, in 1930 and 1932, made the government cautious in its dealings with foreigners and more rigid in control of the press at home. The police gained the power to censor foreign reporting about military and diplomatic matters, while censors reviewed printed materials entering Japan. The authorities frequently seized copies of *Time* magazine and cut out key stories with scissors. Publications thought to have communist connections were confiscated. In 1935, when the American magazine *Vanity Fair* published a caricature of Emperor Hirohito, the Japanese government filed a formal protest with the U.S. Department of State. So worried were the Japanese authorities regarding potential harm that in 1935 the military physically attacked at least three publishers and arranged for the destruction of the presses of another. In 1935 the government took control of the NHK news agency, and in 1936 merged two other private news agencies into a government-controlled entity, the Allied News Agency (Domei Tsushin-sha, or Domei), subsidized by the Ministry of Communication.

By 1936 Japan was under the control of a military government. That same year the Japanese signed the Anti-Comintern Pact opposing the Soviet Union and creating the Rome-Berlin-Tokyo Axis. By this time the Japanese regarded most foreign correspondents as spies, and both foreign correspondents and Japanese newspaper staffs and owners were becoming accustomed to being warned not to file reports giving the impression that the Japanese were warlike.

In 1937, when Japanese forces attacked China, some five hundred Japanese reporters accompanied the troops. In September 1937 the Japanese made a highly brutal attack on Nanking. The Japanese aerial bombardment of the city that year is generally regarded as the first large-scale airplane attack in history on an urban civilian population. Although the bombardment of Guernica in the Spanish civil war preceded it, the assault on Nanking was on a much greater scale. Brutality increased as the Japanese army entered the city in December. They rounded up large numbers of Chinese men for execution and then dumped the bodies into the river. The Japanese held killing contests to see who could use a sword to chop off the most heads. Large numbers of Chinese women and girls were subjected to multiple rapes and then killed in a bestial manner. Reporting of all these events was extensive. The Japanese supplied news bulletins, photographs, and newsreel films to the home islands. Western residents of Nanking, massed together in the International Safety Zone created by the Japanese to avoid overtly provoking the Western nations, were able to send out descriptions of what they had witnessed. Among the Westerners in the city were not only journalists but also large numbers of articulate missionaries. The Japanese made some attempt to censor foreigners but, strangely, seem not to have considered the fact that, even with full censorship, Westerners could still learn of events from copies they received of the newspapers and films being circulated in Japan. The Japanese government was extremely proud of its success in Nanking and did not think that violence on such a scale was improper in war, whether in combat or in the treatment of civilians, whom the Japanese tended to see as extensions of the enemy's military capacity. When photographs of the Japanese soldiers engaging in their beheading contests appeared in Japanese newspapers, families in Tokyo celebrated the victory by enjoying specially prepared meals of Nanking noodles. Only after news reports in the Western media led to international condemnation did the

Japanese attempt to sanitize the story of the invasion with hastily arranged propaganda. The truths initially available in the Japanese media were reinforced by the reports from the International Safety Zone. Journalists such as Frank Tillman Durdin of the *New York Times* and Archibald Steele of the *Chicago Daily News* risked their lives to obtain information in Nanking, help the Chinese, and then make their way to Shanghai to file stories. Two American newsreel cameramen, representing Universal and Fox Movie Tone, recorded the Japanese bombing and sinking of the U.S. gunboat *Panay* in the Yangtze River, then smuggled their film to the West, where excerpts were shown in hundreds of movie theaters.

To stem the tide of such reports, the Japanese soon instituted extreme censorship of Western reportage. President Roosevelt assisted them in a way. In 1937–38 the United States and other Western nations were preoccupied with events in Europe and were not eager to be dragged into a war in Asia. Roosevelt pronounced himself "shocked" by events in Nanking, which was no doubt true, but he sought to keep the worst of the news from Western audiences. He asked one of the U.S. newsreel men to excise some thirty feet of film—which showed Japanese planes strafing the *Panay* at deck level—from the version shown to U.S. audiences, fearing that the images would arouse war fever among Americans. The failure to include these images made it easier for Western audiences to believe the claim of Japanese propagandists that the bombing of the *Panay* had been an accident. Reporters and clergy in the International Safety Zone refused to surrender to censorship. Mobilizing their considerable rhetorical skills, they leaked reports out of Nanking that made their way into Western publications such as *Time*, *Reader's Digest*, and the *Manchester Guardian*. Western outrage never rose to the degree necessary to prompt action against Japanese methods of war in the 1930s. Many viewers were disturbed by the images recorded on film, which were undeniable. But many others categorized the events in Nanking as something happening far away, typical of the behavior of "inferior" Asian races, and in any case not worth shifting the United States from isolationism into a war in the East. In response to the print reports, many readers took refuge in denial and dismissed the information as reminiscent of the propaganda that had been ubiquitous in the Great War.[19]

By 1939 Western correspondents in Japan were experiencing even more hostility than before owing to a Japanese perception that they favored the Chinese. In 1939 and 1940 several U.S. correspondents in Tokyo were arrested and forced to undergo intimidating interrogations; one was murdered. In Manchukuo (Japanese Manchuria) several were abducted and simply vanished.

As late as 1938 Japanese newspapers still struggled to maintain some degree of independence. In December, when the prime minister delivered an important policy address over the radio and did not invite the press to cover it, a group of prominent editors and publishers protested, helping to hasten the resignation of the government. But the following year, under the new but also very militarized government, control of the press became stricter, with extensive powers given to local courts and the ministries of war and the navy. By the end of 1939, some six hundred newspapers and periodicals had been suppressed; many had been forced to merge; supplies of newsprint came under government control; proofs had to be shown to censors before publication; and reporters could be arrested simply for being "uncooperative."

By 1940 a highly articulated publicity structure was in place to serve official needs. The information offices in the ministries of war, the navy, and foreign affairs worked with the cabinet's Board of Information, which had the power to approve all press releases both foreign and domestic. The board had a staff of about one hundred. Foreign correspondents could now sense that the population of Japan had been told to avoid them. Many international journalists left the country. Around the same time, the Japanese began to put pressure on foreign owners of newspapers and periodicals to sell. In February 1941 the Japanese Diet, or parliament, approved a law imposing severe penalties, with no rights of appeal, against anyone suspected of revealing state secrets, a concept defined so broadly that it included almost all military, diplomatic, and commercial matters, even simple reports of government meetings. In early 1941 a new Board of Censorship was established in Tokyo. By this time government officials were in the habit of declaring that a major object of Japanese foreign policy was to drive the white man out of Asia.[20]

The Media Intensify a Crisis

After Hitler annexed Austria in March 1938, he more forcefully reiterated claims he had been making for some time that the Sudetenland, the German-speaking area of Czechoslovakia, ought to be joined to the Reich as well. His aggressive posturing raised the possibility of war. Hoping to preserve peace, the British prime minister, Neville Chamberlain, met with Hitler, Mussolini, and the French premier, Édouard Daladier, in Munich in September 1938. After intense negotiations Germany received the Sudetenland in exchange for a promise not to attack the rest of the country. Newsreel films captured Chamberlain's dramatic return by airplane to Britain and his declaration that the agreement augured "peace for our time." But "appeasement," as it was called, did not prevent war. Hitler annexed the rump portions of Czechoslovakia in March 1939 and then attacked Poland in September, leading Britain and France to declare war.

Advances in mass communication intensified the international attention focused on the Munich conference. One innovation was a new technique of still photography pioneered by the German photographer Erich Solomon. He was already by this time a recognized master in the use of the 35-millimeter camera. At Munich he contributed to the sense of drama through his "candid camera" technique, which captured close-up images of famous conference participants even when flash photography was not possible and he had to make use of available light.

The Munich crisis also marked a greatly enlarged role for radio. From the early 1930s on, shortwave broadcasts had been added to regular broadcasts by the BBC in Britain, Radiodiffusion Française in France, the NHK in Japan, the NBC, CBS, and MBS radio networks in the United States, and other organizations. Millions of people, the largest news audiences ever reached, listened simultaneously to reports in real time during the dramatic negotiations of 1938. They could hear the actual voices of world leaders and background sounds. By this time broadcasters had developed ways of constructing suspenseful narrations and descriptions, delivered by reporters who had learned their trade in the print world but had a special ability to modulate their voices and project a sense of drama. Some spoke extemporaneously, some worked from their own scripts, and some had scripts written for them. Protocols for in-depth analysis were also in evidence, as broadcasters commented on the news at length, either individually or in on-air groups usually gathered together in the same studio. H. V. Kaltenborn, one of the newscasters at NBC, made the technique more elaborate. He dramatically occupied a central studio and from there orchestrated the broadcast of a sequence of commentaries and reports by radio journalists who transmitted their remarks to him from the various countries where they were stationed.

World opinion eventually assigned Chamberlain almost sole blame for the erroneous concessions at Munich, and for sacrificing Czech military and industrial resources. But the popular openness to fascist appeals in the media was also a cause of Hitler's aggressiveness. During the Ethiopian war of 1935–36, French papers accepted bribes to publish stories sympathetic to the Italian Fascists. In Britain the editors of *The Times*, the *Sunday Observer*, and perhaps the *Daily Telegraph* all supported appeasement in principle. Geoffrey Dawson, the editor of *The Times*, wrote privately of the Germans in 1937, that he did his utmost, "night after night, to keep out of the paper anything that might have hurt their susceptibility." Dawson also aggressively edited dispatches from his paper's correspondent in Berlin, Norman Ebbutt. In 1938, when Hitler annexed Austria, Dawson wrote approvingly, in an editorial in *The Times*, about Hitler's "triumphal progress" into the country and said there was "no room for doubt about the public jubilation with which he and his army were greeted everywhere," even though *The Times* was simultaneously publishing dispatches from its own correspondents in Vienna that largely contradicted Dawson's analysis. In 1938, during the diplomatic maneuverings at Munich, the German government was able to bribe many French newspapers to publish stories favorable to its purposes. *The Times*, directed by Dawson, voiced approval for Hitler's demands; Dawson also printed slanted reports on parliamentary speeches opposing appeasement. Even more overt was the manipulation of news by Lord Beaverbrook's papers leading up to and during the Munich crisis. Another influential figure who failed to voice concern about German aggressiveness was Lord Reith, head of the BBC.[21] When the press in democratic countries did so little to protest Hitler's actions in Austria and Czechoslovakia, it became much easier for the führer to think he could get away with almost anything.

5 THE BATTLE FOR THE MIND DEEPENS

1939–1945

In ALL of the dictatorships, by the outbreak of the Second World War, elaborate governmental structures for the manipulation of media were already in place. When war broke out, the democracies worked hastily to mobilize their informational resources and soon were able to use mass communication as a powerful weapon. In every country, old strategies of persuasion remained and new ones appeared. The intangible aspects of war came to matter almost as much as the physical factors, as combatants developed new, often disturbing ways of penetrating the mind.

Hitler Perverts Psychology

Hitler's vast propaganda apparatus had been preparing for war since 1933. Certain features took on particular prominence once the war began. One area of great expansion, not surprisingly, was military propaganda. Each major army, air force, and naval unit had its own staff, numbering in the thousands, responsible for publicity, as did Hitler's elite corps, the SS. An example of the extensive reach of German military propaganda was *Signal*, one of the magazines the army (Wehrmacht) wrote and printed. It had a circulation of 2.5 million at its height and was translated into twenty-five languages, making it the most extensively circulated of the hundreds of German propaganda magazines produced during the war, resembling civilian publications in Allied nations such as *Life* magazine in the United States and *Paris Match* in France. Most issues included color photographs. Images exploited by *Signal*, touching on a wide range of propagandistic themes, included German fighter planes flying over the English coast above Dover, a German soldier on the Eastern Front writing a letter to his mother, a map showing the progress of German soldiers through Holland and Belgium, captured Russian prisoners, a scuttled French battleship, a heroic portrait of Admiral Erich Raeder in his finest dress uniform, and the compassionate rescue of torpedoed British sailors.

Nazi propagandists made extensive use of the motion picture. The authorities required all filmgoers to view the weekly newsreel, the *Deutsche Wochenschau*, which exploited combat footage recently taken at the front. The German secret police, the Gestapo, monitored audience reactions to this and other documentaries, which seem to have increased home front morale. Showings in urban locations predominated, but the films also reached rural audiences and schools. There were numerous propagandistic feature films as well. For example, *Mein Leben für Irland* (1941) exploited stereotypes about British treatment of the Irish, while *Ohm Kruger* (1941) advanced the German interpretation of the Anglo-Boer War. Russia became a subject of films when the Germans invaded that country. *GPU* (1942) portrayed the cruelty of the Russian secret police. The official production of films subsided dramatically after the German defeat in 1943 at the Battle of Stalingrad. Only four feature films appeared that year, three in 1944, and one in 1945, *Kolberg*, which focused on the theme of resistance.

An especially perverse development in Nazi wartime propaganda was the attention given to children and adolescents. This emphasis had begun in the early 1930s with the establishment of groups such as the Hitler Youth (Hitlerjugend) for teenage boys and the Jungmädelbund for girls. Young people encountered ultranationalist propaganda face-to-face in group meetings and rallies and in thousands of books, pamphlets, and posters, as well as in films like *Hitlerjünge Quex* (1933), the first in an often exploited genre idealizing German boys who died for the cause. The Hitler Youth had its own marching songs and flags. The Nazis directed anti-Semitic propaganda at children just as much as they did at adults. In Austria, for example, the German occupying authorities made certain that at the beginning of every school day all children recited in unison, "The Jew is guilty of the war." After the conquest of France and formation of the Vichy regime in 1940, the Nazis used children's fiction to stimulate sympathy for German rule and the collaborationist cause, for example, circulating a manipulative fairy tale about the beautiful marriage of Princess Europa and Prince Germain. Other media reinforced the message of this literature. A 1940 poster showed a sturdy, kindly faced German soldier giving bread to one French child and wrapping his protective arm around two others. The caption read, "You abandoned populations, have faith in the German soldier!" During the First World War, all nations had made use of children's propaganda. The British published boys' adventure stories written in the Kipling style that made a tour of duty at the Western Front sound like a summer at camp, while in the Soviet Union, both Lenin and Stalin directed propaganda at young people. But the Nazis targeted not only the home population in Germany but also children in conquered nations. And the deceptiveness of their manipulation of young minds was especially cruel. During the same years when fairy tales about Germania were being circulated in France, the Nazis were removing Jewish children from their French families and killing them in concentration camps.[1]

The Nazis also made extensive use of radio. In the years after 1934, new laws required that all Germans utilize officially approved radio receivers that did not pick up broadcasts from outside the country except in border areas. The radios had very simple dials; they were tuned to German frequencies and did not receive shortwave signals, thus revealing Nazi fears of a recurrence of the devastating effects of Allied propaganda during the First World War. Domestic audiences received a never-ending stream of mass persuasion from twenty-six official radio stations controlled by the Reich Radio Society.

For a while it remained possible to report news to other countries from within Germany. In 1939 at the time of the invasion of Poland, and in the French campaign in 1940, the German military allowed foreign correspondents to file reports from the front. This situation changed in June 1941, when, disregarding the Nazi-Soviet Pact of August 1939, Germany invaded Soviet Russia. When German troops began their advance into the USSR, Goebbels took to the radio and read a proclamation to the German people from Hitler justifying the war as a proper response to accumulating violations of the treaty. Within a few hours, reports of the proclamation and the invasion reached radio listeners around the world, and within twelve hours most newspapers in major cities carried lengthy coverage and in many cases printed special editions with extensive background material. Nazi censorship of foreign reporting, previously indirect at times, now became explicit. The army also became stricter; it kept correspondents away from military activity and forced them to rely on reports from Wehrmacht press units. In November 1941 the German authorities told the representatives of the three U.S. radio networks in Berlin that their work was unsatisfactory and asked the networks to send replacements. All U.S. broadcasting from Germany stopped in December 1941 after the Japanese attack on Pearl Harbor brought the United States into the war on the side of Britain and the Soviet Union. This also ended any chance that reporters from Allied nations had of going to the German front. The Nazis arrested many Allied correspondents, while others had to struggle to get out.

Though very powerful, the German propaganda machine was not without its problems. At the outbreak of war in 1939, Goebbels and other controllers of information squabbled among themselves and competed for Hitler's favor. Goebbels also had to deal with the fact that the German people were ambivalent about the war at first, until successes in Belgium, Holland, Denmark, Norway, and France followed the initial victory in Poland. The population favored war as long as Germany was winning. Goebbels exploited the chain of victories and gave it a mystique of destiny. But persuasion became more difficult after Germany began to experience defeats and victory seemed less certain. As in all the belligerent countries, German propagandists had to adjust quickly when their messages seemed to contradict reality or there were sudden changes in policy. For example, Nazi publicists had to revise their messages when, in contradiction to extensive propaganda, Hitler curtailed his plans for an immediate invasion of Britain, and then when he suddenly repudiated his pact with Stalin by the surprise attack on Russia. A major setback for German propaganda was the parachuting into Scotland in May 1941 of Rudolf Hess, one of Hitler's close advisers, who soon appeared in Western newsreels in a call for peace that appeared to be motivated less by reflection than by derangement. The propagandists were often surprisingly ingenious. For example, in 1943, when Hitler's paratroopers plucked Mussolini from Allied captivity, German newsreels diverted attention from the fact that the operation was a desperate measure by emphasizing that it displayed German military skill, which indeed it did.[2]

In the Second World War, Germany led the way in exploiting a radically new conception of mass persuasion. In each belligerent country in the First World War, wartime propaganda was, for the most part, *mythic*. This is a useful rubric for mass persuasion rooted in the large-scale sagas that unite nations and other groups and express their highest values in story form. As myth, it is not necessarily untrue. But it does resort, in part, to fictional narration intended to provide connection and meaning, a cause-and-effect understanding of large questions that cannot be answered scientifically or in a completely factual manner but that concern, and often preoccupy, the society. Propaganda rooted in myth often refers to the culture's central, defining narratives. It is usually directed by elites and is sometimes manufactured by them, although it arises from the collective consciousness of all parts of the society and can move the masses if employed skillfully. The effective use of mythic propaganda requires extensive knowledge of the culture. The strategy underlying propaganda in Germany in the 1930s and even more clearly in the Second World War was much less focused on cultural referents and relied on tactics markedly different from those of myth-based persuasion.

One can describe the new kind of German propaganda as *bio-behavioral*. The term is also useful as a description of Soviet opinion manipulation during the time of Stalin, and somewhat useful for categorizing techniques seen at times in Japan and China, as well as the United States and Britain. Bio-behavioral propaganda reserves some space for the knowledgeable references to great national epics that had been the dominant approach to mass persuasion in the First World War. One thinks, for example, of the German film *Triumph of the Will* (1935), directed by Leni Riefenstahl. It records Hitler's dramatic landing by airplane at Nuremberg, his triumphal progress as adoring crowds welcome him, and his appearance at one of the huge rallies of the Nazi Party. The film is morally repugnant in its glorification of Hitler, and yet it is a work of genius, not only in its mastery of cinematic techniques but also in its stirring use of symbols from Germanic literature and Wagnerian opera. But high-minded reference to great cultural traditions was not the chief characteristic of propaganda in Hitler's Germany. His propagandists started not from the Enlightenment premise that people are fundamentally rational and altruistic, nor from religious premises that view people as capable of kindness and moral vision, but from a posture that defined all humans except a small elite as little better than animals.

In the 1920s and 1930s new insights about human nature, based on the emerging science of psychology, were making their way into the cultures of all the industrialized countries. In the minds of demagogues, the influence of notions picked up from psychology was perverse. In *Mein Kampf*, Hitler compared the mass of humanity to dogs that could function only in packs commanded by their strongest members. Never an original thinker, Hitler was drawing on notions that were circulating, by his time, throughout society. One line of thinking drew on the general interest in what was coming to be called the subconscious: the term is today a commonplace but was new at the time. As Sigmund Freud and a number of other thinkers maintained, there are two areas of the mind that operate just below the level of those thoughts of which people are usually aware. One is the unconscious portion of the mind, which regulates basic functions like breathing and heartbeat. Above it, and accessible by special techniques, is the subconscious, consisting of supposedly forgotten childhood memories, ambitions, and desires we might not want to admit to ourselves and society, and warped ways of thinking developed to cope with traumatic experiences.

Another general area of awareness, discussed with care in works like Freud's *Totem and Taboo* (1913) but employed much less honorably by the Nazis, focused on the carryover into modern industrial society of behavior observable in members of "primitive" tribes, who had a deep need to organize themselves into clans led by potent figures who seemed to possess powers drawn from nature. As long as the leader could preserve authority over the clan, people would do whatever the leader asked in order to relieve their everyday insecurities, no matter whether the command was moral or not. A third line of popular thinking that affected Hitler and his propagandists linked back to research by the Russian scientist Ivan Pavlov, who discovered that by repetition, he was able to train animals to associate items arbitrarily and illogically. For example, dogs salivated involuntarily after Pavlov conditioned them to associate the ringing of a bell with receiving food. Another thinker who greatly influenced Hitler was the French physician Gustav Le Bon, who had written about crowd behavior in the late nineteenth century. Medical figures of Le Bon's era had studied how diseases such as cholera and tuberculosis spread rapidly in big cities because of the packing together of large populations. Observing urban riots, Le Bon and many of his contemporaries hypothesized that masses of people became "infected" emotionally by rumor, strategic construction of messages in the media of the era, and orators experienced in techniques of agitation.

Hitler assiduously put the popularized views of theorists like Freud, Pavlov, and Le Bon into practice. He sought to use propaganda, censorship, and terror to turn all of Germany into a herd, a pack, a crowd, a credulous tribe that would fall under his command. His aim was to overwhelm an individual's capacity for internal reflection and voluntary action, and to control each person by means of external stimuli. The result was a form of mass communication that continued to exploit myth but put much greater emphasis than in previous wars on heavy-handed repetition, deception intended to manipulate people's understandings of reality, assertion of the importance of unquestioning obedience, and messages that spoke to people's fears and their concern for basic survival.

Perhaps the most obvious bio-behavioral technique of the Nazis was crowd manipulation. Whipping the mob into a frenzy was a centuries-old technique of politics. One thinks, for example, of Marc Antony's funeral oration in Shakespeare's *Julius Caesar*, or the mania of crowds in the French Revolution. The Nazis used bio-behavioral techniques to intensify large-group experience. At outdoor rallies or in large halls, organizers packed spectators together in strategically bounded spaces, in the belief that bodily electricity and energizing smells would transfer more easily from one person to another. Lighting, music, and swastikas displayed on colorful backdrops helped to flood people's senses. To build suspense, organizers delayed the arrival of the führer, often by an hour or more. When he finally appeared, the impatience of audience members dissipated, and they felt relief and gratitude. The speaker's voice was an instrument. His oration seldom emphasized logic but instead repeated trigger words and animalistic sounds. Listeners participated actively, shouting "Hail! Hail!" in response to loud perorations. All the while, Hitler's propagandists were broadcasting the speech and the audience interaction on radio and filming it for additional circulation via newsreels.

Even truthfulness became a tool of bio-behavioral crowd manipulation. Late in the war, at a mass rally in the Sports Palace in Berlin, broadcast throughout Germany, Goebbels went so far as to share detailed information about setbacks in Russia and to call for "total war" involving much greater sacrifice on the home front. Even at this moment of seeming candor, however, bio-behavioral techniques were in use. Goebbels stationed operatives throughout the crowd at the Sports Palace. At preselected points in the speech, when Goebbels asked the crowd if it was willing to make the sacrifices he advocated, his agents cheered and applauded loudly, prompting the rest of the audience to follow reflexively. In the twenty-first century we have become familiar with oratorical techniques of this kind. In Hitler's era they were newer, and people were less practiced in defending against them.[3]

Another bio-behavioral technique used extensively by the Nazis was the portrayal of the enemy as a beast intent on stealing the territory of Germanic populations, or as an individual intent on reducing the home population's status and fragile sense of emotional well-being. This was a major reason why Hitler's speeches so frequently mentioned Germany's need for *Lebensraum*, or "living space." It was also a factor in the Nazis' focus on supposedly threatening populations such as Jews and Gypsies, whom propagandists repeatedly compared to lice, cockroaches, and rats that would endanger not only German culture but also public health unless exterminated.

Nazi propaganda also manifested great ingenuity in the use of visual techniques designed to circumvent the conscious mind. A striking example was a poster circulated before the war, during the election of 1933, urging Germans to vote for Hitler. It showed nothing but a photograph of Hitler's face against a black background, staring directly at the viewer like a floating image from a dream. The aim was to fix a memory of the führer in the viewer's mind whether the viewer wanted it to be there or not. The Nazis used similar techniques in 1943 in an eight-page folder dropped by the Luftwaffe over airbases in England where Americans were stationed. The front page mimicked the cover of an issue of *Life* magazine, complete with the familiar red and white rectangular logo containing the name of the magazine in the upper-left corner and a full-page photograph of American airplane crews that had served as an actual cover of the magazine in July 1943. But this time the query "life?" appeared in white against a small, dark rectangle at the bottom of the cover, and the seven pages within showed frightening photographs of U.S. airmen who had died over Germany, along with remarks about the folly and consequences of continuing to conduct air raids.

The bio-behavioral exploitation of imagery included not only still photography but also cinema, as the Nazis drew on the latest developments in German filmmaking, including montage, slow fadeouts, and dream sequences intensified by haunting music. An example was *Der ewige Jude* (The Eternal/Wandering Jew), perhaps the most infamous of all the anti-Semitic Nazi films, which appeared in 1940. The film is myth-based propaganda in the sense that it exploits centuries-old cultural stereotypes. But it emphasizes bio-behavioral techniques. For example, it ends with a dreamlike sequence of blond Aryans posed in front of the sky, and flowing images of flags and banners and Nazi salutes. In addition, the film evokes visceral fears by including supposedly authentic images of Jewish ritual slaughter. The announcer prefaces these with a warning that the pictures are "among the most horrifying that a camera has ever recorded."[4]

Another important aspect of bio-behavioral propaganda was the exploitation of sexual drives. For example, in 1941, at the start of the invasion of Russia, Nazi propagandists were able to arouse the Germans' will to fight by means of propaganda that referred to the image of the "gun woman" (*Flintenweib*), that is, Russian women—there were hundreds of thousands— who fought at the Soviet front lines with male troops. Germans feared the "gun woman" partly for cultural reasons, because she contradicted the centuries-old domestic ideal of the *Hausfrau*, who stayed at home and cooked and raised the children. But their anxieties were also biological. German men were fascinated by the image of a cruel, untamed woman but were also repelled by the *Flintenweib* because she threatened male domination, and this increased their desire to defeat the Soviet troops.[5]

Radio was an especially powerful medium for bio-behavioral propaganda. Electrically transmitted sound physically affected the listener's body, and radio audiences brought their own fantasies to broadcasts as their minds worked to supply visual detail. Many listeners in Allied countries regularly tuned in to the broadcasts of Germany's Lord Haw-Haw and Axis Sally, who served up doctored news reports and insinuated frightening images of death and failure into the minds of Western audiences.[6] Over time, Allied listeners tuned in to Haw-Haw and Sally mostly for amusement. But there was an undercurrent of anxiety. The broadcasters circulated false information about Allied defeats and played on soldiers' fears of sexual unfaithfulness among their wives and girlfriends at home. The broadcasts ingeniously exploited sound. For example, in 1944, when all sides knew that some kind of invasion of the coast of western Europe was in preparation, Axis Sally interlaced her broadcasts with recordings of the kinds of deafening explosions and screams of pain that Allied troops would experience as they went ashore on the beaches and cliffs. Within Germany, radio was a bio-behavioral tool for repetitive conditioning of the home population. Every day, for example, German broadcasters exploited the device of the *Sondermeldung*, or special announcement, which frequently interrupted regular broadcasts with a blast of trumpets followed by the announcement of a dramatic military victory and the playing of a stirring song such as "We're Marching against England."

Democratic countries also made use of bio-behavioral approaches to mass persuasion. On the Allied side, the most skilled practitioner was Sefton Delmer, who produced "black" propaganda broadcasts from Britain— propaganda that falsely identified the source or simply left it unidentified. Born in Berlin in 1904, Delmer had been a foreign correspondent for a British newspaper, the *Daily Express*, before the war. He became director of the German-language broadcasts of the BBC and was soon using information picked up from German radio broadcasts and espionage reports, as well as outright lies, to corrode German morale. Reciting the names of actual German soldiers, he spread rumors that hospitals in the Reich were giving wounded infantrymen lethal injections to avoid the bother of rehabilitating them. With Allied military cooperation, Delmer's office interviewed captured German submarine crews about brothels in the harbor cities of Brest and Kiel, then broadcast the information, disgracing the officers among their family members and in some cases leading to suicides. Delmer's propaganda emphasized the difference between the Nazi leadership and the German people. The sheer repetition of messages of this kind was one source of their power. German authorities warned the populace not to listen to enemy broadcasts, but both military personnel and civilians still did so.

Reflecting the influence of bio-behavioral thinking, a new term, "psychological warfare," made its way into the language during the Second World War. (Variations eventually included "psych-war" or "sykewar" and the military shorthand "PsyOps" for "Psychological Operations.")[7] But the democracies used it only to supplement techniques that assumed the capacity for voluntary choice. In liberal constitutional states, where some degree of free circulation of information was always present, bio-behavioral approaches to wartime communication never supplanted the more traditional myth-based techniques that had been dominant in the First World War. There was no official use of media in fascist and communist countries as noble as Churchill's oratory; Edward R. Murrow's wartime radio broadcasts to America; the film version of Shakespeare's *Henry V* (1944), with its evocations of heroism in battle, which Laurence Olivier produced in Britain; or the wartime broadcasts that the great German author Thomas Mann, in exile, addressed to his countrymen.

One important question about bio-behavioral propaganda concerns its ultimate effectiveness. The German experience is probably the most instructive. The Nazis regularly analyzed the mood of the population through "situation reports" (*Lageberichte*) and "mood reports" or "morale reports" (*Stimmungsberichte*) prepared by local and regional party officials. Exceptions notwithstanding, censorship was strict. For many people, rumor, gossip, and secret conversations were the only sources of alternative information. These had to be pursued at risk of execution for saying the wrong thing or being reported by informants. Alternative information did penetrate through Allied radio broadcasts, leaflet drops, and other means. Moreover, ordinary Germans could see that much of the government's reporting did not square with the reality of their immediate surroundings. In the dictatorships, those in uniform as well as the civilian population grew tired of the mechanical repetition of information, and they evolved ways of using gossip and private conversation to transmit the facts they needed for a clearer understanding of their situation.

In a famous study written after the war, William Sheridan Allen showed how residents of a small town in northern Germany quickly became suspicious of, cynical about, and bored by the deluge of controlled information manufactured by the local Nazi authorities. In parades, posters, radio broadcasts, speeches, newspaper articles, and other venues, the Nazis kept telling the town's residents that the economy was prosperous, troops at the front were experiencing few casualties and many victories, and the utopia foretold by the leader was just a few years away. None of this fit with what the townspeople knew about wounded soldiers returning home, food scarcities, supply shortages, and news of the outside world relayed by gossip and rumor. Studies of this kind suggest that the Nazis' control of information was never "totalitarian." But it was disturbingly effective in many ways. Some sectors of society, such as members of the Hitler Youth and the army, never completely lost faith in the führer. One can accept that information about the Holocaust then in progress did not reach some people, although it certainly reached most. And one can understand the claims by many Germans immediately after the war that news of the outside world was so disorienting that recipients felt they were awakening from a spell.[8]

A powerful irony is that bio-behavioral propaganda often disoriented its producers more than its recipients. By the time Hitler and Goebbels took shelter in an underground bunker in Berlin during the last weeks of the war, the two were unable to reconcile the contrast between their propaganda and reality. Their distress was partly based in myth. Defeat did not fit with the tawdry Wagnerian motifs they believed in. But they had also duped themselves by their own repetitious assertions—the way they had conditioned themselves to believe in their inevitable victory. The symbolism of their final actions reveals that they feared not only the consequences of capture but also the negation of their propaganda. Unable to go on, Hitler chose his propaganda minister, Goebbels, rather than anyone else in the Nazi hierarchy, to be his companion during the last weeks of the Reich. In their bunker, the führer and his mistress Eva Braun committed suicide. Goebbels and his wife then killed their children and themselves.

Stalin Evokes Mother Russia

In response to the German attack in June 1941, Russia reoriented and geared up its propaganda. It continued to some extent to use media in support of its allies the United States and Britain. By the time of the German invasion, so many foreign correspondents had left Russia that there were only about twenty left in Moscow. The Soviets hastily worked to build up their numbers, easing visa clearances, offering assistance with lodgings, travel, and facilities, and liberalizing policies for interviews and commentary. Among the print journalists who now entered Russia were Wallace Carroll and Cyrus Sulzberger of the United States and Alexander Werth from Britain. The American novelist Erskine Caldwell represented the magazine *PM*, and his wife, the photographer Margaret Bourke-White, represented *Life* magazine. She had been in Russia in the 1930s and had already gained fame for her work.

German troops met unexpectedly effective resistance from Russian troops and then got bogged down in the Russian winter of 1941–42 and were not able to renew their offensive until the spring. During this period, government media offices were directed at the top by the Council of People's Commissars and the Political Bureau of the All Union Communist Party. They were supervised by the Directorate of Propaganda and Agitation of the Central Committee and managed on a daily basis by the new Soviet

Information Bureau (Sovinformbureau), which had been established in June 1941, within a few days of the German invasion. Through this bureau and its press department, foreign correspondents regularly received dispatches from Tass, the Soviet news agency, as well as access to improved telegraph services. It was possible to make shortwave radio broadcasts from the summer of 1941 on, and airmail service was available for photographs. But there were still censorship problems. Censors were often slow, there were frequent disagreements as to what constituted sensitive information, and travel restrictions were severe. Between September 1941 and March 1943, foreign correspondents had the right to make eight visits to the front as long as they were in supervised groups. But in general, access was difficult. When the Germans bombed Moscow in October 1941, the Soviets evacuated foreign correspondents eight hundred miles east to the medium-sized city of Kuibyshev (about 300,000 residents), where the reporters lived in a former schoolhouse; here they stayed for seven months, until May 1942, out of touch with Soviet leaders, who remained in Moscow. From then until the end of the war in 1945, correspondents again operated from Moscow. Throughout the war, in addition to Moscow, reporters could transmit news from the northern port of Murmansk, whether by radio or via the ships that made the dangerous supply runs across the Atlantic. In the winter of 1942–43, the total number of foreign press and broadcast representatives in Moscow was around twenty-five, about half of them from the United States. In spite of all the difficulties, foreign correspondents were generally satisfied with the degree to which the Soviet authorities allowed unfettered transmittal of information out of the country; most thought it was about as liberal as could be expected from any nation that had to protect itself in war. By late 1944, nevertheless, the Soviet authorities were again beginning to treat the foreign press strictly. They had less need of their Western allies and were beginning to plan for a postwar world in which the USSR would want to go its own way.[9]

After the German invasion, the Soviet Union concentrated mainly on domestic propaganda, which was particularly necessary at the start of war until aid from Britain and America was available in quantity. Given the difficult circumstances, Soviet use of media on the home front was impressive. Germany's quick conquest of parts of the western Soviet Union handicapped media capacity. The number of Soviet newspapers dropped from 8,806 in 1940 to 4,561 in 1942; the weekly cinema audience, which totaled 17 million in 1940, fell to 8 million in 1942. To address home audiences in such circumstances, the Soviets used a variety of methods. News from Tass and *Izvestia* circulated widely. Soviet reporters had extensive access to the front and produced readable, informative copy in spite of great risks and a high death rate. In its official newspaper, *Krasnaya Zvezda*, a four-page tabloid, the Commissariat of Defense also provided reliable reportage on the fighting.

The Soviets made very effective use of films. Newsreel production crews quickly went into action and produced over 500 newsreels and 120 documentary films between 1941 and 1945. The most widely viewed was *The Defeat of the German Armies Near Moscow* (1942; released in the United States as *Moscow Strikes Back*). Soviet filmmakers and censors were much less reluctant than their counterparts in the West to show images of death and severe injury. By 1942 the Soviets had halted production of films strictly for entertainment purposes. Feature films reflecting the emphasis on sober purpose included *District Party Secretary* (1942), *She Defends Her Motherland* (1943), *Invasion* (1945), and *Girl No. 217* (1945). Immediately after the German invasion, within twenty-four hours the Russians moved all their feature film production studios to eastern locations. The studios for newsreels and documentary films were not moved. As in the West, films made frequent use of history to inspire their audiences. Sergei Eisenstein's *Ivan the Terrible* (1942–1946) is the most notable example. Within six weeks of the defeat of Germany at Stalingrad (1943), Soviet filmmakers turned out a stirring seven-reel film of the same name, combining actual film of combat, staged but realistic scenes of street fighting, and informative use of diagrams and maps. Films reached city audiences for the most part, but *agit* trains took them to peasants in the countryside. As in earlier decades, posters were an important element of visual propaganda.[10]

As in other countries, the Soviet use of media had to resolve logical contradictions created by changes in policy. Propaganda depicted the Germans as allies until they attacked Russia. When Soviet troops attacked Japan in August 1945 after the dropping of the atomic bomb, Russian audiences were surprised to find that the Russo-Japanese nonaggression agreement was no longer in effect. The greatest contradiction arose in 1941, when Stalin ordered a shift in propaganda themes from an emphasis on spreading and defending communism to a focus on defending Mother Russia. He did not totally eliminate the defense of communism as a theme. But he deftly began comparing the Nazi dictatorship to tsarist Russia. At the same time, Stalin evoked images of the defense of Russia against Napoleon in 1812. The locus classicus was Stalin's "Holy Russia" speech of November 1941, which was widely reprinted in newspapers and leaflets and mined for quotations that were then included in thousands of posters.

Stalin's greatest propaganda challenge involved sustaining the morale of the military. The army and air force had to function in the harsh natural conditions of eastern Europe and to reckon with German military skill and tenacity. Germany also had an overall superiority in technology, in spite of gradual Russian improvements in areas such as tank manufacture and airplane design. The Soviets purchased their victories with enormous losses of personnel. By February 1942, for every German killed in the war on the Eastern Front, twenty Soviet soldiers had died. Motivation was crucial, especially among units composed of fighters from the least loyal areas of the Soviet Union, such as the Ukraine, Belarus, and the Tatar settlements of the Crimea. The shift to propaganda emphasizing defense of Mother Russia involved risks. The compromise was tenable at first. Most members of the military were Russian, and non-Russian members were united with them in hatred of the German invader. By 1944, however, as the Germans were retreating from Russia proper and many Soviet units were now on their native, non-Russian soil, maintaining unity became increasingly difficult. Propaganda emphasizing hatred of the Germans—even in its most virulent form, including specific instructions to the Red Army to exact brutal revenge—was not sufficient to sustain unity. Desertions among minority groups increased. Some fighters, like those from the Ukraine, prepared to launch postwar guerrilla rebellions against Soviet rule. Throughout the war the Soviets had to use special measures to preserve cohesion. Uniformed party agitators accompanied all units of the Soviet army. In addition, whenever the army advanced into battle, units of the secret police followed a short distance behind with instructions to shoot deserters and stragglers.

In his propaganda and his negotiations with allies, Stalin never tired of emphasizing that the Soviet army was sustaining the largest number of casualties of any of the fighting forces. He did not admit that the losses were in part due to his inadequacies as a commander. Nor was he forthcoming about the army's systematic use of atrocity, like the slaughter of four thousand officers of the Polish army at Katyn in the forest east of Warsaw in the first year of war, and the raping and pillaging that accompanied the infantry's progress through Germany and into Berlin in 1945. During the last months of war, the propaganda no longer even emphasized Mother Russia. Protection and extension of the Soviet system again became the dominant theme. Veterans had few opportunities to address the basic human need to talk about traumatic experiences, as the party began circulating and enforcing its doctored version of events.[11]

The experience of the Soviet army throws into high relief an important question about the effects of propaganda. Researchers have pointed out that more needs to be known about the effects of mass communication on military personnel at the battlefront. Some research has suggested that the fighting spirit of soldiers is not appreciably affected by propaganda efforts such as dropping leaflets from the sky, directing radio broadcasts at troops, or circulating films. To a greater extent it is physical realities, from the casualty rate to the provision of adequate food, as well as home front sociological factors that determine small-group cohesiveness in battle, that is, loyalty to one's unit. This appears to have been the pattern in the German army in the Second World War. Less is known about the role of small-group dynamics on Soviet battlefields such as the German-Russian front in the Second World War, where death rates were so high that formation of any cohesiveness was problematic.[12]

Japan Peddles Deliverance

In East Asia the Second World War began, in many respects, in July 1937, when military conflict broke out near Peking between Chinese troops and Japanese forces encroaching from Manchuria. By this time the Japanese were already mobilizing elaborate propaganda efforts to accompany and justify their more overt uses of physical and economic weaponry. In a perversion of rhetoric about improving understanding among nations, the Japanese used leaflets, posters, radio broadcasts, and other means of communication in an attempt to persuade China and the Western nations that Japan was seeking a benign synthesis of cultures for the greater good of all the peoples of East Asia. Disregarding the irony that Japanese aircraft were bombing libraries, museums, schools, and publishing companies in addition to military targets, the Japanese repeatedly spoke of the "cultural operations" they were conducting to bring about "the awakening of Asia." When the Japanese opened a university in Manchuria, they issued a propaganda leaflet describing it as a place for the training of "pioneering leaders in the establishment of a moral world." Clearly this was hypocrisy to cloak Japan's imperialism. But the fact that the Japanese were at such pains to utilize culturally oriented propaganda demonstrates their belief in its power as a weapon and as a stabilizing force.[13]

The same irony was visible in Japan itself. Throughout the 1930s, even as the Japanese government pursued war in East Asia and prepared to widen that conflict, it was also energetically pursuing cultural exchanges with the United States and the nations of western Europe, such as lecture tours, language teaching initiatives, and book exchanges with overseas libraries. At the same time, Japanese intellectuals sympathetic to the military regime were propounding convoluted arguments to the effect that the nation's martial spirit contained such a large element of harmony that

Japan's military activity was for the ultimate purpose of peace, synthesis among cultures, and eventual creation of a superior society for all of humanity. In Germany, intellectuals sympathetic to Nazism were offering similar arguments.

Japan's entry into the Second World War was greatly facilitated by an American failure of communication. In Washington, D.C., throughout the 1920s and 1930s, the Department of State received regular reports on activity in Asia. By 1940 U.S. military officials were seriously considering the possibility of a Japanese surprise attack against one or more U.S. bases in East Asia. The president, the secretary of state, and the secretary of war regularly received the latest intelligence. Nevertheless, the attack on Pearl Harbor on December 7, 1941, came as a surprise. The Americans did not adequately evaluate the coded messages from Japan to Washington that they intercepted and did not give the information to the right decision makers in time.

The Japanese established an elaborate government information bureau (Naikaku Johobu) in 1941 the day before Pearl Harbor. It had an advisory committee made up of ten members from the armed forces and the media, including the president of the Japanese News Agency (Domei), and the president of the National Broadcasting Corporation (NHK). An already existing Greater East Asia Ministry managed media strategy for the countries that had come under the control of Japan (Manchuria, parts of China, and various islands in the Pacific), as well as proximate areas such as Indochina and Thailand on which the Japanese had designs. Moreover, in Tokyo, the imperial headquarters oversaw production of propaganda directed at the Japanese armed forces.

Although shortwave radio was banned in Japan itself, and residents were forbidden to listen to foreign radio broadcasts, Japanese officials made effective use of shortwave to reach the vast geographic areas where Japan was now active. They established broadcast facilities in Saigon, Batavia, and Singapore. The signals reached not only into the Pacific and China but also into India and Australia, broadcasting in twenty-two foreign languages. The best-known Japanese broadcaster heard abroad was Tokyo Rose. Like Axis Sally and Lord Haw-Haw in Germany, she addressed her commentary to enemy troops, playing Western music interrupted by sultry, insinuating warnings of imminent military defeat and suggestions that wives and girlfriends back home were being unfaithful.[14]

Both at home and in foreign propaganda the Japanese government made extensive use of film, which it controlled completely. A Motion Picture Law dating from 1939 called for all scripts to be submitted to official censors in advance of filming. Two large combines, the Shochiku company and the Toho company, were responsible for nearly all production. The major producer of newsreels was the Nippon Eigasha. A typical newsreel was titled *Capture of Burma and Occupation of Sumatra*. As in other countries, historical themes appeared often in feature films, for example, *The Day England Fell* (1942), which depicted the British in Hong Kong as cruel racists, and *The Opium War* (1943), which claimed—not completely inaccurately—that the British had conquered the Chinese by addicting them to drugs. In 1943, Japanese filmmakers protested the extent of censorship, causing a brief drop in production, but they were soon brought back into line. The leading wartime maker of Japanese films was Kajiro Yamamoto, director of *General Kato's Falcon Fighters* (1943). A film demonstrating the extent of Japanese ambitions was *Forward! Flag of Independence* (1943), which sought to foment revolt against the British in India. The increased Allied bombing of Japan in 1944 led to a sharp decrease in film production.[15]

The greatest challenge faced by Japanese opinion manipulators during the Second World War was that they had to address three vast audiences simultaneously: their own people, the Chinese and other Asian peoples, and the West, particularly Americans. The Japanese were most successful in domestic propaganda, where they benefited from censorship and built on already strong patriotism. Ever since the 1890s, when they had begun their highly focused, unified effort to adopt Western methods, the Japanese had been propagandizing themselves through a collective discussion regarding the importance of national development and imperial expansion. Even as late as the 1930s, by which time military control of the state was far-reaching, this project of modernization allowed for extensive public dialogue within Japan. Questioning fundamental assumptions could result in imprisonment and death, as evidenced by the harsh treatment accorded to communists and to some of the liberal politicians who were imprisoned or assassinated when they pushed back too hard against the military's influence in the civil sphere. But within this framework a surprisingly high degree of participation was also evident. Through the media and in face-to-face dialogue, the government sought and often adopted suggestions from newspaper publishers, trade associations, agricultural societies, charitable organizations, authors' clubs, and similar groups regarding important issues such as food distribution, workers' salaries, methods for improving industrial production, and colonization of Manchukuo and other conquered areas. Domestic support also flowed from the fact that Japan's rapid overseas expansion created job opportunities for the home population, for example, when women were recruited to assume salaried factory positions left vacant as men entered the army and navy, when engineers obtained government contracts, when university graduates found employment conducting opinion polls or crafting plans for colonial economic development, or when the military contracted with Tokyo-based advertising agencies to enhance its propaganda efforts. Together all these developments yielded a home population that viewed Japan's overseas expansion as just and remained remarkably cohesive not only during Japan's years of military success but also during the years 1943–1945, when the tide turned.

The task of maintaining home front morale was also made easier for the Japanese by the failure of Westerners to understand them. The major actors in wartime propaganda against the Japanese home population were the Americans, who directed their messages in Asia through various units such as the Office of War Information and U.S. Army communications specialists under the direction of General Douglas MacArthur. Exploitable opportunities were available. The surprise air raid over Japan launched from naval aircraft carriers in 1942 by General James Doolittle did not square with Japanese home front propaganda. By 1944 the Japanese press felt forced to tell the public of setbacks in defending the areas of the Pacific that the nation had so recently conquered, and the need for the populace to prepare a "front behind the front," that is, to get ready for combat on the home islands. It was impossible to deny the existence of the bombs that American B-29s were dropping on Japan by that time, and Japanese opinion manipulators were coping with the millions of propaganda leaflets that B-29s were now also dropping on their country. But in proportion to the effort expended, American propaganda against the Japanese home front was unimpressive. Viewing the Japanese as "docile," the Americans focused on their demand for unconditional surrender instead of attempting to energize sectors of the population that might petition for a negotiated peace. This forced the Japanese into a frightening either-or choice: to die nobly without surrendering or accept defeat and the horrors of retribution that occupation forces might unleash. By 1944 the Americans were sufficiently puzzled by the ineffectiveness of their anti-Japanese propaganda that they sought advice from the Chinese communists, who were having significant success in persuading Japanese soldiers on the mainland to desert and collaborate. In October of that year American military and diplomatic representatives traveled to Chinese communist headquarters in Yenan as part of a general effort to improve ties with the communists and learn from their experience. The Chinese advised them to soften their propaganda emphasis on U.S. military strength and to make greater use of Japanese POWs, who were usually well treated in captivity and were often willing to assist in making radio broadcasts assuring their fellow Japanese that surrender should not be a horrifying prospect because the Allies desired only to remove the military clique from power and did not intend to colonize Japan. But by the time the Americans were able to redirect their propaganda along these lines, the war was nearing its end.

The Japanese were generally less successful in addressing foreign audiences than in propagandizing themselves. To be sure, Japanese overseas propaganda was extensive. It sought to foment rebellion against the British in India, urged the inhabitants of the Philippines to accept supposedly benign conquest, and advised the peoples of Malaya, Borneo, and Indonesia to fight against the Australians and the Dutch. Japanese efforts at overseas opinion manipulation were most extensive in China, employing a large arsenal of devices including films, pamphlets, radio broadcasts, sound trucks, and, as was often the case in other wartime environments, illustrated materials. A color propaganda poster printed in Chinese, designed to consolidate Japanese rule in Manchukuo, depicts a Japanese soldier shaking hands with a happy Chinese peasant. The soldier says, "Come, my brothers. Change the bad and install the good, for peace and prosperity," while a contingent of loyal peasants cheer in the background. A Japanese color leaflet directed at the Chinese shows a Japanese soldier spraying insecticide into foliage to eradicate the communist pests hiding there, with captions reading, "Defend against communism" and "Only with the removal of harmful insects will China be safe." A Japanese color propaganda poster consists of a sequence of panels in which Chinese Nationalist military forces destroy a beautiful pagoda and attack the local population but are then routed by Japanese soldiers and cooperative Chinese peasants, who together force the local warlord to bow his head in shame.[16]

Though extensive, Japanese propaganda directed at Asian audiences was generally ineffective. One source of difficulty was that the Japanese did not know many foreign languages. Even in China, where they had a long history of contact, the propaganda revealed a lack of mastery of local idioms, while Japanese broadcasters spoke Chinese with a foreign accent. Another problem was their resistance to understanding other cultures. Somewhat like the Germans in both world wars, most Japanese could not understand why foreign populations did not simply acknowledge the superiority of their civilization. Nor did the militarists among them appreciate the usefulness of dialogue as an alternative to abrupt commands. Another problem was the Japanese tendency to issue reports about fictitious victories, causing propaganda setbacks when they were exposed. Moreover, the contradictions between the content of their propaganda and the actual behavior of the Japanese were grossly conspicuous. The Japanese circulated leaflets offering safe conduct to enemy soldiers who surrendered, but it was widely known that they slaughtered or enslaved almost all captured troops, even those who came over to their side voluntarily—a contrast to Chinese communist treatment of Japanese prisoners, and to a lesser extent Chinese Nationalist treatment. The Japanese were racist and hierarchical in their relationships with other Asians. Their propaganda preached that all Asians would experience harmony and equality after the great co-prosperity sphere was created, but it was evident from their actual behavior that the Japanese regarded other Asians as inferior and had no plans to allow shared rule.[17]

The Japanese were even less successful in their propaganda directed against Westerners. This was attributable in part to their cultural limitations, but also to the bigotry of Westerners. One interesting question about the use of media in the Second World War is what might have happened to further dehumanize participants if the conflict had gone on much longer. The battle of media stereotypes between Japan and the Allies raised the issue of long-term effects in its most sobering form. On both sides of the Pacific war, and among both private and governmental organs of mass communication, the struggle encompassed a form of racism—Asians against Europeans, whites against yellow-skinned peoples—that set it apart from the war in Europe. In their films, newspapers, posters, radio broadcasts, and all other communication arenas, each side dehumanized the other with ever-increasing virulence. Westerners spoke repeatedly of "Japs," "Nips," "little men," "monkey folk," and members of the "horde" that would carry off naked white women and dilute the racial strength of the West. Late in the war, this dehumanization had gone so far that David Low, the distinguished editorial cartoonist for British newspapers, advocated "war without mercy" against the Japanese. On the Japanese side, there was a fixation on ancient cultural values of purity and purification. Western leaders were compared to the power-hungry ogres familiar to those versed in Japanese literature. Black Americans were described as eager to help the Japanese so they could be liberated from the tyranny of light-skinned races. Images of Japanese swords (and, by extension, bayonets), long understood as tools of purification, were widespread. Japanese propagandists continually evoked centuries-old fears of invasion by foreign demons. On both sides, by the last year of war, the hateful use of symbols was almost as egregious as the portrayals of Jews in Nazi media. It remains an open question just how vicious the media battle might have become in a longer conflict.

An encouraging element in this story is that much of the hatred transformed itself after 1945. In Europe, many French, British, and eastern Europeans continued to dislike the Germans. But others made their peace, and among the Americans there was a new friendship with Germany in the postwar period, encouraged by the economic aid provided through the Marshall Plan. So too in Japan, the former combatants worked together to craft a postwar reconciliation. Westerners now portrayed Japanese "little men" fondly and expressed an eagerness to protect them from communism, while the Japanese in turn welcomed the strength and assistance of the West. And yet the tendency to dehumanize did not entirely go away. Japanese and Westerners both found new overseas enemies toward whom they could direct their symbolic disrespect. Western media started referring to communist Chinese and North Koreans in racist terms; imagery of this kind even began to appear in children's comic books. Accordingly, Westerners found it difficult to see the North Vietnamese as real people when war expanded in that part of Asia.[18]

China Exhorts from the Edge

By the time of its attack on Hong Kong on December 8, 1941, Japan already dominated most of China. Manchuria had been renamed Manchukuo. The Japanese controlled the major cities of Shanghai, Tientsin, Peiping, Nanking, Hankow, and Canton. Foreigners at the "settlements" in Shanghai, Tientsin, and Peiping were restricted in their movements. Japan controlled news reporting in all the parts of China where it held power. Chinese who found themselves in areas controlled by Japan could do little more than submit. In a situation roughly comparable to that of the French under Nazi occupation, some Chinese formed resistance groups within Japanese-held territory. And as in the Vichy regime, some Chinese collaborated, although the number who did so was conspicuously small—a commentary not only on Japanese barbarity but also on the ineffectiveness of Japan's foreign propaganda.

The new center for information about the Nationalists, especially after the Japanese took over Hong Kong, was Chunking, which had not been conquered by the Japanese. Many of the Nationalist leaders, such as Hollington K. Tong at the Ministry of Information, had spent time in the West and were able to maintain a skillful balance: reading Western attitudes, professing concern for foreign correspondents, making services and amenities available, while also maintaining a subtle form of censorship and spreading propaganda. Tong assisted correspondents stationed in Chunking and also hosted the many visitors eager for up-to-date information.

His star performer was the Chinese-born, Wellesley College–educated Madame Chiang Kai-shek. She charmed representatives of the Western media, like Henry Luce, the owner of the Time-Life empire, who gave the Nationalists slanted, highly favorable coverage in his publications. The number of reporters and visitors increased after Pearl Harbor and the movement of Allied military forces into India, Southeast Asia, and western China.[19] To the north, from his headquarters at Yenan, Mao Tse-tung directed the communist forces, cooperating on a selective basis with the Nationalists and the Allies and hoping that conditions would become favorable for a complete takeover of China.

Britain Projects Courage

At the start of war in Europe in 1939 the Germans were preoccupied in the east and did not attack Britain. Prime Minister Neville Chamberlain entertained hope that the German people would rise up and overthrow Hitler. He did not recognize the need to ramp up war production quickly and to begin detailed economic planning. He also put too much faith in a blockade of German shipping as a key to success. Chamberlain's weekly speeches in Parliament were uninspiring: "dull as ditchwater," Harold Nicolson commented. Noting the frustration and sense of drift in the British population, American observers called this period the "Phony War," while the English called it the "Bore War." Discontent was intensified by the coldest winter in Britain in forty-five years. Then the British suffered failure in their attempt to outflank the Germans through an invasion of Norway. The operation, which began in April 1940, initially appeared to be successful, resulting, for example, in the loss of ten German destroyers. But German air operations limited British gains on land, and the British began evacuations in May. Although the operation injured the German war effort, the British public perceived it at the time as an enormous victory for the enemy.

Chamberlain resigned as prime minister on May 10, and the king named Churchill to assume the post. Although the new PM had not been particularly effective as a politician in peacetime, and was in many ways a man of the nineteenth century, Churchill was, as everyone sensed, the perfect choice to lead his nation in wartime. There was an almost immediate change in the national mood and, abroad, a much stronger confidence that Britain would survive. Moreover, oratory now became available to Britain as a weapon of war. In the first of the many great speeches he was to deliver over the next several years, Churchill declared that he had "nothing to offer save blood, toil, tears, and sweat," continuing: "You ask, What is our policy? I will say: It is to wage war, by sea, land and air, with all our might and with all the strength that God can give us. . . . What is our aim? . . . Victory—victory at all costs, victory in spite of all terror; victory, however long and hard the road may be."[20]

This new spirit was very much needed. The first German bombs fell over Canterbury in May 1940; raids intensified over the summer, and sustained attacks began in August. In the face of heroic action by the Royal Air Force, Hitler canceled his plans in late September for a full-scale invasion of Britain, although massive bomber attacks continued over London and other cities. Moreover, beginning in June 1944, England had to endure attacks from the air by German V-1 and V-2 rockets. Churchill's leadership and the possibility of Nazi conquest unified British public opinion throughout the war. Membership in pacifist groups declined. Leftist writers who had been gadflies in the 1930s enlisted or became air wardens and firefighters. All the major newspapers strongly supported the war effort, not only in the content of their lead articles but also in their conduct. They vigorously exercised their right of free speech and regularly criticized government policies but were also steadfast in support of the war effort. For example, when Printing House Square was bombed during the Blitz, *The Times* still managed to reach the streets the next day, reassuring the populace not only by its presence but also by avoiding alarmist headlines and continuing its usual format of all advertisements and no news on the front page.

Churchill had his own particular views of the role of mass communication in wartime. He assigned less importance to propaganda than Hitler or Goebbels did. In November 1939, noting the torrent of propaganda the Nazis were directing at Britain, he told a radio audience, "If words could kill, we would be dead already." Churchill also cautioned people not to attribute the power of his oratory solely to him. It was, he said, the common people who had "the lion's heart. I had the luck to be called upon to give the roar."[21] Moreover, although he was a strong believer in the importance of establishing a large propaganda apparatus, he preferred to leave management of it to others, and he was fortunate that a small cadre of civil servants and military officers were available to expand official mass communication. At the start of the war, they saw to it that the British immediately established a Ministry of Information (MOI) to deal with the challenge of maintaining home front morale. Plans for such a ministry had first been drafted in 1935 but were sketchy. The waiting time provided by the "Phony War" allowed propagandists to develop their plans.

Censorship played a large role in MOI strategy. Officials worried that bombing raids might lead to panic among the civilian population unless there was strict control of information. In its early years, moreover, the MOI made the error of not trusting in the common sense of the people. The ministry staff consisted mostly of gentlemanly amateurs and products of the Oxbridge network. Revealing their top-down mentality, one official counseled that the thinking of the lower classes should be controlled by feeding them opinions first developed by their betters at the upper social levels: "We must, in short, start in a Rolls-Royce way and not in a Ford way."[22] There were many mistakes made initially. In 1940 the authorities did not tell the public that the British Expeditionary Force had arrived in France. People learned of it through a brief lapse in censorship in the form of a radio announcement from Paris. Then censorship quickly resumed, but only after British papers had published the news in their morning editions. Scotland Yard occupied Fleet Street buildings and seized newspapers from readers on the streets. Other fiascos followed. For example, when a reporter asked the MOI for a copy of a leaflet that had been dropped by the millions on German troops, the MOI refused and warned him not to disclose information that might be of use to the enemy. By the summer of 1940, however, an effective censorship system was in place. The MOI reviewed war-related information before it was distributed to the press, which was then free to use the material as it judged best, with no censorship of opinions about the information. There were relatively few clashes between government and the media during the rest of the war.

Harmony increased greatly after Brendan Bracken became minister of information in July 1941. His predecessors, Lord Reith and Duff Cooper, were unimaginative and also proved unable to counter efforts by the Foreign Office, the Admiralty, and the War Office to go their own ways in press relations. Bracken was an old friend of Churchill's and thus in a better position to make the MOI's case. He was more energetic and effusive than his predecessors. He also had some knowledge of the advertising industry and was the owner of several newspapers that served the financial community. He did not win all bureaucratic battles, but he did make the MOI more of a presence in decision making, and he changed the pattern of the ministry's home front propaganda from exhortation by the upper classes to the provision of basic information and clear explanation that everyone could respect. The people themselves did the rest.

The MOI used posters extensively. As with censorship, the effort had a rocky start. One early poster sought to inspire the populace with the words "*Your* Courage, *Your* Cheerfulness, *Your* Resolution Will Bring Us Victory." This created a feeling of separation between the home front on the one hand and the fighting forces and government on the other. The MOI also had difficulty finding the right tone for posters intended to remind people of the need for caution in conversation, as in "Careless Talk Costs Lives," "Keep Mum—She's Not So Dumb," and "Tittle Tattle Lost the Battle." To many these had the ring of a nagging auntie. Similar problems appeared when the MOI issued a poster that showed a British battleship with the words "Mightier Yet." It did not inspire average people. Many failed to connect the image with the literary allusion to A. C. Benson's poem or the evocation of Sir Edward Elgar's music. Even those who did make the connection often found the message too abstract. But the MOI also produced more unifying posters, like the ones showing Churchill with captions such as "Let Us Go Forward Together" and "We're Going to See It Through." Also very effective were posters that spread important advice about daily habits in simple, direct terms, such as "Coughs and Sneezes Spread Diseases." The people responded well to themes of steadiness and sacrifice, as in "Women of Britain, Come into the Factories" and "Back Them Up." As the war went on, the visual quality of many posters approached that of great art.[23]

Another medium of great importance on the home front was radio. Domestic audiences gained inspiration from the commentaries of C. S. Lewis and the wartime broadcasts of J. B. Priestley in his "Postscripts." Priestley garnered an enormous audience. His voice, which was especially well suited for radio, became a builder of morale in its own right. He had a knack for using reassuring detail, as in his references to a freshly baked pie visible through a shop window, or the "little holiday steamers" that still managed to ply the waters of British lakes and rivers even in wartime.[24] As popular as he was, Priestley also engendered controversy. He accused the War Office of not appreciating the value of mass communication, and many Conservatives regarded him as a troublemaker because one theme of his broadcasts was the importance of raising the standard of living for the common people after the war. Although many Tories agreed with such a goal, they thought that talking about it before war ended was disruptive.

Another well-known BBC broadcaster was George Orwell, who worked for the Indian Section of the Empire Service from 1941 to 1943. Given his leftist leanings, he could have been even more of a troublemaker than Priestley, but he made his peace with the idea of being an official propagandist, arguing that in times of emergency, compromises had to be made. Orwell's stint at the BBC gave him material for his two great postwar works about dictatorship, *Animal Farm* (1945) and *1984* (1949).

All of Churchill's major wartime speeches were broadcast via radio. He made brilliant use of the BBC and strongly preferred speaking on the radio to appearing before newsreel cameras, which made him uncomfortable. Churchill's use of radio was highly important overseas as well as at home. He showed how inspirational he could be on October 21, 1940, when, entirely in their language, he broadcast a long and respectful speech to anxious French listeners for the first time after the fall of their country, beginning with the words "C'est moi, Churchill, qui vous parle."[25]

Like the Ministry of Information, the BBC could at times be overbearing in its reminders to people that they should conduct themselves dutifully. *Punch* satirized this tendency in 1942 in a cartoon that showed a suave BBC announcer getting ready to play a phonograph recording, speaking into the microphone and saying, ". . . and in the beautiful second movement comes a passage in which the strings make a last appeal to us to use cold water for washing."[26] For the most part, however, the BBC earned great respect. Its news broadcasts, though at times egregiously slanted, were generally thought to be the most reliable and truthful in the world. People greatly appreciated the BBC's "talks" on practical subjects like growing food in one's garden and preserving order in bomb shelters. And its entertainment programs, ranging from big band concerts to serious drama, became staples of life on the home front. An example of the way the BBC could strike just the right note with listeners was its comedy series *ITMA* (for "It's That Man Again"), the most popular program during the years of conflict, which made its first wartime broadcast in September 1940. The comedian Tommy Handley and his cast satirized practically everything, not least of all governmental officials like the "Minister of Aggravation" from the "Office of Twerps." On each broadcast Handley assumed the role of head of some fictitious but recognizable institution of British society who was barely able to cope with wartime challenges, for example, His Washout the Mayor of the seaside town of Foaming at the Mouth. Regular supporting characters who moved in and out of each week's show included Funf the incompetent German spy and Mrs. Mopp the Corporation Cleanser. The characters' taglines, like "I go—I come back" for Ali Oop the Pedlar, and "Can I do you now, sir?" for Mrs. Mopp, became leitmotifs of daily wartime conversation.[27]

The British got off to a slow start in using film as a weapon. The first major propaganda film of the war, *The Lion Has Wings* (1939), a tribute to the Royal Air Force, came about through the private initiative of the eminent producer Alexander Korda. By 1940, however, the MOI had developed an agenda for production and acquired the old GPO film facility, renaming it the Crown Film Unit. Going to the cinema remained a popular pastime; by 1945 half the British population were attending regularly. Even though

80 percent of the films came from Hollywood, the British film industry made heroic efforts. The Americans conferred special Academy Awards on two British films, Noel Coward's *In Which We Serve* (1942) and the production of *Henry V* (1944) by Laurence Olivier, and an Academy Award nomination went to Roy Boulting for the documentary *Desert Victory* (1943).

Feature films dealing directly with the war did not appear in great numbers; the public still wanted escapist films. But many excellent films dealt directly with war themes. These included Michael Powell and Emeric Pressburger's *Contraband* (1940), *One of Our Aircraft Is Missing* (1942), *The Life and Death of Colonel Blimp* (1943), and *A Canterbury Tale* (1944). Carol Reed directed *The Young Mr. Pitt* (1942), *The Way Ahead* (1944), and *The True Glory* (1945). Anthony Asquith made *Freedom Radio* (1940), *We Dive at Dawn* (1943), and *The Demi-Paradise* (1943). Examples of great documentary films of the war period include *Listen to Britain* (1941), *Fires Were Started* (1943), and *A Diary for Timothy* (1945), all by Humphrey Jennings.

The MOI also produced films with propagandistic themes, like *The Foreman Went to France* (1942), about the recovery of vital machinery, and *Miss Grant Goes to the Door* (1940), which cautioned the population to be alert for the appearance of fifth columnists and German paratroopers. British filmmakers found ways to partner with the American film industry. Alfred Hitchcock went to Hollywood, where there was already a British community. There he directed *Foreign Correspondent* (1940). Powell and Pressburger sought to arouse American support with *Forty-ninth Parallel* (1941), about a Nazi submarine crew that lands in Canada and meets its deserved end.

The British directed propaganda at enemy countries through their Political Warfare Executive (PWE), which they established in September 1941 to resolve disputes among the MOI and other already existing offices. The PWE supervised all British propaganda work against the enemy from then on, and it also coordinated relations with American propaganda offices. The PWE produced both "black" and "white" propaganda. White, or largely factual, propaganda circulated mainly in two ways: through leaflets dropped into enemy territory by British and American bombers and the broadcasts of the BBC to Europe. Some leaflets dealt with recent news, such as information about the latest battle. Other leaflets addressed less time-bound subjects, like the inevitability of Allied victory. The PWE used BBC radio extensively. By 1942 the BBC was offering broadcasts in twenty-three languages. A famous example of the BBC's many broadcasts to Europe was the "V for Victory" Campaign, begun in January 1941, which inspired resistance fighters. The PWE halted it in May 1942, however, in response to worries that it was arousing false hopes of quick success.

BBC white propaganda usually emphasized dignity, resolve, and a foundation of truth, though not always the whole truth. The black propaganda produced by the PWE for radio was fundamentally untruthful: it sought to create the belief that it was being broadcast from Europe, although in fact it originated in England. It did, however, try to give the illusion of truth by mixing facts about battles and Allied policies with misleading information. Initially the PWE transmitted its black propaganda using BBC equipment, but since this risked damaging the credibility of the BBC's white propaganda, the PWE set up its own stations for the purpose and described them as "research units," or RUs; the best known was Gustav Siegfried Eins, known as GS1. By use of ingenious technology, the RUs were able to monitor German wireless printer news transmissions on the continent; this enabled them to know what the Germans and their allies knew at the same time they knew it.

British propaganda was sometimes racist and hate-filled—a phenomenon known as "Vansittartism" after Lord Vansittart, permanent undersecretary at the Foreign Office, who made a series of broadcasts on the BBC in 1940 claiming that the German national character was historically violent and aggressive, with Nazism merely its most recent expression. The MOI followed that year and later with a so-called Anger Campaign, especially in pamphlets, marked by statements such as: "The Hun is at the gate. He will rage and destroy. He will slaughter the women and the children."[28] After the policy of demanding unconditional surrender was announced at the Casablanca Conference in January 1943, it was more tempting to make such statements, although atrocity propaganda was never as extensive as in the First World War because people had come to distrust it since that time.[29]

Commonwealth countries assisted with the propaganda effort. For example, the Canadian government helped the British make the documentary films *Canada Carries On* and *The World in Action*, a series of spirited wartime newsreels. The Canadians distributed home front propaganda aimed at ensuring loyalty among the nation's many ethnic groups. Canada also provided the home for a secret British base that trained propagandists for radio broadcasting in Europe. The government of Australia assisted the Allied propaganda effort with the usual assemblage of hortatory materials for home front consumption, but it also had to caution the minority of Australians who were willing to collaborate with the Japanese in the hopes of preventing an attack on their country. Collaboration did occur in the case of Major Charles Hughes Cousens, a well-known radio broadcaster from Sydney who was captured during the fall of Singapore and was forced to work closely with the infamous Tokyo Rose. In India, the British faced the challenge of persuading those agitating for independence to put their activities on hold until after the war. They censored Japanese shortwave broadcasts that played upon Indian nationalist sentiment. Newspapers that downplayed coverage of Gandhi's Congress Party received extra supplies of newsprint and enjoyed favored access to news sources. The government asked Indian filmmakers to include officially approved material in their productions.[30]

As in the First World War, the British made a special effort to persuade the United States to enter the conflict on their side. This required ingenuity, because isolationist sentiment was strong and well organized in America even as late as the middle of 1941, when Germany ruled most of the continent, Hitler was attacking Russia, and there was a real possibility of the Germans' invading Britain. Moreover, appeals to America had to be made with great delicacy, since so many U.S. citizens were aware of the seductive propaganda used by the British in the earlier world conflict. The British pursued a variety of strategies: for example, securing placement of favorable stories in the press, sponsoring speaking tours by prominent British intellectuals such as A. J. Ayer and Isaiah Berlin, and arranging showings of British film documentaries about the war at the New York World's Fair in 1939–40.[31]

Many influential Americans helped. Probably the most powerful supporter in the media was Edward R. Murrow. He first came to London in 1937 to direct the European operations of CBS radio. He and his wife, Janet, were in their twenties at the time. Murrow's major duties were to select topics and recruit guests for the network's radio programs, which were transmitted to the United States by shortwave, processed at the CBS engineering center in New York City, sent by land telephone lines to CBS stations around the country, and then broadcast on local frequencies. At first Murrow was not yet an on-air broadcaster. He had little training in such work. But he gradually found a role in on-air news reporting and, by the time Britain went to war with Germany in 1939, was a well-known voice in American homes. Initially he was not as prominent as other radio personalities such as Raymond Gram Swing, H. V. Kaltenborn, and William L. Shirer. But Murrow soon became a master of techniques like the use of street sounds as background and speaking in a way that made him seem a trusted guest in a listener's living room. His reports on German bombs dropping on London and the courage of the British as they endured the attacks and simultaneously fought back made it much more difficult for Americans to feel that they could ignore the war in Europe. One typical broadcast was his report, in May 1940, on British defenses constructed near the coast of the English Channel in anticipation of a German invasion: "Buses, old cars and trucks are parked all over the place, as though left there by drunken drivers, but when you look carefully you see there's not a spot where an airplane can land without plowing into an obstruction of some kind." Murrow added a description of the young British fighter pilots, "the cream of the youth of Britain," who had just returned from battling Germans in the skies above Dunkirk. "There was no swagger about these boys in wrinkled and stained uniforms," Murrow commented. "The movies do that sort of thing much more dramatically than it is in real life." Broadcasts of this kind helped to prepare Americans psychologically for the possibility of entering the European war and made them more comfortable with President Roosevelt's increasingly extensive efforts to provide Britain with economic aid and much-needed military materiel. When the United States finally declared war on the Axis powers after December 7, 1941, and the Japanese attack on Pearl Harbor, Murrow continued to report from Europe. He personally covered major events such as the V-1 and V-2 rocket attacks over London in 1944, as well as profoundly important developments on the continent, including the entry of Allied troops into the concentration camps in 1945.[32]

Once the United States entered the war, the British and the Americans were able to work as partners in many areas of propaganda operations. The exchange of intelligence increased the ability of propagandists to design materials for specifically targeted audiences and made additional radio transmittal possible. The U.S. Army Air Force made available an entire squadron of Flying Fortress bombers to drop leaflets over German troops.

France Copes with Conquest

Germany attacked France in May 1940 and was in control of most of the country within six weeks. The causes of this stunning defeat continue to be debated. Because of the demographic devastation of the First World War, France had probably lost the will to fight. Military planners relied too heavily on the Maginot Line of fortifications built along the German border. Attacking through Belgium, the Germans circumvented the line and advanced quickly into France owing to their innovative use of motorized vehicles and coordination by radio.

As part of their strategy of defense, the French had formed a governmental commissariat of propaganda in 1939. It did not encompass military propaganda, and it suffered from policy confusion: for example, no propaganda could be directed at Italy, because the French hoped that Mussolini would split off from Hitler. To lead their propaganda effort, the French chose the famous playwright Jean Giraudoux. He wrote stirring essays but was not creative in the use of non-print media; in addition, he was a poor manager.

In the face of German occupation, many French decided that collaboration, even if ethically difficult to defend, was the best way to preserve some degree of control over Nazi barbarity. Marshal Philippe Pétain, one of the heroes of the Great War, consented to lead a pro-fascist French state based at Vichy. Collaborationist propaganda was anti-Semitic; it urged the people to embrace rural values, portrayed the British as war criminals, and claimed that Germany had invaded to save France from the Bolshevik menace. Newspapers, newsreels, posters, books, and speeches all disseminated this message.

Although some French collaborated in the face of conquest, the nation became the prime example of Allied efforts against the dictatorships through mass communication by clandestine resistance movements. The French people relied on sources outside France—like the *Ici Londres* radio broadcasts from Britain and Free French broadcasts from Algiers—for much of their knowledge of activity in other countries. But they also managed, at considerable risk, to evolve organs of print-based communication within occupied France. The editors of these makeshift journals faced many of the same problems as official propaganda agencies, for example, whether to emphasize truthfulness in the information they published or to employ exaggeration and lies; how to inspire members of the Resistance by reference to unifying narratives of French culture; and whether to make long-term promises regarding postwar policy.

Publications of the Resistance press were usually four typewriter-size pages, written on whatever stock could be obtained amidst the general shortages. They came from communist and socialist groups, and, as the war went forward, from groups of younger fighters who sought to mediate among older factions and to adopt new techniques. These papers offered local news as well as editorials. They exhorted French citizens to drive out the enemy but took care to say that the form of government established in postwar France should not simply pick up where prewar governments had left off. A typical socialist paper was *Populaire*, which managed to offer seven regional editions and reach a million people. The major communist paper was *L'Humanité*, which also appeared in regional editions. All the Resistance papers emphasized that the blood shed by Resistance fighters constituted a debt to be repaid. The papers were also united in their love of French civilization and the assertion that France remained great even in its time of need and peril. Sometimes the publications were remarkably specific in the advice offered on matters related to covert combat, such as how to kill collaborators or cause train wrecks. The religious press was also represented in Resistance journalism, for example, in the monthly *Cahiers du Témoignage Chrétien*, offering the Catholic point of view. All the papers regularly included vows of revenge. For instance, *La Voix* carried a story relating how French police had surrounded a house in Flanders where a communist member of the Resistance was hiding. When the man tried to escape through an attic window, the police shot and killed him. "We know them," *La Voix* said resolutely.[33]

The United States Expands Communication

The Japanese attack on Pearl Harbor unified nearly all sectors of American public opinion in favor of war. There was almost no dissent among members of the public or in the press even when Roosevelt initiated the profoundly immoral policy of placing Japanese Americans in custody in isolated camps. The general climate of opinion made it easier for the government to impose censorship of mass communication, which began immediately. Although the vague Sedition Act passed during the First World War had been repealed in 1921, the Espionage Act and the Trading with the Enemy Acts of 1917 were still in effect. The postmaster general used these laws to suppress publications sympathetic to fascism, such as Father Coughlin's *Social Justice*, as well as many German-language newspapers. Army and navy censorship began immediately. Within two weeks of Pearl Harbor, Congress approved the first War Powers Act, giving the president broad control of information. Roosevelt quickly created an Office of Censorship and even went beyond the powers of the act by strongly suggesting to its director that he urge the press and radio to pursue strict voluntary censorship of any material that might aid the enemy. Roosevelt nevertheless showed great wisdom in his choice of director of the office by picking Byron Price, the executive news editor of the Associated Press, who was widely respected. Price assembled a staff of veteran reporters and developed a reasonable, effective Code of Wartime Practices for the American Press; beginning in January 1942 it brought order to the information process and perhaps inspired some reporters to err too much on the side of cooperation with the government. Journalists voluntarily avoided mention of matters like the president's health and his schedules for cross-country travel and public appearances. At its height, Price's Office of Censorship had 14,462 staff members to enforce the legally mandated control of all postal, cable, and radio communication in and out of the United States and the guarding of vital war secrets. News of vast programs such as the development of the atomic bomb and the advance planning for the D day invasion of France was successfully kept out of the media.[34]

Initially, Roosevelt hoped that official propaganda could emphasize the provision of information without resorting to manipulation. Toward this end he established an Office of Facts and Figures directed by the prizewinning poet Archibald MacLeish. But the president soon decided that he needed to use more aggressive persuasion. In June 1942, by executive order, Roosevelt created an Office of War Information (OWI), which consolidated and expanded MacLeish's work and that of three other small federal offices that had been created in 1939 and 1941 to respond to press and public interest in America's potential engagement in the war already taking place abroad. To direct the OWI Roosevelt appointed Elmer Davis, a veteran reporter who had worked for the *New York Times* and the Columbia Broadcasting System. Like Price, Davis was widely respected and soon developed an effective method of operation. About 40 percent of the news reports generated by government departments and war agencies continued to be issued with no control by the OWI. This allowed the news to be timely and to be circulated widely. The OWI stepped in when there were interagency disputes, when agencies were suppressing information that did not need to be suppressed, or when the circulars were inaccurate, lacking in context, or amateurish. The OWI coordinated its efforts with army and navy news operations. It offered facilities and services to reporters in the United States and also produced a steady stream of news releases, photographs, cartoons, and other forms of information. One unit made motion pictures; another engaged in audience research. A division of campaigns organized war bond drives, victory gardens, fuel conservation efforts, and scrap gathering.

The overseas activities of the OWI were much more extensive than those of George Creel's Committee on Public Information in the First World War. They were directed by Robert E. Sherwood, the Pulitzer Prize–winning playwright and speechwriter who had been a personal assistant to President Roosevelt, and Joseph Barnes, foreign editor of the *New York Herald Tribune*. In addition to print, radio was a large part of operations. The OWI incorporated the already existing Voice of America, which predated the OWI by a couple of months. Also in contrast to Creel's CPI, the OWI placed much greater reliance on propaganda techniques that utilized recent research in psychology and other disciplines of the social sciences, which the OWI was developing in cooperation with the military and the Office of Strategic Services. For example, the psychiatrist Walter Langer developed a personality profile of Hitler, diagnosing him as a paranoid schizophrenic; it reinforced the belief of military leaders and propagandists that mass communication should be directed at the German people, not their leader, who was beyond persuasion. The anthropologists Ruth Benedict and Clyde Kluckhohn provided studies that seemed to offer scientific substantiation of stereotypes depicting the Japanese people as conspicuously docile. The analyses influenced propagandists to avoid urging revolt against the emperor during the war and were a factor in the decision to keep him on the throne during U.S. reconstruction of Japan after the war.[35]

At the height of their operations in 1943, the overseas news and feature bureaus of the OWI cabled 65,000 words each day to all parts of the world, mailed hundreds of thousands of words of feature material, and provided 2,500 pictures by airmail or radio transmission. In 1943 its annual budget was $43 million, of which $27 million was for overseas operations. Two-thirds of the overseas budget was for radio. When the United States entered the war, the government was making only one radio broadcast per day, through facilities of the British Broadcasting Corporation. By the end of 1942, the OWI was operating twenty-one shortwave transmitters and sending 2,700 programs a week in twenty-four different languages to Europe and Africa alone. Transmission to Asia increased as the war went on.[36]

White propaganda was directed by the Office of War Information. Black propaganda was directed by the Office of Strategic Services (OSS), which was also in charge of espionage. By 1945 the Americans were dropping more than 7 million leaflets a week over enemy-occupied areas. The OWI used leaflets extensively to prepare the way for the invasion of Sicily and the Italian mainland. The OWI published a French newspaper, *L'Amérique en Guerre*, and dropped it in large quantities over France. Over Germany the OWI dropped its newspaper *Sternebanner* (The Star-Spangled Banner). Many of the newspapers and leaflets included safe conduct passes, like those from the First World War, to tempt enemy soldiers to defect.

In 1943 the OWI experienced radical cuts in its domestic budget on the basis of a judgment that home front morale was not as much in need of its services. Throughout the rest of the war the OWI emphasized overseas work, especially newsreels for the military. During this same period the military was increasing its own propaganda capacities. The American commander in Europe, General Dwight Eisenhower, attached great importance to the role of morale in warfare. In autumn 1942, for the invasion of North Africa, Eisenhower established a Psychological Warfare Branch, under his command, to drop leaflets and conduct other forms of propaganda. For the invasion of France, he enlarged this unit, gave it greater authority, and coordinated it with British units as the Psychological War-fare Division of Supreme Headquarters Allied Expeditionary Force. In London, the Americans and the British created a special OWI-PWE committee to ensure that the propaganda they directed against the enemy coordinated with the messages of home front propaganda.

When the Allies captured the powerful transmitter of Radio Luxembourg after their invasion of the continent in 1944, they were able to send radio propaganda directly into Germany. The broadcasts could involve only general themes, like the inevitability of German defeat and the evils of Nazi leadership. Stronger messages—for example, promises of magnanimity toward defeated soldiers and civilians—would have been possible if there had been clearer statements of Allied intentions for Germany after the war, but Stalin, Churchill, and Roosevelt were reluctant to say definitively what they would do. This left German audiences worrying whether they would be treated as severely as their Nazi leaders.

As in the First World War, soldiers' journalism was an important presence. The military newspaper *Stars and Stripes* was revived in 1942, and *Yank* was also influential. The war led to the use of other media pioneered in the First World War as well. Still photography played a large role. For *Life* magazine, Margaret Bourke-White produced powerful images of Russia's participation in the war. Photographs taken at the Normandy invasion in 1944 by Robert Capa and the famous image of marines atop Mount Suribachi on Iwo Jima in 1945 taken by Joe Rosenthal became icons.[37] Popular comic strip and comic book heroes mobilized for war, including the Masked Marvel, Secret Agent X-9, and Batman.

Another sector of communications that had been important in the First World War, advertising, now also "enlisted" for service. By the time of the Second World War, commercial advertising had become a significant industry in all the Western nations and a presence throughout the world. As in World War I, advertisers' responses to the Second World War were a mixture of patriotism and profiteering, and their activity carried with it the danger of reducing public discourse about war and citizenship to lazy sloganeering, equating purchase of a commodity with selfless social responsibility.

The pattern was clearest and most elaborate in the United States, which had the largest advertising industry. Businesses strained to draw connections to the war. A magazine ad for Lucky Strike cigarettes described the logo on the packs as "the smart new uniform for fine tobacco."[38] In July 1944 the humorist S. J. Perelman wrote a piece on advertising for the *New Yorker* magazine. Recounting his perusal of an issue of *Vogue* magazine, he wrote: "I turned the page and beheld a handsome young aviatrix, crouched on a wing of her plane. 'Test Pilot—Size 10' read the text. 'Nine thousand feet above the flying field, a Hellcat fighter plane screams down in the dark blur of a power dive. Holding the stick of this four-hundred-mile-an-hour ship is a small firm hand.' The owner of the small firm hand, I shortly discovered in the verbal power dive that followed, is an enthusiastic patron of Du Barry Beauty Preparations."[39]

While tie-ins of this kind were excusable, even if contrived, some efforts to connect commercial products to the war verged on the morally indefensible. For example, the manufacturers of Talon slide fasteners published an ad that pictured the transparent plastic turret on the underside of a B-17 bomber with the belly gunner inside firing at enemy planes. The ad carried the caption "Giving 'Em Hell from a 'Goldfish Bowl,'" and below the picture a block of text promoting "the little slide fastener and its 123 fighting jobs at war," like making the packing of canvas bags easier, preserving body warmth inside flight clothing, and of course lessening the time it took a gunner to get into and out of his flight clothing. The ad misleadingly glamorized the turret gunner's dangerous experience in a questionable effort to associate a product with wartime virtues.[40]

The dramatic effects of war on advertising became evident on the night of April 30, 1942, when, as part of the national strategy for protection of the home front, the lights went out on the "Great White Way" along Broadway and Seventh Avenue in New York City. Advertisers discovered, with great relief, that their revenues did not fall significantly during the war. But they did conclude that they needed to protect against seeming opportunistic. As a result, they ran ads on topics like observing rationing by prolonging the life of automobile tires and the importance of buying war bonds; and they proclaimed their patriotism in print media, over the radio, and on billboards. Early in 1942 representatives from ad agencies, major business corporations, and the media came together to form the War Advertising Council. The council worked closely with the Office of War Information, organizing over one hundred campaigns in the period 1942–1945 on home front matters as diverse as planting victory gardens and donating objects that contained materials such as steel or brass that could be salvaged for vital war needs. Through the activities of the council, advertisers gained great prestige during the war and helped to lay the basis for postwar cooperation between business and government, in addition to increasing public support for corporate America in its disputes with organized labor.[41]

The American motion picture industry played an enormous role in the wartime battle for hearts and minds and for this reason deserves detailed discussion.[42] Statistics cited by Philip M. Taylor show the international power of Hollywood. By 1919, U.S. companies owned more than half of the film theaters in the world. In 1923, 85 percent of the films screened in France were American made. By 1925, only 2 percent of the films appearing in Britain were actually produced there. Even in 1939, after energetic efforts by other countries to change the balance, Americans still owned 40 percent of all film theaters around the world. During the Second World War, over 80 million Americans went to the movies each week; worldwide as a whole, the figure was in the hundreds of millions.[43]

In the 1930s Hollywood had played two civic roles: affirming the long-term viability of the United States, and acquainting citizens with the possibility that America might soon need to defend itself against powerful foreign enemies. The fact of U.S. involvement in a new war, from Pearl Harbor onward, created challenges that could not be addressed simply by repeating the patterns from the First World War, when the movie industry was young and had not yet permeated American life. The heads of the Hollywood film companies knew their studios would be exerting a large influence. But initially they did not know what they wanted Hollywood's role to be, or whether they would even be the ones to define it.

Whether the studios would control their own activities was not at first clear. President Roosevelt's speedy declaration that Hollywood was "an essential war industry" suggested the potential for a complete governmental takeover.[44] The government decided, however, to leave Hollywood's operations pretty much under private control. The studios were not nationalized. There was, however, control around the edges. The Office of War Information established a film advisory unit that worked closely with the studios. The unit had no authority to censor films made for domestic audiences, but it did have power to approve content for overseas distribution. Because foreign markets were important for almost all films, even in wartime, this gave the government very strong control. The censors used their powers carefully for the most part, forbidding obvious transgressions such as sympathetic portrayals of the enemy, and downplaying but not forbidding acknowledgment of wartime differences of political opinion among citizens. Because the censors were appointees of a Democratic administration, censors tended to encourage New Deal values like respect for labor unions and trust in the efficiency of large government agencies. A manual for filmmakers issued by the OWI in 1942 placed minimal restrictions on the industry, mostly having to do with national safety, but asked filmmakers to focus on five aims: explaining the Allied cause, supporting the idea of a United Nations and portraying the peoples of many parts of the world, encouraging diligence among workers and business leaders, building up home front morale, and recording and praising the heroism of those in battle and those who supported them. The government also influenced the studios financially. The OWI, the army, the Treasury Department, and other agencies had large budgets to commission documentaries and training films, and they were in a position to save the studios money by lending equipment and personnel the filmmakers otherwise would have had to pay for.

Motivated by patriotism and the desire to preserve a degree of independence, Hollywood found many ways to assist the war effort voluntarily. The studios supplied celebrities for bond rallies and USO shows, arranged for wartime charitable appeals in theaters before each showing of a film, established the Hollywood Canteen in Los Angeles where military personnel could socialize with stars, and undertook many similar actions. They also tried to create a feeling of welcome and comfort at theaters, for example, by featuring speakers during intermissions and decking the stage with flowers, aware that going to the movies was an important form of relaxation and an expression of community that was now more necessary than ever.

In terms of film content, the war had a very great impact. Escapist films—sheer entertainment—continued to be produced, and everyone agreed that they were needed. Examples include the musicals *Springtime in the Rockies* (1942) and *Coney Island* (1943) with Betty Grable, as well as *Going My Way* (1944), featuring Bing Crosby's Oscar-winning performance as an optimistic big city priest. But new emphases were conspicuous. One very noticeable change was the profusion of films seeking to provide details about the enemy. There were relatively few such productions depicting Mussolini's armed forces. One rare example was *Sahara* (1943), a saga of American tank commanders in North Africa, which included a portrayal of a not especially competent Italian soldier played by J. Carroll Naish. By contrast there were numerous depictions of the Japanese. Every combat film about the Pacific war included buck-toothed, maniacal soldiers, sailors, and pilots who wore thick-lensed glasses, mispronounced their "r's" and "l's," and mounted suicidal attacks. None of the films explored Japanese humanity. In *Gung Ho* (1943), U.S. Marine raiders mercilessly slaughter barely human Japanese soldiers on a Pacific island. In scenes of combat against the Japanese in *The Fighting Seabees* (1944), John Wayne shouts out his hatred of "Tojo's bug-eyed monkeys." Films portraying the evil Germans include *Hitler Dead or Alive* (1942), *Hitler's Children* (1943), *Women in Bondage* (1943), and *Enemy of Women* (1944). Hollywood's Nazis were pompous, harshly autocratic, sadomasochistic, bumbling, and dense. Depictions of the enemy were almost always cartoon-like. Even the exceptions were unforgiving, like *The Moon Is Down* (1943), in which a Nazi lieutenant expresses remorse to members of the Norwegian resistance movement; the Norwegians do not trust him, and soon kill him. At a time of great fear and perplexity, when mobilization, persistence, and unity were essential, filmmakers and audiences needed to put a face on the enemy but also needed to belittle and dehumanize him. A few productions attempted to use comedy to mock the Nazis, such as *To Be or Not To Be* (1942) and *Once Upon a Honeymoon* (1942). But the results were mixed. Even cartoons, with characters like Bugs Bunny and Donald Duck mobilizing for war, had difficulty using humor. The Nazis seemed too dangerous for many such films to be made.

Another major purpose of wartime films was to justify America's participation. Nearly every Hollywood production of the time helped to perform this function, whether by depicting the suffering of victims of enemy attack; alluding to the possibility of the homeland being conquered by evil invaders; including friendly portrayals of British, Chinese, Russian, and French characters; or featuring classic symbols like the flag and the Statue of Liberty that reminded audiences of America's duty to bring freedom to the world. A few productions attempted to present the logic behind U.S. involvement in foreign policy terms, for example, *Mission to Moscow* (1943), Warner Brothers' exposition of the work of Ambassador Joseph Davies. Many films explicitly justified involvement in the war, in case anyone missed the point. In *Desperate Journey* (1942), a bomber crew consisting of a Canadian (Arthur Kennedy), an American (Ronald Reagan), a Scot (Ronald Sinclair), an Anglo-Irishman (Alan Hale), and an Australian (Errol Flynn) is shot down behind German lines. The men escape from imprisonment and then fight their way across four hundred miles of enemy territory before hijacking a bomber and returning to England. When Flynn and Reagan accuse Kennedy of being too tense, he delivers an oration of the kind that was to make its way into hundreds of wartime films: "I didn't get into this war for fun, or adventure, or because it was expected of me. I got in because it was a hard, dirty job that has to be done before I can go back to doing what I liked—before a hundred million other people can get back to doing what they liked. It's no bright game to me. It's a job—a job that has to be done as rapidly and efficiently as possible."[45]

One ethical contradiction never adequately addressed by Hollywood was America's failure on the home front to completely support the values for which it was fighting. Filmmakers occasionally attempted to praise interethnic unity at the battlefront. In *Guadalcanal Diary* (1943), during a religious service on the deck of a transport ship, marines sing the hymn

"Rock of Ages," led by a Catholic priest substituting for his buddy, a Protestant chaplain, while in *Pride of the Marines* (1945), a machine gun shared by comrades in a foxhole is decorated with a shamrock and a Star of David. There were also a few films cautioning against overly conformist behavior, like the Preston Sturges comedy *Hail the Conquering Hero* (1945), which satirized mindless flag-waving on the home front and cautioned against overreliance on government control. Nevertheless, wartime productions did not honestly acknowledge faults like the widespread presence of poverty in America, the fact that many Americans were anti-Semitic, or the extensive prejudice against African Americans.

Another theme evident in wartime films involved models of conduct. Many productions depicted the virtues expected from members of the armed forces: bravery, patriotism, sacrifice, comradeship, stoicism, good humor, and ingenuity. Films in this category include *Wake Island* (1942), *Guadalcanal Diary* (1943), *Bataan* (1943), *Corregidor* (1943), and *Destination Tokyo* (1943). Slitting throats and incinerating Japanese soldiers with flame-throwers were depicted as examples of admirable U.S. military conduct. Portrayals were sometimes more nuanced, for example, in one of the greatest romances in the history of cinema, *Casablanca* (1943), in which Rick, the disillusioned saloonkeeper who fought the fascists in Spain and Ethiopia, rises to the challenges of moral courage presented by the sudden appearance of his former lover and her statesman husband. Another great film that explored models of conduct was *They Were Expendable* (1945), John Ford's tribute to the quiet heroism of a torpedo boat crew in the Pacific. Especially by the last two years of the war, Hollywood was also offering models of conduct for the home front. One film that sought to perform this function indirectly was *Dragon Seed* (1944), based on a novel by Pearl Buck. Intended as a compliment to America's ally China, it depicted the courage, family loyalty, and support for the Allied cause manifested in a Chinese village after it is attacked by evil Japanese soldiers, and implied that Americans should demonstrate the same virtues stateside. Audiences seem not to have been bothered by the fact that the central Chinese characters in the film were played by longtime Hollywood stars like Walter Huston, Katharine Hepburn, Akim Tamiroff, and Turhan Bey.

Another example of an artful film that provided models of conduct was *Since You Went Away* (1944), which the famed producer David O. Selznick regarded as on a par in importance with his prewar epic *Gone With the Wind*. Claudette Colbert played the part of a courageous mother who holds the family together after the departure of her husband for the war in January 1943. Colbert finds a constructive outlet for her anxiety by taking a job as a welder at a local factory, where she works on the assembly line with other women. She develops a close friendship with one particular woman who is an immigrant from Czechoslovakia. The woman describes her feelings upon first seeing the Statue of Liberty and tells the heroine, "You are what I thought America was." In the last scenes of the film, word is received that Dad is alive and will be coming home. In spite of this perhaps overly sentimental ending, *Since You Went Away* was widely praised at the time and remains one of the great achievements of wartime filmmaking.

In addition to its effects on feature film production, the war stimulated many new developments in the documentary genre. In comparison to prewar output, the number of documentaries increased enormously. To produce them, facilities had to be enlarged at all the studios. In addition, documentary film units became a presence in all combat operations, thanks to the development of more portable cameras. Back home, specially designed labs added battlefield sound effects, music, light enhancements, and narration. Protocols for documentaries soon became standardized. For example, cameramen always shot enemy action from left to right and action by the United States and its allies from right to left, to facilitate editing that would keep audiences oriented and help them to sense the clash of opposing forces. Similarly, editors refrained from cutting battle sequences in which the camera jiggled or there was too much or too little light. Anomalies of this kind heightened the audience's appreciation of the chaos and danger of battle, especially when excitedly placed in context by the film's narrator.

Several prominent directors who had been commercially successful in making feature films turned their talents to wartime documentaries. John Ford directed *December 7th* (1943) and *The Battle of Midway* (1942). John Huston directed *Report from the Aleutians* (1943) and *The Battle of San Pietro* (1945). William Wyler directed *The Memphis Belle* (1944) and *Thunderbolt* (1944). Probably the most effective maker of documentaries was Frank Capra, who was already famous for award-winning films from the prewar era, including *It Happened One Night* (1934), *Mr. Deeds Goes to Town* (1936), and *Mr. Smith Goes to Washington* (1939). General George C. Marshall, the army chief of staff, asked Capra to produce a film explaining America's reasons for going to war. *Why We Fight*, the seven-film series that resulted, has been called a masterpiece of propaganda by many. The studio magnate Jack L. Warner called it "the greatest gangster movie ever made."[46] President Roosevelt directed that the films be released to civilian audiences. Churchill filmed a special introduction for British viewers. Stalin allowed the film in the series which dealt with Russia to be shown there.

Writing in the *Nation* magazine in 1943, the prominent film critic James Agee gave generally good marks to Hollywood documentaries and orientation films but complained that Hollywood's fictional war movies did little to help home front audiences understand the reality of life for American military personnel, in contrast to British feature films about the war, which he found to be more mature, intelligent, and honest.[47] With some exceptions, this was a fair and accurate summary. It was, however, the view of a professional critic. It is also important to gauge the reactions of mass audiences, even though such an exercise is difficult. According to the best research as analyzed by Nicholas Reeves in his pioneering work *The Power of Film Propaganda: Myth or Reality?* (1999), the influence of war movies is often overrated but does tend to be significant when a film offers radically new information or reinforces beliefs already widespread in a society at the time the film appears. In the late 1930s and early 1940s, Hollywood did acquaint audiences with the international crisis, even if much of the presentation was sanitized. This helps to explain why even second-rate productions usually generated ticket sales large enough to repay their costs and turn some kind of profit. Of course, other factors also exerted influence, like the need for people to get out of the house, and the growing purchasing power of Americans as the war economy ramped up. By 1942, in any case, Hollywood's total film earnings were at their highest point in fifteen years. Perhaps more interesting is the way ticket sales reveal that the public could make astute judgments about quality. *Sergeant York*, released in 1941 before the United States officially entered the war, not only received praise from the professional critics and generated an Academy Award for Gary Cooper but also was also the top moneymaking picture of that year, a clear indicator of the audience's ability to recognize quality. *Casablanca* (1942) is another example of a film that earned both critical and popular approval. It won Oscars for best picture, best director, and best screenwriting, and was highly successful at the box office. Reactions of this kind are rough but important indicators that film sometimes had the power not only to reinforce the public's perceptions of war but also to broaden them.[48]

War Becomes Intimate

In physical terms, all wars have dimensions of distance and nearness. Soldiers and sailors and airmen may be fighting far away, but they and the people at home are physically in contact through supply chains, the comings and goings of those in uniform, return of the dead and injured, and other means, including the encroachment of the fighting on the home front. There is a similar pattern in the nonphysical realm. News of battles reaches the people at home, loved ones send letters to the troops, and so on.

During the Second World War, connections between those in battle and those at home became so intense and complex that one is tempted to speak of an "intimate" war. Several factors combined to give the conflict this characteristic. The war was total: it involved entire societies. Mass communication was possible: the technologies and societal infrastructures for such communication were elaborate. The importance of communication as a tool of warfare, both in battle and on the home front, was widely appreciated. The combination of these three factors resulted in an odd kind of closeness that has not been noticeable to the same extent in any other war. And an important fact about the intimacy is that it was mediated. An intense personal exchange of ideas and emotions took place, but it was not the same as the kind of intimacy experienced directly among individuals and in primary groups such as families, clubs, and small religious groups. The exchanges occurred via highly controlled channels of communication and were shaped by hundreds of thousands of professional intermediaries, including censors, reporters, entertainers, planners of propaganda, and political and military strategists.

The First World War was "intimate" in some ways. Troops came home on leave and told their stories. There was regular and extensive news of battles, not only in print, including illustrations, but also in other media such as photography, the motion picture, and posters. In spite of censorship, an extensive personal correspondence was possible because of more advanced postal services and higher levels of literacy compared to earlier wars. There were camp shows for the troops, starring famous entertainers of the era. Beautiful songs were written and recorded. Certain political leaders and generals evidenced some of the characteristics of symbolic personalities. In France, Premier Clemenceau was "the Tiger"; General Joffre incarnated the virtues of the French peasant; at the siege of Verdun in 1916, General Pétain became known as the "savior" of the symbolically important fortress. In Britain, Prime Minister David Lloyd George won over the crowds with his dramatic oratory. In Germany, General Hindenburg and General Ludendorff captured the public's imagination as personifications of the virtues of the Prussian officer class, and they understood the importance of carefully written press releases. The leader of the American forces, General "Black Jack" Pershing, had a bit of a symbolic aura too. In all the belligerent countries, daring aviators like the "Red Baron" in Germany and the American members of the Lafayette Escadrille were known by name and were seen as sports heroes and knights of the sky. The war was also intimate in a grotesque sense, in that so much of the fighting involved face-to-face combat, including bayonet warfare. Nevertheless, in most respects the Great War was not an "intimate" conflict. The monarchs of the various countries may have been majestic, but they were distant. President Woodrow Wilson was inspiring but monumental and at times priggish; he reminded John Maynard Keynes of a "Presbyterian minister." Admirals kept as far away from the press as they possibly could. General Kitchener may have been the icon on the famous recruitment poster, but he detested the press. The typical military officer, in terms of publicity, was the British general Douglas Haig. He may have been sentimentalized after the war, when he toured hospitals and schools and the press depicted him as a grandfather figure. But during the war he was stiff in front of reporters, the troops, and audiences at home, and he never really understood the role of news and propaganda in modern warfare.[49]

By the time of the Second World War, much had changed. The role of news and publicity was widely understood: certainly by the purveyors of propaganda, and intuitively at least, by most of the population. Older technologies like the newspaper and the poster were used much more extensively. Newer technologies like radio and the motion picture camera increased the links among all those involved in the war. Because of the airplane and speedier ships and trains and wheeled vehicles, written correspondence was more extensive; motion picture films could be shipped to the front, wherever it might be; and sound recordings could be transported to double and triple the impact of what had been broadcast a few weeks before.

All the means of communication reinforced one another. The effect was noticeable, for example, in the entertainment industry, which played an especially large role in personalizing the conflict compared to the First World War. The radio singer Kate Smith gave her powerful rendition of Irving Berlin's song "God Bless America" at bond rallies in American cities; the performances were broadcast nationally and overseas; film and sound recordings followed soon thereafter. In Hollywood, at the Stage Door Canteen, the troops met movie stars face-to-face, while a feature film of the same name was produced and shipped abroad. The comedian Bob Hope was the host of the radio program *Command Performance*, during which famous singers like Frances Langford performed songs requested in letters received from the troops at the front. Here again, filmed versions and sound recordings were shipped overseas. Hope and Bing Crosby, his partner in popular feature films, appeared in hundreds of camp shows at the front, earning the gratitude of their audiences. At every performance the audience asked Crosby to sing "White Christmas," with its nostalgic lyrics about home and loved ones, familiar because of the sales of sheet music and phonograph recordings, and numerous radio broadcasts. At the camp shows, Crosby always complied but was ambivalent because of the sadness everyone felt by the time the song was done. A similar melancholy on the part of millions was experienced at the front and at home whenever news was received of the death of a famous personality who had entertained the troops, like the singer Jane Froman, the actress Carole Lombard, and the bandleader Glenn Miller, all of whom died in plane crashes on the way to or returning from war-related activities. And there was always a sense of deep longing when, all over the world, British soldiers and sailors tuned in to the BBC to hear their favorite singer, Vera Lynn, "the Forces' Sweetheart," offer her latest rendition of "We'll Meet Again" and "White Cliffs of Dover," reaffirming the ties of the men in the armed forces with their women at home.

In at least one case, intimacy crossed the lines of battle. The song "Lili Marlene" began as a poem written by a German in 1915, to which a German composer added music in 1938. In the Second World War, with help from the media, the song was adopted by soldiers, sailors, pilots, and civilians on both sides of the conflict. It was an especially powerful reminder that throughout the long history of the relationship between war and mass communication, the media have always had the potential to help people transcend hatred and imagine a less violent world.

Another form of intimacy that was characteristic of the Second World War was personal photography. Portable "snapshot" cameras made by Kodak and other manufacturers had been in existence since the beginning of the century. But by now they were much more portable and more widely available. Family photographs from home accompanied many letters to the troops. Erotic photographs also made their way to the front by this means, often with help from the censors, as well as through commercial photography. Erotic illustration had been a feature of the First World War, notably in postcards. But it became much more extensive commercially in the Second World War. Hollywood was a large supplier. Almost every soldier's tent and every sailor's quarters had its display of "pinup" photographs of motion picture stars like Hedy Lamarr, Ann Sheridan, Ava Gardner, and Betty Grable. It seemed that no opportunity for erotic communication was overlooked. Late in the war a photograph taken at the National Press Club in Washington, D.C., became famous. It showed Lauren Bacall in a tailored coat and skirt sitting in a leggy pose atop a piano, singing wartime melodies being played enthusiastically by President Harry Truman.[50]

The sense of intimacy during the Second World War also involved military leaders. Most generals and admirals knew that they could not rise in the hierarchy or do their jobs adequately unless they were willing to put themselves on stage. Within the limits of censorship, all made themselves available to reporters. Some commanders, like Admirals Chester Nimitz and Raymond Spruance in the Pacific and General Omar Bradley in Europe, took the route of conveying quiet dignity. General Dwight Eisenhower—"Ike" to the troops and reporters—projected the image of a powerful, wise, protective uncle. Most of the commanders had nicknames, like General James "Jimmy" Doolittle, who led the daring air raid on Japan in 1942, or Admiral "Bull" Halsey in the Pacific, and General Joseph "Vinegar Joe" Stillwell, who commanded troops in Asia. Some of the military leaders were highly theatrical. In Europe, General George Patton wore cowboy-style holsters and carried revolvers with ivory handles. His flamboyant remarks provided extensive material for the many reporters he courted. Among British commanders—indeed, all commanders—no one was more skilled in the arts of publicity than General Bernard Montgomery—"Monty"—who joined with Patton to drive General Erwin Rommel from North Africa and then went on to brilliant service in Europe. The many characteristics for which he was known included his clever repartee with reporters, the witty, masterly briefings he gave to his troops, and his insistence on wearing two badges on his cap, one his general officer's badge and the other the tank regiment badge.

For a detailed example of "intimacy," or at least the illusion of such, in the Second World War, one cannot find anything more striking than the imagery surrounding General Douglas MacArthur. He was serving as Allied commander in the Philippines when the Japanese launched their attack there on December 8, 1941. After battling against the Japanese unsuccessfully, MacArthur made a dramatic escape to Australia in March 1942 under orders from Roosevelt, who appointed him supreme commander of Allied forces in the Southwest Pacific area. American newspapers reported that the Allies had extensive military forces in Australia and that MacArthur was one of America's finest generals. In fact, neither the Australians nor the Americans in the area had extensive numbers of troops or planes available at the time. The general reported this fact privately to Roosevelt, but neither the president nor MacArthur so apprised the press; nor did they disclose the decision that had been made by Roosevelt and Churchill to concentrate on the war in Europe. Knowing the importance of imagery in such a situation, MacArthur assembled a large publicity staff. They quickly exerted their influence. On his arrival in Australia, MacArthur had commented, "I have come through and I will return." The staff changed this to "I shall return," which became one of the most famous comments of the war. It was repeated in hundreds of correspondents' reports and was printed or stamped on matchbooks, blotters, buttons, and bars of soap that were dropped over the Philippines. Appearing at a press conference in Canberra, MacArthur wore thirty-six medal ribbons. In the days and months that followed, his personal photographer supplied hundreds of images of him hard at work at his desk or among the troops, often with his trademark corncob pipe, aviator sunglasses, and silk scarf around his neck. Later in the war, when MacArthur was able to return to the Philippines, his arrival on the beach was elaborately stage-managed. He waded ashore numerous times, on several different beaches, to provide the most advantageous images for the many still photographers and newsreel cameramen who accompanied the general and his staff.[51]

Heads of state and government projected a special kind of intimacy. All sensed the need for a certain tone and manner. In Britain, the monarch and his family circulated among the people to an unprecedented degree, and the king spoke to his subjects regularly by radio. Churchill's magnificent speeches achieved added impact via radio and newsreels, and everyone was familiar with the visual symbols he cultivated, like the cigar, the homburg hat, and the two fingers held up in the "V" sign for "victory." Roosevelt enhanced the power of his amazing oratory via radio and newsreels and cultivated his own symbols, including the cigarette holder held at a jaunty angle and frequent references to his faithful beloved dog Fala. In China, where technologies of communication were less industrialized, Mao and Chiang Kai-shek still managed to be presences among their followers. Pictures of the two leaders appeared everywhere, on posters and postage stamps and in newspapers and on propaganda leaflets. In Japan, in the early years of war and in accord with religious doctrine, the emperor was never seen by his people, but he was a ubiquitous spiritual presence. Then at the end of the war, in an attempt to improve morale, he took the historic action of appearing in public with cameras present, a strategic use of intimacy with his people.

In all the dictatorships—and, in some senses, even in the democracies—there was a perverse quality to this sense of intimacy with wartime leaders because of the evils carried out at their command. This was less so in Italy than elsewhere. Mussolini was a thug who made use of murder, torture, and atrocities in battle. But at least in the early years of his rule, he shared poetry with his fellow Italians, and invoked a usually sane form of humor in his speeches, radio broadcasts, and appearances before the camera. Perversion of intimacy was much more pervasive in the case of Stalin and Hitler. Their derangement gave them a genius for sensing and exploiting the emotions of the people around them. Stalin's approach was relatively plain. He projected himself to his subjects in terms of cultural archetypes they knew well: the bear, the axe-holding villager who might go berserk at any moment, the secretive monk. These were not invoked directly, but they were powerfully implied. Stalin's image was everywhere. While not especially articulate, he also made use of radio, usually with his voice emanating from loudspeakers in village squares because so few Russians owned receivers. In spite of the stone-like delivery, the people became familiar with Stalin via these broadcasts. Although he read from a script, Stalin sometimes paused strategically, thereby helping listeners to visualize him drinking from the glass of water they knew he had at his elbow. As the war went on, Stalin broke with his earlier, more formal manner and began addressing his audiences as "brothers and sisters, friends" to inspire them and make them believe he cared.[52] Hitler's cultivation of intimacy was much more elaborate. Whereas Stalin had risen by means of backstage intrigue, Hitler was the product of street politics and mass demagoguery, as well as the controller of a vast, technologically sophisticated apparatus of communication. Every aspect of his personality—or so it was made to seem—was shared with the people through all available media.

In all cases, however, this intimacy was carefully controlled. Pictures of Roosevelt on his crutches were not made public. There were no stories in the press about Churchill's frequent battles with depression, his drinking, or the fact that he had to overcome stuttering, a lisp, and chronic stage fright to become the great orator that he was. The fact was never admitted that Hitler was ineffective and boring when speaking alone in front of a microphone in a radio studio. After experimenting with this approach, Goebbels simply halted it and thereafter made certain that a crowd was present whenever Hitler spoke over the radio. Nor was the public told about Hitler's tirades during planning sessions, any more than Stalin's murderous habits were officially reported. In all the belligerent nations, according to the specific norms of each, the head of state was portrayed as a protector, a totemic idol, a savior, a sleeping hero roused to rescue the faithful and lead them to triumph. This is the situation in all wars. But the phenomenon was unusually powerful during the Second World War because of the converging facts that entire societies were involved, elaborate tools of communication were available, and the potential for using such tools was recognized and exploited.

In very important ways, to be sure, the Second World War was not at all intimate. Some feelings could not be shared. They were too primal or complex. Russian soldiers were usually silent when asked to describe the horrors done to them and by them in combat against the Germans. The first Western journalists to enter the concentration camps agreed that what they saw there was beyond description. Those who survived imprisonment in the camps were, to say the least, of the same view. Moreover, the intimacy of the conflict was frequently involuntary. The average participant in the war often felt unable to control intrusively inaccurate portrayals. Generals and heads of state could greatly influence how the media depicted them. They had large staffs and bureaucracies and cooperative reporters to assist with information management. But the average soldier, sailor, airman, or civilian had almost no power to shape the way he or she was portrayed.

This was not a problem as long as the media fit the person into a framework that was welcome. But because of the large role of media, there were numerous occasions when average people felt uncomfortable or insulted in response to media depictions. One of the reasons why the 1944 Hollywood film *Since You Went Away* rose above typical productions of the era was that it sensitively acknowledged this fact. In one scene a male character sits in a half-darkened theater watching an upbeat newsreel. Tanks, trucks, and smiling troops parade across the screen as the narrator proclaims the inevitability of Allied victory in an almost giddy tone of voice. The man in the theater rises from his seat and walks out. In the half-light we see his gaunt face and notice that he is wearing a black armband. Tying this to information provided in earlier scenes, we suddenly realize that, in the last few days, the character has received word of his son's death in battle, and we understand the pain that a selective portrayal of war has caused. Such reactions were not confined to America, as indicated by the Hollywood production *Mrs. Miniver* (1942), an attempt to portray British heroism, which was a hit in the United States but which the British found to be saccharine. The Hollywood film *Objective Burma!* (1945), Britons protested, exaggerated the role of U.S. forces in South Asia. There was a similar, less understated reaction to the forced jollity of entertainers, who sometimes tried to suggest that their sacrifices were on a par with those of the troops. A striking example involves the comedian Bob Hope. Military personnel were grateful for his hundreds of camp shows at and near zones of battle. But at times they found him to be presumptuously chummy, forgetful of the fact that he wasn't the one doing the fighting. At one show in Tunisia, where Hope was in the midst of a performance for soldiers, sailors, and medical personnel preparing for the invasion of Sicily, a heckler shouted from the audience: "Draft dodger! Why aren't you in uniform?" Always quick on his feet, Hope fired back: "Don't you know there's a war on? A guy could get hurt." But this quip did not resolve the tension.[53]

No episode of the war better epitomized the burden of being intimately yet inaccurately portrayed than the moral drama that resulted from a series of coincidences and choices about symbolism that occurred in February 1945 on the small Pacific island of Iwo Jima. The island was urgently needed as an airbase and staging area for the planned invasion of Japan. In the battle for control of Iwo Jima, more than 20,000 Japanese and 6,821 Americans died during six weeks of hand-to-hand combat that ended with an American victory. On the fifth day of battle, U.S. troops controlled enough of the island to climb to its highest point on top of Mount Suribachi, where six marines planted a makeshift pole with an American flag. Observers on the beach and in a ship offshore decided that the flag was not sufficiently visible and ordered that it be replaced. As soon as the first flag was removed, six other men at the top of the mountain put up a second pole and a larger flag. Their image was captured in a photograph snapped hastily by the seasoned, respected combat photographer Joe Rosenthal. He sent his rolls of film back to the U.S. mainland for the usual military processing and clearance. A technician in the lab noticed the image of the second flag-raising, and remarked, "Here's one for the ages." The photograph was soon being reproduced around the world and was on its way to becoming the most iconic American image of the entire war, and one of the most stirring symbols of human steadfastness in all of history. Three of the six men who had raised the second flag were ultimately killed in the battle for Iwo Jima. The three who survived were ordered back to the United States for a nationwide publicity tour to build morale and aid the sale of war bonds. All three were thus forced to put themselves on display and simultaneously bear an enormous burden of irony. They felt guilt at having had to desert comrades who were still in battle, believing, like all warriors, that the true heroes were those who had died. They felt the shame of hypocrisy, knowing that the six soldiers who had raised the first flag were not being honored. They felt anger when faced with the cheap oratory at banquets, papier-mâché replicas of the flag-raising, hundreds of small town parades and big city rallies cluttered with politicians and autograph seekers, and the censorship that kept the images of bayoneted guts and burnt bodies—their reality—away from the public eye. All three of the marines suffered long-term depression.[54]

The two portrayers of war who were probably the most sensitive to the warrior's burden of irony—at least among American media professionals—were the combat cartoonist Bill Mauldin and the frontline correspondent Ernie Pyle. Mauldin worked for the army newspaper *Stars and Stripes*. He was only twenty years old when, serving overseas, he created the characters Willie and Joe, two infantrymen who endured mud, rain, rats, and enemy bombardments with courage, humor, and bravery. Mauldin depicted a world that, he and his fans believed, the officers and politicians did not understand, a world where cigarettes were always wet, the larger purposes of battle were not entirely clear, and comradeship was the key to staying alive. Typical of Mauldin's humor was a cartoon published midway through the war showing an exhausted, unshaved Willie preparing to board an airplane. Greeting him is a boyish figure with pilot's wings and a colonel's eagles on his clean uniform. The caption reads, "Uncle Willie!" The cartoon captures the enlisted man's sense of bewilderment and injustice, and prompts a viewer to wonder what has happened to the older pilots. Have they all been killed, or has the war has expanded to such a scale that hasty inductions have become necessary to expand the supply of fliers?[55]

Like Mauldin, Ernie Pyle also adopted the perspective of the enlisted man. His prose was spare and direct, very much a product of the world of the working newspaperman, similar in style to that of Ernest Hemingway, who had begun as a journalist, but without Hemingway's bravado and overdone stoicism. Pyle's reports appeared regularly in some three hundred daily newspapers and ten thousand weeklies. When he issued a complaint on behalf of fighting men, generals and politicians paid attention. Commanders feared the damage Pyle could do to them, but they also loved his articles as much as the enlisted men did and understood his immensely positive effect on morale. From his position with the soldiers at the front lines, Pyle wrote about everyday concrete concerns of enlisted men: the wounds of battle, their feelings of sadness and fear, the arrogance of officers, individual bravery, shortages of supplies, and the importance of letters from home. He was the defender of the non-com, "the GI's friend." At Pyle's urging, Congress increased the rate of pay for soldiers in combat. General Omar Bradley once commented, "Our soldiers always seemed to fight a little better when Ernie was around." Pyle's closeness to the troops was epitomized by the way he died: from sniper fire on a Pacific island in 1944.[56]

The Media Cope with Enormity

In the Second World War, democratic countries faced new challenges regarding regimentation of the media. This resulted from such factors as enlarged use of espionage and the need to keep knowledge of scientific and industrial processes out of the hands of the enemy. Heads of propaganda bureaus had to sign confidentiality agreements; publishers, filmmakers, and other controllers of opinion in the private sector knew they ought to be discreet; and extensive censorship, though never as severe as in fascist and communist countries, made full and accurate reportage difficult.

But the Western media also voluntarily censored themselves, for better or worse, without governmental prompting. In China, for example, reports on the setbacks of Chiang Kai-shek and the Nationalists submitted to his employer Henry Luce by the American journalist Theodore H. White were regularly rewritten by Luce to build home front morale and discredit the Chinese communists.[57]

In an article for *Harper's* magazine in February 1942, E. B. White expressed concern about the excessive, misleading optimism prevalent in America's war reportage. Among many examples, he cited a United Press story that carried the large headline "ALLIES SINK JAPANESE CRUISER." The reference was to a ship sunk by the Allies in the Netherlands East Indies. The story went on to include the clarification that the sinking took place during action in which the Japanese gained control of large parts of the area. White commented, "You certainly wouldn't know, from looking over your neighbor's shoulder in the subway, that the second largest naval and air force base in the Indies had been taken by Japan."[58]

American journalists disagreed among themselves about how best to support the war effort. An episode that typifies the way the journalistic community could break down took place near the end of the war in Europe. Associated Press reporter Edward Kennedy was one of sixteen reporters from Allied nations invited to military headquarters in Reims to witness the German surrender. All promised not to release their stories before an officially designated time. Kennedy became angry when he learned that German radio was announcing the surrender earlier. He made an unauthorized telephone call to London, and the AP published the details of the German surrender a day before V-E Day. In Paris, fifty-four American reporters charged Kennedy with committing "the most disgraceful, deliberate, and unethical double cross in the history of journalism." Kennedy retorted that he was legitimately protesting censorship. But his reputation among colleagues was never the same.[59]

Great journalism was produced in spite of censorship. Usually it focused on selected aspects of the war, with no attempt to see the larger strategic perspective. The American A. J. Liebling produced outstanding reportage by evoking a sense of place and atmosphere, being honest about mistakes and human weakness, and reminding readers of the folly that was seen in all wars, even the most just.[60] Among British journalists, an example of great reportage was that of V. S. Pritchett, who served as a correspondent for the *New Statesman and Nation*. In April 1945, during the last months of the war in Europe, he filed a dispatch that brilliantly met the challenge, common to all correspondents on the winning side at that time, of recalling the evil the Germans had caused while also preserving compassion for their suffering and describing the rubble that was visible for mile after mile. "We have become connoisseurs of ruin in this war," he wrote. "But in England," he added, "we have never seen a town that has been killed . . . a place as empty as Pompeii . . . where the only sound is the drip of water from the broken roofs. . . . This is negation. The mind and heart have got to begin at the beginning again and learn all they knew once more."[61]

The two events of the Second World War that probably challenged reporters most intensely both took place during the last year of the conflict, one in Japan and the other in Europe. The Second World War in the Pacific officially concluded in Tokyo Bay on September 2, 1945, aboard the battleship USS *Missouri*, one of the hundreds of vessels assembled for the ceremony. The commander of Allied forces in the Pacific, General Douglas MacArthur, arranged for extensive press coverage. Numerous reporters were among those crowding the decks of the *Missouri* as the surrender papers were signed. But MacArthur was by no means as open about the events that had precipitated the surrender, namely, the dropping of atomic bombs on Hiroshima on August 6 and Nagasaki on August 9—one of the major stories not just of the war but of the century. President Truman announced the bombing of Hiroshima sixteen hours after the event. The military had provided press releases and photographs internationally within a few days of the bombings. The military also undertook a campaign of leaflet drops and propaganda broadcasts directed at Japanese audiences, though because of logistical confusion these did not begin until August 10. But MacArthur declared southern Japan off-limits to reporters and tried to divert them to the north to cover the less disturbing story of the opening of POW camps— what one reporter called the "look-Mom-I'm-free" story.[62] This was not because of fear of radiation poisoning; little was known about that at the time. Instead MacArthur wanted to maintain control over the portrayal of the bombings in view of the horror of the events and the resulting deaths of more than 200,000 people. Entire blocks of buildings had been flattened. Human silhouettes were burned into walls. Skin peeled from the bodies of survivors, and they endured hemorrhages, infection, and hair loss. Patients crowded into hospitals. People walked the streets in shock.

The first Western journalist to disclose these effects was Wilfred Burchett, an independent reporter from Australia. Defying MacArthur's orders, he boarded a train and traveled for twenty hours to reach Hiroshima. His article, headlined "THE ATOMIC PLAGUE," appeared on September 5, 1945, in the *London Daily Express*. It shocked readers throughout the world and created a public relations disaster for MacArthur and his military censors. In a clumsy attempt to recover, MacArthur and his staff asserted that Burchett was under the influence of Japanese propaganda, denied the existence of radiation sickness, and underplayed the number and severity of human casualties. Four days after Burchett's story broke, the director of the atomic bomb project in New Mexico, Major General Leslie Groves, gave a tour of the test site to thirty reporters and repeated the assertion that there was no need to fear atomic radiation. One of the reporters was William L. Laurence, who represented the *New York Times*. On September 12 the *Times* published his report on the tour after it had been cleared by military censors. It downplayed the possibility of death by radiation. In additional articles that appeared soon thereafter, Laurence glorified the technological accomplishments that had produced the atomic bomb and glossed over the extent of human suffering it had caused.

Laurence was one of the pioneers of science journalism, a field he had begun to cover during the 1920s. For his reporting on the atom bomb project Laurence received a Pulitzer Prize. But he was too credulous. Laurence had been in the pay of the Manhattan Project since March 1945, when General Groves hired him to begin preparing press releases for future use. Laurence had also been on one of the planes that flew over Nagasaki when the bomb was dropped there. The *Times* had revealed Laurence's dual status in a story published on August 7, but the paper did not question his capacity for objectivity.

In any case, the public's desire for more information about the human effects of the atomic bomb continued to grow. To address this need, in May 1946 the *New Yorker* sent the author and seasoned war correspondent John Hersey to Hiroshima. The magazine devoted its entire issue of August 31, 1946, to Hersey's thirty-thousand-word account, which described the arrival of the atomic era in terms of the suffering of six Japanese survivors of the bombing. The issue sold out within hours and was serialized in other publications and read over the radio in the United States and Britain. Albert Einstein ordered one thousand copies. Key information about the bombings nevertheless remained unavailable to the public. A team of thirty Japanese cameramen had made a documentary record in Hiroshima and Nagasaki between August and December 1945. The American authorities confiscated this film and sent it to Washington, D.C., with orders that not a single copy was to remain in Japan. Not until 1950 were any Japanese allowed to publish visual representations of the bombings; that year two artists obtained permission to publish a small book of drawings depicting what they had seen or been told. The first official exhibition of actual photographs of the two cities in the days after the bombings did not take place until 1952, after the Allied occupation ended.[63]

An even larger challenge to reportage during the Second World War involved the Holocaust, one of the great crimes of human history, and certainly the greatest crime of the Second World War. The systematic, industrialized extermination by Nazi Germany of millions of Jews and other minorities went almost unnoticed by other nations at the time. Why this was so is a difficult question—one of the many surrounding a historical event that continues to arouse very deep emotions and generate important debates. A helpful discussion of the issue can be provided, however, by relying on two works that have earned great respect: Deborah Lipstadt's *Beyond Belief: The American Press and the Coming of the Holocaust, 1933–1945* (1986), and Laurel Leff's *Buried by the Times: The Holocaust and America's Most Important Newspaper* (2005).[64]

From the 1930s, when Nazi Germany first established the concentration camps, then later when the press reported events such as Kristallnacht, until 1942, by which time the existence of the Final Solution was no longer a secret, the media gave the Holocaust only fragmentary attention. There were many reasons. After the First World War, skepticism in response to atrocity stories was widespread. The moral enormity of the crimes the Nazis contemplated, and the large-scale organization they instituted, were always difficult to comprehend. Isolationist groups in the United States and Britain sought to downplay assertions of Germany's aggressive aims. The desire to avoid disturbing information was also widespread among people in those countries and in France who still felt exhausted by the last war. In some sectors of governmental bureaucracies, such as the U.S. Department of State in the 1930s, tacit anti-Semitism was part of the organizational culture. Government leaders, including Roosevelt, who knew through espionage reports about increasing German brutality toward Jews and other minorities chose not to circulate the information for fear of complicating public discussion about issues they deemed more important, like domestic economic recovery during the depression of the 1930s.

Factors such as skepticism about atrocity stories, isolationism, and in-house anti-Semitism also operated in the world of mass communication.

Some influential figures, including even the Jewish publishers of the *New York Times*, believed that they should not single out Jews for attention over other war victims. Among Western reporters, editors, and publishers an important additional factor was the day-by-day, segmented, empirical approach to journalism. The code of "objectivity," while admirable in many respects, could also deteriorate quickly into a lazy, unreflective lack of willingness to consider unfamiliar patterns. And except among some columnists and veteran correspondents, the ability to fit information into larger analytical frameworks was scarce. All of these problems produced an audience of news consumers who were either ignorant of the existence of the Final Solution or confused, doubtful, and poorly equipped to understand the significance of what little they did know. Allied leaders greatly intensified the problem by deciding not to divulge all they were aware of by 1942 in the belief that the information would produce a public demand for diversion of military resources from the essential task of winning crucial battles.

When the Allies liberated the concentration camps in 1945, horrified journalists struggled to make the facts of the Holocaust known in their full context. Marguerite Higgins, the correspondent for the *New York Herald Tribune*, was with the troops who entered Dachau. She sought to convey what she witnessed by describing the rage of surviving prisoners who beat one of the SS guards to death. Ronald Monson, another correspondent, who was with the first soldiers to enter Belsen, chose to report in tones of understatement, which conveyed an observer's extreme shock but did not adequately address the moral enormity or express righteous anger. Gene Currivan, reporting for the *New York Times*, successfully conveyed much of the reality of Buchenwald by describing the reactions of the 1,200 Germans from nearby Weimar who were forced by U.S. military authorities to walk through the camp and witness its horrors. Larry Solon of the *London News Chronicle* went a long way toward capturing the moral significance by describing the children who were among the survivors at one camp. Radio was in many ways the most effective medium for conveying what reporters were witnessing. When he spoke of his entry into Belsen, Richard Dimbleby, the respected and experienced BBC broadcaster, broke down on the air for the first time in his career. Edward R. Murrow told his American listeners: "I pray you to believe what I have said about Buchenwald. I reported what I saw and heard but only part of it. For most of it I have no words."[65]

The public was rightly and deeply disturbed by such information, but most were still disoriented, unprepared to digest what journalists and governments were now disclosing. The decision to allow intensive reporting of the war crimes trials at Nuremberg was, among other things, an attempt to assist the public in the task of comprehending. A major legacy of the war was the burden of guilt it placed on all those who had failed to alert the world when they could have done so.

6 SYMBOLIC WAR TAKES PRECEDENCE

1945–1991

IN THE YEARS after the Second World War, two power blocs of nation-states gradually formed. One group, led by the Soviet Union, with the People's Republic of China as its main partner, sought to spread communist forms of government and economic organization. The other group, led by the United States with western European nations as major partners, sought to spread liberal constitutional forms of government and capitalistic economic organization. Mass communication reflected this new bipolar alignment. By this time, all the industrialized nations had extensive media structures, and developing nations were working to gain access to these networks and also create their own. Moreover, many technologies were highly developed and continued to be used energetically, including print, radio, and film, with television quickly emerging. Strategies for using these technologies were also highly organized, involving journalism, advertising, public relations, feature and documentary filmmaking, and official propaganda. From its inception in the late 1940s to its end in 1991, many nation-states and many media played active roles in the cold war. But especially in its first three decades the story of mass communication during the cold war tended to be mostly about the Soviet Union and the United States, and the strategies of persuasion they adopted.

When the Second World War ended, the victors quickly dismantled the highly regimented structures of media coordination that had existed in Germany, Italy, Japan, and other countries. They at first hoped to establish the kinds of relations between governmental and private organs of mass communication that were familiar in peacetime in liberal democratic countries. But no one could force the Soviet Union to abolish regimentation in Russia and countries such as Hungary and Poland that came under Soviet control. Nor did any of the victors have the power to dissuade China from mobilizing its mass communications when the communists created the People's Republic in 1949. For these reasons, the Western powers did not radically dismantle

143

their structures of wartime media coordination as they had after the First World War. Instead, they modified what already existed and even went so far as to export the model to other countries—not only ones that had recently been enemies, like Germany and Japan, but also states in other regions such as the Middle East and Latin America. Manipulation of opinion now took place in an environment where, because of the possibility of nuclear annihilation, everyone struggled to avoid another world war, but where localized wars like the ones in Korea (1950–1953) and Algeria (1954–1962) were acceptable; violence took place behind the scenes in the form of covert action; and a worldwide effort to win over populations through mass persuasion was regarded as essential. The central consideration was the prospect of total physical annihilation. The media helped people to visualize the consequences of such an event and strengthened their resolve to avoid it. As a result, war became proportionately more symbolic than ever before.

Peacemakers Revisit the Media

In August 1941, on a ship off the coast of Newfoundland, Churchill and Roosevelt composed the first drafts of what became known as the Atlantic Charter. One item in the document called for full collaboration by all nations in efforts to abandon the use of force after the war. In January 1942, meeting in Washington, D.C., representatives of the twenty-six nations allied against the Axis signed the Declaration by United Nations, laying the foundation for what would become the UN. Details of the work such an organization would undertake were elaborated during the remaining years of the war, for example, through establishment of a Food and Agriculture Organization in 1943 and international financial structures agreed upon at Bretton Woods, New Hampshire, in 1944. A United Nations Conference on International Organizations met in San Francisco in April–June 1945 and drafted the United Nations Charter. Some 2,636 correspondents representing all types of media from numerous countries were present, making this the most thoroughly reported—perhaps overreported—conference in history. The United States and other countries adopted a policy of maximum possible openness to the press. There was little censorship of the event; most media problems were due to the crush of reporters, who filed some 6 million words of copy via telegraph during the conference. Among the correspondents were some who had been present in Paris in 1919 or in Geneva for early meetings of the League of Nations, including Erwin D. Canham of the *Christian Science Monitor*; Walter Lippmann, who was on the staff of the *New York Herald Tribune* at the time; and the French journalist André Géraud ("Pertinax"). The ceremonial honor of printing the actual charter document went to the University of California Press across the bay in Berkeley, in part because it was the home of master printer A. R. Tommasini and his staff. The charter was signed in the San Francisco Opera House on June 25, 1945, and the first meeting of the UN General Assembly took place in London the following January.[1]

Mindful of the importance of media, the founders of the UN included a large office of press and publicity in its Secretariat and designed its headquarters building in New York City to accommodate television, radio, motion picture production, still photography, telegraph, and print journalism.[2] The desire for a lasting peace led world leaders to consider many tools for reaching such a goal. Some looked to economic integration, others to international political organization via the UN and regional political structures. One of the tools that opinion leaders began to consider energetically was use of mass communication to foster trust and understanding among diverse cultures and polities. A dramatic effort of this kind was the adoption of the symbol of a "doomsday clock" from the cover of the *Bulletin of the Atomic Scientists*. With the hands set at a few minutes before midnight, and occasional adjustments to reflect a lessening of or an increase in world tensions, the clock became a reminder to millions of the importance of finding alternatives to war in an era when violence between states could lead to the destruction of the entire planet.

In 1945, to help stimulate mutual understanding as an alternative to war, the founders of the UN established UNESCO (the United Nations Educational, Scientific and Cultural Organization), a unit of international government specifically mandated to include considerations of culture in its work. (The League of Nations charter had not mentioned culture.) Its founding document stated that UNESCO was addressing the by now accepted principle that "wars begin in the minds of men."[3] UNESCO designed educational curricula for schools in developing nations, published textbooks, led efforts to preserve historic monuments that expressed a nation's cultural heritage, and sponsored scientific and cultural exchanges that brought great minds together. Other UN agencies pursued similar work. For example, UNICEF (the United Nations International Children's Emergency Fund) sponsored hundreds of projects such as the international sale of holiday greeting cards, and world tours, reported in television documentaries, by noted entertainers like Danny Kaye and Audrey Hepburn, who were strongly interested in protecting endangered children and educating audiences about the need for world peace.

UNESCO eventually ran into major obstacles. Like other offices of the United Nations, it was gradually weakened by cronyism and political patronage in the hiring of staff and awarding of contracts, strong philosophical differences among various cultures, periodic budgetary crises, behind-the-scenes intrigues between member states, and the continuing propensity of humans to resort to violence as a solution. But even with these many problems, the organization accomplished a great deal. In 1948 UNESCO issued a Universal Declaration of Human Rights, which proved to be highly influential over the years. In addition, it convened hundreds of scientific conferences—for example, meetings of atomic physicists worried about the possibility of nuclear war—and sponsored international encyclopedias and countless speaker tours. UNESCO was less elitist in its cultural efforts than the League of Nations, and was able to draw upon broader energies because of the inclusion of science in its mandate. It had access to a wide variety of communications technologies and, paradoxically, found itself consumed by debates over the years about how to guarantee access to all communications technology by developing nations while still retaining the support of the major world powers, which were reluctant to give up any of the control they had enjoyed historically.[4]

At the same time the UN was being established, the World War II victor nations concluded that extensive counterpropaganda would be needed to reduce the emotional tensions that had been stimulated by the use of mass communication during the war. In the countries it controlled, the Soviet Union imposed Stalinist ideology, portraying it as the surest way to guarantee continued peace. In China, after the communist victory over the Nationalists in 1949, Mao propagated an Asian version of the same worldview. In western Europe there was an extensive effort to replace the values of dictatorship with those of liberal constitutionalism, free market capitalism, and moderate socialism.

In Germany the Allies created special military units and assigned thousands of civilian officials to undertake "denazification." The effort mobilized all media, including newspapers, film, and radio, and included special curricula for German schools. How concerned the Allies were by the lasting effects of wartime propaganda was suggested by *Your Job in Germany*, one of the U.S. films used to orient American soldiers. (It won an Academy Award in the documentary category in 1946.) The film cautioned American soldiers not to fraternize with Germans: "You'll be offered the hand of friendship. Don't take it. It is the hand that heiled Hitler." The film called the Nazi propaganda effort "the greatest educational crime in history."[5]

In Japan, after the Allied victory in the summer of 1945, the newly created occupying regime under General Douglas MacArthur attempted to rid the Japanese press of war criminals and others judged to have assisted too vigorously in the war effort. Hundreds of members of the Japanese press were removed from their jobs. In the 1950s the occupying authorities allowed many to return because of fear of communist influence. Then, in a reverse game of musical chairs, some seven hundred members of the press thought to be communist sympathizers were sacked. In 1948 the occupying authorities also instituted press censorship. By the end of the 1950s, with economic improvement and growth in purchasing power, total sales of morning and evening papers in Japan reached over 50 million. Only in the United States were more papers purchased. The press included a significant sector advocating radical politics. Many of the papers, of all political persuasions, were owned by their employees, a policy encouraged by the occupying authorities. It meant that the concentration of ownership of the press was not a large problem. Nevertheless, at many of the papers, relations between editors and politicians were often cliquish, with a great deal of information exchanged behind the scenes.[6]

Another effort to promote peace involved the tardy disclosure of the full extent of the Holocaust. After the liberation of the concentration camps, the criminality of Nazi leaders became evident. Many influential figures, including Churchill, advocated the traditional practice of just shooting the barbarians. But proponents of international cooperation, echoing the principle of the UN, sought a judicial forum in which to assert the old Stoic idea of the law of humanity, and they wanted the precedent established by such action to be widely publicized. The Allies knew that such publicity would also help compensate for their failure to disclose the extent of the crimes during the war. For all these purposes, the victors convened war crimes tribunals in Germany and Japan. Both at Nuremberg and in Tokyo extensive structures for press relations were put in place, and prominent journalists covered the proceedings. In Germany, for example, U.S. radio broadcasters included William Shirer and Walter Cronkite. The proceedings at Nuremberg were well conducted. This eased the task for reporters and produced large audiences for press accounts for some time. The trials in Tokyo were not as well managed. The American occupation authorities, MacArthur especially, allowed politics to play much too large a role, most conspicuously in exempting Emperor Hirohito from prosecution. Western audiences did not stay with the reportage for as long as they followed Nuremberg. But Asian audiences were attentive. The Chinese communists exploited the proceedings for propaganda purposes. The Japanese followed the Tokyo proceedings in detail and used domestic media as a means of coming to terms with the record of their nation's conduct.

The Soviet Union Plays the Media Card

The Western democracies and the Soviet Union were allies in the Second World War, and at the wartime conferences at Yalta and Potsdam, both government and private media described participants as cooperative in spirit, heralding the start of a new era of peace. But immediately after the war, severe tensions developed. The USSR detonated its first atomic bomb in 1949, and aid from the USSR helped Mao and the Chinese communists drive the Nationalists out of China in the same year. Stalin began installing his agents and puppets in the states of eastern Europe which the Soviet army had conquered in the later years of the war, where Churchill, Roosevelt, and Truman had agreed to give him a relatively free hand. In 1948 Stalin engineered a coup in Czechoslovakia, the only Eastern Bloc state that still had a democratic structure; a civil war broke out in Greece between communists and groups aligned with the West, with the Western-allied forces prevailing only after great struggle; and liberal constitutional politicians in Italy won a hard-fought election campaign against a communist-socialist coalition. Moreover, in 1948 Stalin attempted to take over the Western-controlled sectors of Berlin by instituting a blockade of the city. The Allied powers surprised him by undertaking the Berlin airlift. News reports of Allied constancy and the bravery of West Berliners resulted in a major propaganda setback for the Soviet Union.

The Soviets established an elaborate postwar media strategy that built on propaganda structures already in place. It was coordinated by Agitprop (the Administration of Agitation and Propaganda of the Communist Party Central Committee) and also, from 1947 on, by Cominform, which had replaced the Comintern. Media in the Soviet Union were closely controlled by the government, which granted all licenses, provided all funds, trained journalists, controlled access to officials, and exercised censorship. The Politburo of the Central Committee of the Communist Party, which was the ruling body of the Soviet Union, was in direct control of the chief censorship body, Glavit. The Politburo appointed the head of the state news agency, the head of the national radio agency Gostelradio, and the editors of *Izvestia* and the Tass news agency. Television, which played only a minor role, began in Russia in 1949 and slowly expanded, although it did not reach most of the USSR until the 1970s.

Within its borders the Soviet Union had the propaganda advantages of an ability to restrict information from abroad and monopoly control of the media. This tight control also made it very difficult for the United States and other Western nations to survey public attitudes in the Soviet Union in order to judge the effects of information they sought to send in. Abroad, the Soviet propaganda strategy included the use of many front organizations. Toward this end, the World Peace Council was established in 1949. The Soviet Ministry of Culture made extensive use of cultural exchanges, such as those begun in France in 1957, and others with the United States and Britain.

The USSR undertook major efforts to win over opinion in the "Third World" or "developing" nations that were experiencing decolonization. The Soviets generated extensive propaganda to exploit French misconduct in the war in Algeria (1954–1962), the expulsion of the British from Egypt in the Suez Crisis (1956), and the French defeat in and withdrawal from Vietnam after the battle of Dien Bien Phu (1954).

The United States Responds

In a speech delivered in 1946 at Westminster College in Fulton, Missouri, alluding to an "iron curtain" that had appeared between communist nations and the West, Churchill signaled the start of the "cold war." He did not use the latter term in his speech, but it quickly gained currency as the most apt capsule description of the world situation. In his journalism George Orwell had spoken of a "cold war" as early as 1945. Walter Lippmann used the term in his influential newspaper columns and published a book in 1947 titled *The Cold War*. Ironically, Churchill's Conservative government had been voted out of office in 1945. He was in America on a speaking tour to earn money. President Harry S. Truman, who had assumed office in 1945 after Roosevelt's death, picked Fulton as the location for a Churchill speech as a favor to one of his party cronies, an alumnus of the college. A poll soon after the speech indicated that the public favored Churchill's view by a small margin. But an opinion survey taken a month later indicated 85 percent approval.

Some part of the difference must be credited to word of mouth and delayed reaction. But the U.S. government and press also played large roles in intensifying the public's attitudes toward the USSR. Truman made widely reported inflammatory speeches, and Undersecretary of State Dean Acheson fanned the flames whenever he met with journalists. Gradually the influential newspapers fell into line. The result was reorientation, polarization, and demonization. Truman's oratory paved the way for issuance, in 1948, of the Truman Doctrine, a policy he had been developing in his thinking and in draft form for several years previously. It characterized the world as divided into two camps, communist and noncommunist, and warned that America reserved the right to intervene in the affairs of other nations if they appeared to be in danger of succumbing to anti-Western autocracy.[7]

The democracies soon developed official structures to mobilize makers of opinion and sentiment. The British built on experience that went back to the founding of the British Council in 1934, supporting libraries, sponsoring speakers and artists, and promoting the teaching of English around the world. American efforts, already vigorous in the private sector, were greatly stimulated by passage of the Smith-Mundt Act in 1948. It authorized the pursuit of governmental activities for promoting understanding of America abroad, and protected this activity against political criticism at home by prohibiting the use within the United States of any offices or materials developed for overseas information purposes. During the Truman era, many analysts called for a more assertive use of media in cold war foreign policy. For example, the prominent *New York Times* reporter Wallace Carroll authored the influential book *Persuade or Perish* (1948), and in the mass-circulation *Saturday Evening Post*, the influential writer Milton Lehman published "We Must Sell America Abroad" (November 1947). Representative of a large body of opinion within official circles, the distinguished diplomat George Kennan warned that the State Department had to realize that propaganda had become a major tool of international relations and ought to be given high priority in all agency planning.

Truman pursued the propaganda agenda on many fronts. One initiative involved exploitation of the publicity potential of the Marshall Plan, the ambitious program of American economic aid for European postwar recovery. First announced by Secretary of State George Marshall in 1947, the plan had an important informational component. Availability of the aid had to be made known, and its distribution involved instructing many people in many languages with regard to procedures and regulations. The need for an additional publicity dimension became apparent as the Soviet Union launched propaganda attacks against Marshall aid, portraying it as economic imperialism cloaked in charity. In 1949, in response, Congress and the president approved legislation expanding the publicity mandate of the plan, which now used information not only to facilitate reconstruction but also to praise American values and the free enterprise system. Host European countries assisted by providing local facilities and funding.

On another front, Truman made known his intention to continue the work of the Voice of America (VOA), the official U.S. overseas broadcasting service, which had been established in 1942. He also supported creation in 1949 of Radio Free Europe (RFE), an ostensibly private organization established by prominent internationalists to mobilize refugees eager to make anticommunist broadcasts into eastern Europe. RFE began operations in 1950, and in 1951 it merged with Radio Liberty (RL), a separate organization originally established by Russian refugees to focus on propaganda directed at the Soviet Union. Most of the funding for RFE/RL came secretly from the newly established American espionage organization, the Central Intelligence Agency, which had begun operations in 1947 to build on the work of the wartime Office of Strategic Services. The CIA also began its own clandestine propaganda operations, which were to grow considerably over time. In 1950 propaganda received additional endorsement as a tool of foreign policy when the National Security Council issued NSC 68, a complex policy document that sought to orchestrate all aspects of federal activity in the fight against world communism. Truman and his advisers made sure that NSC 68 identified the strategic use of information as one of the functions marked for continuous attention.

In 1950 Truman inaugurated a "Campaign of Truth," intended to battle communist propaganda. Significantly, he announced it that year at a meeting of the American Society of Newspaper Editors, declaring: "We must make ourselves heard around the world in a great campaign of truth. This task is not separate and distinct from other elements of our foreign policy. It is a necessary part of all we are doing . . . as important as armed strength or economic aid." In 1951 Truman created a Psychological Strategy Board at the National Security Council.[8]

The assertiveness evident in all these actions involved a considerable irony. By the 1950s the United States was in the habit of viewing itself as a "can-do" nation, flush from victory and able to manage all its problems. Popular culture reflected the triumphal attitude, for example, in the multi-episode television documentary *Victory at Sea*, which first aired in 1952–53 and was rerun many times thereafter, and in the Broadway musicals of Rodgers and Hammerstein, which evoked myths of American pastoral innocence and explored Western encounters with other cultures. But the United States was in fact still naïve on the world scene and suddenly faced puzzles it could not solve. It decided that others were to blame, not Americans themselves, which would have been a frightening admission. Reflecting the popular mood, the U.S. Congress decided to hunt for hidden enemies. The Senate had an Internal Security Committee, and the House of Representatives had its Un-American Activities Committee (HUAC), originally founded in 1938 to scour the nation for Nazi agents. Both these bodies conducted hearings after the Second World War, and when the proceedings began to be televised, from 1948 on, they caused a "Red Scare" even greater than the one that had occurred in the 1920s. This "Great Fear," as it later came to be called, was intensified by the paranoid, vitriolic Senator Joseph McCarthy, the Wisconsin Republican who in 1950 announced to the nation that he would undertake his own personal campaign against the spread of communism.

In one of his several investigations, in 1953 McCarthy turned his attention to the Voice of America and the State Department's overseas library program. He was convinced that the nation's foreign propaganda operations were insufficiently zealous, a result, he believed, of infiltration by Americans who sympathized with communism, as well as foreign-born members of U.S. staffs who were collaborating with the enemy behind the scenes. McCarthy pursued some aspects of his investigation secretly, for example, in interviews of potential malefactors by his staff in hotel rooms in several American cities, and in closed executive session of his Senate committee. But he also held extensive hearings which were broadcast on national network television and created a sensation. A typical witness was the novelist Howard Fast, who had attracted McCarthy's attention because his writings, sympathetic to communism, could be found in overseas U.S. libraries. At the first hearing, held in Washington, D.C., Fast angrily defended himself against McCarthy's grilling but was soon cut off by the senator, who said he would not permit his committee "to become a transmission belt for the communist party."[9] At the second hearing, in New York City, McCarthy heavy-handedly tried to win the support of New York Jews by railing against the VOA's attempted abolition of its Hebrew broadcasting desk. At a third hearing, back in Washington, D.C., McCarthy conducted an erratic, unfocused cross-examination of Reed Harris, the acting administrator of the Voice of America, accusing him of mismanaging the agency and condemning a book about football that Harris had written in 1932, which McCarthy characterized as sympathetic to communism.

A few journalists courageously fought back. Throughout the McCarthy period the veteran reporter I. F. Stone produced eloquent print journalism defending privacy and individual freedom. And there were criticisms in more specific instances. For example, in response to the VOA hearings of 1953, the *New York Times* condemned "the television carnival produced, staged, and directed by Senator McCarthy." The *Washington Post* noted the unfair practice of placing a citizen in legal jeopardy as a "hapless witness summoned to judgment before television cameras." And the *New York Post* praised the "dignified and valorous performance" of Reed Harris. Moreover, television itself made some attempts to fight back. In 1953 the popular CBS television program *You Are There* used its device of on-the-scene broadcasts of historical events for a mock coverage of the Salem witch trials of 1692, loosely based on Arthur Miller's hit play *The Crucible*, which had opened on Broadway just a month before McCarthy's VOA hearings. CBS was fully aware of the historical parallel it was implying, as evidenced by Walter Cronkite's portentous signoff, which spoke of the "deep shame" and "angry resistance" eventually provoked by the witch trials.[10]

But media complicity in the panic was widespread, exemplified by the treatment accorded experts on China. By the time of McCarthy's fall in 1954, twenty U.S. Foreign Service experts on China had retired, been forced to resign, or been reassigned to work involving other countries. The press had reported extensively on all these transitions. During these same years the American press also published many editorials strongly criticizing McCarthy's conduct. But American publishers did much less to examine the degree to which they had skewed the content of their coverage of China to avoid provoking McCarthy further. For example, between 1945 and 1950 respected authorities on China based at the Institute of Pacific Relations, an object of McCarthy's wrath, were the authors of twenty-two of the thirty books on China reviewed in the *New York Times*, and in the same period were the authors of thirty of the thirty-five books on China reviewed in the *New York Herald Tribune*. But from 1952 to 1955, the period overlapping the McCarthy era, not one of these authors was invited to review a book in either paper—this at a time when these were the two most prestigious forums for book reviews in the nation. Commenting on such contradictions, the respected journalist James Aronson wrote that hypocrisy was "commonplace in an industry where the least vicious and most respected publications are perhaps the most efficient adjuncts of established power because they disarm and mislead their readership with greater sophistication."[11]

The most effective media counterattack against McCarthy came from Edward R. Murrow. After his distinguished service in Europe during the Second World War, he had returned to CBS in the United States. By the early 1950s, as a result of his programs on radio and television, he was the most distinguished news broadcaster in the nation. Murrow and his producer Fred Friendly were deeply troubled by the spread of McCarthyism and increasingly looked for opportunities to counter it. In 1953, for example, they used Murrow's television program *See It Now* to condemn unfounded accusations of disloyalty against an officer in the U.S. Air Force Reserve, who had served with distinction during the Second World War and whose only sin appeared to be his central European name, Milo Radovich. Murrow's broadcast prompted the secretary of the air force to restore the officer's security clearance. Later in 1953 *See It Now* devoted its full thirty minutes to a recapitulation of the service of General George Marshall, who had just received the Nobel Peace Prize. McCarthy had been accusing Marshall ever since 1951 of taking part in a vast conspiracy to undermine the United States. Murrow used the occasion of the Nobel award to condemn McCarthy indirectly. The *See It Now* broadcast even included an on-camera comment from President Truman, who opined, with clear, even if not specific, reference to McCarthy, that anyone who accused the great wartime leader of conspiracy "isn't fit to shine General Marshall's shoes."[12]

By early 1954, criticism of McCarthy by the press and Congress was sufficiently strong for Murrow and Friendly to believe that the moment was right for a more direct assault, and they began putting together material for the soon-to-be-legendary broadcast of *See It Now* that aired on March 9 of that year. The program was mostly a review of strategically edited film clips showing McCarthy as he went about the business of cruelly accusing witnesses and mobilizing half-truths. The close-ups of McCarthy's facial expressions were especially damning. As the half-hour neared its end, the cumulative impact had become astonishingly powerful. Murrow reinforced it by looking straight into the camera and delivering a measured peroration, in almost Shakespearean cadences, that deftly underlined the harm that the senator was inflicting on the republic. This and later Murrow broadcasts which were almost as powerful went a long way toward neutralizing McCarthy. The senator helped the process along when he took on the U.S. Army in televised hearings in April and June 1954 that turned millions of citizens against him and prompted an on-air condemnation from the army's legal counsel, Joseph N. Welch, that seemed to provide the final blow necessary to bring down a demagogue whose successes had been dependent on the mass media.[13]

In 1954, after McCarthy had been censured by the Senate, James O. Eastland carried on his predecessor's approach as head of the Senate Internal Security Subcommittee and the Senate Judiciary Committee. The Mississippi Democrat called prominent journalists to testify and utilized the same devices of insinuation and intimidation. Neither the television and radio networks nor prominent newspapers did much to defend their representatives. The major actor to fill the breach was the American Civil Liberties Union. The ACLU was a long-established presence in American civic life. It now began to go beyond its emphasis on the courts by developing an extensive structure of media relations.[14]

China Enlarges Its Role

The establishment of the People's Republic of China in 1949 meant that the West now had to fight communist propaganda that originated not only from

Moscow but also from Peking. Chiang Kai-shek and his Nationalist government retreated to the island of Taiwan (Formosa as it was then called in the
West). The threats and counterthreats exchanged by the communists and
Nationalists became the subject of frequent news stories in the Western media, as did the overblown oratory regarding Asian communism among Western political figures. The communist leader Mao Tse-tung was in any case
a brilliant propagandist. Although he utilized brutal repression, censorship,
and strategic lies to make people more receptive to his ideas, he also knew
how to employ persuasion to obtain voluntary support. The propaganda
that the Nationalists and Western nations directed against the communists
tended to emphasize materialistic values, which was perhaps unavoidable for
capitalism. This propaganda spoke of justice and freedom from tyranny, but
even more so of the attractions of a higher standard of living that would come
quickly once communism was defeated. Such a message did not immediately
convince Asians. They were the heirs to many centuries of suffering and deprivation and held to worldviews that were skeptical of claims that history
would change its path quickly. Mao did not promise easy solutions. Instead
he offered meaning and a sense of purpose, a message that present-day suffering would be *for* something, namely, the gradual realization of a better
society, free from Western domination and corruption.[15]

The outbreak of war between North and South Korea provided a focal
point for Western fears of the Chinese communists.[16] That the war took
place while Senator McCarthy was at the height of his activity further increased tension. Fighting broke out in Korea on June 25, 1950. Immediately
there was debate as to who had started the conflict. In any case, within a
few days the United States had pressured the United Nations into approv-
ing a "police action," moved the Seventh Fleet into the Taiwan Straits, increased its military activity in the Philippines, and stepped up cooperation
with the French in their pursuit of colonial war in Indochina. Some evidence suggests that South Korea instilled panic into the United States after
the crushing election defeat of President Syngman Rhee in May 1950.
The coalition that defeated Rhee was in favor of the reunification of Korea, which had been partitioned into communist and pro-Western sectors
of influence as part of the World War II surrender agreements. Rhee may
have ordered South Korean troops to take provocative actions against
North Korea at the Thirty-eighth Parallel, the line dividing North from
South Korea.

To emphasize U.S. resolve, John Foster Dulles, who was a special assistant to President Truman at the time, flew to Korea and, wearing business
dress and a homburg hat, posed in the trenches for what would soon become

a famous photograph. Key interest groups in the United States very much welcomed the possibility of war, which would gear up the arms industry and perhaps help to ward off an economic depression that many saw as not too far away. The U.S. government began circulating propaganda stating that the Soviet Union had masterminded an attack on South Korea. A major actor in the propaganda activity was Edward W. Barrett, assistant secretary of state in charge of press relations. (It was a sign of the times that he later left the State Department to found his own public relations firm, which was purchased in 1954 by the established firm of Hill & Knowlton.) Later, when UN troops crossed into China, prompting it to enter the war, the United States claimed that China had been a significant partner in instigating the conflict. Throughout the war the Office of Public Information of the South Korean government assisted with news releases, radio broadcasts, and other activities.

The communists countered with propaganda of their own. Using the communist-dominated World Peace Council (WPC) and its affiliates, they systematically circulated rumors that the United States was engaging in biological warfare. In 1952 the People's Republic of China sent a telegram to the head of the World Peace Council, after which a member of the French Communist Party organized a worldwide protest campaign. That same year an Austrian affiliate of the WPC circulated a pamphlet purporting to offer evidence of such charges. These accusations were recirculated in youth-oriented newspapers published by communists in several countries, including the United States.[17]

The outbreak of the Korean War made it easier for the American press to assist in Red-hunting. When the FBI announced roundups of suspicious persons, *New York Daily News* columnist Ed Sullivan—also at that time the host of a widely viewed television variety program—expressed approval for the jailing of "dangerous jerks," and the columnist Westbrook Pegler called for execution of all communists. This pattern continued to be the dominant one for the duration of the war. There were nevertheless journalistic voices of dissent. Perhaps the most influential was I. F. Stone. Though a seasoned reporter, he at first accepted the U.S. government's portrayal of the conflict. But then, on overseas assignments in August 1950 and later, he noticed the contrast between American press coverage of Korea and accounts in papers in London and Paris. Stone expressed his skepticism in articles published in several European venues but had difficulty attracting notice, even in London, where several editors told him they did not want to alienate the U.S. government, in spite of the fact that Stone's evidence was taken from public sources like United Nations and U.S. government documents. Stone's efforts to market the book manuscript he had prepared on U.S. government portrayals of the war met refusal from twenty-eight American publishers. Not until the fall of 1951 did he succeed in getting his evidence released in the United States—by an independent socialist publisher. But his views had little influence because the mainstream press generally ignored him. American journalism gave itself over almost entirely to articles and books claiming the existence of a worldwide communist conspiracy of which Korea was just one part. An example of the extremes to which the American press went was a photograph published on October 28, 1950, in the *Los Angeles Mirror.* It showed three smiling Asian soldiers exhibiting machine guns. The caption read, "THEY MAY BE FIGHTING IN KOREA TODAY. Grinning Chinese Communists display late model heavy machine guns of Russian design. Many reports of Chinese intervention in Korea battle are pouring in." The *Mirror* failed to mention that the photograph dated from 1945 and showed Chinese soldiers who were fighting the Japanese, from whom they had captured the machine guns. The photo had originally appeared in a 1945 book, *Report from Red China*, with a caption describing the three soldiers as "heroes." On the same page in the *Mirror* where the photo was reproduced were stories with headlines such as "China Reds Aid Commies; Stem Big Advance" and "Christ Lives on 'Mid Red Terror."

When peace talks began in an attempt to end the Korean War, censorship of the press was much in evidence. American and other correspondents were not permitted to talk with UN negotiators but had to be content with briefings by U.S. Army press liaison officers several hours after the negotiating sessions ended. Access to documents related to the negotiations was strictly limited. Some American reporters found a way around the censorship by cooperating with two British journalists, Alan Winnington and Wilfred G. Burchett (who had played a role, after the defeat of Japan, in reporting on the effects of the atomic bomb). Both men had been assigned by London papers to the North Korean–Chinese command.[18]

Mind Control Seems Possible

In the years after the Second World War people continued to ask themselves where the increase in the use of mass persuasion would end. Propaganda was by now a recognized and powerful element of warfare. Might it become the most powerful weapon of all? Could wars be fought exclusively by nonphysical means, at low cost and with no harm except, ironically, to the mind and spirit? Could mass persuasion become so potent a tool of war that, by a kind of hypnosis or thought manipulation, one side could not simply defeat but completely control the other?

George Orwell brought these questions to the public's attention in two widely read novels published shortly after the Second World War. *Animal Farm* (1945) was an allegorical fable that raised the possibility of Stalinism's being replicated outside the Soviet Union. At the head of the society described in the novel is a tyrannical pig named Napoleon. He is aided by his propaganda minister, Squealer, who helps to keep the other animals in line through classic techniques of persuasion like rumor-mongering, the re-writing of history, and executing dissidents. In *Nineteen Eighty-four* (1949), Orwell issued a more general warning, portraying a dictatorship that ruled through its propaganda-based Ministry of Truth and relied on hate-fuelled war against other societies as its major instrument of control. So mesmerizing were Orwell's novels that terms drawn from them like "newspeak," "thought police," "doublethink," and "Big Brother" quickly entered daily conversation throughout the world.

Other writers explored similar themes. Robert Heinlein's best-selling science fiction novel *The Puppet Masters* (1951) tells the story of aliens who come to Earth and, one mind at a time, very nearly take control of the population. Journalists also produced best-selling works, like *The Hidden Persuaders* by Vance Packard (1957), which charted the inner workings of the advertising industry. Social scientists pursued the subjects of mind control and techniques of persuasion in thousands of reports, conferences, and research projects funded by foundations and government agencies. Many observers sketched scenarios for the use of mind control to defeat enemies who were oblivious to thoughts of peace.[19] The CIA and the U.S. military conducted secret experiments that involved using mind-altering chemicals on soldiers and prisoners without telling the subjects what was being done to them.

Both symptomatic of the strong interest in mind control and a contributor to that interest was the scare that arose in the United States and parts of Europe regarding an Asian phenomenon that came to be called "brainwashing." During the Korean War, reports began to appear in Western news media that the Chinese communists were experiencing great success in extracting fabricated confessions from American prisoners, who stated, sometimes on film or into tape recorders, often with observers present, that they despised their country and the capitalist system and believed that the North Koreans and the Chinese were justified in defending themselves against military aggression. The techniques used to obtain the confessions resembled the party indoctrination sessions that Mao had developed over the decades. Moreover, they involved some measures that were being used covertly in the West, such as sleep deprivation, along with techniques that were familiar to readers of any private eye novel. But these facts were not sufficiently appreciated by Western observers. In 1951 a book by the journalist Edward Hunter, *Brainwashing in Red China*, gave wide currency to a misleading word. "Brainwashing" was seen to be a combination of sinister, mysterious oriental trickery and sophisticated adaptation by Asians of the techniques of mind control supposedly created in refined form by Western social scientists and medical professionals. The term entered into Western popular culture and took its place in the constellation of anxieties already occupied by McCarthyism, fear of communist domination of the world, and the terrified contemplation of possible nuclear annihilation. Reinforcing all of this was an older fear, dating from the nineteenth-century era of imperialism, regarding the takeover of Western civilization by dark-skinned races, in this case the "Yellow Peril."[20]

A symbol of this cluster of fears was *The Manchurian Candidate* by Richard Condon, a work of imaginative fiction in the thriller genre. It appeared in book form in 1959 and became a best-seller. In 1962 it was made into a film directed by John Frankenheimer. The densely plotted, complex story concerns a group of American soldiers captured during the Korean War. They are "brainwashed" and conditioned to act out scenarios favorable to the communists after covert reintegration with their units and their return to America. Their obedience to those who brainwashed them is subconscious. One of the brainwashed soldiers is directed, by means of mental triggers, to assassinate the presidential candidate of one of the political parties at the nominating convention so that the party's vice presidential candidate, who is secretly in league with the communists, will take his place. The scenes in the film that depict the initial brainwashing and later flashbacks are a strange mix of torture, military courts-martial, social science jargon, and pidgin English worthy of Edgar Wallace and Dr. Fu Manchu. The actors who play the brainwashers are recognizable to moviegoers as the same Asian Americans who played the parts of the evil "Japs" in Second World War movies. The film is nevertheless well crafted, thought-provoking, and frightening. *The Manchurian Candidate* was premiered nationally in theaters in 1962, coincidentally during the Cuban missile crisis. An urban legend holds that the film was withdrawn from theaters in 1963 when President Kennedy was assassinated, because the producers worried that the film would cause mass unease. A more probable explanation is that the film was no longer generating large ticket sales by 1963. It was shown on late-night network television in 1965 and 1974 but did not reappear in theaters for some time thereafter because of legal disputes about licensing rights. The film was revived in theaters in 1988 and a remake appeared in 2004.

Excess Becomes the Norm

In 1953, concurrent with the waning of McCarthyism and the end of the Korean War, Dwight Eisenhower took office as president. Eisenhower had seen the importance of psychological operations in the Second World War and was experienced in their use. He placed as much emphasis as Truman did on employing the media in foreign policy. Eisenhower even added a personal adviser on psychological warfare to the White House staff. But he took information policy in directions different from Truman's and, though conscientious, soon found that his efforts were leading to great harm.

Under Eisenhower, public diplomacy continued but was reorganized. In his first year in office Eisenhower moved information functions that were at the State Department to a new, independent agency of the executive branch, the United States Information Agency (USIA), which was known overseas as the United States Information Service (USIS). This was a major show of support for the active use of mass communication in foreign relations. But a significant ambivalence was also evident: Eisenhower did not give the USIA permanent membership on the National Security Council, though he frequently invited a representative of the agency to participate informally in NSC meetings. But he tended to treat mass communication as a tool of foreign policy, not as an essential component on a par with traditional geostrategic elements like military planning, high-level diplomacy, and international economics. This ambiguity about the exact role of mass persuasion in U.S. foreign policy would persist throughout the cold war.

The radio component of the USIA was the Voice of America. It was already a going concern and was now folded into the USIA structure. The new arrangement intensified the possibility that VOA would veer away from its emphasis on objective news reporting, modeled on the BBC, and succumb to the more partisan approach that the USIA sometimes had to adopt in response to pressure from strident anticommunists in Congress and CIA offices who wanted to use the USIA for cover. VOA fended off many such pressures by diverting them to the explicitly partisan Radio Free Europe. Soon it was regarded as the "crown jewel" of the USIA. By 1950 VOA was broadcasting five hundred hours a week, offering thirty programs in twenty-five languages. Early efforts concentrated on the Soviet Union and eastern Europe. A VOA Farsi service was begun in 1949. Culturally sensitive in its use of Iranian literature, music, and extracts from the Koran, it was nevertheless co-opted when the broadcasts were used to set the stage for the eventual rule of Iran by the shah, who was seen as more sympathetic to the West than the incumbent leader Mohammed Mossadegh. Not until the 1970s were there regular VOA broadcasts to China and Southeast Asia. All VOA efforts of the 1950s were part of the so called Crusade for Freedom advocated by Eisenhower's secretary of state, John Foster Dulles.[21]

Eisenhower used government funding for public diplomacy in conjunction with private-sector funds and organizations. For example, for a major international trade fair held in Moscow, he mobilized American companies to have their PR offices convey well-crafted messages and display American products alluringly. Soviet citizens were astounded by this evidence of America's industrial capacity and the multitude of products available to average people in the West, in contrast to their own standard of living. Communist Party leaders worried that increased exposure to Western products would undermine the Soviet system. They were also worried by Hollywood's projection of American values, which lent great allure to Western ways.[22]

Immediately after Stalin's death in 1953, the Soviet Union began a new phase in the use of media, greatly aiding Eisenhower's information policy. Even Russians who had hated Stalin felt anxious and adrift without their father figure. Stalin's successors knew that major psychological changes would be needed. Nikita Khrushchev began a "de-Stalinization" campaign designed to do away with the "cult of personality" that had been built around his predecessor. The revised use of media included extensive indoctrination of schoolchildren. Khrushchev and his colleagues also knew that some degree of openness toward the West would be advisable. They were aware, as Western propaganda increasingly penetrated the USSR during the 1950s, that Soviet home propaganda was becoming less effective. The leadership therefore allowed a degree of openness to the West but countered it with internal commentary.

After Stalin's death the Soviets became less confrontational in foreign relations. Rhetoric directed at the Western press was sometimes conciliatory. The Soviets exploited not only the press but also other venues, trumpeting their successes at the Olympic Games, in space, and in medical research. Khrushchev's visit to the West in 1959, extensively reported in the media, exemplified his efforts to indicate a greater desire for decreased tensions between communist and noncommunist countries.

Eisenhower never trusted the Soviets, but in response to their gestures of compromise he did seek to lessen suspicion through careful reciprocity. An example was his invitation to the USSR to join in an "Atoms for Peace" initiative. He proposed that the two countries stockpile an equal amount of enriched uranium that would be available to all the countries of the world for peaceful development of atomic energy, as long as those countries joined with the United States and the Soviet Union in halting further production. The proposal was disingenuous, since the United States had the largest stockpile and would have supplies left over when no other nation would. But it garnered some goodwill.

Relations between the United States and the USSR underwent setbacks in 1956 when, with behind-the-scenes encouragement from the West, anti-Soviet groups staged a revolution in Hungary. They were brutally crushed by Soviet military forces. This was a propaganda disaster for the USSR, but it was also a propaganda setback for the West and for President Eisenhower in particular, as word emerged concerning his last-minute change in strategy. Eisenhower had made secret promises of support to the Hungarian revolutionaries, but when they rose up, he failed to send assistance. In that same year, however, America's reputation was improved somewhat by its actions in Egypt when that country's revolutionary leader, General Gamal Abdel Nasser, took over the Suez Canal and sought to expel the British. When Great Britain and France threatened to go to war, Eisenhower intervened, personally scolding Prime Minister Anthony Eden and threatening to cut off American financial assistance to Britain. Egyptian independence, achieved shortly thereafter, was seen as a propaganda victory for the United States because it undermined Soviet claims that America was unfailingly imperialist. Another development in 1956, the Sino-Soviet split, proved to be a more difficult challenge for the West. After Stalin's death, Mao defended Stalin against Khrushchev's attacks and concluded that Khrushchev was diluting the power and unity of the worldwide communist movement. The Soviet Union and the People's Republic initiated a propaganda war against each other, and Western powers faced the dilemma of antagonizing one communist state whenever they sought to lessen tensions with the other.

In spite of his best efforts, Eisenhower's management of mass persuasion gradually intensified the difficulties that had developed under Truman. America's official use of mass persuasion increasingly lacked a sense of proportion, mirroring and exacerbating the arms race that was going on in the military realm. Symptomatic of the growing lack of moderation was the mingling of information policy and espionage. In the United States, the Central Intelligence Agency worked behind the scenes with the USIA. Despite loud disclaimers, libraries and other USIA units overseas became locales for American espionage activity. The CIA provided secret information that became a factor in the shaping of USIA strategies, for example, in deciding which speakers to send overseas and how to determine the content of government-sponsored publications, radio broadcasts, and exchange programs.

Propaganda was a major element in the mixture of activities—clandestine information gathering, economic subsidy of front organizations, and the organized use of violence—that increasingly defined the agency's work, first under Truman and then to an even greater degree under Eisenhower. For instance, the CIA financed attacks along the coast of communist China in the early 1950s and engineered the overthrow of democratically elected leaders in Central America, Indonesia, and Iran during the same period. Each operation involved the secret financing of political groups, airdrops of propaganda leaflets, the planting of stories in the local press, and inflammatory radio broadcasts from specially created stations posing as spontaneous supporters of overthrowing the ruling regime.

In the United States, through the National Student Association, the CIA recruited American college undergraduates to help spread anticommunist thought abroad. Eminent figures in higher education, like Gordon Gray, the president of the University of North Carolina, served as consultants to the CIA. In 1959 Hank Ketchum, creator of the internationally popular comic strip "Dennis the Menace," decided to take a trip to Moscow as part of the "People to People" campaign then being sponsored by President Eisenhower as an initiative to promote international goodwill. In advance of his visit, Ketchum was approached by the CIA, briefed on techniques for spying, and asked to draw pictures of Soviet military installations while he was in flight. Ketchum willingly assisted. The CIA channeled funds for international projects through trusted philanthropic organizations like the Ford Foundation and, as necessary, helped establish additional philanthropies, such as the Asia Foundation. Radio Free Europe secretly received major funding from the CIA. Unknown to most of its staff, including George Orwell, the respected intellectual journal *Encounter* accepted cash payments from the CIA. The agency had secret contacts at hundreds of newspapers, magazines, and wire services around the world; owned printing companies in India, Italy, and Japan; and held a controlling interest in the newspaper *Daily American* in Rome. Even in countries publicly acknowledged as aligned with the United States, the CIA pursued secret political action. For example, in Japan in the early and mid-1950s the agency invested in selected motion picture and television projects designed to increase support for the center-right Liberal Democratic Party. All these operations violated America's frequent public avowals of support for national self-determination and free, open elections. In its use of information as a tool of international power politics, the United States operated on two

policy tracks: public proclamation of liberal constitutional values and secret use of illegal, nondemocratic methods that were supposedly needed to
protect the cause of freedom in a brutal world.[23]

The Soviets for their part also mingled information policy with espionage. The most spectacular examples involved forgeries. The communists
had employed this tactic during the Bolshevik Revolution to lure émigré
counterrevolutionaries back to Russia for execution. Forgery became widespread during the cold war. In the early 1960s the Soviets circulated a false
U.S. State Department document ordering American diplomats to sabotage negotiations for a proposed summit conference on disarmament. In
1960, after an American U-2 spy plane was shot down in Russia, the Soviets
sought to add to the embarrassment by circulating a forged American communiqué outlining plans to resume U-2 flights over Russia from secret
bases in Japan. Another use of forgeries involved fabricated exchanges of
letters among air force officers presenting evidence that pilots of the American planes equipped with atomic bombs were psychotic. There were numerous bogus letters supposedly implicating the United States in plots to
overthrow heads of state such as Sihanouk in Indonesia and Nasser in Egypt.
Though outrageous, all the forgeries played upon an international awareness that at any given time, both sides in the cold war were discussing hy-
pothetical coups and in some cases carrying them out.[24]

One factor undermining diplomatic civility in Western nations was the
feedback effect of battling the bio-behavioral approaches to opinion manipulation that were still dominant in the Soviet Union and were being
adopted by the Chinese communists. Americans in particular felt a need to
counter these influences with more of the same. As a technologically oriented nation with a tradition of isolationism and not much capability in the
foreign languages that are the gateways to other cultures, the United States
found the repetitious, mechanical aspects of bio-behavioral communication tempting. This was particularly so because of three forces in American
society that, by the 1950s, were impinging on foreign relations: political
campaigning, advertising, and public relations. All three relied on repetition, simple slogans, and the manipulation of subconscious drives and fears.
All three had been important before the Second World War. But their undeniable successes in some realms, and the effects of shrewd, extensive, and
continuous marketing of their services, made them major presences by the
time of the cold war. Thus, for example, in 1950, working for the United
Fruit Company, the public relations consultant Edward Bernays played a
significant role in the overthrow of the elected government of Guatemala
by the Central Intelligence Agency.

The Cold War Mobilizes Culture

One of the defining features of the cold war was its pervasive influence over all aspects of cultural life. Such a development was predictable, to a certain extent, because thoughts of total annihilation were not easy for anyone to repress and had a way of producing a common ethos among all people. But the pattern was nevertheless astonishing in its depth and extent. This was evident, for example, in popular entertainment, which reflected and reinforced cold war attitudes to a remarkable degree. The American movie industry, for instance, produced overtly anticommunist films like *The Woman on Pier 13* (1949; originally titled *I Married a Communist*) and *I Was a Communist for the FBI* (1951). The dilemma of dissenting from prevailing conformity was reflected in *High Noon* (1952) and *On the Waterfront* (1954). Fears of being overcome by foreign invaders was evident in science-fiction films like *The Thing from Another World* (1951), about a threatening visitor from the Red Planet, Mars; *Them!* (1954), about an invasion of Los Angeles by giant red ants; and *Invasion of the Body Snatchers* (1956). Satirical commentary on the cold war found its place in *Dr. Strangelove, or How I Learned to Stop Worrying and Love the Bomb* (1964) and the British production *The Mouse That Roared* (1959), in which a small, obscure principality decides to make war against the United States in the hope of receiving economic aid after its defeat. Spy movies offered another reflection of the cold war. A serious entry of great influence was *The Spy Who Came in from the Cold* (1965), based on the novel by John Le Carré. Eventually the films became more gaudy, glamorous, and explicitly commercial, as in the James Bond movies with Sean Connery and the Harry Palmer series featuring Michael Caine.

Television programs reflecting and exploiting the cold war included *Dangerous Assignment* with Brian Donleavy, *I Led Three Lives* with Richard Carlson, and *I Spy* with Robert Culp and Bill Cosby. *Get Smart* with Don Adams was a popular parody of spy movies. Similar British TV programs included *The Saint* with Roger Moore, updating the 1930s novels of Leslie Charteris; *The Avengers* with Diana Rigg and Patrick MacNee; and *Secret Agent* with Patrick McGoohan. In *The Man from U.N.C.L.E.*, television evidenced a capacity for spy drama that transcended cold war stereotypes. One of the leading characters in the series was a sympathetic Russian, played convincingly by David McCallum. By generally treating the cold war as amusement, however, the television and film industries encouraged citizens to indulge in harmful fantasy. When presented with violent or morally ambiguous scenes, viewers could pretend that they were being shown the full reality of the cold war. But many such scenes, compared to their real-life referents, were sanitized, and the endings were usually pat and reassuring. These dramas did not challenge citizens to face up to and take responsibility for all the actions of their nations.

A conspicuous element of cold war media culture in the West was the role of religious themes. They were evident in all formats of communication—for example, in the anticommunist television sermons of Bishop Fulton J. Sheen, which attracted large audiences in the 1950s—but were perhaps most easily noticeable in cinema, whether in films made from original screenplays or in productions adapted from best-selling novels of the period. While many people viewed the cold war as a clash of economic and political systems, it easily lent itself to religious themes, since the world seemed to be divided into two armed camps pursuing a Manichean struggle between good and evil, with one side, communism, endorsing atheism; Armageddon itself seemed to be a real possibility,. Fears of the world coming to an end were realized in films like the science-fiction classic *The Day the Earth Stood Still* (1951), in which a humanoid visitor from another planet lands his flying saucer in Washington, D.C., and warns the peoples of the Earth to end their pursuit of war or face total self-destruction. The possibility of Armageddon was explored less fantastically in *On the Beach* (1959), in which Australian survivors of a nuclear war reckon with the fact that all forms of life will die within a few months. In it's a more direct approach to religious themes, Hollywood experienced great box office success with biblical epics like *Quo Vadis* (1951), an adaptation of the best-selling novel by Henry Sinkiewicz, and *The Ten Commandments* (1956). Both films portrayed the struggles of decent common people—early Christians in the first instance and Israelites in the second—against tyrannical empires, leaving no doubt which side would prevail over time. Communist persecution of religious figures was a theme of films such as *Satan Never Sleeps* (1962), in which a priest involved in missionary work in China attempts to protect his church from communist soldiers who seize it as a headquarters for local operations, rape a woman who has been assisting the church, and force the priest to flee across the border.

Not all film treatments of the cold war involved hysteria, as evidenced by British productions of the era, which were conspicuously more measured than American efforts. British filmmakers already had a long history of cataloguing the faults of the Soviet system, for example, in productions like *Land of Mystery* (1920), which encapsulated fears of the Bolshevik Revolution, and *Forbidden Territory* (1934), which criticized life under Stalin. British films of the cold war era also vigorously criticized communism. For example, the producer Louis de Rochemont accepted financing and technical assistance from U.S. and British intelligence agencies to make cinematic versions of Orwell's *Animal Farm* (released in 1955) and *1984* (released in 1956), both of which were prime examples of energetic anticommunism. A rather solemn portrayal of persecution was presented by the 1955 film *The Prisoner*, made in Britain with American financing. It is a not very well disguised drama about the show trial and imprisonment of the Hungarian cardinal József Mindszenty, who was arrested in 1948 for opposing Soviet repression of Christianity; the film includes scenes in which the cardinal is tortured, though psychologically rather than physically, echoing cold war fears of brainwashing. Most British films of the day were less strident than Hollywood's, frequently questioning assumptions and dissenting from the official line. This is seen, for example, in Anthony Asquith's 1954 critique of cold war paranoia *The Young Lovers*, George Parry's comedy *Friends and Neighbors* (1959), and films that protest state intrusions on privacy, like *The War Game* (1965) by Peter Watkins. Although British filmmakers experienced some official and societal pressures, they did not have to reckon with the "Great Fear" and the blacklisting of creative talents endured by Hollywood during the McCarthy period.[25]

Perhaps the most startling instances of cold war influence on culture occurred in elite circles, where one might have expected sophisticated artists to develop ways of transcending cruder forms of symbolic battle. But even the great cultural figures of the era quickly became enmeshed in the East-West struggle. At times the involvement was almost unavoidable. This was most obvious in the many cases of great artists living behind the Iron Curtain who were persecuted or intimidated. The British philosopher Isaiah Berlin provided a moving record of the effects of such pressure in 1958, when the Soviets allowed Dmitry Shostakovich to journey briefly to Oxford to receive the honorary degree of doctor of music. By that point in the great composer's life, many of his works had been condemned by the Soviet regime. During the visit, handlers from the Soviet embassy accompanied Shostakovich everywhere. Berlin described him as "terribly nervous, with a twitch playing in his face almost perpetually—I have never seen anyone so frightened and crushed in all my life. . . . [T]hroughout the visit he looked like a man who had passed most of his life in some dark forbidding place under the supervision of jailers of some sort, and whenever the slightest reference was made to contemporary events or contemporary personalities, the old painful spasm would pass over his face, and his face would assume a haunted, even persecuted expression and he would fall into a terrified silence."[26]

Artists became enmeshed in the cold war less directly as well. Whenever a Russian symphony orchestra toured Western countries or an American chamber music ensemble traveled behind the Iron Curtain, their impressive performances tended to reflect prestige on either communism or capitalism, as audiences frequently forgot that great art had its origins in traditions that were centuries in the making. The mass media and propaganda agencies encouraged such fuzzy thinking. An instance of the resulting ambiguities occurred in 1958, when at age twenty-three the American pianist Van Cliburn entered and won the International Tchaikovsky Piano Competition in Moscow. The Soviet managers of the event regarded it as a venue for advertising communist cultural superiority. Even after Cliburn received an eight-minute standing ovation from the audience and the judges decided to give him the prize, the organizers still felt obliged to ask Nikita Khrushchev for permission before granting Cliburn his deserved honor. Cosmopolitanism did triumph in the sense that Khrushchev approved the award. But soon thereafter, not only in the Soviet Union but also in the West, most media coverage dwelt on the potential for using art as a weapon of political and economic struggle.

There were also many clumsy, overtly aggressive attempts by governments to turn great art into a political pawn and nothing more. That was the case, for example, in London in 1956, when British authorities arrested the visiting Russian discus thrower Nina Ponomereva on a charge of shoplifiting. Under orders from the Soviet government, the Bolshoi Ballet threatened to cancel a planned visit unless the charges were dropped, but Prime Minister Eden nevertheless decided, after weighing the propaganda benefits, to pursue the case. How reductive some political leaders could be was evident in 1958, when Secretary of State Dulles gave his reaction to *Dr. Zhivago*, Boris Pasternak's Nobel Prize–winning novel about a writer's struggle to retain his authenticity during the Bolshevik Revolution. After being told that the book could not be published in Russia and had been smuggled out to the West, Dulles commented: "The system of international Communism insists on conformity not only in deed but in thought. Anything a little out of line they try to stamp out." This prompted the respected American literary critic Edmund Wilson to reply: "*Dr. Zhivago* is not merely a little out of line with the assumptions of the Soviet Union; it presents a radical criticism of all our supposedly democratic but more and more centralized societies."[27]

There were numerous cultural figures who enlisted in the war of symbols of their own free will. Pablo Picasso, Aaron Copland, and Jean-Paul Sartre were among the great artists living in the West who frequently expressed admiration for the communist system even though their works were censored or suppressed in the Soviet Union. Conversely, Mikhail

Baryshnikov, Rudolf Nureyev, and Mstislav Rostropovich were among the many Russian cultural figures who defected to the West out of a legitimate desire to escape the stagnation of Soviet society, even though they were well aware that most people would view their actions as simply political and not understand the higher cosmopolitan loyalties to culture that motivated them.[28]

Television Expands Its Influence

Although he projected youthfulness and was elected on a platform that promised a change from the ways of the ailing Eisenhower, John Kennedy, who became president in 1961, manifested much the same pattern of mixed success in the cold war use of media as his predecessor. The new president won great popular approval during his visit to West Berlin, which was eagerly covered by the media; and Jacqueline Kennedy was regarded approvingly in her extensively reported world tours as an almost royal first lady. But Kennedy lost face during the 1961 Bay of Pigs disaster in Cuba, when the United States bungled a badly planned effort to invade the island and start a counterrevolution, and only regained it later, at high risk, during the Cuban missile crisis of 1962. From the perspective of mass communication, the most important development of his administration was the increasing influence of television.

The concepts underlying the medium of television dated from the late nineteenth century, when inventors had first become interested in the idea of electronically transmitting images, either moving or stationary, perhaps accompanied by sound. Engineers and science-fiction writers spoke of a "telephonoscope" that would build on technologies already available for radio, the telegraph, and the telephone. At first it was assumed that images would be transferred by wires (what later came to be called closed-circuit television), but interest gradually developed in the possibility of broadcast transmission. The concept of "scanning" an image—that is, using a light-sensitive device to convert an image into electronic dots that could be sent as electrical pulses—also dated from the late nineteenth century. A cathode ray tube was used to display the reconstructed image after it was received. Creation of the first sophisticated television system is usually credited to the American inventor Philo Farnsworth, who demonstrated it to the news media in 1928, televising a motion picture film. The first widespread television broadcasting took place in the 1930s through the BBC. But television did not achieve much influence until after the Second World War, when its use expanded in western Europe and the United States. The U.S. War Production Board had halted manufacture of TV and radio equipment for nonmilitary use from April 1942 to October 1945. After the war, television became an increasing presence in both entertainment and news broadcasting. During the Korean War, newsreel films were flown to broadcast studios in the United States and Europe, to be included in nightly news programs. During the Eisenhower years, television intermittently captured the nation's political attention, for example, during coverage of Senator McCarthy's anticommunist hearings. Eisenhower discovered that television was an effective means to build public support for his domestic policies, and he sometimes included brief remarks in his broadcasts that served as signals to the communists about his foreign policy. By Eisenhower's time, television viewing was a major pastime in most Western countries, even more so after the arrival of color broadcasting, which debuted in 1967 in the United States.

The influence of television in domestic politics was confirmed during the presidential election contest of 1960, when Richard Nixon lost popularity because he seemed dour and menacing during televised debates with Kennedy, while Kennedy projected charm and crisp competence. The medium's importance for international relations increased significantly after Kennedy took office, though gradually at first, as television jockeyed with and then surpassed the print media in influence.

In the first major crisis of the new president's administration, however, the print media played the larger communications role. Evidence suggests that key individuals in the major American news organizations, including James Reston of the *New York Times* and the syndicated columnist Walter Lippmann, were aware in advance of Kennedy's secret plan to invade Cuba but did not publicize what they knew. In spite of such cooperation, Kennedy remained so afraid of the press's power that he became deeply angry when newspapers catalogued the errors leading to the debacle after CIA-organized forces were decimated at the Bay of Pigs. In one speech, in 1961, to a group from the Newspaper Publishers Association, he asked reporters to reexamine their standards in view of "our country's peril." He acknowledged that the United States was not at war in the traditional sense. Nevertheless, he said, "our way of life is under attack." It was the duty of the press to practice "the self-discipline of combat conditions" because America and its allies were "opposed around the world by a monolithic and ruthless conspiracy that relies primarily upon covert means for expanding its sphere of influence." Even more emphatically, he added that the American press should ask itself, before publishing any story, "Is it in the interests of national security?" Because it was so sweeping, this was in effect a call for the press to become an assistant to the government and to ignore its responsibilities under the First Amendment. Retorts from the press were, however, weak. Not until several years later, in 1966, was there an admission of such weakness by Clifton Daniel, who had been an editor of the *New York Times* in 1961.[29]

One of the people Kennedy initially kept in the dark about preparations for the Bay of Pigs invasion was his own USIA director, Edward R. Murrow, for fear that Murrow would resign if he knew. Murrow did not learn of the invasion plans until two weeks ahead of the operation, first through his deputy Don Wilson, who had been tipped off by his friend Tad Szulc of the *New York Times*, and then when Kennedy's chief security assistant, McGeorge Bundy, provided background in response to Murrow's concerns. Murrow felt betrayed that the USIA had been kept out of the loop. He correctly predicted that the operation would create a major propaganda disaster. Nevertheless, Murrow kept the invasion plans secret from his own staff; his VOA director, Henry Loomis, obtained his first news of the invasion while listening to his car radio on the way to work. Murrow stayed on at the USIA after the invasion but remained deeply troubled by Kennedy's treatment of official information functions as peripheral to conducting foreign policy.[30]

Television came to the fore in 1962. In October of that year, after the discovery that there were Soviet missiles based in Cuba, and following extensive consultations with his advisers, President Kennedy went on television, dramatically displayed photographs of the Soviet installations taken by U.S. spy planes, and warned both the Cubans and the Soviets to remove all the missiles or risk nuclear attack. The Cuban missile crisis solidified the importance of television as a factor in military and diplomatic affairs. Kennedy's dramatic speech, viewed by anxious audiences around the world, raised the possibility that, because of human folly, a nuclear conflagration might actually occur. The U.S. government kept secret its behind-the-scenes activity before the broadcast, which was understandable. Less understandable was the failure of the press to protest increased censorship by the State Department and other branches of the U.S. government after the crisis ended.[31] In any case, the withdrawal of Soviet missiles from Cuba was a major victory for the United States and a clear example of the power of the media to complement other tools of warfare. The Soviet capitulation came about because of a genuine threat of physical annihilation combined with the Americans' sophisticated use of media to undermine the enemy's confidence and make certain consequences clear. There were also significant aftereffects. The missile crisis hastened Khrushchev's fall from power. By this time the Kremlin's inner circle was already worried about the consequences of his having allowed the Berlin Wall to be constructed, as well as his internal management of agriculture. Members of the power structure forced him into a peaceful retirement in 1964. His successors, Alexei Kosygin and Leonid Brezhnev, turned the USSR inward, toward dealing with emergencies in the Soviet economy, and found it convenient to initiate the process of looking for ways to lessen international tensions which came to be called détente.

Ironically, additional propaganda advances—indeed, enormous sympathy—for America came in 1963, when President Kennedy was assassinated. News media all over the world interrupted their routines to disseminate the latest information related to the assassination and the funeral attended by thousands of dignitaries. The USIA garnered additional goodwill for the United States by doing some of its best work ever when it produced a feature-length documentary film about the president's funeral, *John F. Kennedy: Years of Lightning, Days of Drums*, which premiered simultaneously in 1964 in Washington, D.C., Rome, Mexico City, and Beirut, with showings worldwide thereafter. The film became the most widely viewed agency production ever. Gregory Peck narrated the English-language version and Maximilian Schell the German version. Congress had to grant special permission for the film to be shown in the United States.[32]

While always working in tandem with other media, television nevertheless increased its influence in the years after Kennedy's assassination, proving to be a major factor in the undoing of both President Lyndon Johnson and President Richard Nixon. Johnson, who succeeded to the presidency on Kennedy's death, received international praise for his support of civil rights and racial harmony, and America's struggle to attain these goals was reported by media around the world. His invasion of the Dominican Republic in 1965, when Johnson went on television to inform the world that he was sending U.S. forces to that country to prevent a communist takeover, was controversial but generally accepted. So too was his management of America's response to the events that took place in Czechoslovakia in 1968. Aided by their brilliant, eloquent political leader Alexander Dubček, the Czechs bravely undertook to liberalize their government and align it more to the West. But the hopes of their "Prague Spring" were stifled when troops from the Soviet Union and Warsaw Pact countries invaded Czechoslovakia and installed heavy-handed rule. Some 300,000 Czechs eventually fled their country, but the West could do little because it was not willing to undertake military engagement. The episode was nevertheless a propaganda victory for America and other liberal constitutional states because the Kremlin's actions so dramatically contradicted Soviet claims of benign rule.

President Johnson labored under the public's suspicion that he had fabricated the evidence that was the basis for his escalation of the Vietnam War in 1964, after U.S. ships were attacked in the Tonkin Gulf and he went on television to claim, in effect, that international disaster would occur unless Congress gave him the war powers he needed to respond. As the war dragged on, Johnson's frequent comments about winning the "hearts and minds" of the people of Southeast Asia seemed deluded.

Johnson also undermined his international reputation by failing to make effective use of the USIA publicity apparatus. After becoming president, Johnson appointed Carl Rowan to assume direction of the agency. Rowan was a respected journalist with admirable values, a veteran of print media and television. But the president's interest in the USIA was sporadic (for example, during the Dominican crisis, when Johnson requested psychological situation reports from the agency several times a day), and tensions with his director soon developed. Rowan did not like the direction the Vietnam War was taking. But instead of overtly protesting, he decided to work from within the government, thinking that he could use the USIA to alter the course of the undeclared war and hasten peace. Rowan's calculation proved to be a case of overestimating the power of information. He failed in his quiet crusade and left the agency in bitterness. Rowan's successor, Leonard Marks, also encountered difficulties. He advised Johnson that America's reputation in the world would not improve until the U.S. withdrew from Vietnam. The president's response was one of extreme anger, and he broke off relations with Marks for several months. In 1968 Johnson memorably used television as the medium for delivering his dramatic announcement that because of growing opposition to his Vietnam policy, he would not seek reelection.

Richard Nixon, who became president in 1969, had a double-edged experience with the media similar to Johnson's. He scored a propaganda victory with his opening to China in 1972, which marked a major realignment of the balance of world power. The People's Republic enlarged its cultural and economic relations with the United States and signaled that it would not automatically follow the Soviet line in foreign relations. Nixon's visit to China was covered by all the news media, with television playing the dominant role. Every detail from the president's handshake with Chou En-lai when the prime minister greeted the American president on his arrival at the Peking airport was carefully choreographed by Nixon's trusted aide H. R. Haldeman, who had been an advertising executive before coming to the White House.[33] Nixon enjoyed another public relations coup in 1973, at least temporarily, when he benefited from the reflected glow of the Nobel Peace Prize awarded to his national security adviser and secretary of state Henry Kissinger for attempting to end the war in Southeast Asia. But especially after he ordered carpet bombings in Southeast Asia—films of which were broadcast on television—while talking of peace, Nixon was seen as a symbol of American evil by much of the world. The resignation of his vice president, Spiro Agnew, in 1973 in the face of news reports of Agnew's cheating on his income tax also hurt America's prestige.

The print media became a major antagonist for Nixon in 1971, when the *New York Times* published the so-called Pentagon Papers—thousands of pages of secret documents, dating from 1967, illegally Xeroxed by the military planner Daniel Ellsberg—which seemed to confirm a longstanding intention by the Pentagon to pursue the war in Vietnam regardless of public preferences and even in the face of tremendous setbacks. Shortly thereafter the Watergate scandal, implicating Nixon himself and soon leading to his resignation, was another major setback for the president's international reputation, even while the conduct of the legislative branch of government was much admired. In 1972, in the early months of the scandal, the print media dominated the coverage as Carl Bernstein and Bob Woodward, reporters for the *Washington Post*, regularly published stories about illegal campaign activities involving Nixon political operatives who had broken into a Democratic Party office in the Watergate apartment building in Washington, D.C.

Then in 1973–74 television took center stage by broadcasting the dramatic, long-running, revelatory hearings of the Senate committee appointed to investigate the Watergate incident, and subsequent hearings in the House of Representatives regarding possible impeachment of the president. Television cameras were also on the scene in the summer of 1974 when, after choosing to resign rather than risk being impeached, Nixon gave his farewell speech on the back lawn of the White House and was transported into private life by helicopter.

Nixon's uses of the publicity machinery of the USIA were even more turbulent than President Johnson's. Nixon read very few of the reports produced by the agency, except for an occasional poll or press summary after a major speech. He acquiesced when Kissinger allowed the director of the USIA to participate only in subcommittee work of the National Security Council; Kissinger believed that the USIA was imprisoned in a cold war mindset that was not helping his efforts to bring about détente. During the Watergate scandal Nixon was not pleased to see the Voice of America offering extensive reports about the matter to audiences around the world—an initiative that earned the VOA great respect.

The one area of media activity that worked almost completely in Nixon's favor was "space journalism," a category of news coverage that had developed in the early 1960s but reached its apogee during Nixon's administration. In April 1961, aboard its *Vostok 1* rocket craft, carrying Air Force Major Yuri Gagarin, the Soviet Union launched the world's first man into orbit in outer space. In August 1961 the USSR followed with a longer space journey by Major Gherman Titov. Both launches took place in secret, but news of the successful completion of the two projects, provided by Soviet sources, stimulated excited print and radio reporting worldwide. In addition, the USSR allowed limited television coverage of the landings. But television played a much larger role in February 1962, when a U.S. rocket launched the *Friendship 7* space capsule that successfully carried Lieutenant Colonel John Glenn into orbit and back. Hundreds of reporters representing numerous countries witnessed the entire event from Cape Canaveral, Florida, where the U.S. government provided them with extensive facilities. While print and radio journalism were much in evidence, particularly in providing background information, television dominated through its dramatic visual coverage of the launch, the landing, and the excited reactions of spectators. The same pattern of media coverage continued in later American spaceflights, including Commander Scott Carpenter's flight in May 1962 and Commander Walter Schirra's flight in October 1963. In each case media attention brought propaganda success to the nation involved and prestige by association to whoever happened to be the political leader at the time. The process culminated during Nixon's presidency with the *Apollo 11* mission in July 1969, when the American astronauts Neil Armstrong and Edwin "Buzz" Aldrin became the first humans to land on the moon, and billions of people viewed the event as it happened, a profound experience made possible by advanced television technology.

Portrayals Compete

With so many sectors of society experiencing growing contact with mass communication during the cold war, it was probably inevitable that even more new ways would be explored to shape audience perceptions of great international events advantageously. The Vietnam War accelerated and made more evident the search for effective strategies of portrayal.

Throughout the Vietnam conflict, from the beginning of open U.S. involvement in 1964 until final disengagement in 1975 with the fall of Saigon, reporters were given remarkably open access by military personnel, whether behind the lines or in battle zones. In spite of misgivings expressed by President Johnson, and later attempts by Nixon to increase censorship, military leaders used their frontline authority to test the proposition that nearly unfettered journalistic access to battlefield information would help rather than hinder operations by eliminating the need to shepherd reporters and increasing the probability that coverage would be more sympathetic to the military's point of view. Tragically, the new arrangement led to a high casualty rate among reporters, both injuries and deaths. But it did nevertheless stimulate a variety of strategies for framing the war as various groups thought best.[34]

Under both Johnson and Nixon, the U.S. government assumed a large media presence during the Vietnam War. Official American advisers, including a small number assigned to propaganda activities, had been in Southeast Asia ever since 1950. The use of mass persuasion increased greatly from 1964 onwards. For example, the U.S. Army and the USIA undertook advisory operations to support the work of the South Vietnamese Ministry of Information, helping to produce millions of leaflets and a number of films, and also attempting to cure the ministry of clumsy habits like confiscating foreign magazines and newspapers as they entered South Vietnam. In response, the North Vietnamese ramped up their own production of propaganda, very effectively using radio broadcasts, posters, and word-of-mouth publicity. In 1965, to coordinate its ever-expanding informational presence, the United States established JUSPAO (pronounced "juss-pow," the Joint United States Public Affairs Office) in Saigon, combining official journalistic functions and psychological warfare, with over five hundred personnel from the USIA, the CIA, the U.S. military, the U.S. Agency for International Development (USAID), and a large contingent of Vietnamese. JUSPAO pursued a large range of initiatives to spread the American message, from leaflet drops, radio programs, and posters to village-level indoctrination, tours for visiting dignitaries, and low-altitude flights over enemy territory by helicopters broadcasting over loudspeakers. These many activities were not well managed, however. When asked how the acronym JUSPAO should be pronounced, one staff member quipped, "chaos." In addition, the office could not balance its two roles: it gradually veered away from providing objective news and became increasingly propagandistic. The daily U.S. press briefings in Saigon came to be known as the "five o'clock follies."[35]

The Vietnam War was another landmark in the growing influence of television. Films and videotapes shot in great number during the Vietnam

War were flown to the United States and western Europe, where they appeared on TV screens very soon after the events they recorded. Because of advances in the technology of film and TV cameras, which became smaller and more portable, and now included the capacity to record electronic tapes of images for TV, as well as the freedom given to reporters, it was possible to photograph the war up close and capture startling details of combat and suffering. For example, at the village of Cam Ne, in response to a single burst of gunfire, U.S. soldiers used cigarette lighters to torch the huts of local Vietnamese in front of a TV reporter, who was present with cameramen and a microphone. This event, regarded by many as an atrocity, was broadcast to an audience of millions of American viewers by CBS News in August 1965 and became one of the iconic images of the war. Each night, viewers in many countries could learn about the progress of the war and, in the numerous cases where censorship did not succeed, observe the true violence of battle. There were also great print journalists, like the Americans David Halberstam and Frances Fitzgerald and the British reporter Jon Swain, who personally covered the Southeast Asia conflict and the communist takeover of Phnom Penh, Cambodia, in 1975. But because of the ubiquitous television cameras, this was, as commentators pointed out, the world's first "living room war," and widespread questioning of the worth of that war was one by-product.[36]

The Vietnam War may have been the first in which media portrayal of the home front population was a major factor. By this time most people in influential positions appreciated the importance of directing well-crafted messages to civilians: not only those within enemy territory but also those in one's own country. Propaganda of both these types was widespread. The CIA funded clandestine radio stations in Southeast Asia, and American planes dropped millions of leaflets over North Vietnam. Likewise, the U.S. government assiduously directed favorable information about the war at American citizens through televised speeches by Presidents Johnson and Nixon and extensive interviews with generals, among other means. This pattern, at least with regard to print media, had been common since the press conferences of the Second World War. But in the Vietnam War era the U.S. government and nongovernmental interest groups also worked to shape the characterization of the receivers of propaganda. During Nixon's two election campaigns for the presidency, the Republican Party funded television commercials that characterized the majority of Americans as in sympathy with its emphasis on societal order and, by showing antiwar protesters in confrontations with police, framed them as unpatriotic threats to the nation. In his speeches and campaigns for the governorship of California, Ronald Reagan profited from the same approach by making constant derogatory references to protesters at the University of California campus in Berkeley.

Conversely, groups that opposed the war realized they were in the media spotlight and developed strategies in response. Initial communication among protesters was often inward-looking, limited to activities like face-to-face recruitment and the circulation of brochures. But their tactics soon became more sophisticated. Protesters systematically accused the "establishment" media of bias and fed information to newer media outlets that were profiting from reporting on the counterculture, including radio stations that featured musicians like Bob Dylan and Joan Baez, and the magazines *Mother Jones*, *Ramparts*, and *Rolling Stone*. Learning from the freedom marches of the civil rights movement, radical groups like SDS (Students for a Democratic Society) made effective use of stage management during confrontations with police. In 1967, in the presence of television, radio, and print reporters, a group of protesters numbering at least 35,000 marched from downtown Washington, D.C., across the Potomac River to the steps of the Pentagon and provoked an armed retaliation, hoping to frame the government as a Nazi- or Soviet-style agent of repression. Contesting portrayals of a home front population by those who were themselves the home front had never before been such a large factor in war.[37]

Who ultimately won the battle of portrayals was never clear. Some analysts concluded that the antiwar movement, like the counterculture movement generally, was "made" and then "unmade" by establishment media organizations such as the *New York Times*, the *Washington Post*, and the major television networks. According to this theory, the media initially publicized the protesters in a generally favorable way because the novelty, creativity, and drama of the movement made journalists curious and increased circulation. But then as protests expanded and became more violent, the media and the corporate powers that controlled them became uneasy and joined with conservatives in portraying antiwar activity as a threat to society. This theory is partly accurate. But it has to be qualified. Walter Cronkite, the most trusted television newscaster, used one of his CBS broadcasts to accuse the government of lying about the war and to question the worth of America's presence in Southeast Asia. The public was even willing to hear out some radicals. In his book *The Armies of the Night* (1968), Norman Mailer charged that the media had been biased in their coverage of the 1967 march on the Pentagon, for example, by intentionally failing to record the most violent police reactions. Mailer was regarded as a left-wing sympathizer, but *The Armies of the Night* earned him a Pulitzer Prize—a clear sign of the establishment's approval—and became a best-seller, proving that it resonated with the general public. In any case, all contestants in the battle of portrayals knew that the degree of credibility they possessed among media audiences greatly affected their ability to influence voter perceptions and the elected members of government, who ultimately determined the future of the war.[38]

As the Vietnam War proceeded, military leaders concluded that by stimulating dissent in America, television handicapped their efforts to achieve victory. This came to be called the "Vietnam effect." The military was especially angered by media coverage of the Tet offensive. In 1968, by means of bravery, skill, and a huge, almost foolhardy sacrifice of men and resources, North Vietnamese forces were able to make great advances into the South. American military leaders viewed this offensive as only a temporary success and believed that its long-term effect would be to further weaken the North. At the same time, U.S. leaders accused American media, particularly television, of giving the public the impression that Tet was a major defeat for the South. They accused the media (the same media that were being accused by radicals of building support for the war) of undermining public support and diverting the military's energies away from day-to-day management of the conflict. In fact, the influence of television on the conflict was probably less direct. Although opinion polls did show a lessening of public support for the war after Tet, the major cause of the military's inability to pursue the war as it wished was a growing division of opinion among elite members of the U.S. government, some at the Pentagon, more at the White House, and still more in Congress and in other civilian sectors of government. This led to contradictions in decision making and in some cases to decreases in funding. But the information on which this ambivalence was based was known to the policymaking elite before television coverage began to fuel home front skepticism. Nor did television decrease support for the war among newspaper publishers. In 1968 the *Boston Globe* sponsored a survey of thirty-nine major U.S. papers, with a combined circulation of 22 million, to learn more about the attitudes of the print media. The survey showed that some papers had become more strongly in favor of the war, and others more skeptical about it, but not one of the papers advocated U.S. withdrawal from Vietnam even though millions of Americans were by this time demanding such action.[39] Nevertheless, belief in the "Vietnam effect"—that is, the power of readily available negative coverage to handicap effective pursuit of a military operation—became widespread at the Pentagon. Ironically, this conclusion resembled the "stab-in-the-back" legend that had been exploited by Hitler after the

First World War. In any case, military leaders started to plan for greater censorship in future wars, and they began to expand the public information function within the Pentagon bureaucracy so they would not have to rely on the USIA or private-sector media to communicate the military's interpretations in the future.[40]

The efforts of the armed forces to control public perception were becoming so aggressive that in 1970, after extensive televised hearings, Senator J. William Fulbright published a widely read book titled *The Pentagon Propaganda Machine*, in which he noted that during the late 1960s all the service branches had broadly expanded their use of public speakers at military and civilian locations in the United States. Their speeches were so heavily in favor of the war that Fulbright accused the Pentagon of violating the federal laws that prohibited the government from engaging in domestic propaganda. Fulbright also noted a troubling increase in assistance provided by the Pentagon for production of war-oriented films. The practice had become common during the Second World War and had expanded thereafter. In the 1950s, for example, the Pentagon had made navy personnel and an aircraft carrier available for filming *The Bridges at Toko-Ri* (1955) and in the 1960s had assisted with production of the submarine-oriented spy thriller *Ice Station Zebra* (1968). The Pentagon also aided production of the James Bond film *Goldfinger* (1964), dealing with an attempt by vaguely Soviet-like forces to detonate an A-bomb at Fort Knox. Help of this kind was generally regarded as part of the legitimate public information function of the military. But then, Fulbright noted, in 1967, for production of John Wayne's pro–Vietnam War film *The Green Berets*, Pentagon assistance became extraordinarily extensive. The list of equipment provided by the army was eight pages long and included jeeps, captured North Vietnamese weapons, guns of many types, tanks, helicopters, and scout dogs. Filming was allowed at Fort Benning, Georgia, and other installations for ninety-eight days. Some 358 army personnel appeared on camera as extras, and hundreds of additional troops were provided for support functions, such as operating bulldozers and cranes. For all these expenses Wayne's production company reimbursed the U.S. government slightly less than $56,000.[41]

In hindsight, an assumption has become widespread that the war in Vietnam was greatly affected by Hollywood. This was true in a limited sense. Many powerful figures in the movie industry sought to end the war through political contributions and private conversations with contacts in Washington. Celebrities also were active in public speaking, notably Jane Fonda on the antiwar side and John Wayne on the pro-war side. For the most part, however, filmmakers started late in the war, hardly visited Southeast Asia, and imposed their own fantasies on events.

The only major Hollywood film production dealing directly with Vietnam that appeared during the war was *The Green Berets* (1968), John Wayne's glorification of American elite forces battling the communist menace. The film was a box office success, and helped to prolong the sales of a hit song with the same title written in 1965, but received mostly negative reviews and lacked credibility among American combat forces actually serving in Southeast Asia. The action includes American defense of a stockade that could have taken place in any Hollywood movie about the cavalry and Indians. One of the characters in the drama is an American reporter who is skeptical about the worth of the war; he is subjected to harangues by Wayne and other military characters that are so hyperpatriotic as to strain credibility. *The Green Berets* was an unreflective attempt to recycle old formulas.

Antiwar advocates flocked to see *MASH*. Robert Altman's film, which premiered in 1970, was based on *MASH: A Novel about Three Army Doctors*, by Richard Hooker, published in 1968. Altman's film was ostensibly about the Korean War and portrayed the characters and crises at a mobile army surgical hospital during that era. But it was intended as a commentary on the absurdity of all wars, and its irony and dark comedy seemed to capture much of the frontline experience of the Vietnam conflict, even though the film did not address the deeper antiwar concerns that were fostering student protests on campuses. The film was so popular that it became the inspiration for a television series that premiered in 1972 and ran until 1983, garnering numerous awards and earning a reputation as one of the best TV shows of all time. As an allegory for the Vietnam War, *MASH* provided the combination of emotional distance and honesty necessary for contemplating some if not all of the implications of America's military activities during years of great tension and distress on the home front.

The three films that did the most to shape moviegoers' images of the Vietnam War were *The Deer Hunter* (1978), directed by Michael Cimino; *Apocalypse Now* (1979), directed by Francis Ford Coppola; and *Platoon* (1986), directed by Oliver Stone. *Platoon* was the most realistic of the three. Stone saw military service in Southeast Asia and was a decorated veteran who, like many of his comrades, became deeply disillusioned by the contrast between American actions and officially stated purposes in Southeast Asia. The other two films were more impressionistic. All appeared after the U.S. withdrawal from Southeast Asia. The time lag probably was due to the difficulty of absorbing the shock of the Vietnam experience and the challenge of evolving new cinematic formulas to address that experience. All three films are powerful works of art and are significant explorations of war on their own terms. In view of their timing, they could not have influenced the American decision to withdraw from Southeast Asia, although they served as important warnings from the antiwar point of view about the high emotional costs of war and the risks of similar involvements in the future.

Even as warnings, however, the films had only a limited effect in military circles. The three productions bore little resemblance to the reality of war. An immense amount of detail about the conflict was available from the extensive reportage that had taken place. But military authenticity was subordinated in favor of portrayals that fit the agendas of the filmmakers. For example, in *Apocalypse Now*, the props were not always accurate, the Philippines location undermined geographic authenticity, and the use of Philippine military equipment further compromised verisimilitude. The central act of the film—the secret murder of an American officer sanctioned by American generals—almost certainly would never have been ordered, since medical treatment was the typical response during the Vietnam War to the problem of unstable officers. The film contains instances of insane, sloppy fighting, and even combat *between* groups of Americans, as if all American soldiers were bitter, bored, and technically incompetent. There were indeed problems of drug use and "fragging" (grenade attacks on one's own troops) during the war. But military experts have pointed out that if U.S. forces had operated as they do in *Apocalypse Now*, the American army would not have lasted two weeks. The film may perhaps be plausible as the depiction of a rare occurrence. But most veterans found it to be misleading, disrespectful, and ill-informed. The film that probably won the greatest respect among veterans was *Coming Home* (1978), an authentic, respectful portrayal of one injured soldier's return to America.[42]

Theorists Challenge Authority

Around the time of the Vietnam War there was a flowering of theory related to war and mass communication. Because of its close ties to governments and the tendency for ownership to be concentrated, mass communication became identified, in the minds of many, with excessive control that had the potential to militarize all of society. Examples of the widespread desire to scrutinize this control are provided by the work of three theorists who attracted scholarly respect and large audiences, and provoked widespread debate, by analyzing media from antiauthoritarian perspectives.

Marshall McLuhan (1911– 1980), director of the Centre for Culture and Technology at the University of Toronto, probably played a larger role than any other writer during the period 1960–1980 in making general readers aware of the importance of media. He combined serious analysis with humor, quotable aphorisms, and arresting generalizations that were overstated but held elements of truth. McLuhan became famously associated with the phrase "the medium is the message." The central point in all his writings was that people must look more closely at the astonishing degree to which the system used to deliver information affects its content and impact. Some saw this as technological determinism, a manifesto to ignore content entirely. But McLuhan believed that since people were the creators of their tools they could in the end control them. Looking at history, McLuhan saw printing as a divisive force, since the portability of books and newspapers made it possible for each reader to spend large amounts of time in a private, isolated world. But he regarded electronic media as a force for the reconstruction of community. They were interactive, encouraged group participation, and would create a "global village." McLuhan did not live to see the merging of print text and electronic interaction via the Internet. Furthermore, McLuhan distinguished between "hot" and "cool" media. Print was hot: it had high resolution, was authoritative, and was low in audience participation (interactivity). Electronic broadcast media were cool: they had low definition and were less authoritative in the sense that the reader had to fill in much of the content.

McLuhan was influenced by the Catholic philosopher Pierre Teilhard de Chardin, who maintained that the use of electricity extended the human nervous system. At the beginning of his career McLuhan thought that electronics would bring people closer to God. Later he came to believe that the electronic media were evil and held the potential to militarize all of society. In *War and Peace and the Global Village* (1968), he described the Pentagon disparagingly as "the biggest filing cabinet in the world" and expressed his anxiety regarding the military's vast mobilization of information. One of McLuhan's beliefs was that major changes in technology lead to collective stresses that stimulate armed conflict. "Every new technology necessitates a new war," he declared. As examples of a technology that was part of the physical infrastructure of communication and that directly contributed to the outbreak of war, McLuhan cited the railway in the American Civil War and the First World War, because it made the massing of armies and weapons easier. An example of technology that specifically carried information was radio in the Second World War, because it "awakened tribal energies."[43] Such broad generalizations are typical of McLuhan's writing.

Another analyst of media who attracted notice in the 1960s was Noam Chomsky (b. 1928). By that time he was already regarded as the world's foremost authority on linguistics, dubbed by many as the successor to Descartes. Revulsion against the Vietnam War, and against Western treatment of the Third World generally, led Chomsky to analyze the connection between power and the use of information. He came to believe that the mass media nearly always served rich and powerful elites and tended to suppress information not favorable to these groups. In Chomsky's framework of analysis, elites usually are able to make the citizenry believe that dissent and broad consultation with the general population are genuine elements of the political process. But when the discussion turns to questioning vital underlying assumptions, the state responds first with the strategic use of tools of persuasion and then if necessary with coercion and violence. The media participate in this collusion because the people who own and control them are members of the elite and do not want to give up the accompanying wealth and power.

Chomsky argued that "filters" have been created to serve elites and prevent significant sharing of dissent and disturbing information. One filter was costs of entry. Establishing a newspaper or TV station requires a large amount of funding, which has to be obtained from investors who are members of the elite. Broadcasting licenses are controlled by government commissions that are influenced behind the scenes by lawyers and lobbyists in the employ of the elites. Advertising is expensive; most of it is purchased by those who already have economic power. Another filter is media self-censorship. Editors and reporters know that they will lose their jobs if they offend the elites. Some criticism is allowed, but there are unstated boundaries. For example, papers seldom report scandals related to the personal lives of individuals who control newspaper chains or television networks, and they seldom disclose details regarding the wealth of members of the elite. Yet another filter is the supplying of surrogates to propagate the views of elites. Government agencies and large corporations arrange a steady stream of "press conferences" that maintain the illusion of openness and access, and pay for the "experts" who write so many of the stories that appear in print and compose so much of the punditry on television. Chomsky never claimed that the system of information control he described was a conspiracy. Rather, he saw it as an inevitable by-product of the capitalist system. Chomsky also maintained hope that the system could be changed through education, vigilance on the part of each citizen, and support of alternative media. But he cautioned that as small organizations grow and gain power, they often take on the characteristics of those already among the elite. Chomsky was a vocal opponent of the Vietnam War who assisted many protest groups. He maintained that violence would be present in international relations as long as elites were allowed to retain the kind of control he ascribed to them.[44]

The French thinker Jacques Ellul (1912–1994) was the author of *Propaganda: The Formation of Men's Attitudes* (1965). His work spanned several decades but received its greatest attention in the 1960s. Ellul carefully studied earlier theorists of propaganda such as Walter Lippmann and Harold Lasswell and concluded that they had treated propaganda as an independent variable created by certain groups to gain power over other groups. Ellul saw propaganda as something deeper and more pervasive. It was not so much created as it was simply *there*, the inevitable by-product of a society that had come to be ruled by the technology it had created. Propaganda appeared not so much in the form of lies or distortions as in the form of half-truths, qualified truths, and truths taken out of context. Even Goebbels had believed, whether he always put his belief into practice or not, that carefully utilized truth was the best propaganda. Mass persuasion of this kind often catered to real needs that people felt, like the need for food and shelter. But it also created "pseudo-needs" to make people dependent. Ellul argued that propaganda was most powerful when it sharpened and intensified existing opinions. He singled out two categories of propaganda related to action that were especially important. One was *agitation propaganda* (a term that Ellul probably got from Lenin), which caused people to go beyond the repetition of ideas to acting on the basis of the ideas. The other was *integration propaganda*, which led people to conduct themselves according to the patterns required by society. Propaganda was important not only in war but also in peace, to secure the gains of war.

New Squabbles Break Out

The period 1979–1991 is often called the "new cold war." The term is misleading in some ways, because there was continuity throughout the entire period 1945–1991. Communists and capitalists did not halt their maneuverings against each other in 1979 and then, after making peace, decide to begin another fight. But it is accurate to say that there was a decrease in antagonism in the 1970s followed by renewed tension, and that the later years of the cold war became significantly different from the earlier ones as the final burst of antagonism paradoxically led to the end of the great standoff. The change was due in part to mass communication.

In 1972, after Nixon's visit to China, Soviet leaders decided that they needed to find ways of counterbalancing the growing assertiveness of the People's Republic. That year, as a result, Nixon was able to conclude two major arms limitation agreements with the USSR. From 1972 to 1974, moreover, the United States and the Soviet Union increased their economic ties. This was also the period of *Ostpolitik*, the successful effort by West German chancellor Willy Brandt to improve relations between his country and the Eastern Bloc. An important factor in lowering anxieties was that major American involvement in Southeast Asia ended in 1975. In addition, in the same year the United States and the Soviet Union signed the Helsinki Accords, which led to further disarmament. President Jimmy Carter followed in 1979 with the Salt II agreement limiting manufacture of medium-range and long-range missiles. All of these developments augured well for more benign relations between East and West. But tensions appreciably reawakened by the end of the decade. In 1979, to prop up a local communist takeover that had occurred there, the Soviet Union invaded Afghanistan, leading to widespread condemnation of its brutal methods and arousing American fears that communists might push southward all the way to the Indian Ocean. In response, the United States began arming Afghan guerrillas who were working to repel Soviet troops. At the same time, Carter announced that the United States would boycott the 1980 Olympic Games in Moscow.

Developments in the arena of international communication took place within this larger framework of events and gave it many of its features. The pattern of movement from decreased to increased tension is visible in the strategies of mass persuasion used by the two U.S. heads of state who followed Richard Nixon. Nixon's immediate successor, Gerald Ford, who became president in 1974 when Nixon resigned, suffered stereotyping as unintelligent and inept after he lost his place during speeches in state dinners abroad, and he suffered embarrassment when his remarks to foreign audiences were inaccurately translated in ways that insulted those audiences. But perhaps because he was somewhat bland, Ford at least experienced no propaganda disasters. He relied on Henry Kissinger, who was a shrewd employer of media, for most of his foreign policy strategy, including a decision to attack Khmer Rouge ships in a minor skirmish off the coast of Southeast Asia to defend the USS *Mayaguez*. Ford also saw great potential in the USIA and sought to use it to restore America's reputation globally after Nixon's disgrace and the American defeat in Vietnam.

Under Ford, in 1976, the United States celebrated the bicentennial of the Declaration of Independence. USIA publicity played a large role in making the event a spectacular success worldwide. The agency sponsored a major museum exhibition on the world of Franklin and Jefferson that opened to very favorable reviews in Paris in 1975 and in 1976 moved on to equal success in Warsaw, London, New York City, Chicago, San Francisco, and Mexico City. In another distinguished effort, the USIA arranged international broadcasts via satellite of the thrilling fireworks displays that took place in Washington, D.C., on July 4 and 5, 1976. The celebration helped to improve America's image after Vietnam and Watergate.[45]

Jimmy Carter succeeded Ford as president in 1977. By his frequent isolated retreats to Camp David, which were given great attention in the media, Carter created concern at home and abroad about his skill as an executive. But he brought the United States worldwide praise for bringing together Israel's leader Menachem Begin and President Anwar Sadat of Egypt, using mass communication extensively to emphasize the importance of this initiative. Like President Ford, Carter saw great potential in the USIA, using it to improve America's international reputation. Assisted by his secretary of state, Zbigniew Brzezinski, Carter mobilized the agency to publicize his emphasis on human rights as an aspect of American foreign policy; he renamed it the U.S. International Communications Agency (ICA), in the belief that such nomenclature would emphasize America's desire to listen to other countries as well as speak to them. Carter was also very effective in public diplomacy in Latin America. He made a well-received tour there in 1978, adding to the good impression because he spoke some Spanish. Through the ICA, and with congressional approval for funding, Carter established an educational exchange program offering college scholarships for study in the United States to poor but deserving students from Latin America, in memory of the recently deceased senator and former vice president Hubert Humphrey.[46]

Carter became the object of criticism, probably unfairly, as a bumbler during the Iran hostage crisis of 1979, when the religious regime that had overthrown America's ally the shah took a group of Americans prisoner and forced them to appear before television cameras. The influence of the crisis on Carter's administration, and indeed on international conceptions of foreign policy, was intensified by the extensive reportage. In response to the event, the ABC television network began a new late-evening program, *Nightline*, which covered the crisis under the heading "America Held Hostage." The program heralded the increased ability of television, from the 1980s on, to present images of war and foreign policy crises "live"—that is to say, in real time—because of technological advances such as portable cameras and satellite transmission. (During the Vietnam War, film and videotape had to be flown to broadcasting stations in the United States or Europe before airing.) An ominous fact was that the creator of *Nightline* was Roone Arledge, ABC's director of sports programming. Arledge used skills he had developed during coverage of the Olympic Games and on *Monday Night Football* to package the hostage crisis in a highly suspenseful manner. Viewers were encouraged to feel the great human drama of the crisis but received background analysis only in snippets. ABC's *Nightline* program was also a step toward the later practice of covering international news twenty-four hours a day, seven days a week, adopted within a few years by CNN (Cable News Network), established by Ted Turner, who saw an opportunity to chip away at the monopoly of the three broadcast television networks, ABC, CBS, and NBC, by offering programs fed to viewers along the landlines of telephone companies and other providers. Carter's prestige was much less affected by the Soviet Union's invasion of Afghanistan; for in spite of the intense criticism of the USSR in many Western capitals, and Carter's aggressive use of symbolism in ordering the American boycott of the Moscow Olympics, the media decided, at least initially, that the Afghan conflict was not sufficiently newsworthy to justify the risk to journalists and the expense and difficulty of covering a war in an isolated, mountainous area. This was an important example of the media's capacity to affect public perceptions of foreign affairs.

The Soviet Union Collapses

The "new cold war" was fully in evidence by the time Ronald Reagan took office as president in 1981, and he at first conducted himself in ways that led observers to wonder if the long East-West conflict would ever come to an end. Initially Reagan played his role in the cold war confrontationally. Conservative in his ideas of foreign policy, and a product of Hollywood, Reagan saw information as a valuable tool for a strategy of actively challenging the Soviet Union. His first media success was a matter of luck: the hostages came home from Iran on the day Reagan was inaugurated as president. Strategic moves that were more the result of his doing followed. In response to growing Soviet influence in Afghanistan, Reagan enlarged the psychological warfare capabilities of the Pentagon and used them covertly. Reagan also exploited public diplomacy. He appointed an old friend, Charles Z. Wick, as director of the USIA. Like Reagan, Wick was a product of the entertainment industry, a former bandleader, though he also held a law degree and possessed considerable experience as a political organizer. Wick's management of the USIA reflected this background. It was vulgar but sensitive, ingenious in ways that directors from more elite backgrounds might not have been, sometimes ridiculous, sometimes unconstitutional, and in its way effective in countering the effects of Soviet propaganda. Reagan frequently invited Wick to sit in as a guest at meetings of the National Security Council. The two men brought an aggressive style to U.S. international information policy that had not been seen since the Truman era. The USIA vociferously supported the Solidarity movement in Poland and the buildup of America's missile capacity, and sought to exploit the public relations disaster suffered by the Soviet Union in 1986 when its atomic reactors at Chernobyl experienced deadly meltdown, and as the gradually increasing media coverage of the inability to achieve military victory in Afghanistan harmed Moscow's international reputation. Wick's highly ideological approach led to many resignations at the Voice of America, which had always struggled to protect its role as a purveyor of objective reporting. In a Hollywood-style flourish, appropriate for a president who believed in the importance of business and the private sector, Reagan and Wick established an advisory council composed of five hundred of the richest business leaders in the world along with the world's most powerful political leaders.

Reagan openly used war as an instrument of policy in the Caribbean in Grenada in 1982, when he ordered an invasion of the island in response to reports of a communist takeover. Victory came easily. Many observers wondered why the operation had even been necessary. From an information point of view, the most important aspect was the evidence it provided that belief in the Vietnam effect was widespread in White House and military circles. There was intensive news management and an almost complete blackout of information until after military success was assured.

Another example of belief in the Vietnam effect occurred the same year. It involved an operation in which the United States was not directly involved, but of which it was an active supporter via Reagan's public endorsements and through assistance behind the scenes: the Falklands War. The British successfully defended their South Atlantic possession from takeover by Argentina, which had attacked the Falkland Islands (the Malvinas in Spanish usage, a reversion to the name used before British settlement in the nineteenth century) to divert attention from domestic problems. The stout defense of the Falklands by Prime Minister Margaret Thatcher made her hugely popular in Britain and the United States and allowed the British to relive fantasies of imperial glory, complete with use of Gurkha knife fighters brought in from Nepal. The Argentines were no match for the British navy and amphibious units. The war was over so quickly that it might not have earned much of a place in history except for the accompanying information strategy. Influenced by their beliefs about the role of the media in Vietnam, the British almost completely closed off access to reporters.[47]

The United States was the major Western actor in late-twentieth-century international relations, and under Reagan, image management became a very large component of U.S. foreign policy. In some ways this was merely the continuation of a centuries-old pattern. Political leaders have always tried to portray their actions on the world stage to maximum possible advantage. But as pursued by Reagan in the era of television, the management of imagery seemed at times to become almost the totality of foreign policy at the expense of any substance.

The American system of government assigns not only a managerial but also a large ceremonial role to the office of the president. This is in contrast, for example, to the British system, in which a political technician, the prime minister, concentrates on managing the state and doing battle against the opposition, while a ceremonial leader, the monarch, concentrates on being well liked by the population as a whole, incarnating the unifying traditions of the state and remaining apart from day-to-day controversies. Most American presidents have understood the importance, under the U.S. system, of combining the managerial and ceremonial functions. Some, like Abraham Lincoln and the two Roosevelts, have done so brilliantly. Others have combined the two functions successfully but with difficulty. Eisenhower, as a war hero, tilted toward a ceremonial emphasis but, as an experienced general, knew the importance of guiding and monitoring his staff. Nixon, in contrast, relied on his political and managerial skills but also knew the importance of overcoming his social awkwardness and regularly attending ceremonial events. Reagan, however, was a president who relied almost completely on a strategy of ceremonial rule, made possible by a century's worth of developments in mass communication that preceded his ascension to office.

During the Second World War, Reagan was an up-and-coming, reasonably competent actor who made inspirational documentaries for the Hollywood film industry. After the war he continued to act in films but also became interested in California party politics. When his film career declined, he landed a job as a corporate spokesman for the General Electric Company, doing television testimonials and touring the country to speak at banquets and conferences. Originally a member of the Democratic Party, Reagan gradually became more conservative and, by the early 1960s, was giving powerful speeches on behalf of Republican political leaders like Barry Goldwater. Reagan's ability to arouse mass audiences attracted the attention of party organizers and rich businessmen in California. They were well aware that Reagan lacked experience or talent as a manager. They also knew that although he had a keen sense of social factors, he was not mentally agile when pressed to discuss issues in detail. But they also noticed that he was bright enough to have developed a set of core beliefs in the importance of checking the growth of government, lowering taxes, and supporting a strong military. They saw as well that he could powerfully articulate these beliefs by continuously repeating and recombining the appealing catchwords and artful phrases that had become the memorized essence of his thousands of set speeches over the years. They recognized that he was a handsome, good-humored, very likable personification of the Middle American values he had absorbed while growing up in Illinois before moving to California. And like just about everyone else, they could see that he had near-genius-level ability to magnify his influence through the skillful use of film, radio, and television. Republican operatives and financial backers decided they could use Reagan to expand their power by splitting the two traditional functions of an executive in the American political system. They provided Reagan with a highly competent staff of handlers who knew the public policy issues and could craft the programs to address them. Then they also provided him with a large staff of political campaign organizers, advertising executives, and public relations consultants, who were responsible for writing Reagan's scripts, planning his appearances, and shaping the overall message. Reagan's indispensable but limited role was to deliver the message with charisma, act the part of the executive once elected, and field impromptu questions from the press and public as well as he could, in the knowledge that his overall attractiveness would trump any specific mistakes he made.

This strategy enabled Reagan to become governor of California and eventually president. Nor was it lacking in positive effects. After the turmoil of the 1960s, the shock of Watergate, and four years of Jimmy Carter's self-righteous manner, Americans were reenergized by a leader who helped them see virtue in the nation's core values. And thanks to the competence of Reagan's staff, most managerial functions went on smoothly, first in Sacramento and then in the White House. His actions were not always pleasing to liberals. Reagan severely cut funding for welfare programs and education, and many analysts accused him of propagating a selective, sugarcoated version of the nation's history, one that encouraged Americans to feel good about themselves without deeply examining any faults or ironies. But most voters assigned the greatest importance to the cuts he made in their taxes, his anticommunist rhetoric, his emphasis on military preparedness, and the economic prosperity of his years in office, even though it masked a growing national debt. Reagan might well have been elected to a third term as president if such a possibility had been allowed under the Constitution.

And yet it is an open question whether the Reagan approach to leadership was ultimately good for the nation. The record in the area of foreign policy showed a mixture of clear successes, dangerous failures, and instances in which success would not have been possible without fortunate turns in external circumstances. Examples of nearly undeniable achievements in foreign relations included Reagan's 1984 visit to Ireland and his several journeys to London during his early years in office. The Irish trip, which created great goodwill, was a stage-managed return to the president's "roots," as he was hosted by the mayor of Dublin, toured his ancestral village of Ballyporeen, and acted out tried-and-true motifs that had become familiar to audiences of numerous Hollywood films about Ireland. His visits to London were marked by cordial conversations with Britain's Conservative prime minister, his friend Margaret Thatcher, and a well-received address to members of Parliament and other dignitaries at the Palace of Westminster that said little about policy issues and much about Anglo-American friendship and shared memories of the Second World War. A spectacular example of success in building international amity was Reagan's visit to Normandy in June 1984 to commemorate the fortieth anniversary of the D-day invasion. At two stops on the beaches where brave American troops had landed, Reagan brilliantly delivered magnificent addresses that had been prepared by his excellent speechwriter Peggy Noonan. The veterans and international leaders in attendance were deeply moved, as were the viewers in many countries who watched the ceremonies on television.

Reagan may have reaped his greatest dividends from image-centered foreign policy during the celebration in New York harbor on July 3–6, 1986, which the president's staff arranged to honor the centennial of the Statue of Liberty. President Reagan and French President François Mitterand jointly opened the four-day, $32 million extravaganza of music, fireworks, and patriotic orations. The celebration was attended by three thousand corporate donors who paid $5,000 each, and a thousand journalists from forty nations. It was watched by an estimated 1 billion television viewers around the world. Reagan gave Medals of Liberty to a dozen naturalized citizens, including Henry Kissinger, Bob Hope, and Elie Wiesel. A variety show boasted such stars as Gregory Peck, Elizabeth Taylor, and Frank Sinatra. In an animated speech Reagan proclaimed, "We are the keepers of the flame of liberty; we hold it high tonight for the world to see."

Reflecting the enormous public approval that Reagan garnered from the festivities, both for himself and for America, *Time* magazine made Reagan's appearance at the Statue of Liberty its cover story for the week. Exulting, "Ronald Reagan has a genius for American occasions," *Time* called him "a magician who carries a bright, ideal America like a holograph in his mind and projects its image in the air. . . . Looking at his genial, crinkly face prompts a sense of wonder: How does he pull it off?"[48]

That Reagan did not always "pull it off" was evidenced by a visit to Germany in May 1985. It was productive in the sense that Reagan's staff, as authorized by the president, was able to update and reaffirm various defense agreements behind the scenes. But the public aspects of the trip proved to be very harmful when Reagan sought to manage things by himself. The visit included a speech at the Bergen-Belsen concentration camp, where the president movingly paid his respects to the sixty thousand prisoners—Jews and others—who had died there. But on the same day, at his insistence and against the advice of most of his aides, Reagan also went to the nearby military cemetery at Bitburg for a wreath-laying ceremony intended as a gesture of reconciliation to honor Germany's fallen fighters. Forty-nine members of the SS were among the two thousand German soldiers buried there, and as a result, the event caused enormous international outrage. Reagan knew in advance about the SS graves, and everything in his personal history indicated that he sympathized with the victims of the Holocaust. But in deciding to go to Bitburg, Reagan did great damage to America's standing in the world by so badly overestimating his ability as an actor to keep audiences focused on certain aspects of a drama and not others.

An even more startling instance of image-reliant leadership gone wrong occurred during Reagan's second term of office in 1986, when the "Iran-contra" scandal became intense. After a growing number of disclosures by the media, Reagan had to go on television and confess to the world that he was unaware of illegal funding provided over the period 1983–1986 to right-wing forces in Nicaragua who were working to overthrow the communist government there, and that he did not know of secret U.S. shipments of arms to Iran intended to secure the release of Americans held hostage by pro-Iranian groups in Lebanon. Nor did he know of the bizarre connection between the two operations, specifically, that clandestine American operatives were overcharging Iran for the arms and using the profits to provide the funds for Nicaragua. All of this activity had been coordinated by Reagan's staff, who received general approval from the president after telling him what was going on in purposely vague terms. The behind-the-scenes intrigue was a striking example of the damage that could occur when the chief executive of the nation was so lax about his managerial duties that powerful factions supposedly accountable to the president could secretly commit the United States to actions that broke the law and contradicted many of his stated principles of foreign policy, for example, that his administration would never negotiate with terrorists.

In March and again in November 1987, by which time a good deal of information had been leaked to the press, Reagan offered televised apologies for not having known about the Iran-contra scheme except in a general way. The president mobilized all his skills as a communicator, but his attempts to appear candid and convey remorse were not convincing. Opinion polls after the speeches indicated that he had lost the confidence of a majority of the American people and had seriously harmed the country's reputation abroad. Reagan made the problems worse by his ineptitude at a televised prime-time news conference in November. He was not able to master the information given to him in advance by his aides and, as a result, was rambling in his replies to reporters. Nor did he realize that almost every answer he gave was at variance with facts that were by then available to the media. At times Reagan simply lapsed into denial, for example, when he insisted that all the arms shipped to Iran could fit into a single cargo plane, and when he adopted the strategy, pursued even more vigorously in the weeks that followed, of blaming media leaks for the failure to secure the release of more hostages.[49]

It is nevertheless testimony to his skills as a manipulator of images that Reagan was able to survive Iran-contra. He never again enjoyed the trust of a majority of the American people. But there was no move to impeach him; and his public apologies, his sheer likeableness, and the short attention spans of the voters allowed him, during the last two years of his second term, to regain his footing and move on to new challenges. It was fateful that one of these challenges, involving nothing less than the conclusion of the cold war, emerged under circumstances that happened to be ready-made for mobilizing Reagan's particular talents.

Because of his skill in using the media during the period when the cold war was winding down, there has been a tendency to give Reagan full or major credit for ending it. To be sure, he made important contributions. In spite of his characterization of the Soviet Union as an "evil empire" and other occasionally bellicose rhetoric, Reagan was by nature a peace-loving person, and he kept more belligerent members of his administration in check. His optimistic personality led him to see opportunities where many longtime members of the Washington establishment habitually projected geostrategic gloom. It is arguable that Reagan effectively pressured the Soviets to come to the negotiating table by means of his widely publicized "Star Wars" initiative calling for construction of an elaborate U.S. satellite defense system in outer space. Moreover, Reagan supplemented USIA publicity efforts by using the CIA and other resources to pump clandestine radio propaganda and more overt television broadcasts, via satellite, into Soviet-dominated areas, especially Poland, where the Solidarity movement, led by Lech Walesa, was winning rights for workers and causing consternation in the Kremlin.

But events in central and eastern Europe had their own internal dynamic. For example, the Chernobyl atomic reactor disaster resulted from Russian mismanagement, not Western maneuvering, and an underground revival of Christianity in Russia was turning the Orthodox Church into an important anti-Soviet force. And no one, not even Reagan, was more central to ending the cold war than the Soviet leader Mikhail Gorbachev, who worked to reform the Soviet Union internally and decrease the burdens the USSR was bearing as a result of its standoff with the West. As the historian Melvyn Leffler has stated, "Gorbachev came to feel that Soviet security was not threatened by capitalist adversaries; it was far more endangered by communist functionaries, economic managers, and demoralized workers than by any external foe."[50] Moreover, Gorbachev was probably even more masterly than Reagan in his use of mass persuasion. Within the Soviet Union, he created a constructive context for active debate about the future through his policy of glasnost (transparency). Beyond the borders of the USSR, he turned himself into a highly attractive personality on the world media stage, charming audiences in his press conferences and personal appearances. Journalists coined a new term, "Gorbymania," to describe his international popularity. Even more important, it was Gorbachev who took the initiative in proposing arms reductions and more open relations with the West. Reagan deserves great credit for listening closely, but essentially he functioned as the responder. The cold war did not even end on Reagan's watch. The Berlin Wall was dismantled—without opposition from Gorbachev—in 1989, while Reagan's successor, George H. W. Bush, was in office. Within another two years, democracy and capitalism came to Romania, Hungary, Poland, and Czechoslovakia. These events marked the beginning of the end of the cold war, which "officially" ended in 1991 with the dissolution of the Soviet Union. Thus, in the middle of his term in office, President Bush faced the challenge of responding to a historic transition.

The Icons Change

A conspicuous feature of the cold war was its iconography. During its entire forty-five years, a combination of powerful images functioned to excite apprehension, influencing in the process perceptions and actions worldwide. Picked up, circulated, elaborated, and re-elaborated by the channels of mass communication available at the time, the icons affected the way everyday citizens organized their lives and provided fundamental concepts that world leaders used in making life-and-death decisions about war and peace.

Oddly, the image that gave its name to the era was not one of the major icons. During all the years from 1945 to 1991, it is difficult to find any public discourse about international relations that did not use the term "cold war," or that did not voice fear of the war becoming "hot." Moreover, the term made its way into daily life as a metaphor. So, for example, a magazine might refer to the "cold war"—meaning a standoff or stalemate—in the competition between two business corporations and speculate whether the conflict might "heat up." But the imagery seldom became more detailed than that. Probably this was because of the abstraction inherent in the term.

There were, however, many other images that proved to be rich sources of description for the cold war experience. Among the more notable was the idea of borders or divisions. In 1946 Winston Churchill fixed this imagery in the world's consciousness in his famous speech in Fulton, Missouri, when he declared that an "iron curtain" had gone up from north to south in central Europe, dividing the world between Soviet dictatorship and Western democracy, slave and free, an economically creative West and an economically backward East. Within a few years, references to the "curtain" began to be associated with images of barbed wire, watchtowers, guarded gates that were raised and lowered at border crossings, and strips of empty land that bisected forests, crossed rivers, and cut through farmers' fields to mark the fortified boundaries between nations dominated by the Soviet Union and those loyal to the West. Stories of heroic attempts to cross the border became a staple of cold war journalism.

The imagery of division took on additional permutations in 1948 when Stalin attempted to aggrandize Berlin by denying the Western powers all land access to it, and in response the Allies organized the Berlin airlift. The media became filled with images of C-47 cargo planes landing at the airports of Berlin, anxious Berliners staring up at the sky, and delighted children catching the packets of candy that Western pilots dropped with miniature makeshift parachutes. Then in 1961 came images of the Berlin Wall, constructed by the East German government to stanch the flow through the relatively unguarded border between the Soviet zone of Berlin and the three Allied zones, which had become the conduit used by thousands of residents of the Eastern Bloc, notably the young and the highly skilled, to flee the communist system. The West knew it could not succeed in a military response to the fact of the wall. Symbolic behavior became the preferred option. With news cameras recording the scene, the U.S. commander, General Lucius Clay, ordered tanks to advance to within a few feet of the new fortification and aim but not fire their cannons. The West German press magnate Axel Springer built the skyscraper headquarters of his media empire almost flush up against the wall and covered the building with gold-colored metal to symbolize unapologetic capitalism. The news media provided dramatic accounts of the attempts by brave individuals and families to sneak over or under the wall or crash through it or smuggle themselves past checkpoints by hiding under the seats of automobiles or inside packing boxes. President John F. Kennedy visited the wall in 1963 and, to a large crowd that roared its approval, declared, "I am a Berliner." Symbolic visits on the same pattern became rites of passage for other political figures in succeeding years. By the 1980s such visits seemed to take on renewed power as world leaders sought to use the imagery of the wall as a tool for humiliating the East into hastening the end of the cold war. That was President Reagan's strategy in 1987 when he journeyed to Berlin and, posing for the cameras with the historic Brandenburg Gate in the background, exhorted Mikhail Gorbachev to "tear down this wall."[51]

Then, in the last two years of the cold war, the imagery of borders seemed to fade gradually away. As the Soviet Union began to break up, the great physical reminders of division were dismantled. In no particular sequence, and in almost random episodes, sections of the Iron Curtain were deconstructed. Border guards abandoned their watchtowers and gates, people cut down and hauled away the fences and marketed the pieces of barbed wire as souvenirs, and human traffic in both directions radically increased. In Berlin, the East German authorities suddenly stopped guarding the wall, and the population of the city proceeded to dismantle it as television cameras streamed images of the event to the world. That led eventually to the final stage of the iconography of division, in the decades after the cold war, as the peoples of East and West struggled to overcome what came to be called the "mental borders" created by forty-five years of cultural, socioeconomic, and political differences that complicated and slowed down the process of European reintegration.[52]

The iconography of division was not absolute. It allowed for the possibility that borders could be vague and ambiguous, could be penetrated, and could be used to advantage if one were ingenious and perhaps a bit reckless. Such was the symbol world of cold war espionage. In the beginning the imagery emphasized moral and political ambiguity more than actual spying. One of the most famous films of 1949 was *The Third Man*. It took place in a postwar Vienna governed in sectors by the four victorious powers and told the story of a murky, predatory world of black marketers. During the early cold war years, in popular thriller novels and in films like *Diplomatic Courier* (1952), audiences were introduced to the lives of agents who carried important information back and forth for their governments and risked getting beaten up or killed by thugs from other governments who usually operated brazenly. But the iconography soon included an element of real deception, as trained operatives from the intelligence services of all the major states used disguise, lies, and recruitment of turncoats to discover official secrets involving codes, bomb specifications, agents' identities, possible military attacks, even plans for overthrowing governments. The imagery associated with such activities could evoke memories from the past, as, for example, in Graham Greene's novel *Our Man in Havana* (1958; adapted as a film in 1959), which told, in a sometimes comic and sometimes frightening way, the story of a member of British intelligence who finds himself in a semitropical backwater that resembles the old world of British imperialism more than that of the contemporary twentieth century. Alternatively, the imagery might focus on the unique predicament of espionage agents in the new conditions of the cold war, as in the best-selling novels of John le Carré, especially *The Spy Who Came in from the Cold* (1963; film adaptation 1965), which told the profoundly tragic story of a British operative unable to cope with the emotional strain of his work, who is shot down at the Berlin Wall.

The human face of the enemy was also an important aspect of cold war iconography. The people who lived on either side of the East-West divide were never able to see each other completely as abstractions, even though they might have wished to do so to relieve worries about their moral obligations. In the early years of the cold war, Westerners remembered the Russians as their allies, and one could find occasional references to brave Russian soldiers. With the passage of time, such imagery became less widespread, as anticommunist hysteria caused most people in the West to see the average Russian in cartoon fashion—not without some accuracy, but with great simplemindedness—as little more than a wretched victim of tyranny or a supporter of a regime ready to do violence to all democracies. Moreover, there was a tendency to envision most Russians as peasants or heavy-bodied, regimented factory workers. This was not a totally unrealistic stereotype either, given the economic hardship behind the Iron Curtain. And indeed Soviet newspapers and magazines regularly glorified their country's everyday laborers and frequently carried stories about Western farmers and factory workers as well. Then, by the later years of the cold war, portrayals began to soften. The changing attitudes could be seen in mass market fiction. One best-selling detective novel was *Gorky Park* by Martin Cruz Smith (1981; film adaptation 1983), about a hardworking member of the Moscow city police force who is just as ingenious, as full of human foibles, as brave, as frustrated by bureaucracy, and as dedicated to justice as any of his counterparts in the West. A similar indicator was the worldwide best-seller *The Hunt for Red October* by Tom Clancy (1984; film adaptation 1990), which tells the story of a naval officer on a Soviet submarine who defects to the West with his ship and its secret stealth propulsion system, in the hope of preventing the Soviets from being tempted to use the weapon to deliver nuclear missiles.

Imagery related to political and military leaders was also conspicuous. From the Soviet perspective, the iconography was relatively simple. In the early cold war years, Stalin and his successors as rulers of the Kremlin saw the West as decadent, but they also worried that the communist movement might be seduced by its allure. When Nikita Khrushchev visited the United States in 1959, he went out of his way to learn about American consumer culture and material prosperity, and he became angry when his hosts told him he could not visit Disneyland in southern California because of the potential security risk. As the cold war went on, some of the flash of the West made its way into Soviet leaders' conceptions of themselves. By the time of Mikhail Gorbachev, Soviet leaders had adopted Western business styles in their choice of clothing, and they had beautiful, fashionably dressed wives or mistresses.

The development of the Western perspective during the cold war generally mirrored the Eastern process. Western leaders and journalists were struck by the contrast between themselves and Stalin. He was Marshal Stalin, who never wore civilian garb except perhaps when he wanted to look like a peasant, and though dressed in uniform, he seemed more like an abstraction or archetype from Old Russia: a demon out of Russian folklore, or a priest of the Orthodox faith without his robes. Westerners noticed that group portraits of Soviet leaders eerily resembled traditional Russian paintings of groups of religious figures. When, after Stalin, Soviet leaders began appearing in ordinary business clothing, Western reporters were amused. The duo who succeeded Stalin—Nikolai Bulganin as chairman of the Council of Ministers and Khrushchev as first secretary of the Communist

Party—seemed like "portly, waddling, jovial men, in silly hats with up-
turned brims, brightly coloured suits with voluminous jackets billowing
over the paunch, and eighteen-inch trouser bottoms flapping around the
ankles."[53] Truman and Eisenhower and West German chancellor Konrad
Adenauer may not have been fashion plates, but they managed to look pre-
sentable in their double-breasted suits. By the 1960s, John Kennedy, Prime
Minister Harold Macmillan, and West Berlin's mayor (and later West German chancellor) Willy Brandt were dapper in their dress and constantly
asked themselves how they would appear in news photographs and on television. Reagan projected the glamour of the movie star he once had been,
and Prime Minister Margaret Thatcher, though sometimes dowdy, could
also be quite striking in the impression she created for the media. One of
Gorbachev's many assets as a negotiator was that by his time, Soviet political leaders and those in their circle looked and acted like their Western
counterparts. After her first meeting with Gorbachev, who was accompanied by his wife, Margaret Thatcher was pleased to note that Raisa Gorbachev was "often seen in public and was an articulate, highly educated and
attractive woman." She was dressed, Thatcher observed, "in a smart, Western style outfit, a well tailored grey suit with a white stripe—just the sort
I could have worn myself, I thought. She had a philosophy degree and had
indeed been an academic." And, in the ultimate capitalistic compliment,
Thatcher described Mikhail Gorbachev as "a man with whom I could do
business."[54]

An aspect of cold war iconography that changed surprisingly little, however, was the imagery associated with everyone's greatest fear: nuclear annihilation. The iconographic constant of the period was The Bomb. From
the time of Hiroshima and Nagasaki, everyone was familiar with the
vision—obscene, not fully describable, menacing, powerful—of the mushroom cloud, rising first from the atomic bomb and then, in the 1950s, from
the newer, even more powerful hydrogen bomb. This image and its
accompaniments—the flash of light, the enormous rumbling sound, the
wind that swept away all objects, the metal gnarled by intense heat, the
peeling skin of victims of fire and radiation poisoning—were continually
circulated and recirculated by the media and became a permanent fixture
of human perception throughout the cold war, at both the conscious and
subconscious levels. At the same time, however, some of the imagery
around the edges of this central icon did change over time. Air raid shelters
and civil defense drills were common preoccupations early in the cold war,
but the media gave them less coverage in later years, when resorting to
them came to seem pointless. Big military aircraft like the B-29, the B-36,

and the B-47 were regularly seen in newspaper photographs, television broadcasts, and feature films during the early cold war years. But by the late 1960s, as missiles became the preferred means for delivering nuclear "warheads," these were more noticeable in the iconography of the period, eventually fusing, by the late 1980s, with Reagan's imagery of defending against nuclear destruction with "Star Wars," his proposed system of space satellites to guard against an enemy's first strike. And to all this, by Reagan's time, was added the development of chemical and biological weaponry: cheaper, more portable, more easily concealed, shockingly more deadly even than nuclear weaponry—and, oddly, less image-laden, because people seemed to have difficulty visualizing exactly what such warfare would look like.[55]

The other major element in cold war iconography had to do with what actually prevented the war from ever becoming "hot": negotiation. Imagery associated with foreign policy discourse went through two stages. Initially the images related to threat and counterthreat. Eisenhower's secretary of state John Foster Dulles became famous for something the journalists called "brinksmanship," that is, menacing rhetoric accompanying carefully calibrated action designed to make the other side believe that the United States was more than willing to resort to nuclear war unless concessions were forthcoming. Khrushchev practiced a similar form of grand opera, becoming notorious for his use of overheated rhetoric in comments like "We will bury you," and a controlled mixture of feline purring and loud rants at diplomatic conferences, especially when reporters were present. One of the major theaters for the use of threats and counterthreats was the United Nations headquarters in New York City. Here, for example, in 1960, in a meeting of the General Assembly, playing to the TV and newsreel cameras, Khrushchev pounded his shoe on the top of his delegate's desk in feigned anger at the West. That same year, during a meeting of the UN Security Council, the U.S. ambassador to the United Nations, Henry Cabot Lodge Jr., displayed a carving of the seal of the United States removed from the wall of the U.S. embassy in Moscow, antagonistically revealing the tiny microphone that the Russians had planted in the beak of the eagle to eavesdrop on secret discussions.

A second phase of iconography relating to negotiations had to do with what became known as "summitry." This phase overlapped with the threat/counterthreat phase but extended all the way to the end of the cold war as East and West sought to develop methods for more effective dialogue. "Summitry" was essentially the age-old diplomatic device of specially arranged meetings involving heads of state. The term was sometimes used during conferences of the Allies, like those at Casablanca and Yalta, in the Second World War. By 1955, at the Geneva summit, journalistic coverage of such gatherings had become melodramatic. The public hoped that high-level discussions among charismatic personalities would somehow break the pattern of shared nuclear fear. World leaders would travel by airplane from one highly publicized encounter to another, always accompanied by large staffs and numerous reporters, who thrived on leaks of information and briefings that made them feel important. Leaders, too, were affected by the rarefied atmosphere. "The darting microphones, blazing arc lights and clicking cameras encouraged them to reduce intricate issues to simple formulae suitable for a fireside chat on radio, a strong headline for the newspapers, or a stabbing gesture at a globe in a television studio," writes the historian Ann Tusa.[56] The pattern was visible all the way through the cold war, up to and including the last major "summits" of the era, between Reagan and Gorbachev at Geneva in 1985 and Reykjavik in 1986. But by this time the two leaders were able to talk realistically and to bring about lasting changes that helped to end the decades-long standoff.

Developing Nations Assert Themselves

Throughout the forty-five years of the cold war, the United States and the Soviet Union were the dominant players in international communications. But other countries, never inactive, pursued their interests within the larger framework, and by the last decade of the period they were competing with the two most powerful nations in efforts to influence world audiences.

That such a turn of affairs would eventually come about had been accepted in principle as early as 1946, when UNESCO, in the preamble of its founding charter, endorsed "the unrestricted pursuit of objective truth" and "the free exchange of ideas and knowledge." As decolonization occurred in the 1950s, with Britain's loss of possessions from Kenya to Malaya, and the French withdrawal from Algeria and Southeast Asia, newly independent nations sought to increase not only their political and economic power but also their access to the communications technologies that had been developed and were still dominated by the West and the Soviet Union. Thus in 1956 Nasser promoted Egyptian nationalism via radio through the Voice of the Arabs network. In 1955, in a major declaration of assertiveness, twenty-nine developing nations in Africa and Asia formed the Non-Aligned Movement (NAM) at the Bandung Conference in Indonesia. A number of Latin American countries later joined. The NAM focused chiefly on economic and political independence; but its members knew that growth in these sectors would not be possible without modernized structures of mass media, and they also wanted to defend themselves against being smothered by U.S. and Soviet ideologies. With these goals in mind, developing nations began to expand their own communications capacities. This was a slow process. Fledgling countries had to buy much of their equipment from the two great power blocs, had to learn how to use the equipment and organize its use, and had to wean their home audiences away from providers like the BBC World Service, foreign newspapers and magazines, and dominant wire services such as Tass, Agence France Presse, and in America the Associated Press.

Developing nations pursued many strategies to achieve maturation. Press alliances served consortia of developing nations, including the Inter Press Service, established in Latin America in the 1960s; the Non-Aligned News Agency Pool, founded in 1975 to assist press services in more than one hundred countries; the Caribbean News Agency, which began in 1976; and the Pan-African News Agency, founded in 1979 by the Organisation of African Union. Developing nations also introduced their own television networks. These at first used traditional broadcast techniques but soon developed satellite capacities. For example, Indonesia began its satellite service in 1976, and the Arab League created Arabsat, which launched its first satellite in 1985.

Inspired by achievements of this kind, developing nations began to speak of a "New World Information and Communication Order" (NWICO), or in shortened usage, a "New World Information Order." Calls to make international communications more pluralistic had been coming from UNESCO planners since the early 1970s. Additionally, a conference of nonaligned nations in Tunis in 1976 called for a "decolonization of information." In 1980 a much-publicized UN working group, the MacBride Commission, recommended a "mighty cooperative effort" to increase Third World access to basic communications resources like the telephone, postal services, printing presses, and TV sets. And it was evident by this time that developing nations were indeed making progress toward their goal of establishing a new world information order. On the one hand, in 1980 ten North American and European countries possessed 80 percent of the world's telephones, and in Japan, where Western aid had created a thriving economy, Tokyo alone had more telephones than all of Africa. On the other hand, in 1979, operating from Paris, the Ayatollah Khomeini successfully overthrew the shah of Iran by, among other tactics, smuggling audiocassette recordings of his speeches into the country for wide circulation.[57]

In a somewhat ambiguous position between the United States and the Soviet Union on one side and newer developing nations on the other stood the People's Republic of China. The PRC drew upon resources that had evolved from the victory over the Nationalists in 1949 supporting its own broadcasting services and an extensive propaganda apparatus. The very powerful competitor to Western and Soviet wire services, the China News Service, was established by the People's Republic in 1952. Even older was the Xinhua News Agency, which dated from 1931 and was originally named the Red China News Agency. In 1958 the PRC established China Central Television.

In the 1950s and 1960s Mao used these networks of mass communication belligerently, focusing on a message of aggressive export of revolution to other countries. This caused unease not just in the West but even in the Soviet Union and among nations of the nonaligned movement, because Mao went so far as to support very autocratic groups like the genocidal Khmer Rouge regime in Cambodia. After succeeding Mao, Deng Xiaoping attempted to improve China's reputation by using relatively less force and softer rhetoric. But he followed the same pattern of mistrust of compromise in the war China pursued against Vietnam in 1974. And even after Deng passed from power in 1994, the People's Republic continued to make threats against Taiwan and wildly asserted that it possessed legal control of the entire South China Sea.

The West and the Soviet Union responded to such developments mostly with alarm. The two blocs reflexively feared the loss of influence. At this time they could not clearly foresee how opportunities to sell their communications technology and expertise to developing nations might in fact be used to their advantage. Between Western nations and developing nations there was also a conflict of values with respect to the role of news. Western Europeans and Americans were inheritors of a tradition that saw journalism as not simply a tool of propaganda but also a way of keeping politicians honest, a constitutionally necessary gadfly. Developing nations, by contrast, viewed talk about the free flow of information as a way to mask domination by the rich. They preferred to think of mass communication as a means for hastening the growth of their nations and believed that news reporting and indeed all cultural discourse should subordinate itself to such a goal even if that involved censorship. As the cold war approached its end, the increasing influence of developing nations on international communications was one indicator that the bipolar configuration of power which had existed since 1945 was about to become multipolar.

New Technologies Appear

Several highly influential technologies hastened the transition from a bipolar to a multipolar distribution of power in the realm of international mass communications, as the computer, satellite transmission, the World Wide Web, and the Internet revolutionized society. The computer had its origins in diverse sources, from the ancient abacus to the nineteenth-century "calculating machine" of the Englishman Charles Babbage, punch-card machines developed in the 1890s, research at MIT in the 1920s by Vannevar Bush, and the "Enigma" codebreaking machine developed in Britain in the Second World War by the mathematician Alan Turing. In the 1950s, private companies like Remington-Rand (which pioneered the Univac system) and IBM (International Business Machines) worked with the U.S. government to develop computers controlled by binary electrical signals that could process both mathematical and verbal information through elaborate systems of code (software). Computers were soon adapted to many military and scientific uses, and highly effective marketing, particularly by IBM and other companies such as Hewlett-Packard and, later, Wang, resulted in a rapidly expanding consumer market, culminating in enormous sales of small, easy-to-use Apple computers in the 1980s, with their reliance on graphic interfaces and the hand-directed command device that quickly came to be known as the "mouse." The 1980s also saw the birth of "laptop" or "notebook" computers that were easy to carry from place to place and could be powered by a battery or plugged into the nearest available electrical outlet. Computers made it much easier for organizations and individuals to store, categorize, retrieve, and package large amounts of information. They also facilitated the exchange of information among computer users, initially as large computers were connected via telephone lines, and then as distributional capacity expanded, first through the use of portable discs, and then directly from computer to computer as satellite transmission became possible.

Computers grew in importance during the years when satellite communications were developing. In 1957 the Soviet Union launched *Sputnik*, the first earth-orbiting satellite, causing great anxiety in the United States. The Americans followed with *Explorer 1* in 1958 and then later the same year launched *Score*, the first satellite to carry an explicit propaganda message: a Christmas greeting from President Eisenhower expressing America's wish for world peace. In 1962 the United States launched its first communications satellite, *Telstar*. During the 1960s, the United States developed Intelsat and the USSR established Intersputnik, the first international satellite consortia. Cost considerations slowed further development until the 1970s, when refinements in technology and market opportunities made it possible for satellites to become important international conduits for telephone traffic and news transmission. In the same decade, cable news providers like CNN shifted from reliance on landlines to the use of satellites, while new companies like Sky News also appeared. During the 1990s many developing countries launched their own satellites to establish communications independence from the networks controlled by the United States, the USSR, and western Europe.

An important indicator of the influence of satellite communication on foreign relations came in 1989 with the mass demonstrations against political regimentation in Tiananmen Square in Beijing. Organizers timed the protests in part to take advantage of news coverage of the visit of Mikhail Gorbachev to the People's Republic that year. Television images of the demonstrations—notably the iconic episode of a single protester bravely facing down a tank—swiftly made their way around the world via satellite transmissions. For the ruling elite of the People's Republic, the Tiananmen Square experience was sobering. It set off internal discussions. By the late 1990s China was making greater efforts to win international approval, viewing this as an asset in the quest for world power. Using satellite technology, the Chinese increased their overseas radio and television programming, emphasizing news and entertainment that portrayed a soft, favorable image of their country.

The effects of computers and satellite transmissions were intensified by the emergence of yet another new technology. The beginning of the Internet is traceable to 1969, when the U.S. Department of Defense created its Advanced Research Projects Agency Network (ARPANET) to link computer activity at key military and civilian branches of the government as a safeguard against possible Soviet strikes. ARPANET split into military and civilian divisions in 1983, with the latter providing an infrastructure for linkage among American universities and scientific research institutes. Use of the Internet increased enormously in 1989 with the creation of the World Wide Web, a network of large-capacity computers (servers) that could interact extensively (interface) with one another and, through common codes (interface protocols), enable any individual to establish a personal address and a "home page" that could be a locus of conversation with thousands of other Web users all over the world, thanks to the possibilities for satellite transmission of signals that had expanded so greatly since the beginnings of the space programs in the 1960s. By 1992 the World Wide Web had 3 million users. There would be over 1 billion unique Web pages by the end of the twentieth century.[58]

7 MASS COMMUNICATION BECOMES MULTIPOLAR
1991 and After

WITH THE ENDING of the cold war, tensions dating back to 1945 lessened. Simultaneously, as many observers have noted, the restructuring of international relationships into a multipolar pattern presented new challenges. In the realm of mass communication, the main problem for the United States involved adjusting to the fact that the disappearance of the Soviet Union did not translate into worldwide American hegemony. America's resources of mass communication were vast. But by the 1990s, many countries had developed their media, others were working energetically to do so, and nongovernmental organizations, both political and economic, were entering the communications picture. In some ways, the new configuration in world communications resembled the pluralistic environment of the 1920s and 1930s. America could not assume that it would dominate world communications. Indeed in the governmental realm, the United States soon appeared to be making serious errors in its use of mass communication that weakened its standing in the world, while quasi-governmental and private-sector actors attempted to fill the void.

Wars Are Packaged

If President Reagan received the credit for ending the cold war, this was in part because his successor, George H. W. Bush, was much less competent in the use of mass communication. As a political favor, Bush appointed an old friend, Bruce Gelb, to be director of the USIA; Gelb proved an ineffective advocate. The president was seen as cavalier in his treatment of many of America's allies and, when accused of lacking an overall plan in foreign policy, dismissed this criticism as "the vision thing"—a phrase given wide circulation by the media. When Bush fainted from exhaustion during a state dinner in Japan, the intense press coverage left the impression that he might no longer be fit to hold office.

The exception to this media pattern was Bush's conduct in the Persian Gulf War. Led by the dictator Saddam Hussein, Iraq attacked Kuwait in 1991. President Bush went to the United Nations and formed a coalition of states that launched a counterattack, receiving high praise for his skill in gathering allies and encouraging thoughtful debate in Congress, which was extensively covered by the media. Bush communicated effectively with journalists and used the USIA to explain his pursuit of the conflict to nations abroad.

The Gulf War brought major changes in the relation between war and mass communication as the new technologies that had begun to develop in earlier years started to exert broad influence. One such change was the speed and freedom with which print reporters in war zones were able to transmit their stories. Earlier they had used landline telephones or short-wave radio for instantaneous filing. These methods were cumbersome. Getting to a land phone or a radio was not always easy. Moreover, access to phone lines could be denied, and radio transmissions could be jammed. With the arrival of the Internet, however, filing stories became easier. Working with a laptop computer, the small, easily portable phones that were by now available, and a satellite hookup, a reporter could file a story almost anywhere and at any time. After being edited at the home office, the story could be quickly integrated by computer into the paper's layout and distributed in hard copy and on the World Wide Web.

The Internet and the Web also expanded the capacities of television news coverage. The Gulf War was notable for the 24/7 coverage, presented live by CNN. By this time CNN was no longer cable-dependent; instead it made extensive use of satellite transmissions from combat areas, turning on-the-scene correspondents like Peter Arnett and Christiane Amanpour into media stars.[1]

The sheer amount of information made available by the media during the Gulf War was unprecedented. Whether there was any depth to the coverage is, however, debatable. The military gave journalists nearly open access to some areas of the conflict but subtly directed them away from others. For example, CNN reporters were allowed to remain in Baghdad while missiles were falling, and to report from Jerusalem when it was under bombardment. Similarly, at press briefings the military provided arresting videotapes, taken from cockpit-mounted TV cameras, which showed American missiles being launched from fighter planes and precisely obliterating their targets on the ground thousands of feet below. But television news reporters were kept away from the gory slaughter of Iraqi troops retreating from Kuwait and southern Iraq. The amplitude and immediacy of the coverage fed the illusion that the "real war" was being reported, when in fact audiences were getting a carefully skewed version.

During the Gulf War there was a revival of U.S. military use of propaganda directed specifically at enemy combatants. Encouragement to renew attention to psychological operations had begun under President Reagan. In the Gulf War, the general in command, Norman Schwarzkopf, openly declared that PSYOPS would be a critical factor. American forces used white propaganda extensively, through radio, leaflets, and loudspeakers. Black propaganda took place via clandestine radio stations that appeared to be operated by discontented factions of Iraqis advocating an end to combat and the overthrow of Saddam Hussein.

President Bush also oversaw two military operations that did not involve full-scale war but closely resembled it. Toward the end of the Gulf War, in response to American propaganda urging them to rebel, the Kurds in northern Iraq took up armed resistance against Saddam Hussein and were soon in danger of being slaughtered by his troops. In April 1991 the United States began a massive relief effort, extensively reported by the media, to provide protection and supplies to the Kurds. In December 1992 attention turned to the east of Africa. In response to extensive news coverage of Somalia, which was being devastated by civil war and famine, U.S. troops intervened with the hope of ending the violence and suffering. But they were soon trapped and, in 1993, decided to retreat. The media covered both stories dramatically.

During the Somalia crisis there was widespread international speculation about the possible influence of something called the "CNN effect," that is, potential distortion of the foreign policy process due to the relentless drumbeat of coverage of an international event arousing the sympathies of mass audiences. Television now clearly possessed the capacity to bring unsettling images of local wars, famines, and the slaughter of innocents into billions of homes simultaneously. Somewhat in the manner of communications pressures on the eve of the First World War, coverage of this kind impelled national leaders to do something, anything, to quiet the crowd quickly. Governmental decision makers were convinced for the most part that the "CNN effect" was real and was institutionalizing haste. But many researchers argued that the pressures of television were no greater than those created by the media in earlier eras and that numerous variables came into play. Key factors included the varied responses of different segments of audiences, the slant of the verbal content accompanying images, whether an audience personally identified with the culture of the population being depicted, the amount of attention drawn to a crisis by figures such as entertainers and heads of charities, competition from other news stories receiving media attention at the same time, and a political or military leader's ability to exploit the media as a source of information and a tool of influence.[2]

Bill Clinton succeeded Bush as president in 1993. In September 1994, in response to a breakdown during the previous year of order in Haiti and the flight of refugees to the United States, Clinton sent U.S. troops to the country and installed a civilian regime. Before, during, and after invasion, the U.S. military conducted psychological operations, a further confirmation of the large role such activities were assuming at the Pentagon.

In 1994 Clinton had to decide how to respond to reports from Rwanda, where a civil war accompanied by genocide was in progress. Influenced by the Somalia experience and worried about overextending U.S. resources, he chose not to intervene. He continued this policy during the humanitarian crisis in Zaire in 1996. The president encountered severe criticism for inattention to Africa and offered no convincing rebuttals. He later expressed extreme remorse for not intervening.

Problems in Yugoslavia dating from 1992 presented a major challenge. After the fall of the Soviet Union, Yugoslavia began to break up into its ethnic components, and the regions fought among themselves. Atrocities took place as old racial hatreds revived. The crisis and the dramatic reporting of it confronted the United States with yet another question of whether to intervene.

Beginning while Bush was still in office, intensive media coverage of war in the Bosnian region of the former Yugoslavia carried over into Clinton's presidency. Bush did not believe that U.S. interests were sufficiently affected by the war to send in troops, and Clinton at first agreed. Media coverage of the killing and suffering in Bosnia continued, and became a factor in the change in thinking that took place within the Clinton administration. Influenced by French diplomats working behind the scenes, by internal memos from Secretary of State Warren Christopher, and by the opinions of Madeleine Albright, then U.S. ambassador to the United Nations, Clinton decided that military intervention in Bosnia was advisable. Planning for such action was already in progress when, in February 1994 in Sarajevo, the Bosnian capital, sixty people were killed and almost two hundred others severely injured by a mortar shell which exploded in the central marketplace. Bosnians loyal to neighboring Serbia were thought to be responsible. Indicative of the growing proliferation of video equipment and its effects on the news process, a witness caught the events in the marketplace on videotape, which was shown by media all over the world. The outrage this caused boosted support for the Clinton administration's new policy of intervention. The media also played a role when Ambassador Albright appeared on television at the UN immediately after the "marketplace massacre" to argue the case for the administration's new policy. The media by themselves did not cause the change in Clinton's policy, but they were a seemingly inextricable part of the process.[3]

The presence of television during the Yugoslav conflict greatly increased the medium's dominance over other media in the coverage of military activity. It also had the paradoxical effect of making the war both more and less real to viewers. On the one hand, images of death and destruction, victory and defeat, strategic decision making, and legislative debate could all be viewed as they were happening, in an almost intimate manner. On the other hand, the opportunity to feel as if one were part of the action, to enjoy the suspense and yet know that one's own life was not at risk, created an appetite for war as media drama, along with a habit of pretending that the violence of war was not real.

What had become apparent by the time of the Yugoslav conflict was the growing tendency of television viewers to regard war as an electronic game. Increasingly the images of war appeared on TV screens in formats like those found on computer screens. To increase viewers' understanding while also feeding their appetite for excitement, television packaged real conflicts as phenomena similar to the war games one could purchase for recreation. This unreality became even more pronounced as military organizations expanded their use of computer-based techniques such as sighting targets through global satellite positioning, enhancing night vision, and directing bombs and missiles by means of heat-seeking devices. On their television screens, viewers were able to watch all of these devices in actual use. Now, in the era of cyber war, there were two barriers insulating people from the reality of pain, maiming, terror, and death. Those who fired the missiles and dropped the bombs were no longer in face-to-face combat with the people being killed. And those who viewed it all on television or on their computer screens were yet another step further removed.[4]

The Yugoslav conflict revealed that military forces around the world were becoming increasingly interested in using their psychological operations units in support of humanitarian activities, whether by military or nongovernmental groups. In 1995, after the fall of Srebrenica and the crafting of the Dayton peace agreement, American PSYOPS personnel joined the international Implementation Force in civil reconstruction operations, seeking to counter the effects of hate propaganda. The PSYOPS personnel began regular radio and television broadcasts of news about reconstruction; published a dual-language newspaper, *Herald of Peace*, which attained a circulation of 100,000 in Bosnia; distributed peace-oriented coloring books for children; circulated information about land mines; and produced posters advising local inhabitants about official sources of protection against harassment. These activities prompted extensive dialogue among military personnel, civilian planners, and decision makers in publications like *British Army Review*, *Jane's International Defence Review*, and *National Guard* magazine regarding the long-term potential of PSYOPS as a tool for peacemaking. At that time a movement began to grow among military figures in support of large-scale inclusion of psychological operations in the work of United Nations peacekeeping forces. Theorists envisioned a future in which PSYOPS personnel would work in cooperation with peace-oriented journalism and the publicized efforts of nongovernmental organizations focused on refugee relief and international provision of medical care.[5]

President Clinton generally raised the reputation of America abroad—a view of the United States as, in Madeline Albright's frequently used words, "the indispensable nation." In spite of the moral scandal during his presidency, related to media disclosure of an adulterous affair with one of his assistants, Monica Lewinsky, and the subsequent impeachment process, Clinton remained in high favor overseas. But it was during Clinton's presidency that funding for public diplomacy functions at the Department of State was severely cut, in the mistaken belief that such activity was less necessary with the ending of the cold war. Clinton followed the pattern of George H. W. Bush by appointing an old friend, Joseph Duffey, to head the USIA. Duffey was an unimpressive leader. This did not much concern Clinton; he was a masterly politician who relied on his own skills to sway international opinion. During the Lewinsky scandal, in any case, he had little time to spare. By the time Clinton became president, because of the influence of political conservatives in Congress and elsewhere in power who mistrusted internationalist activities, the United States had gone several years without paying its dues to the United Nations. Clinton made a deal with one of the most powerful conservative legislators, Senator Jesse Helms, who agreed to release funds to pay the dues, in exchange for which Clinton ended the status of the USIA as an independent agency, subsuming it under the State Department in 1999.[6]

Ironically, Clinton's cutbacks in diplomatic propaganda occurred during the same period when military and private-sector analysts were advocating even greater attention to the strategic use of information. In the 1990s, war planners at the Pentagon were manifesting a growing interest in concepts like "information war," "cyber war," "neuro-cortical warfare," and "digitizing the battlefield." These terms were amorphous and faddish. But they did reveal emerging trends in military thinking. In some cases the planners were doing little more than advocating renewed, increased attention to the tactical potential of propaganda directed at the frame of mind of enemy combatants on the battlefield and civilians in enemy nations. Planners were intrigued by the possibility of using the growing power of tools such as computers and satellites for this time-honored purpose. The Pentagon was also interested in methods of sending signals that would disable an enemy's software. This was an area of strategy that seemed to combine the tangible and intangible aspects of information warfare: destroying an enemy's equipment while simultaneously sowing confusion. In other cases, military planners did not talk about intangibles at all but focused on the use of electronic and physics-based devices strictly as military hardware, that is, as new forms of physical weaponry. This resulted in many expensive studies, for example, on using electronic pulses and laser beams transmitted from satellites to destroy an enemy's material resources and employing laser beams to neutralize or obliterate an enemy combatant's nervous system.[7]

Continuing civilian interest in the relationship between war and mass communication was evident in the writings of Alvin and Heidi Toffler. Alvin Toffler had begun his career as a journalist for *Fortune* magazine. By the 1990s, through several best-selling books and the activities of their consulting firm, he and his wife had become highly influential, especially in conservative business circles. Their clients included not only Mikhail Gorbachev but also Presidents Nixon, Ford, and Reagan, and Newt Gingrich, the influential Republican majority leader of the U.S. House of Representatives. The Tofflers were less confrontational than the antiauthoritarian theorists of the 1960s, but they still cautioned against overlooking the morally ambiguous influence of media. Beginning in the 1970s, in *Future Shock* and other books they posited the existence of three successive "waves," based on the most important activities of production in a society, as the keys to historical development. Oddly, the economic determinism of their approach echoed the writings of Karl Marx. In any case, in the first wave described by the Tofflers, societies are organized around agricultural production, in the second around factory-based industry, and in the third around knowledge-based industry. Tensions occur as the waves overlap, and the two earlier kinds of societies continue to exist in backwater regions of the world. But increasingly the "Third Wave" is creating a society in which the use and production of information leads to new social structures, personal interactions, forms of business organization, strategies of education, ways of creating and obtaining wealth, and techniques for making war and seeking peace that are much less physical. They maintained that this emerging Third Wave society must develop ways of using information benignly. The influence of television during the Vietnam War and the emergence of the computer as a tool of combat were for the Tofflers confirmations of the changes that would challenge analysts to re-imagine terms like "propaganda" and "information war," integrating ideas about information into every aspect of decision making.[8]

Another theorist of communication who became influential during the 1990s was Joseph Nye Jr., a member of the faculty at Harvard's Kennedy School of Government. In his book *Bound to Lead: The Changing Nature of American Power*, published in 1990, Nye introduced the concept of "soft power" to call attention to the fact that America was hampering its ability to be a leader in the world by failing to understand that it was the strongest nation not only in military and economic power but also in a third, nonmaterial dimension that could not be ignored in its quest for success in international relations. This was the ability to get other nations to do what one wanted without resorting to payment, economic sanctions, or physical force. "Soft power," in Nye's formulation, was based on attraction, not coercion. It emerged from a nation's culture, political ideals, and thoughtfulness in the formulation of policies. America's soft power could be debased if the nation's leaders were arrogant, or if the only expressions of American values projected abroad were products like Coca-Cola, fancy cars, and crime movies. But the nation's ability to win allies and to operate in the world would be enhanced if it made use of the attractive potential of the best expressions of American values, as in Franklin Roosevelt's articulation of the Four Freedoms during the Second World War; the respect for individuality embodied in the Bill of Rights; the international respect earned by great American writers, musicians, and visual artists; and U.S. support for education in numerous countries. In some ways Nye's ideas were simply reiterations of principles articulated by others who had studied the connection between mass communication and international relations over the previous century. But he brought added impact to the discussion because of his skill as a writer and speaker, his mastery of the terminology and research literature in the field of political science, and his ability to bolster his arguments with case material gained from the practical experience he had accumulated during periods of high-level government service in Washington, D.C. The term "soft power" startled many policymakers and theorists into realizing that they were excessively materialistic and culturally tone-deaf. Nye augmented the effectiveness of his argument by stating that "hard power" (that is, military and economic weaponry) plus "soft power" (that is, culturally based persuasion) was "smart power." By the end of the 1990s, Nye's terminology had become highly influential in public discourse.[9]

9/11 Confirms Multipolarity

In 2001 George W. Bush, the son of George H. W. Bush, succeeded Bill Clinton as president. America's prestige in 2001, in the eyes of the world, was at one of its all-time highs, increasing the nation's ability to project influence in a period when strategic thinking about "soft power" was becoming an increasingly important element of foreign policy. The United States had prevailed in the cold war and was generally perceived as having acted wisely and responsibly during the Gulf War, the Balkan crisis, and other recent military episodes. There was frequent criticism, but it was outweighed by praise.

Much changed, however, on September 11, 2001, when hijackers used passenger planes to destroy a wing of the Pentagon and the two towers of the World Trade Center in New York City. Reports of the disaster, including many still photographs, sound recordings, and videotapes supplied by amateurs at the scene, made their way around the world in minutes. It soon became clear that the perpetrators were operatives from the Middle East tied to the Taliban faction in Afghanistan and the Islamic fundamentalist al-Qaeda organization led by Osama bin Laden, who was seeking to neutralize Western influence worldwide by the use of terrorism. The attacks showed how very much had been learned about propaganda in developing regions of the world, which for several decades had been eager to obtain greater access to Western-dominated networks of international communication.[10] The Pentagon and the World Trade Center were symbols, in the eyes of many people, of Western and capitalist oppression. Destroying them was an evil but brilliant exploitation of the power of mass communication. Although the terrorists did not officially represent any nation-state, analysts worried that 9/11 might become as tragically significant as the assassination of Archduke Franz Ferdinand by terrorists in 1914, which had sparked the terrible sequence of wars in the twentieth century.

In the days immediately after 9/11 there was a massive wave of sympathy for the United States. The queen of England bestowed an honorary knighthood on the mayor of New York City. Reflecting the opinions of billions of people, the French newspaper Le Monde, not always a friend of the United States, commented, "We are all Americans now." In Iran, a million people marched in the streets of Tehran to express support for the United States.

George W. Bush initially helped the United States earn additional respect. Favorable images circulated around the world of the president speaking personally with firemen at the World Trade Center, conferring in Hollywood with leaders of the movie and television industries about the importance of projecting a better image of America abroad, visiting American mosques to make clear his respect for Muslims, and delivering an emergency address in Congress that was widely regarded as eloquent, honest, and intelligent. When the United States then quickly routed the Taliban in Afghanistan, where the terrorists had most of their bases, and asked other nations to help track down terrorists, criticism both at home and abroad was minimal.

Soon, however, the White House began to make very serious errors in its use of mass communication related to foreign policy. The miscalculations fell into two categories. The first involved leading the nation into a war in Iraq on the basis of inaccurate information and manipulation of public opinion, with grave implications for the responsible use of the power to make war delineated in the U.S. Constitution. The second category of errors emerged once the war in Iraq began, as the administration's mismanagement of international communication regarding the conflict contributed to a rapid decline in America's reputation that made it much more difficult for the nation to operate effectively on the world scene.

The White House Sells War

During the Gulf War of 1991, the elder President Bush and his advisers decided not to exploit fully the advantages that military victory over Saddam Hussein gave them. After gaining control of the southern portion of Iraq, U.S. forces could have gone all the way north to Baghdad, hunted down Saddam Hussein, and established a colony or client state with a new government more dedicated to liberal constitutional principles. But the administration chose instead to stay put in the south and maintain a nominal force that would use international monitoring, a "no-fly zone," and other means to prevent Saddam from again encroaching on the sovereignty of neighboring states. Bush did not want to expend additional lives and treasure to replace the dictator with a new, artificially democratic regime that probably would have disintegrated within a few years as Iraq's political and religious factions squabbled among themselves and eventually engaged in a bloody civil war that might destabilize the entire Middle East.

Many conservatives in the Republican Party were displeased by his course of action and continued to look for a way to remove Saddam. They believed that Iraq was indeed fertile ground for planting a regime on the

Western model. They also believed that such a government would inspire other countries in the Middle East to become more democratic, thereby improving chances for overall peace in the region and increased security for Israel. The most extreme of the conservative strategists were so convinced of the rightness of this view of the Middle East that they were willing to take the United States into a renewed war in Iraq even if a majority of the American people did not endorse such action.

After the attack on the World Trade Center and the Pentagon in 2001 and broad support for America's subsequent invasion of Afghanistan, right-wing Republicans believed that the time was now opportune for toppling Saddam. Their conclusion was in many ways a priori. The grandiosity of their theories seemed to provide them with sufficient reassurance for starting another war. But they also sought justification on the basis of several claims that seemed to them supported by intelligence available from the CIA, the Pentagon, and groups of Iraqi refugees. These were that Iraq was building a nuclear weapon, that Iraq possessed mobile biological and chemical laboratories that were developing warfare capability, that Iraq had close ties to the al-Qaeda terrorists who had engineered the World Trade Center attack, and that pro-democracy factions secretly operating within Iraq would rise up to overthrow Saddam and help create the new democracy once U.S. forces attacked. The evidence for all these assertions was highly questionable. For example, scientific experts in several countries undermined a claim that Iraq was buying special aluminum tubes from Niger to use for uranium enrichment by showing that the tubes were much better suited for constructing artillery rockets. Similarly, classified reports produced by the Pentagon and the U.S. Defense Intelligence Agency said that most of Iraq's chemical warfare weapons had been destroyed in 1991 and there was no conclusive evidence that Saddam was producing or stockpiling new ones. Assertions of close ties between Saddam and al-Qaeda were also highly debatable. They proved to be based on rumors and intelligence provided by various shady international characters who wanted to curry favor with the Americans or were being pressured by interrogators.

The president and his advisers chose to discount such doubts. By late fall of 2001 they were preparing to move the United States into war in Iraq. Toward this end they began pursuing a several-pronged strategy. One element, directed at American public opinion, involved classic public relations techniques. Through the use of focus groups, market research, and media analysis, PR organizations hired by the White House developed carefully crafted messages to be directed at target audiences through third-party entities like the Committee for the Liberation of Iraq, the Middle East

Forum, and the Washington Institute for Near East Policy. Eminent figures associated with the administration, such as the journalist William Kristol, former UN ambassador Jeane Kirkpatrick, former CIA director James Woolsey, and the longtime defense intellectual Richard Perle gave alarmist speeches on the banquet circuit and appeared on radio and television. Major figures from the administration did their part. Around the time of the first anniversary of 9/11, national security adviser Condoleeza Rice appeared on a TV talk show to dramatize Iraq's nuclear capability, commenting: "There will always be some uncertainty about how quickly [Saddam] can acquire nuclear weapons. But we don't want the smoking gun to be a mushroom cloud." Also appearing on TV, Defense Secretary Donald Rumsfeld said: "Imagine a September eleventh with weapons of mass destruction. It's not three thousand—it's tens of thousands of innocent men, women and children."[11]

Another audience the Bush administration targeted was the United Nations, with the goal of obtaining an official resolution—eventually provided—endorsing military action against Iraq. Much of this activity took place through diplomatic channels behind the scenes, both at UN headquarters and in foreign capitals, as the United States sought to garner potential allies for a multinational invasion force. But it also became very public in February 2002, when Secretary of State Colin Powell made the administration's case before the UN Security Council. Although he did not deliver all of the remarks the White House had written for him—he thought much of the prepared speech was an exaggeration—Powell did claim there was a "potentially sinister nexus between Iraq and the Al Qaeda terrorist network, a nexus that combines classic terrorist organizations and modern methods of murder."[12]

The other challenge to the administration was the U.S. Constitution, which stipulates that only Congress can declare war. The younger President Bush knew that his father had gone to Congress for endorsement of the Gulf War in 1991. And he hoped that even if he could not get a full declaration of war, he might still obtain a favorable vote for a congressional resolution supporting emergency action. The White House therefore sent its parade of message carriers to Capitol Hill. Rice, Rumsfeld, and other administration representatives all appeared repeatedly before the relevant committees. At first they encountered obstacles. In 2002, for example, CIA director George Tenet faced aggressively skeptical questioning from two Democratic senators, Bob Graham of Florida and Dick Durbin of Illinois, when he testified before the Senate Intelligence Committee, which was at that time controlled by Democrats. But opposition of this kind weakened in 2003 when Republicans gained a majority in the Senate. Meanwhile, the president himself was exerting rhetorical pressure. In October 2002, in a much-publicized speech in Cincinnati, one of many given in the same vein, Bush laid out the administration's case for going to war and urged Congress to approve the resolution that was by now pending. This and all the other rhetorical volleys being fired from the White House had their intended effect. Bush got his war resolution from Congress in October. Then in March 2003, after elaborate preparation, the United States and a small number of allied forces attacked Iraq, overran the country, and installed a provisional government in late April.[13]

America Loses Face

As soon as the United States began its march toward war in Iraq, and then even more so as that war proceeded, it increasingly squandered the goodwill it had accumulated immediately after 9/11. This caused a freefall in its competence in information management at a time when "soft power" had come to be recognized, after more than a century of experience, as an essential element in handling international crises and determining comparative influence among nations. The increasing difficulty the United States faced in winning the war in Iraq probably would have led to a loss of prestige in any case. But its incompetence in the area of "soft power" exacerbated rather than ameliorated the difficulty of meeting international challenges. "We've got to do a better job of making our case," President Bush told reporters shortly after the 9/11 attacks.[14] This was obvious. The comment would prove to be a tragically, unconsciously ironic statement, as the Bush administration soon began to reveal enormous ineptitude in its discourse related to 9/11.

Immediately after the attacks, while seeking support for the USA Patriot Act, which tightened domestic national security procedures, the White House spoke in broad-brush terms about vast overseas conspiracies, conveying the suggestion that all foreigners were somehow involved. Lapsing into stereotypes drawn from his home state of Texas, the President cast Osama bin Laden as an outlaw from the American Wild West who was "wanted dead or alive." His cowboy swagger made foreign leaders wonder how sophisticated the president was in his understanding of world affairs. Many observers also objected when the White House began speaking of a "crusade"—apparently not realizing the medieval images it thus evoked and the ways in which such rhetoric played to Western stereotypes of Arabs—and advocating a "war on terror" as the proper response to the problems presented by 9/11.[15] Critics noted that an alternative and more sophisticated approach would have been to speak in terms of an international police action, which would have conveyed an awareness that the response to terrorists was not likely to have a neat beginning, middle, and end, but ought to be fought like a serious epidemic of crime appearing simultaneously in many neighborhoods, which cannot be eradicated simply by capturing one leader. "Terror" is a state of mind—and in this case it was a condition of the mass mind. But "terror" is not an action, let alone a nation-state or a group of people. How the conspicuously material instruments of a military machine could be used to battle a form of consciousness was not made clear. The president sometimes spoke of battling "terror*ism*" but this was also a vague idea as propounded. The term "terrorism" might have had some usefulness if carefully defined, as the term "communism" sometimes had been during the cold war, when the need to counter an ideology and a system of politics and economics was often discussed. Calling for a war against "terror*ists*" might have made sense as well. But the president did not offer clear criteria for identifying terrorists or defining their legal standing. Or a guiding statement could have been issued to the effect that the military was going to shift into propaganda mode and do battle against ideas in conscious acknowledgment of the growing importance of "soft power." But neither was this clarification offered.

The White House did additional damage by the manner in which it pursued its quest for international support for an invasion of Iraq as a response to the threat of terrorism. Not only within America but also abroad, the president had great difficulty winning adherents for such a war. In all the countries invited to join the United States as allies, there were great divisions of political opinion. The administration made the problem worse with its divisive rhetoric at the United Nations. National security adviser Condoleeza Rice further antagonized other nations by asserting a new foreign policy doctrine: that the United States reserved the right to launch wars against other countries merely on the basis of secret intelligence which might suggest that those countries were preparing a surprise attack. America's go-it-alone rhetoric added to the burden of proof placed on Secretary of State Powell when he went before the UN to offer evidence that Saddam Hussein possessed and was preparing to use weapons of mass destruction against his enemies, including the United States and Israel. It was the secretary's immense personal prestige, not any strong belief in the quality of the evidence presented or any broad agreement that invading Iraq would solve long-term problems, that was the key factor leading to a resolution in favor of the invasion.

When U.S. and coalition forces swept through Iraq and drove Saddam from power, foreign observers were just as mesmerized by U.S. military efficiency as they had been in the case of Afghanistan. The general respect earned by this physical mastery was symbolically undercut, however. By immediately raising the American flag in Iraq, the United States created suspicion that its goals were imperialistic. This damage could not be undone even though the Americans eventually took down the flags. The United States also looked culturally insensitive in failing to secure and protect the museum in Baghdad that contained irreplaceable artifacts dating back to ancient times; this suggested that protection of the world's common heritage was not part of America's conception of itself. An even greater error was the president's decision, once Iraq was overrun, to put on a fighter pilot's flight suit, land on the deck of a U.S. aircraft carrier a few miles off the coast of San Diego, and proclaim "Mission Accomplished." This media stunt may have increased the president's support among conservative voters in the United States. On the world stage, however, it reinforced the belief that he viewed international affairs through the eyes of an unreflective, cocksure Texas gunslinger. In the months that followed, as suicide bombers and guerrilla fighters prevented America and its allies from stabilizing Iraq, the image of Bush in the flight suit became an embarrassment.

Reporters Lose Their Way

Through most of his first term, and in spite of military setbacks, President Bush enjoyed overall support both at home and abroad for his pursuit of the war in the Middle East. This support, though genuine, was magnified by the absence of vigorous, critical investigative reporting. The press was supine.[16] The reasons have yet to be fully determined. Certainly American reporters felt a desire to protect their country at a time of danger. Journalists and, even more, media owners probably feared they would lose readers, listeners, and viewers if they questioned the rush to defend the nation. They may have been predisposed to feel intimidated because of right-wing accusations that had been extensive before and during Bush's election campaign against Democrat Al Gore, to the effect that the media were controlled by "liberals" who did not give conservatives fair coverage. A longer-term cause of press passivity may have been a selective form of nostalgia for the Second World War that was widespread in the United States at the time, and was reflected and reinforced by the media. Many Americans who were children or grandchildren of World War II veterans were by now in their fifties and sixties, and were in influential positions. They were old enough to appreciate the great sacrifices and accomplishments of the Second World War generation and felt a duty to affirm this awareness. They also felt that remembrance of World War II could inspire America as it faced new complexities and uncertainties in the years after the cold war. A reflection of this attitude was the lavishly produced best-selling book *The Greatest Generation* (2001) by the prominent NBC television reporter Tom Brokaw. The nostalgia often led to an inaccurate assumption that the United States had single-handedly won both the Second World War and the cold war. In the days after 9/11, American news media were awash in references to Pearl Harbor, and reporters, just like most other Americans, were eager to repeat, in selectively remembered form, stories of the nation's earlier, united mobilization.[17]

Gradually, however, the media became less compliant. In the election campaign that took place in 2003 during the president's fourth year in office, Senator John Kerry, the Democratic candidate, began to chip away at voter support for the war, and the media disseminated his comments. Around the same time, an independently produced documentary film, *Fahrenheit 9/11*, caused damage to the White House. It was made by Michael Moore, the populist director known for earlier films exposing General Motors and analyzing the Columbine High School tragedy. Moore accused President Bush of a failure to heed advance warning of 9/11, a tardy response to it, concealment of secret ties to Saudi Arabia, and insensitivity to the poor people of America who were being enlisted in large numbers to fight the war in Iraq. He also charged the president and his allies in Congress with failing to tell the American people how extensively their liberties were being compromised by the hastily passed Patriot Act. For this film Moore won a major prize at the Cannes Film Festival. *Fahrenheit 9/11* was also a subject of great attention at the 2004 Academy Award ceremonies in Hollywood, which enjoy a global viewership.[18] This worldwide attention to a movie highly critical of the Bush presidency and its war in Iraq contributed significantly to the decline in the president's reputation.

The initial hyperpatriotism of the U.S. press was also countered by sources of reportage that originated in the Middle East and that were part of a new distribution of power in the control of information. Throughout the twentieth century, questions about war and the media had been pretty much questions about interactions between highly industrialized societies. But the destruction of the World Trade Center and subsequent battles in Afghanistan and Iraq revealed a new reality. Wealthy but not broadly industrialized or urbanized societies in the Middle East, like Saudi Arabia and Qatar, proved to be developing considerable capacities for the use of mass communication and were training publicists to make the views of non-Western nations known. Moreover, the exploitation of media could now be asymmetrical. It was no longer routinely on the model of Tokyo Rose against Bob Hope, *Pravda* against the Voice of America, large nation-states against one another. Now, nongovernmental organizations, including terrorists, were gaining access to communications networks and circulating information that often challenged the portrayals of events coming from American sources and the White House.

The most potent new source of information on this model was the Arabic-language television network Al Jazeera. Based in Qatar, it was funded by wealthy Middle Easterners, could be received via broadcast or through the Internet, and had an audience numbering in the millions. Al Jazeera followed Western codes of journalistic practice regarding factual accuracy and balance. But in its news stories and editorial opinions it often included information that contradicted or changed the way one looked at portrayals in the Western media, and this information made its way into Western channels. A powerful early example was the network's decision to circulate videotapes of Osama bin Laden castigating the West which had been made available to Al Jazeera through secret sources by the al-Qaeda organization. There were soon hundreds of stations like Al Jazeera, funded by a wide variety of political groups and wealthy individuals. They included Al Arabiya, which was pan-Arab in its news coverage and opinion; Al Masar and Al Forat, which supported the Shiite party in Iraq; Baghdad Television, run by the Sunni party; Ashour, a Christian broadcaster; Al-Hurriya, run by the Kurds; Turkmaniya, established by ethnic Turkomen; and Nahrain, owned by the billionaire Egyptian businessman Naguib Sawiris. These stations sometimes scooped Western media, as in March 2006, when Baghdad Television was the first to feature an appearance by the American journalist Jill Carroll after her release after eighty-two days of being held hostage by an extremist group of Sunnis.

The Downward Slide Continues

Early in the second Bush term there were more blows to the White House in the symbolic realm. Prominent Republicans—members of the president's own party—including Brent Scowcroft and Melvin Laird advocated phased withdrawal from Iraq. Congressman John Murtha further eroded the president's support when he took the same view. Though a Democrat, Murtha was a war hero and a known defender of the Pentagon and the enlisted ranks; he enjoyed broad working-class support among both Republican and Democratic voters. The Republican leadership called him a traitor and a coward, and then lamely apologized, damaging their own cause and America's international reputation as a defender of free speech, one of the liberties that was, presumably, a goal of U.S. involvement in the Middle East.[19]

The growing damage to the U.S. effort in Iraq had spillover effects in other parts of the world. In Iran, the country's leaders were emboldened to escalate their rhetoric against Israel and even deny that the Holocaust had taken place. In Latin America, leaders like Fidel Castro in Cuba and Hugo Chávez in Venezuela exploited the decline in America's international prestige by heating up their anti-U.S. rhetoric as a way to win support from their populations and garner admiration from other nations. In Havana, Castro made systematic use of billboards with anti-American messages related to Iraq, while Chávez established his own television station to attack America and thus add to his stature.[20] In trips to foreign capitals to promote support for the World Trade Organization treaty, the president and other Americans experienced publicity setbacks because of riots and protests during their visits—crowd behavior that was caused mostly by fears of economic injustice the treaty might set in motion, but was greatly intensified by the negativity generated from America's declining prestige on the world stage.

During Bush's second term, Saddam Hussein went on trial in Iraq. His capture had been a temporary propaganda coup for the United States. Putting him on trial also held the promise, at first, of adding to U.S. stature by projecting America's concern for due process and international law. This hope was partly realized during the proceedings. But as the trial progressed, Saddam had many opportunities for engaging in theatricality. Some he did not use effectively. But in others he did gain appeal among Middle Eastern audiences, and terrorists exploited the trial. The White House had no hope of managing the imagery of the proceeding, which was covered 24/7 by Middle Eastern television outlets that had their own press corps.

At the same time, Bush had to go on the defensive in response to media reports that he and his aides were condoning torture. Confidential memoranda became public in which White House adviser John Yoo and others claimed that the president had the right to use torture and should do so. More explicit defenses soon emerged, like those by CIA director Porter Goss, who was frank in detailing the value of torture. In the face of this discourse, the president's responses to queries from the media and Congress were inadequate. "We do not torture," he said repeatedly, without specifically addressing the evidence that had become public in direct contradiction of his words.

Later in his second term, stories appeared in the British press reporting that early in the Iraq war, in conversations with Prime Minister Tony Blair, President Bush had advocated having American planes bomb the Qatar-based Al Jazeera TV network out of existence. Bush denied these accusations, but was curt and dismissive, which left the impression that he had in fact done what the rumors claimed.[21]

Bush's public appearances now became increasingly controlled. Stage management was nothing new. From the beginning of his first term on, at White House press conferences the president took no questions from reporters that had not been presented and approved ahead of time. During the 2004 election campaign, all his appearances before voters were carefully scripted, even to the point of admitting only those attendees whose presence was deemed desirable. But things became even more rigid after his reelection. In his international travel, the president's manner was seen as increasingly royal.[22] His so-called dialogues with the troops, whether on visits to the Middle East or via television hookups between the war zone and the White House, were especially unreal. The troops were seated in carefully posed arrangements and briefed on how to behave on camera, their questions were vetted ahead of time, and in spite of the spontaneous manner he affected, the president's own comments and even some of his gestures and inflections were scripted and looked like they were. Moreover, there were still echoes of the "Mission Accomplished" strategy. In a major speech on November 30, 2005, designed to counter sagging public confidence, the president appeared before midshipmen of the U.S. Naval Academy to announce a "Plan for Victory" in Iraq. The speech exaggerated the readiness of Iraqi troops to secure their own country. "We will never accept anything less than complete victory," claimed Bush, even as reporters were uncovering plans to withdraw U.S. troops at a stepped-up rate in advance of the upcoming congressional midterm elections. In his speech the president repeated the word "victory" fifteen times, following advice from a Duke University political scientist, Peter Feaver, an expert on public opinion in war.[23]

In his arguments offered to justify the Iraq war, from the start of his first term on, the President made grave errors. Style was part of the problem. While he may have been coached to appear humble and judicious, the president never lost his undertone of Texas cowboy swagger. But the bigger problems were substantive. He repeatedly conflated the war in Afghanistan with the war in Iraq, claiming that Iraq was a center of Taliban activity, even as reported facts to the contrary piled up. Especially damaging was the president's attitude toward the idea of national sacrifice. He spoke often of the need for America and its allies to persist, to be patient and resolute, to realize that the "war on terror" was likely to take many years. But he was not credible in his calls for sacrifice. He brushed aside proposals for a national military draft, even when the military did not meet its recruitment quotas, preferring instead to call up the National Guard and extend the tours of duty of those who were already enlisted.[24] He assigned little importance to the fact that at a time when he was obtaining tax cuts for the rich and the distribution of wealth in the United States was growing ever more inequitable, the men and women wearing the nation's uniforms in the Middle East and around the world were drawn almost completely from the least prosperous and most disenfranchised sectors of American society.

The president's difficulties in projecting America's image overseas were compounded by many of his media-related domestic actions. When family members of those killed on 9/11 asked for a special investigation, Bush at first refused, thereby alienating them and appearing insensitive in the eyes of many abroad as well as at home. He appeared obtuse and devious when he procrastinated in creating a special commission to analyze possible reforms of the U.S. intelligence establishment. After creating the Department of Homeland Security in May 2003, he allowed it to set, as one of its major priorities, the hiring of the advertising firm Landor Associates to give the large new federal agency its own "brand" by establishing a typeface and color scheme, designing uniforms for agents, using focus groups to test a department seal meant to convey "strength" and "gravitas," and creating a special lapel pin with Secretary Tom Ridge's signature, which was given to all employees in June 2003 to celebrate the agency's "brand launch."[25]

His troubles continued. The president was evasive regarding the alleged existence of weapons of mass destruction in Iraq, even though evidence to the contrary was mounting. He was similarly embarrassed by the disclosure that a White House operative was being passed off at press conferences as a legitimate member of the press corps with instructions to plant comments and questions favorable to the administration.[26] He gave inadequate answers when it was reported early in his second term that he had been authorizing wiretaps on American citizens in the United States by the National Security Agency, a unit of the espionage establishment specifically required by law to confine its spying to activities outside the country.[27] The president lost face when Kenneth Tomlinson, his appointee to head the Corporation for Public Broadcasting, was forced to resign after allegations that he had broken federal law in his attempts to force the CPB to include more politically conservative programming.[28] He said as little as possible when the press disclosed the existence of overseas installations where the United States outsourced torture to countries more willing to engage in it and directed Secretary of State Condoleeza Rice to meet privately with world leaders to ask their indulgence of this practice.[29]

The Pentagon Takes Command

When he immediately framed America's response to 9/11 as a "war" on terror instead of describing it as the beginning of a long-term police action, President Bush took a large step—seemingly unknowingly—toward ensuring that the country's official international use of mass communication would be dominated by the Pentagon. A major role for the military in propaganda was of course necessary. The invasion of Afghanistan created the need for keeping the public informed and disorienting the enemy. This became even more understandable with the invasion of Iraq. Whether or not one accepted the invasion as a good idea, one knew that once it began, the need for information management had to be met. What was damaging was the Bush administration's decision to entrust the Pentagon with projecting nearly the entire official image of the United States to the world—or perhaps it was not even a decision but rather a lack of awareness of the consequences.

The Pentagon did initially exhibit some sophistication in its concern for world opinion. A few weeks after the 9/11 attacks, the White House established a secret panel to develop strategy and broad operational guidelines for information warfare conducted by the Pentagon, other government agencies, and private contractors. This panel, later named the Counter Terrorism Information Strategy Policy Coordinating Committee (CTISPCC), included representatives from the Pentagon, the Department of State, and intelligence agencies.[30] U.S. troops arrived in Baghdad in April 2003. Six months later, on October 30, Defense Secretary Rumsfeld signed the "Information Operations Roadmap," a seventy-three-page directive to the U.S. military to use the news media, public opinion, and the Internet as weapons of war.[31] Rumsfeld issued directives acknowledging that paying attention to hearts and minds had to be part of American military activity in the Middle East. He expanded existing offices within the Pentagon that were dedicated to performing these functions and made himself and his generals and admirals and press secretaries available for frequent interviews by the media. He skillfully balanced media concerns about access to frontline information with military concerns about the need for secrecy, reviving the system of embedding reporters at the front which had worked well in the Second World War. He saw to it that soldiers and sailors and pilots were given orientation about dealing with the media; he allowed the lower ranks to speak openly with reporters; he was respectful of the needs of troops for informal networks to vent their emotions, for example, by making Web log entries on their personal computers. He supported the inclusion of information warfare units in force deployments, and these units made effective use of certain tried-and-true techniques of propaganda, like dropping well-crafted leaflets over combat areas and posting handbills on walls to counter those of the enemy. In July 2005, in a *Wall Street Journal* article titled "War of the Words," Rumsfeld published a spirited articulation of the importance of enlightened information policy, stating that the United States had to develop "new and better ways to communicate America's mission abroad," including "a healthy culture of communication and transparency between government and public."[32]

But from the beginning there were serious miscalculations. Although the CTISPCC had been established even before the invasion of Iraq and had shown promise of great media sophistication, it was handicapped in February 2002 when news reports disclosed that the Pentagon had initiated a bizarre program called the Office of Strategic Influence, which planned to "provide news items, possibly even false ones, to foreign news organizations."[33] The Pentagon at first denied that the office existed while at the same time abolishing it, then announced that an internal review showed no plans to plant false news items. The publicity made the White House wary of participating in the CTISPCC, and some agencies resigned from its panel. The work of the CTISPCC remained secret, but it appears to have continued through and even after the invasion of Iraq, though with diminished influence and focus. The Pentagon was so slow in gearing up its propaganda planning units that it had to hire consulting firms to fill the gap, with strong urging from the White House. "We were clueless," said Mary Matalin, the communications assistant to Vice President Dick Cheney, in a summation of the White House's preparedness for international information management at the time of 9/11.[34]

To help prepare the American military campaign in Afghanistan, the administration turned to John Rendon for assistance. His firm, the Rendon Group, had been a secret consultant to the CIA in the 1990s, when he was hired to help the exiled Iraqi National Congress conduct public relations warfare against Saddam Hussein. The White House hired Rendon to help the U.S. government respond quickly to Taliban propaganda appearing in foreign media outlets. Around the same time, the Pentagon also hired Rendon, under a $27.6 million contract, to establish focus groups in several countries around the world and to analyze Arab-language media sources like Al Jazeera. For the Iraq war, the Rendon Group received additional contracts to perform such tasks as analysis of media and management of a media operations center in Baghdad. Another consulting firm, the Lincoln Group, also soon appeared on the scene, though by means that were not made public.[35] The total amount budgeted for all consulting firms was not publicly announced. Contracts that are known include those with the Lincoln Group, S. Y. Coleman, Inc., and Science Applications International Corp., for which at least $300 million was budgeted over a five-year period, probably beginning in 2001. The Pentagon's purpose, as stated by the Lincoln Group Web site, was to "inject more creativity into its psychological operations efforts to improve foreign public opinion about the United States, particularly the military."[36] The Pentagon allowed the Lincoln Group to continue its work even after the Pentagon's own units geared up. The outsourcing to private contractors raised important issues of accountability to the laws and norms of warfare between civilized states. And disclosures of some of the practices of the consultants eventually harmed America's reputation. For example, during the second Bush term, news reports revealed that the firms were paying to plant news stories favorable to the United States in Iraqi media—approximately two hundred Iraqi-owned newspapers and fifteen to seventeen Iraqi-owned television stations—thus undercutting American claims of wanting a free press as a step on the road to Iraqi democracy.[37] Some of the initiatives proposed by consultants but not carried out probably would have caused even more damage. In one proposal that was rejected, the Lincoln Group recommended borrowing methods from American popular culture by creating a satirical newspaper called *The Voice*, based on the humor magazine *The Onion*, and producing television comedies on the model of *Cheers* (which took place in a bar serving alcohol, which is forbidden by Islam) and *The Three Stooges*, with three bumbling terrorists as the lead characters.

Secretary Rumsfeld added to all the difficulties with his personal manner. During his first term President Bush allowed Rumsfeld to dominate foreign policy discourse to such a degree that in the eyes of the public the role of Colin Powell and the State Department was downgraded. The president did little to counter Rumsfeld's gratuitous comments when the defense secretary spoke disparagingly of "old Europe" and indulged in anti-French comments. The president also stood by passively as information began to emerge concerning corruption in Pentagon contracting involving the Halliburton company, Vice President Cheney's former employer, and allowed Cheney and Rumsfeld to be unresponsive when the media and Congress sought details about Halliburton. All the while, within the Pentagon,

Rumsfeld overrode the advice of generals and admirals, who understandably became reluctant to work with him. During personal appearances covered by the media, even though Rumsfeld proclaimed his respect for press access, his style was caustic and dismissive. Eventually he even assumed this manner when speaking to the troops in Iraq, for example, when he cavalierly responded to a soldier's request for better body armor by telling him, "You have to go to war with the Army you have, not the Army you want."[38]

A compensatory development was the growing awareness within the Pentagon that communications technology could be a tool for helping injured soldiers. War has, in some respects, always been a public health issue. This is apparent to anyone who has seen the physical effects of armed conflict. By the time of the Iraq war, observers were coming to recognize that the public health dimensions of war included mass communication. It had long been known that face-to-face encounters with violence are likely to be traumatic. But investigators were also beginning to demonstrate that people who encounter images of violence spread by the media during wars may suffer for many decades from limited emotional and social capacity. This had happened over many generations in Latin America, Vietnam, Cambodia, Laos, and the Balkans. It had been happening among the civilians in the Middle East, who were traumatized by factual reports of violence and by violence-oriented propaganda for several generations before the Iraq war. Some U.S. grant programs, like those at the National Institutes of Health, were becoming available for research related to such trauma and ways to stimulate improved methods of responding. In addition, much attention had been given to the mental health problems of troops after the Vietnam War, partly due to public failure after their return home to legitimate their role as warriors. But this effort did not extensively explore the effects of media images as a source of injury. By the time of the Iraq war, however, new therapies using information technology were being developed to counter the effects of violent images of warfare. For example, at the Virtual Reality Medical Center in San Diego, funded by the Office of Naval Research (ONR), personnel returning from the conflicts in Iraq and Afghanistan were being given special assistance to deal with the flashbacks that often accompany acute posttraumatic stress disorder. The treatment used computer-simulated scenarios of battle to help former combatants cope with the stimuli that trigger painful emotional responses. By gradually revisiting the shocks of combat, patients lowered their anxiety levels and gained perspective that they could transfer from the medical environment into their daily lives. Researchers hoped that medical breakthroughs of this kind might be useful in the broader ongoing effort to counter im-ages of violence spread by mass communication.[39]

Another effort to broaden the Pentagon's patterns of information man-agement involved espionage. During his second term President Bush began to explore expanding the use of America's intelligence agencies to partner with but also supplement the Pentagon's role in the war of ideas. In a strat-egy document issued in October 2005, the president listed initiatives to "bolster the growth of democracy" as one of the top three priorities for U.S. spy agencies, along with activities to counter terrorism and reduce the proliferation of weapons. A senior administration official stated that the new priorities were an acknowledgment that the administration needed to improve its understanding of the important role of "soft power" in foreign policy. The strategy included an increased use of what the military had come to call "humint," that is, intelligence generated by human analysis rather than mechanical surveillance, and greater attention to cultural and civic factors in gathering information.[40]

The Internet Surprises the Pentagon

The war in Iraq involved a dispersion of information warfare that in some ways resembled the decentralization of physical resources accompanying the guerrilla warfare tactics of the insurgents. The Bush administration was slow in adjusting. The Internet made the new pattern possible. Its pres-ence was an emerging factor in information warfare, dating to the first Gulf War. By the time of the Iraq war, America's armed forces were highly computerized, and they themselves used the Internet and militarily re-stricted versions of it as a major tool of coordination. But the Pentagon did not immediately understand the extent to which the Internet could be ex-ploited by enemies. Terrorists used the Internet to circulate their propa-ganda worldwide, to build internal morale, and to share coded messages among themselves. The terrorists also created thousands of Web sites that circulated propaganda to the public, which could access the sites from lap-tops or cell phones. By frequently moving to new Web sites, terrorists were able to keep several steps ahead of Pentagon and intelligence service efforts to track them down.[41]

An even larger challenge to the Pentagon's management of information came with the worldwide uproar, in May 2004 and thereafter, in reaction to the circulation of photographs documenting U.S. abuse of Iraqi prisoners at Abu Ghraib prison. The disclosure of the photos was a major blow to America's reputation. In significant measure this was due to the Internet. Within hours of their appearing in the *Washington Post*, the pictures were being viewed all over the world. More followed in the days and months after, from both Western and non-Western sources, as if a war of images was in progress. The velocity of distribution was not unprecedented. Powerful images from earlier wars, like the mushroom cloud over Hiroshima in 1945, were transmitted with equal speed just as soon as they were publicly available. But the saturation of information related to Abu Ghraib was probably comparable only to the circulation of images of the towers in New York City on September 11. Photographs of Hiroshima could be transmitted instantaneously only to specific outlets, for example, by wire among newspaper offices, in rare cases by television, and within a few days by newsreels. Because of new forms of technology, the images of Abu Ghraib reached billions of viewers with amazing speed and were recycled repeatedly.

The photographs were also a major example of the power of public information to alter the course of a war. There had been instances of this phenomenon in earlier eras. In the Vietnam War, for example, disclosures of Americans killing civilians at My Lai made continuation of the conflict more difficult. And as long ago as the Anglo-Boer War, newspaper revelations of British mismanagement had helped to end that conflict. But it is difficult to recall instances in which a specific body of news—in this case a set of images—caused such extensive midcourse changes in the pursuit of a war. In the United States, the Abu Ghraib scandal set in motion revisions to the military command structure; the White House was forced to regroup; Secretary Rumsfeld twice offered privately to President Bush to resign; and voter support for the war in Iraq declined precipitously. There were parallel repercussions in Britain, the strongest and increasingly the only ally of the United States in the conflict.

Simultaneously, international willingness to assist the Americans weakened, and already unfriendly populations in the Middle East brought added pressure on U.S. forces to leave. The Abu Ghraib photographs damaged the honor of the United States, provoking grave doubts about America's claims to be bringing freedom and respect for human rights to the region and making it much more difficult to think of the United States as a moral leader in the world.[42]

The manner in which the photographs became public raised important questions about media ethics. Many of the images were leaked, given illegally to journalists by individuals in the military and other behind-the-scenes intermediaries. The *Washington Post* and other media outlets then had to decide whether to disclose the information to a broad audience when confidential investigations into prisoner abuse were already being conducted by the U.S. military. Disclosure carried with it the potential to humiliate the individuals shown in the pictures, to compromise the rights of defendants, and to make certain lines of investigation impossible. News outlets decided to publicize the photos nevertheless in order to raise larger issues concerning management of the war in Iraq and the possibility of violations of the Geneva Conventions. The ethics of the media's conduct in publicizing the images are likely to be debated for many years.[43]

Two other post-9/11 military scandals might have had equally strong effects on public perception but in fact did not. In both cases, paradoxically, the key factor was not the moral importance of the scandal but the relative lack of images available for circulation. One of involved the slaughter of Iraqi civilians by U.S. troops in the town of Haditha in 2005. The story of the atrocity was broken that same year by *Time* magazine. A small number of photographs were available, and several were soon circulated, both from the *Time* story and from other sources. But the availability of images was limited because one of the American commanders involved in the atrocity had ordered his troops to destroy their photographs. The Haditha incident received extensive verbal coverage in media throughout the world and resulted in courts-martial proceedings. But it never received the same level of attention as Abu Ghraib. A similar situation occurred in the case of the U.S. prison camp for detainees at Guantanamo Bay in Cuba. Existence of the camp was widely publicized in the media from 2003 on. There was extensive verbal reporting, particularly regarding the ethics of establishing the camp, the possibility that torture was taking place, and legal proceedings related to the prosecution and defense of each of the prisoners. These stories, and the unwillingness of the Pentagon or the White House to discuss the installation in detail, undercut America's claims to be a beacon of liberty protected by law.[44] But as in the case of Haditha, attention throughout the world was surprisingly limited in comparison to the attention to Abu Ghraib, because the White House and the Pentagon were able to strictly limit the number of images of the camp available to the public.

Another significant effect of imagery on public perception of the Iraq war did arise in 2006, however, as a result of Internet circulation of videotapes made by American troops. These had been allowed for some time by U.S. authorities as a way to build morale. Initially the videotapes were used mostly for military personnel to communicate with family members and friends in the United States; they played a role in warfare much like that of letters home in earlier wars. Soon the soldiers began shaping the videotapes into artistic forms—a natural transition for young men raised in the era of MTV, consumer technologies like those permitting the individual downloading of music, and iPod and PC software editing programs that allowed each individual user to shape his or her electronic experience. Soldiers were soon swapping their video creations and also sending them home. Leaders at the Pentagon and the White House hoped that the videos would include strong expressions of support for the war and evidence of high morale to counter negative images in the mainstream media. But most of the videos conveyed a different message. Soldiers were careful to mouth the phrases they knew the authorities wanted to hear. But deep cynicism and fatigue were also evident. In one video a soldier claimed that he was protecting freedom and democracy, but then asked why so much of his time had to be spent guarding the property of the Halliburton company, one of the private contractors making huge profits from the war. More grim was the video "Hadji Girl," created by one soldier, about a U.S. marine who falls in love with an Iraqi girl and is then ambushed by her family. Thousands of these videos were produced. They became a considerable informational force in 2006, as soldiers began to upload them to YouTube, with millions of on-line viewers worldwide. The extensive reach thus attained by the videos led some observers to believe that whereas Vietnam had been the "living room war" because of television, Iraq was becoming the "YouTube war," part of a growing tendency for the democratization of information to become an important factor in warfare, as personal communication and mass communication merged.[45]

Public Diplomacy Is Rediscovered

The White House eventually began to notice that publicity related to its efforts in the Middle East was being dominated by the Pentagon, and it took a few hesitant steps to alter the pattern. Toward this end, in the first Bush term the White House hired a talented Madison Avenue advertising agent, Charlotte Beers, to create ads for the United States. She had an impressive track record, but she did not rise to the challenge of addressing foreign audiences and disseminating complex messages. Her first creation was a series of commercials on American television offering rewards for information leading to the capture of terrorists. This was redundant. Most Americans were already eager to provide such information if they had it. Beers failed to emphasize ads directed at foreign audiences that would have reminded viewers of the good things about America. Shortly thereafter, in an equally inadequate response, the president's senior adviser Karl Rove, conferring with Hollywood producers and studio executives, came up with the idea that the boxing champion Muhammad Ali be sent to the Middle East as a model Muslim, even though Ali had no real standing in the Muslim community outside the United States and was not known to audiences that did not follow the American-dominated sport of boxing.[46]

Very little was going on at this time at the United States Agency for International Development, which had become the de facto USIA and was supposed to be the coordinator of public diplomacy (an irony for those who remembered USAID's origins as the locus for agricultural and economic assistance). The elder President Bush and President Clinton had spent $350 million annually from 1991 on to develop independent media in eastern Europe and the former Soviet Union, with positive effects in both areas. In 2004 the George W. Bush administration's USAID budget for democracy and governance activities in Iraq was $380 million annually, with $5 million of that amount going to independent media development. In 2005 spending in the same budget category fell to $169 million. For 2006 it remained at that level. In both 2005 and 2006 the amount for independent media development was proportionally as small as in 2004.[47] By 2005 USAID was covertly financing about thirty radio stations in Afghanistan, had distributed tens of thousands of iPod-like audio devices in Iraq and Afghanistan, and had hired a private contractor who distributed prepackaged civic-oriented messages playable on the units, without public mention of the U.S. source.[48]

A few months into his second term Bush began to take actions designed to broaden the administration's strategy for nonmilitary propaganda. He encouraged his new secretary of state, Condoleeza Rice, to include cultural and social events in her tours. He dispatched his wife, Laura, to the Middle East, not only to visit troops but also to pay calls, highly publicized, on many civilian dignitaries. He appointed his press and campaign aide Karen Hughes to be assistant secretary of state in charge of a newly expanded office responsible for coordinating and reenergizing public diplomacy. She went on American television to emphasize the administration's increased awareness of the importance of this aspect of foreign policy and also made many visits to the Middle East and elsewhere. At first such initiatives received a favorable response. But they were not pursued systematically and soon drew criticism. It appeared that the president perceived public diplomacy not as something pursued by "real men" but as a task for women to dispatch. Interviews with the first lady and Assistant Secretary Hughes were marked by cultural and professional naïveté.

An important activity assigned to the State Department was to establish U.S.-run Arab-language television stations. For example, in 2004 a Virginia-based network, Al Hurra ("the free one" in Arabic), began broadcasting to Arabic-speaking countries. But Arab viewers regarded the station's offerings as bland and sympathetic to Lebanese interests rather than to the Arab world as a whole. By 2005 there were accusations that the station's managers were paying inordinately high fees for some services and inflating audience statistics. The U.S. House of Representatives began hearings on Al Hurra, and the State Department's inspector general undertook an audit.[49] In any case, the Bush administration's rediscovery of public diplomacy came too late and did not solve its many problems of information management.

At least one powerful sector of American society decided to take matters into its own hands. Large business corporations gradually realized that weaknesses in foreign propaganda after 9/11 were diminishing the ability of the United States to compete effectively in the international economic arena. In October 2005, in an article in the business section of the *New York Times*, the editor in chief of *Chief Executive Magazine* described widespread worries among American CEOs concerning the negative effects on business of the country's declining international image. He noted the formation of the group Business for Diplomatic Action (BDA), led by Keith L. Reinhard, chairman of the advertising agency DDB Worldwide. Reinhard was a brilliant businessman known for engineering the merger that created DDB Worldwide and for spectacularly successful management of international advertising campaigns like that for McDonald's organized around the tagline "You deserve a break today," which became one of the best-known ad slogans of all time. Reinhard was also an international visionary, in part because of a Mennonite upbringing that intensified his interest in building peace. His prestige and drive enabled BDA to recruit as board members executives from ExxonMobil, UPS, Microsoft, and McDonald's to push for improved governmental action, and to expand private-sector efforts in world diplomacy. By 2006 Business for Diplomatic Action was distributing a "World Citizens Guide" to corporate travelers, recruiting young Arabs for internships at American companies, working to publicize overseas corporate philanthropy, such as the distribution of medicine to eradicate river blindness, and pushing for increased attention to geography, foreign languages, and world history in U.S. schools. Through the use of overseas focus groups and more culturally sensitive advertising, BDA worked to counter the fact that American brands were becoming less and less welcome worldwide. BDA also mobilized the puppet characters from the television program *Sesame Street* for thirty international co-productions adapted for overseas audiences to include information about the United States. One of the board members of BDA was Gary Knell, who ran the nongovernmental organization Sesame Workshop, which in its own contribution to the cause of building peace pursued "Muppet diplomacy."[50]

Efforts like those of BDA and Sesame Workshop also drew on the energies of an emerging movement called "place branding," which stressed the importance in the twenty-first century of enlisting private-sector sources of advertising and public relations to cultivate favorable organizational images for cities, regions, and nations. One of the leaders in this movement was Dick Martin, author of *Rebuilding Brand America: What We Must Do to Restore Our Reputation and Safeguard the Future of American Business Abroad* (2007). Another leading figure, based in Britain and with close ties to both government and the commercial world, was Simon Anholt, the author of *Competitive Identity: The New Brand Management for Nations, Cities and Regions* (2006). In 2004 Anholt founded the quarterly professional journal *Place Branding and Public Diplomacy.*

Prescriptions Multiply

As the war in Iraq continued, the minority-party Democrats became increasingly vociferous—sometimes in a constructive spirit, sometimes to gain political advantage. By the time of Bush's second term they were finding useful information in widely read journalistic exposés of White House management of the war, such as *Cobra II: The Inside Story of the Invasion and Occupation of Iraq* (2006) by Michael Gordon and General Bernard Trainor; *Fiasco: The American Military Adventure in Iraq* (2006) by Thomas Ricks; and *State of Denial: Bush at War*, part two (2006), by Bob Woodward; as well as disclosures in April 2008 by the *New York Times* that the Pentagon had improperly influenced the commentary of the many retired generals and colonels who had become fixtures on television news programs; and publication in May 2008 of the book *What Happened: Inside the Bush White House and Washington's Culture of Deception* by the president's former press secretary Scott McClellan, who alleged that Bush and his assistants had engaged in a "political propaganda campaign" to build support for the Iraq war, even though the conflict was "unnecessary" and other options ought to have been more carefully considered.[51]

Halfway through Bush's second term, in the congressional elections of 2006, the Democrats were able to secure control of the Senate and the House of Representatives. Encouraged by their victory, and by opinion polls showing strong disapproval of President Bush as a war leader, the Democrats sought to use their new power to broker a different approach to the conduct of U.S. foreign policy, not just in Iraq but in the Middle East as a whole, and elsewhere in the world. Democrats floated a variety of proposals for action, including regional diplomatic conferences, sterner treatment of the U.S.-backed government in Iraq, and phased withdrawal of troops with or without preannounced timetables. The Democrats were seldom specific and often chose simply to let Bush twist in the wind. The president showed some willingness to change course, for example, in accepting Rumsfeld's resignation and replacing him with the less ideological Robert Gates, and an openness to the advice provided by an unofficial advisory commission, the Iraq Study Group, chaired by former secretary of state James Baker. The Democrats examined most matters of obvious urgency, including re-deployment of American forces, U.S. alliances, and behind-the-scenes ne-gotiations, as well as possible changes in strategies for combating terrorism and protecting the homeland. Whether the Democrats would be more so-phisticated in understanding the relation of war to mass communication, and whether the administration that followed the Bush presidency would also make improvements in America's official use of mass communication, remained open questions. During the presidential election campaign of 2008, concern about America's reputation in the world was a topic of fre-quent discussion. The Republican candidate, Senator John McCain, spe-cifically called for enhanced psychological warfare capacity at the Pentagon and a revival in some form of the old USIA as a larger, more independent agency. The Democratic candidate, Senator Barack Obama, did not get into specifics about whether he would create a new information agency, al-though he did say he would intensify public diplomacy activities, for ex-ample by use of the Internet and revival of overseas libraries like those sponsored by the USIA. He seemed to be of the view that the projection of American values was a by-product of the nation's overall behavior and ought to be part of every agency's activity. Obama seemed to be so much a child of the era of mass communication, and so international in his back-ground, that awareness of world opinion was to him a matter of second nature.[52]

In January 2007 a BBC World Service Poll of 26,000 people, taken in twenty-five countries, indicated that only 29 percent of those surveyed be-lieved that the United States was exerting a mainly positive influence in the world, compared to 36 percent in 2006 and 40 percent in 2005. These fig-ures contrasted with earlier polls taken by the Pew Center at the end of the 1990s and in 2002 before the invasion of Iraq, which indicated that most people believed that the world was safer with the United States as the sole superpower.[53] White House management of information strategies was by no means the only factor contributing to the decline in the reputation and influence of the United States. One has to give due weight to the continu-ing increase in power of other nations vis-à-vis the United States as a natu-ral consequence of multipolarity.[54] But a change in American foreign policy that included avoiding self-inflicted wounds in the use of mass communication was very much needed.

In the months and years after 9/11, many observers emphasized that the weaknesses in the government's projection of images of the United States were distressing not only because of the damage they caused to the nation's effectiveness in war and foreign relations but also because of the harm they created in other realms of activity. In a detailed analysis of anti-Americanism in February 2005, shortly after President Bush began his second term in office, *The Economist* commented: "Why, anyway, should America care if a bunch of foreigners dislike it, or affect to? Maybe, as a military and economic power without rival, it should not be too worried. Yet America needs the cooperation of other governments if it is to conduct trade, combat drugs, reduce pollution and fight terrorism. . . . It is striking that Mr. Bush's 49 mentions of liberty or freedom in his inaugural address last month do not seem to have struck the chord round the world that Jack Kennedy's quixotic commitments did in the 1960's."[55]

Observers noted that weaknesses in foreign propaganda were eroding democracy and adherence to the Constitution. In December 2005 David Brooks, the conservative columnist for the *New York Times*, wrote that in contrast to the Second World War, when leaders had inspired a sense of national unity and self-confidence among Americans, the war in Iraq, like the Vietnam War, was contributing to a mood of "sour pessimism" among citizens and a deep cynicism about the capacity of their national government to manage warfare or any other activity competently. Similarly, in June 2005, commenting on the failure of the nation's leaders to win the public's confidence, the eminent Harvard psychologist Howard Gardner noted that trust is perhaps the most important factor in the ability of a society to function productively, and that a critical element in such trust is the presence of leaders who are perceived to be trustworthy.[56]

Many analysts focused on the need for greatly increased training of frontline troops in cultural and propaganda matters, to supplement the limited training that was taking place.[57] Other analysts noted that in the new information age, when the importance of effectively projecting America's image could only grow, there was a need for a high-level body within the national government that could discuss broad policy issues related to propaganda and give these issues added visibility. A major revision in the federal structure for information management seemed to be required. Toward this end a number of analysts called for the creation of a National Academy for Public Diplomacy, on the model of other entities like the National Academies of Science and Engineering. Many commentators argued that additional funding should be made available for training in foreign languages. U.S. governmental agencies, it was widely agreed, were making major mistakes in communication with and about other countries because so few Americans understood other languages and the cultures embodied in those languages. The analysts emphasized that isolationism would not change appreciably until language competency expanded.[58]

Some observers called for restoring or increasing funding to support international cultural and scientific exchange. Face-to-face contact of this kind reinforced and worked in tandem with the use of media. During the cold war the United States enhanced its position in the world and helped to promote peace by a sustained, many-faceted program of cultural and scientific cooperation. Starting in the late 1940s and continuing through most of the 1980s, the U.S. government partnered with groups such as the Rockefeller and Ford foundations to sponsor lectures and conferences on American culture, tours by artists, professorships for American academics, and fellowships for foreign graduate students to study in the United States. Person-to-person activity was emphasized, but the media also played a role. At U.S.-supported cultural centers abroad, like the America Houses in major cities in Germany and Austria, well-stocked libraries spread the U.S. point of view and disseminated factual information. Many of the people involved in exchanges were authors and artists known through their writings and film and television appearances. The impact of their media products was enhanced by the opportunities for foreign audiences to meet such figures personally. Many initiatives, such as the American Congress for Cultural Freedom, received secret financial support from the CIA. But even in these cases, promotion of goodwill and understanding took place. Analysts noted an urgent need to revive a balanced strategy combining media with personal contact, and emphasized that activities must be planned and pursued for the long term, not just in response to the immediate publicity crises of a particular administration, so that foreign audiences received a clear, consistent message about America's values. One activity attracting interest was the possible awarding of grants for college and university programs and institutes focused on diplomacy, like the master's program in public diplomacy begun in 2003 at the University of Southern California, the first in the United States.[59]

Peacemakers Persist

In addition to analyses conceived within the framework of traditional power politics, the post-9/11 era also witnessed the continuation of a more idealistic tradition that called for a paradigm shift through the use of mass communication as one available tool to move international relations away from an obsession with war to employment of nonviolent conflict resolution techniques. Analysts of this persuasion were well aware that many great thinkers have concluded that war is an inevitable aspect of human experience and have cautioned that societies must always be prepared to defend themselves. Saint Augustine and Martin Luther are two examples. But they also knew that other great thinkers such as Kant, Gandhi, and Martin Luther King Jr. have been of the view that the eradication of war is possible if one realizes that peacefulness is a form of power in its own right and need not be mere passivity. That had been the view of the founders of UNESCO in the 1940s; as we saw in the previous chapter, they declared that "wars begin in the minds of men," and they sought to pursue this insight proactively. During the post-9/11 era efforts continued to enhance the peace-inducing capacities of media through research, activism, publicity, and already available societal structures. The strategies carried on a noble tradition as they laid the foundations on which future efforts for the peaceful use of mass communication would build.[60]

One area of exploration involved journalists, who began to reflect more deeply on the ethics of their professional conduct.[61] This development drew on a historic legacy, exemplified by the hundreds of eloquent memoirs written by reporters over the generations. A powerful post-9/11 example was *War Is a Force That Gives Us Meaning* (2002) by the *New York Times* reporter Chris Hedges, who described the emotional effects of battle in the Balkans, the Middle East, and Central America on those who reported it. Moreover, there were efforts to deal with a divide between two groups of investigators. On the one hand, observers noted, much of the writing in journalistic memoirs was impressionistic, mired in the present, anecdotal, narrow in its perspective, and not informed by relevant research in fields such as history, ethics, and psychology. On the other hand, academics tended to be aloof and preachy in their examinations of media. Increasingly, however, opportunities were being created for the two sectors to learn from each other, for example, in conferences and in research studies integrating the insights of both journalists and academics.[62] Important questions were also raised concerning the ways in which information was making its way into the media. For example, a 2002 study by the media analyst Nancy Snow probed the significance of the fact that, from 1995 onward, the United States had more public relations professionals (150,000 at that time) than reporters (130,000), with some 40 percent of the information assumed by the public to be "news" being generated by the former.[63]

A growing body of thought focused on a new field called peace journalism—a term originally coined in the 1960s by the Norwegian sociologist

Johann Galtung to counter the long tradition of glamorizing the image of the war correspondent. Every journalism student and apprentice reporter grows up with the stereotype of the brave, flamboyant figure in a trench coat who risks his life at the front lines of battle and writes the story that is then transmitted back to the main office for processing by hawkish editors and publishers. Observers asked if there could not also be created an image of a "peace correspondent" bravely reporting battlefield negotiations to end conflict (while still respecting the need for behind-the scenes-negotiations) or efforts by courageous doctors and nurses to treat the wounded or to provide medical care for large populations. One hint that such a new genre of reporting might be developing was Tracy Kidder's widely respected best-selling book *Mountains beyond Mountains* (2003), which describes the humanitarian work of the physician Paul Farmer in troubled Haiti. Another bellwether was the widely read book *Non-violence: The History of a Dangerous Idea* (2006), by the American journalist Mark Kurlansky, with a foreword by the Dalai Lama.

Potential for the development of "peace journalism" was suggested by the growing influence of the group Reporters Without Borders. The most fundamental ethical principle of journalism is respect for the truth. In many countries of the world, those who report the truth can be jailed or killed. Based in Paris, Reporters Without Borders was founded in 1985 on the model of the already successful Doctors Without Borders. Reporters Without Borders defended journalists who were imprisoned or mistreated, publicized state actions that undermined press freedom, provided emergency financial aid to journalists and their families, and worked to improve the safety of journalists in war zones. By the early years of the twenty-first century, the organization was active on five continents through national branches, offices in capital cities, and regional correspondents. Every January it published a "Round-Up of Press Freedom in the World," and on May 3 it issued a list of "predators of press freedom." The organization's "Worldwide Press Freedom Index," issued each October, measured the degree of press freedom in more than 160 countries.

In 2000 the United Nations added its prestige to the field of peace journalism by establishing the Media and Peace Institute. Based in Paris as part of the UN's already existing University for Peace, the institute dedicated itself to research, education, and international dialogue to promote new thinking about ways in which the media could help prevent violent conflict and alert decision makers and the general public to looming risks of war. The institute maintained regular contact with regional security organizations such as NATO and the Organization of African Unity, offered courses for executives and career professionals, maintained a news service, and published research articles on topics like the distorting effects of the international arms trade on development and nation building in Third World countries. The first director of the institute was a Canadian, Kenneth Spicer, author of several books on international relations and communications theory, Canada's first commissioner of languages, and an expert on the Internet. The institute had a distinguished board membership, including a former CEO of Agence France Presse, Henri Pigeat; the editor in chief of the *Straits Times* in Singapore, Cheong-Yip-Seng; and, until his death, the prominent Columbia University professor Edward Said, author of influential books on Western stereotyping of the Middle East.

Another area of growing self-examination involved new media. By the time of 9/11, information technology companies were earning huge profits by marketing to the military in many countries, making these companies part of the worldwide arms trade. The companies had been slow to realize this fact, let alone pursue its consequences as part of their social obligations. Gradually, however, some of those who had become rich from success in the information technology business began to support philanthropy. A pioneer in the 1980s was Ted Turner, the founder of CNN, who worked vigorously to establish "Friendship Games" between the United States and the Soviet Union. In addition, Turner gave $1 billion to the United Nations for urgently needed administrative funding.[64] Bill Gates was a later and even more spectacular example. At the time of 9/11, however, infotech companies still had not done much to support studies of the relationship of their activities to war, and ways to lessen the harmful use of information technology while still allowing for defense. But then a gradual change became discernible. An example was the cooperative venture launched in 2007 by the Holocaust Museum in Washington, D.C., and the managers of the Internet search engine Google. The company's geographic search feature, Google Earth, was founded in 2005, and by 2007 it had over 200 million users. An initiative called Crisis in Darfur enabled Google Earth users to observe evidence of the genocide that had been taking place in this region of Africa since 2003, in which more than 200,000 people had been killed and 2.5 million displaced. Internet disclosure of details such as the destruction of villages and refugee migration patterns made it impossible to deny what had been happening and aided the mobilization of worldwide public opinion.[65]

Infotech companies broadened their constructive activity by supporting the emerging interest in "serious games." For example, in 2006 *Peacemaker* appeared. It allowed players to fantasize how they might solve the Israeli-Palestinian crisis, acting in the role of the Israeli prime minister or the president of the Palestine Liberation Organization. Players could launch missiles and had to react to suicide bombers. But strategies available to gamers also included behind-the-scenes negotiations, speeches against militancy, and other nonviolent actions. The MacArthur Foundation, based in Chicago, was by this time awarding million-dollar grants to develop serious games. Game designers included organizations such as the University of Wisconsin and Game Lab, a private firm in New York City. The United Nations developed and marketed *Food Force*, which challenged players to overcome obstacles in the way of delivering food aid to war-ravaged areas. Ivan Marovic, a Serbian who helped engineer the downfall of Slobodan Milosevic, developed *A Force More Powerful*, a game that taught techniques of nonviolence. An international association of peace game designers, Games for Change, held annual conferences in New York City beginning in 2003. Many serious games were given away for free; this strategy resulted in more than 4 million downloads of *Food Force*. Supporters of the serious games movement believed that, especially for young people who had grown up with video technology, the medium could be a powerful teacher of approaches to nonviolent solutions in world conflicts. The games challenged players to put theory into practice and conveyed the complexity of problems. By inviting players to take on varying roles, the games taught appreciation for different points of view. The games that offered both peaceful and war-based techniques allowed players to weigh the values and consequences of these differing routes to conflict resolution. At the same time, games also appeared that offered only war-based responses to emerging conflicts, like *America's Army*, the very popular video game offered for free as a recruiting tool by the U.S. military, and *Under Ash*, a game developed in Syria that allowed players to assume only one role, that of a Palestinian freedom fighter. Even when peaceful solutions were explored, some games aroused controversies over their ethics. *Darfur*, a game developed by MTV, led many to object that it trivialized genocide. Balancing entertainment values against the need for social responsibility emerged as an important challenge for the serious games movement. A belief in its great potential led to establishment of a Serious Games Initiative at the prestigious Woodrow Wilson International Center for Scholars in Washington, D.C.[66]

There were also emerging efforts to use financial techniques to broaden peace-oriented access to media. In 1996 Ventobel, a private Swiss bank, joined with social investment specialists to establish a fixed-interest-return investment fund to promote independent media in developing countries. With assistance from the New York–based Media Development Loan Fund (MDLF), loans were made to independent media outlets in the Third

World to buy printing presses and broadcasting equipment. Access to the Internet could follow. The fund was relatively small by bond market standards but was part of a growing worldwide interest in microfinance as a tool of social development. Investors got a slightly smaller yield than they might with other kinds of funds, but they were attracted by the social return and the creativity of using the capital market as an alternative to direct philanthropy. By 2006 the fund was active in thirteen countries, including Russia, the former Yugoslavia, and countries in Africa and Latin America. The fund was established with seed money from George Soros, the influential financier, who was working to promote civil society around the world.[67]

Peacemakers Confront Hate

In the years after 9/11 there was a great increase in efforts to understand the role of media in the creation of hate, which seemed to be at the center of so many conflicts leading to war. Psychologists knew by this time that violent conflicts can often be prevented if we are alert to the ways in which our capacity for being kind to others is rooted in an understanding of ourselves, that is, in understanding whether our fear of something or someone is based on facts and a clear perception of reality or on projections of our own fears. And they knew that media have played a large role in giving us our facts and projecting our fears.[68] By the early twenty-first century, investigators were helping people to describe more precisely the connection between hate and mass communication and to identify issues that still were not well understood. For example, analysts of media asked how much of the hatred that appears in wartime among civilian populations is induced by media portrayals of events and how much by real events like the death of loved ones, economic privation, and famine? The links between mass communication and anger directed at an enemy that could easily be seen, they determined, were probably the ones that involved censorship and deception. When the media were able to withhold basic information from fighting units and the home front, or to circulate incorrect information unchallenged, then the controllers of those media were affecting people's fundamental constructions of reality, and wartime decisions regarding advisable actions would be made on that basis. A growing body of analysis also suggested, however, that when given even partial access to facts, people were remarkably resourceful in separating the manipulative aspects of messages from those that are true. That was the contention, for example, of James Surowiecki's influential book *The Wisdom of Crowds* (2005).[69]

At many law schools, efforts were in progress to draft model legislation that would prevent the expression of hate while preserving constitutional rights. Much of this work centered on America, naturally so in view of the nation's racial and civil rights struggles. By the early twenty-first century, the effort to define and limit hate speech was gradually being internationalized. Through such means as grants, Justice Department initiatives, and United Nations conferences, efforts were being pursued toward the goal of designating hate speech in support of war as a crime against humanity.[70]

Special efforts were being made to address the role of hate speech in international relations with the Middle East. Middle Eastern governments showed signs of willingness to partner with the United States and other Western states in battling extremist, hate-oriented ideology. In December 2005 leaders of some forty countries, members of the Organization of the Islamic Conference, met at a two-day summit in Mecca to plan reform of textbooks, restriction of religious edicts, and controls over militant preachers and the financing of terrorists, among other actions.[71] Similarly, in 2006 the government of Saudi Arabia promised to review its educational textbooks and deny governmental funds for publishing books that promote intolerance toward Christians, Jews, and Muslims who do not endorse the Wahhabi view of Islam that is officially endorsed in the kingdom. The move came after negotiations with the U.S. State Department, and was part of the work of a human rights commission created by the Saudi government.[72]

The difficulty of balancing press freedom with the eradication of hate speech was illustrated by events that took place in Rwanda beginning in the 1990s and culminating in 2006. In 1993, a year before the war between the Tutsi minority and the Hutu majority, several Hutu journalists founded a talk radio station called Radio Milles Collines and a newspaper, *Kangura* (Wake It Up!). During the three months of 1994 when Hutus committed genocide against Tutsis, the radio station became the most popular in Rwanda, broadcasting hour after hour of hate-filled content that included songs advocating the killing of Tutsis, indecent anti-Tutsi jokes, pseudoreligious exhortations to kill the enemy, frequent comparisons of the Tutsi to cockroaches, and news of the latest death statistics. In 2006 three of the founders of Radio Milles Collines were put on trial before an international tribunal in Rwanda, charged with crimes against humanity like those brought against Julius Streicher, the editor of the Nazi anti-Jewish newspaper *Der Stürmer*, who was sentenced to death by judges in Nuremberg in 1946. UN prosecutors argued that, as in the case of Streicher, Radio Milles Collines directly contributed to the deaths of hundreds of thousands of Tutsis, and was part of a conspiracy organized for this purpose even before the war began. The prosecution's case, however, was based mostly on circumstantial evidence. This led to an international debate. Some observers worried that a guilty verdict would suppress freedom of speech, that it would be like sending the editors of the *Washington Post* to jail for publishing an angry op-ed article or arresting Joan Baez for singing protest songs. Others argued that such comparisons trivialized the enormous crimes of Radio Milles Collines, and that the time was overdue for the United Nations to take a stronger stand against hate speech.[73]

A great deal of activity was being directed elsewhere toward expanding the role of the media in reporting hate-fueled acts of atrocity and genocide. Autocratic regimes usually try to cover up such incidents. Even in more open environments, disclosure involves a number of difficulties: getting information, understanding what is happening, resisting the temptation to ignore problems, giving priority in reportage, continuing to cover the story, defining one's duty to arouse the public, determining how to do so, and defining the meaning of "genocide," "atrocity," and other key terms.[74]

Getting information to the public, even late after the fact, can be an especially vexing problem. That was the case, for example, in publicizing the decimation of the Armenian population in Turkey early in the twentieth century. An example of mass slaughter that was reported in detail in 2005, in a Pulitzer Prize–winning study, was that in Kenya during the Mau Mau uprisings of the 1950s, as described by Caroline Elkins in her book *Imperial Reckoning*. Two other events with disturbing consequences, the Japanese mistreatment of prisoners of war and the Allied firebombings of enemy cities during the Second World War, became subjects of detailed examinations through widely read books published in 2006: George Weller's, *First into Nagasaki: The Censored Eyewitness Dispatches on Post-Atomic Japan and Its Prisoners of War*, and A. C. Grayling's *Among the Dead Cities: The History and Moral Legacy of the WWII Bombing of Civilians in Germany and Japan*.[75]

Investigators also continued to disclose the many permutations in the story of the Holocaust. For example, an aspect of the Holocaust that was not disclosed until 2006 concerned Poland in the period 1945–1970. After the Allies defeated Nazi Germany in 1945 and the USSR was given control over much of central and eastern Europe, the new communist regime established in Poland used anti-Semitism as a tool. In spite of the terrifyingly vigorous efforts of the Nazis, many Jews in Poland had survived. Some remained in the country because they wanted to. Most were simply trapped there because of the swift takeover by the USSR. Poland had a long history of anti-Semitism, which did not abate simply because of regime change. Polish Jews continued to be targets of hate speech, group rejection, and intimidation, all of which was especially cruel because of the horrors just concluded. Instead of exerting leadership to prevent anti-Semitism, the communists exploited it by willful ignorance and failure to discipline police and other officials who participated. The new regime was worried about its future and was willing to use any means available to win favor and redirect discontent. As a result, many Polish Jews were murdered by individuals or by mobs in what amounted to pogroms. Persecution of Polish Jews continued into the late 1960s. Almost no information about these crimes was widely available at the time. The Polish communist regime enforced rigid censorship. Non-Jewish Poles tacitly cooperated to keep the news out of circulation. Western journalists and visiting governmental observers knew little about what was happening. World opinion never became a factor in the playing out of events. But thanks to work published in 2006 by the historian Jan T. Gross, the story began to receive long-overdue attention.[76]

Through her prizewinning book *"A Problem from Hell": America and the Age of Genocide* (2002), Samantha Power made people much more aware of the recurring patterns of outrage and inability to get powerful people to take action, which were visible in the cases of genocide in Armenia, Nazi Germany, Cambodia, Kurdistan, the former Yugoslavia, and Rwanda. She offered no easy solution to the enormously complex problem of preventing genocide. And she emphasized that a variety of strategies would always be necessary, including, for example, focused employment of military force, economic sanctions, and judicial proceedings. But she also helped analysts to understand the importance of mass communication. Energetic disclosure is essential, Power noted, along with insistent repetition of the facts to leaders and mass audiences, who would almost certainly find reasons to ignore or downplay disturbing information. Especially important, Power counseled, is the role of the media in helping audiences understand the spillover effects of genocide. When moral arguments fail to carry the day, people can be reminded that genocide has a way of harming everyone, not just its immediate victims. Genocide creates large populations of refugees who become a cause of political instability in neighboring countries. It creates a need for foreign economic assistance and slows down processes of economic development. It creates public health problems that lead to widespread disease, in some cases contributing to pandemics. Authoritarian political leaders allowed to engage in genocide are emboldened to think that uses of force beyond their borders will go unchallenged. By informing audiences of these considerations, the media help to prevent instances of genocide from being ignored and can bring focus to discussions regarding how best to intervene, so that energies are not misdirected and no one can use misinformation or past experience to argue that effort is futile.[77]

Early-twenty-first-century disclosures of past atrocities took place in tandem with more present-oriented efforts. Celebrities gained a growing understanding of their power to focus attention on international crises, for example, in the Darfur region of Sudan. By 2003, over 200,000 people from that area had already been killed and 2.5 million displaced. Celebrities such as the actor George Clooney and the singer Bono used their media access to call attention to the crisis in Darfur, and sporadic action was taken by the United Nations and international charities. Then in 2007 international pressure on the Sudanese government increased greatly, thanks to sudden diplomatic moves by the Chinese, who were pressured to act by the Hollywood producer Stephen Spielberg and the actress Mia Farrow. In television appearances and newspaper articles Farrow warned China that the 2008 Olympic Games in Beijing would become known as the "Genocide Olympics" if China failed to make constructive use of its influence as a major trading partner of Sudan and investor in the country's oil industry. In his role as an artistic adviser to China for the Games, Spielberg publicly echoed Farrow's exhortations.[78] The approaching Olympics also provided publicity opportunities for the growing movement for independence in Tibet, which had been under Chinese control since the 1950s. Worldwide media coverage of protests by Tibetan monks, and the ensuing Chinese crackdown, created vexing problems of diplomacy for the People's Republic at the precise moment when it was seeking to burnish its image. Nor could the repressive dictatorship in Myanmar (Burma) escape the consequences of unwanted publicity. In 2008, when the country was devastated by an enormous cyclone and Myanmar's rulers brutally limited donations of aid from the world community, international media coverage underlined the government's deep lack of confidence in itself.

One sector of mass communication that was slow to rise to the challenges of defusing hate in a post-9/11 world was the film industry. In the weeks after 9/11, Hollywood powerbrokers held a widely publicized meeting with President Bush and swore an oath that the major studios would produce more films promoting international understanding.[79] This gesture reflected a long Hollywood tradition, since filmmakers have contributed many powerful explorations over the years of the possibility of peace and the need to understand the roots of anger. For example, in *The Grand Illusion* (1937), Jean Renoir showed how fantasies of war based on ideas of chivalric combat became untenable in the conditions of the First World War. *The Watch on the Rhine* (1943), based on the play by Lillian Hellman, offered a haunting examination of efforts to promote peace by one dedicated, eloquent leader whose techniques combined politics and a religious sense of universal obligation. In *Paths of Glory* (1958), set in the First World War, the director Stanley Kubrick showed how nationalism could be manipulated to conceal military corruption and incompetence. *Gandhi* (1982), directed by Richard Attenborough, used the story of the Indian independence movement to inspire renewed efforts to end the cold war. *The Killing Fields* (1984) exposed the horror of genocide in Cambodia and stressed the obligation of its central character, a prominent journalist, to acknowledge that he had become famous in part by reporting on but not actively opposing that genocide. In *Schindler's List* (1993), Stephen Spielberg used the power of film to give audiences a greatly enlarged sense of the evil and pain of the Holocaust and to pay tribute to those who, like the film's hero, risked their lives to save people at moments of great ethical complexity.

The long-term record made it probable that new formulas for the use of cinema to lessen hatred and promote peacefulness would be developed for the twenty-first century. Possibilities were suggested by productions like *Hotel Rwanda* (2005), which chronicled heroism in the midst of genocide; *Babel* (2006), which asked audiences to be more aware of the ways that acts of individual and paramilitary violence could be linked in the contemporary world; and *Pan's Labyrinth* (2006), which mixed fact and fantasy, live actors, and digital technology to explore the long-term effects of war on both adults and children.

Of all the interactions involving peace and mass communication that took place in the years after 9/11, the most interesting may have been the one that occurred in October 2006, when the secretary of the Norwegian Nobel Committee, the body responsible for choosing the winner of the Nobel Peace Prize, disclosed that the committee had recently commissioned a report on the link between eradication of collective enmity and news coverage and was considering the possibility of awarding the Peace Prize to a media outlet. The secretary mentioned CNN, the *New York Times*, the *Washington Post*, *Le Monde*, and *El País* as possible contenders. "Good news coverage, as opposed to propaganda or inaccurate reports, can be essential to peace," the secretary commented.[80] The remark was a powerful reminder that an important aspect of human experience had changed over the course of the previous 150 years. War, peace, and mass communication were now interwoven.

Notes

1. War Encounters Mass Communication

1. John Hohenberg, *Foreign Correspondence: The Great Reporters and Their Times* (New York: Columbia University Press, 1964), 10.

2. On Napoleon, see Philip M. Taylor, *Munitions of the Mind: A History of Propaganda from the Ancient World to the Present Day*, 3rd ed. (Manchester: Manchester University Press, 2003), 153–57. On Wellington, see Antony Brett-James, ed., *Wellington at War, 1794–1815: A Selection of his Wartime Letters* (London: Macmillan, 1961).

3. For an exploration of the origins and changing meaning of this widely used word, see Asa Briggs, "The Language of 'Mass' and 'Masses' in Nineteenth-Century England," in *Collected Essays of Asa Briggs: Words, Numbers, Places, People* (Urbana: University of Illinois Press, 1988), 34–54.

4. On Northcliffe, see Gary S. Messinger, *British Propaganda and the State in the First World War* (Manchester: Manchester University Press, 1992), 144–61.

5. On yellow journalism, see David Nasaw, *The Chief: The Life of William Randolph Hearst* (Boston: Houghton Mifflin, 2000), and W. A. Swanberg, *Pulitzer* (New York: Charles Scribner's Sons, 1967).

6. For an informative discussion of the emergence of public opinion in the newly expanding cities, see Hans Speier, "The Rise of Public Opinion," in *Propaganda*, ed. Robert Jackall (New York: New York University Press, 1995), 26–46. For analysis of the growing importance of the urban press, see Peter Fritzsche, *Reading Berlin 1900* (Cambridge: Harvard University Press, 1996), with its extensive list of citations regarding research in this field. For additional information on journalism in Berlin around the turn to the twentieth century, see Gerhard Masur, *Imperial Berlin* (New York: Dorset Press, 1970), esp. 60–70, 69–73, and 173–87.

7. Useful discussions of the press before 1914 are Stephen Koss, *The Rise and Fall of the Political Press in Britain: The Nineteenth Century* (Chapel Hill: University of North Carolina Press, 1981), and *The Rise and Fall of the Political Press in Britain II: The Twentieth Century* (Chapel Hill: University of North Carolina Press, 1984); and Alan J. Lee, *The Origins of the Popular Press, 1855–1914* (London: Croom Helm, 1976). For extensive statistical information about the press in the late nineteenth and early twentieth centuries, see the article "Newspapers" in *Encyclopaedia Britannica*, 11th ed. (Cambridge: Cambridge University Press, 1910–1911), 19:544–81.

8. Hohenberg, *Foreign Correspondence*, 62.

9. Phillip Knightley, *The First Casualty: From the Crimea to Vietnam; The War Correspondent as Hero, Propagandist, and Myth Maker* (New York: Harcourt Brace Jovanovich, 1975), 20–39; Drew Gilpin Faust, *This Republic of Suffering: Death and the American Civil War* (New York: Alfred A. Knopf, 2008).

10. An invaluable study of the relationship of the press to the state's sphere in making war and peace is Oron J. Hale, *Publicity and Diplomacy, with Special Reference to England and Germany, 1890–1914* (New York: D. Appleton Company, 1940).

11. David Ayerst, *The Manchester Guardian: Biography of a Newspaper* (Ithaca: Cornell University Press, 1971), 273–86.

12. Knightley, *First Casualty*, 67–69.

13. Jacqueline Beaumont, "The British Press during the South African War: The Sieges of Mafeking, Kimberley and Ladysmith," in *War and the Media: Reportage and Propaganda, 1900–2003*, ed. Mark Connelly and David Welch (London: I. B. Taurus, 2005), 1–18.

14. Knightley, *First Casualty*, 66–78.

15. I. F. Clarke, *Voices Prophesying War, 1763–1984* (London: Oxford University Press, 1966); John A. Hobson, *The Psychology of Jingoism* (London: Grant Richards, 1901); Paul M. Kennedy, *The Rise of the Anglo-German Antagonism, 1860–1914* (1980; London: Ashfield Press, 1987); and Anthony Morris, *The Scaremongers: The Advocacy of War and Rearmament, 1896–1914* (London: Routledge and Kegan Paul, 1984).

16. See the seminal analysis by Asa Briggs, "The Communications Revolution," in *Serious Pursuits: Communications and Education*, vol. 3, *The Collected Essays of Asa Briggs* (London: Harvester Wheatsheaf, 1991), 62–76. Also very informative is Anthony Smith, *The Newspaper: An International History* (London: Thames and Hudson, 1979.

17. Stephen Kern, *The Culture of Time and Space, 1880–1918* (Cambridge: Harvard University Press, 1983), 258–77.

2. Mass Communication Enlists

1. Quotations from Edward Timms, *Karl Kraus: Apocalyptic Satirist* (New Haven: Yale University Press, 1986), cited in Niall Ferguson, *The Pity of War* (New York: Basic Books, 1999), 240–41.

2. Quoted in Gary S. Messinger, *British Propaganda and the State in the First World War* (Manchester and New York: Manchester University Press/St. Martin's Press, 1992), 189–90.

3. Quoted in M. L. Sanders and Philip M. Taylor, *British Propaganda during the First World War, 1914–1918* (London: Macmillan, 1982), 211.

4. Prewar press relations are discussed in Harold J. Hanham, *Elections and Party Management: Politics in the Time of Disraeli and Gladstone* (1959; Brighton: Harvester Press, 1978); and Basil Kingsley Martin, *The Triumph of Lord Palmerston* (London: Allen and Unwin, 1924).

5. The increasing role of government in manipulating public opinion is discussed in Messinger, *British Propagada;* and Sanders and Taylor, *British Propaganda during the First World War.* For a catalogue of definitions and varied usages of the

term "propaganda," see Nicholas J. Cull, David Culbert, and David Welch, *Propaganda and Mass Persuasion: A Historical Encyclopedia, 1500 to the Present* (Santa Barbara: ABC-Clio, 2003), 317–23.

6. Marc Ferro, *The Great War, 1914–1918* (London: Routledge, 2001), 111–12.

7. Quoted in Harold Lasswell, *Propaganda Technique in World War I* (1927; Cambridge: MIT Press, 1971), 32.

8. German propaganda is analyzed in Lasswell, *Propaganda Technique*, esp. 22–24 and 32–36.

9. Quoted in Ferguson, *Pity of War*, 212–13.

10. Bethmann Hollweg quoted in Bernadotte C. Schmitt and Harold C. Vedeler, *The World in the Crucible, 1914–1919* (New York: Harper and Row, 1984), 315.

11. See George G. Bruntz, "Allied Propaganda and the Collapse of German Morale in 1918," in *A Psychological Warfare Casebook*, ed. William E. Daugherty (Baltimore: Johns Hopkins University Press, 1958), 96–105; and Bruntz, *Allied Propaganda and the Collapse of the German Empire in 1918* (Stanford: Stanford University Press, 1938). The lack of universal appeal in German propaganda is discussed in Hans Thimme, *Weltkrieg ohne Waffen* (Stuttgart: J. G. Cotta'sche Buchhandlung, 1932). For information on other European analysts of the effects of propaganda, see Everette D. Dennis and Ellen Wartella, *Communication Research: The Remembered History* (Mahwah, N.J.: Lawrence Erlbaum Associates, 1996).

12. On propaganda in France, Belgium, Italy, and other countries, see Peter Chalmers Mitchell, "Propaganda," in *Encyclopaedia Britannica*, 12th ed., vol. 32 (London: Britannica Publishers, 1922), 176–85. A recent detailed study is Mark Cornwall, *The Undermining of Austria-Hungary: The Battle for Hearts and Minds* (New York: St. Martin's Press, 2000).

13. On the participation of intellectuals, see Albert Marrin, *The Last Crusade: The Church of England in the First World War* (Durham: Duke University Press, 1974); Roland Stromberg, *Redemption by War: The Intellectuals and 1914* (Lawrence: Regents Press of Kansas, 1982); Stuart Wallace, *War and the Image of Germany: British Academics, 1914–1918* (Edinburgh: John Donald, 1988); D. G. Wright, "The Great War, Government Propaganda and English 'Men of Letters,' 1914–1916," *Literature and History*, no. 7 (Spring 1978): 70–100; and Mark Wollaeger, *Modernism, Media, and Propaganda: British Narrative from 1900 to 1945* (Princeton: Princeton University Press, 2007).

14. Defence of the Realm Acts quoted in Ferguson, *Pity of War*, 219.

15. The infamous Bryce Report is analyzed in Messinger, *British Propaganda*, 70–84; and in Trevor Wilson, *The Myriad Faces of War: Britain and the Great War, 1914–1918* (Cambridge: Polity Press, 1986), 182–91.

16. On Britain, see Messinger, *British Propaganda*; Sanders and Taylor, *British Propaganda during the First World War*; Cate Haste, *Keep the Home Fires Burning: Propaganda in the First World War* (London: Allen Lane, 1977); and Irene Cooper Willis, *England's Holy War: A Study of English Liberal Idealism during the Great War* (New York: Alfred Knopf, 1928).

17. Ads quoted in J. M. Winter, *The Experience of World War I* (New York: Oxford University Press, 1989), 188–89. For a general discussion of the role of advertising in Britain during the war, see Messinger, *British Propaganda*, 213–24.

18. Sir Gilbert Parker's activity in America is summarized ibid., 53–69.

19. Barbara Tuchman, *The Zimmermann Telegram* (New York: Ballantine Books, 1966).

20. On the run-up to the Great War in the United States, see Edwin Emery, *The Press and America: An Interpretative History of the Mass Media*, 3rd ed. (Englewood Cliffs, N.J.: Prentice-Hall, 1972), 507–11; H. C. Peterson, *Propaganda for War* (Norman: University of Oklahoma Press, 1939); Ralph D. Casey, "The Press, Propaganda, and Pressure Groups," *Annals of the American Academy of Political and Social Science* 219 (January 1942): 68.

21. Debs quoted in Emery, *Press and America*, 517. On American propaganda in the war, see George Creel, *How We Advertised America* (New York: Harper & Row, 1920); Harold Lavine and James Wechsler, *War Propaganda and the United States* (New Haven: Yale University Press, 1940); Alfred E. Cornebise, *War as Advertised: The Four Minute Men and America's Crusade, 1917–1918* (Philadelphia: American Philosophical Society, 1984); James R. Mock and Cedric Larson, *Words That Won the War: The Story of the Committee on Public Information, 1917–1919* (Princeton: Princeton University Press, 1939); Emery, *Press and America*, 511–19; David M. Kennedy, *Over Here: The First World War and American Society* (1980; New York: Oxford University Press, 2004), 45–92; and Geoffrey Stone, *Perilous Times: Free Speech in Wartime; From the Sedition Act of 1798 to the War on Terrorism* (New York: W. W. Norton, 2004).

22. Creel quoted in Philip M. Taylor, *Munitions of the Mind: A History of Propaganda from the Ancient World to the Present Day*, 3rd ed. (Manchester: Manchester University Press, 2003), 183. Pershing quotation, tobacco slogans, and information on Gillette from Michael Schudson, *Advertising: The Uneasy Persuasion* (New York: Basic Books, 1984), 186–87.

23. For the use of gramophones as well as other aspects of the propaganda war in central Europe, see Hugh Seton-Watson and Christopher Seton-Watson, *The Making of a New Europe: R. W. Seton-Watson and the Last Years of Austria-Hungary* (Seattle: University of Washington Press, 1981).

24. Charles H. Brown, *The Correspondents' War: Journalism in the Spanish-American War* (New York: Scribner's, 1967); Frank Freidel, *The Splendid Little War* (Boston: Little, Brown, 1958); Cull, Culbert, and Welch, *Propaganda and Mass Persuasion*, 378–79.

25. Craig Campbell, *Reel America and World War I* (Jefferson, N.C.: McFarland, 1985); Michael I. Isenberg, *War on Film* (Rutherford, N.J.: Fairleigh Dickinson University Press, 1980); David H. Mould, *American Newsfilm, 1914–1919* (New York: Garland, 1983); Nicholas Reeves, *Official British Film Propaganda during the First World War* (London: Croom Helm, 1986). For a fascinating contemporary account, see Lucy Masterman, *C. F. G. Masterman: A Biography* (London: Nicholson and Watson, 1939).

26. Richard M. Barsam, *Nonfiction Film: A Critical History*, rev. ed. (Bloomington: Indiana University Press, 1992), 36–37.

27. Ibid., 37–41. On German film, see Miriam Hansen, "Early Silent Cinema: Whose Public Sphere?" *New German Critique*, no. 29, "The Origins of Mass Culture: The Case of Imperial Germany (1871–1918)" (Spring–Summer 1983): 147–84.

28. See Eric Barnouw, *Documentary: A History of the Non-fiction Film* (New York: Oxford University Press, 1993); Michael Paris, ed., *The First World War and Popular Cinema: 1914 to the Present* (Edinburgh: Edinburgh University Press, 1994); and Andrew Kelly, *Cinema and the Great War* (New York: Routledge, 1997).

29. Jane Carmichael, *First World War Photographers* (London: Routledge, 1989); Stuart Sillars, *Art and Survival in First World War Britain* (New York: St. Martin's, 1978); Meirion Harries and Susie Harries, *The War Artists: British Official War Art of the Twentieth Century* (London: Michael Joseph/Imperial War Museum and Tate Gallery, 1983); Kenneth E. Silver, *Esprit de Corps: The Art of the Parisian Avant-Garde and the First World War, 1914–1925* (Princeton: Princeton University Press, 1989); Maria Tippett, *Art at the Service of War: Canada, Art, and the Great War* (Toronto: University of Toronto Press, 1984).

30. For illustrations and analysis of advertising and postcards, see Winter, *Experience of World War I*, 188–89.

31. The long-term importance of the rhetorical tradition is one of the themes of J. Michael Sproule, *Propaganda and Democracy: American Experience of Media and Mass Persuasion* (Cambridge: Cambridge University Press, 1997).

32. Australian War Museum, ed., *What Did You Do in the War, Daddy? A Visual History of Propaganda Posters*, intro. Peter Stanley (Melbourne: Oxford University Press, 1983); Libby Chenault, *Battlelines: World War I Posters from the Bowman Gray Collection* (Chapel Hill: University of North Carolina Press, 1988); Schmitt and Vedeler, *World in the Crucible*, 214–19.

33. Phillip Knightley, *The First Casualty: From the Crimea to Vietnam; The War Correspondent as Hero, Propagandist, and Myth Maker* (New York: Harcourt Brace Jovanovich, 1975), 87–88.

34. Two fascinating contemporary accounts of attempts to balance military and press priorities are Sir Douglas Brownrigg, *Indiscretions of the Naval Censor* (New York: Doran, 1920); and Sir Edward Tyas Cook, *The Press in War-Time* (London: Macmillan, 1920). See also Colin Lovelace, "British Press Censorship during the First World War," in *Newspaper History from the Seventeenth Century to the Present Day*, ed. George Boyce, James Curran, and Pauline Wingate (London: Constable, 1978), 307–19.

35. See Heywood Broun, *The AEF: With General Pershing and the American Forces* (New York: Appleton, 1918), and *Collected Edition of Heywood Broun* (New York: Harcourt Brace, 1941), for examples of this distinguished American reporter's efforts to cope with censorship.

36. For the regrets of a respected British correspondent, see Philip Gibbs, *Adventures in Journalism* (London: Heinemann, 1923).

37. C. E. Montague, quoted in Messinger, *British Propaganda*, 247–48.

3. The Democracies Try to Demobilize

1. Information on reporters attending the Paris conference is from Robert W. Desmond, *Windows on the World: The Information Process in a Changing Society, 1900–1920* (Iowa City: University of Iowa Press, 1980), 405–27. Two of the many books on the conference are William K. Klingaman, *1919: The Year Our World*

Began (1987; New York: Harper and Row, 1989); and Margaret MacMillan, *Paris 1919: Six Months That Changed the World* (New York: Random House, 2001). The interaction of the journalistic and literary communities is described in Ronald Weber, *News of Paris: American Journalism in the City of Light between the Wars* (Chicago: Ivan R. Dee, 2006).

2. John Maynard Keynes, *The Economic Consequences of the Peace* (1920), in *Collected Writings*, vol. 10 (London: Macmillan, 1972), 3–19; Harold Nicolson, *Peacemaking, 1919* (New York: Grosset and Dunlap, 1965), 60–62.

3. Colorful accounts of the Hague conferences are in Barbara Tuchman, *The Proud Tower: A Portrait of the World before the War, 1890–1914* (1966; New York: Bantam Books, 1967), esp. 292–312 and 324–38.

4. On peace initiatives by Morel and others, see F. L. Carsten, *War against War: British and German Radical Movements in the First World War* (Berkeley: University of California Press, 1982). A sense of earlier activities can be gained from Paul Laity, *The British Peace Movement, 1870–1914*, Oxford Historical Monographs (New York: Oxford University Press, 2001).

5. Desmond, *Windows on the World*, 413–14.

6. Details of the League's efforts to assist journalists are given in Paul F. Douglas, Karl Boehmer, and Emil Dovifat, "Supplement: The Press as a Factor in International Relations," *Annals of the American Academy of Political and Social Sciences* 162, "National and World Planning" (July 1932): 241–72.

7. Nicholas Pronay and Philip M. Taylor, "'An Improper Use of Broadcasting . . .': The British Government and Clandestine Radio Operations against Germany during the Munich Crisis and After," *Journal of Contemporary History* 19 (1984): 357–84.

8. Akira Iriye, *Cultural Internationalism and World Order* (Baltimore: Johns Hopkins University Press, 1997), 62–67, 75. For an argument that the League could have been more vigorous in its use of mass communication, even with limited resources, see Dell G. Hitchner, "The Failure of the League: Lessons in Public Relations," *Public Opinion Quarterly* 8, no. 1 (Spring 1944): 61–71.

9. Escapist media coverage in Britain is described in Robert Graves and Alan Hodge, *The Long Week-End: A Social History of Great Britain, 1918–1939* (1940; New York: Norton Library, 1963). For the American environment, see Frederick Lewis Allen's two social histories, *Only Yesterday* (1931; New York: Perennial Library, 1964) and *Since Yesterday* (1940; New York: Perennial Library, 1986).

10. Thomas J. Knock, *To End All Wars: Woodrow Wilson and the Quest for a New World Order* (Princeton: Princeton University Press, 1992).

11. Palmer quoted in James Aronson, *The Press and the Cold War* (Indianapolis: Bobbs-Merrill, 1970), 29. Villard information from ibid., 30.

12. Nancy Snow, *Propaganda, Inc.* (New York: Seven Stories Press, 2002), 37.

13. Mark Crispin Miller, introduction to Edward Bernays, *Propaganda* (1928; Brooklyn: Ig Publishing, 2005), 9–33. Bernays published his life story in *Biography of an Idea: Memoirs of Public Relations Counsel Edward L. Bernays* (New York: Simon & Schuster, 1965).

14. For additional context covering several media, see D. L. LeMahieu, *A Culture for Democracy: Mass Communication and the Cultivated Mind in Britain between the Wars* (Oxford: Clarendon Press of Oxford University Press, 1988). For a comparative

analysis of radio in the United States, Britain, and other countries, see Alice Gold-farb Marquis, "Written on the Wind: The Impact of Radio in the 1930s," *Journal of Contemporary History* 19, no. 3 (July 1984): 385–415; and Nicholas J. Cull, David Culbert, and David Welch, *Propaganda and Mass Persuasion: A Historical Encyclopedia, 1500 to the Present* (Santa Barbara: ABC-Clio, 2003), 331–34. An essential work is Asa Briggs, *The History of Broadcasting in the United Kingdom*, vol. 1, *The Birth of Broadcasting* (Oxford: Oxford University Press, 1961). Also useful are Asa Briggs, *The BBC: The First Fifty Years* (Oxford: Oxford University Press, 1995); and Asa Briggs and Peter Burke, *A Social History of the Media* (Cambridge: Polity Press, 2002).

15. Arthur Ponsonby, *Falsehood in War-Time* (New York: Allen and Unwin, 1928).

16. Lippmann quoted in Ronald Steel, *Walter Lippmann and the American Century* (Boston: Atlantic Monthly Press, 1980), 182.

17. On the historical context of Lippmann's analysis, and the response of critics, see Steel, *Walter Lippmann*, 171–85 and 211–16.

18. Sidney B. Fay, *The Origins of the World War*, 2 vols. (New York: Macmillan, 1928–1930), 1:47.

19. On the role of Lasswell and other analysts of propaganda before the Second World War, see J. Michael Sproule, *Propaganda and Democracy: American Experience of Media and Mass Persuasion* (Cambridge: Cambridge University Press, 1997).

20. Jonathan Alter, *The Defining Moment: FDR's Hundred Days and the Triumph of Hope* (New York: Simon & Schuster, 2006).

21. *Printer's Ink*, June 18, 1931, quoted in Stephen Fox, *The Mirror Makers: A History of American Advertising and Its Creators* (1984; New York: Vintage, 1985), 117. On Roosevelt's ability to interpret public opinion, see Steven Casey, *Cautious Crusade: Franklin D. Roosevelt, American Public Opinion, and the War against Nazi Germany* (New York: Oxford University Press, 2001), 3–45.

22. Milton Israel, *Communications and Power: Propaganda and the Press in the Indian National Struggle, 1920–1947* (Cambridge: Cambridge University Press, 1994).

23. Raphael Levy, "The Daily Press in France," *Modern Language Journal* 13, no. 4 (January 1929): 294–303.

24. Donald S. Birn, "Open Diplomacy at the Washington Conference of 1921–2: The British and French Experience," *Comparative Studies in Society and History* 12, no. 3 (July 1970): 297–319.

25. Conyers Read, "More Light on the London Naval Treaty of 1930," *Proceedings of the American Philosophical Society* 93, no. 4 (September 1949): 290–308.

26. Robert J. Young, *Marketing Marianne: French Propaganda in America, 1900–1940* (New Brunswick: Rutgers University Press, 2004); William R. Keylor, "How They Advertised France: The French Propaganda Campaign in the United States during the Breakup of the Franco-American Entente, 1918–1923," *Diplomatic History* 17, no. 3 (Summer 1993): 351–74.

27. Arthur Willert, "Publicity and Propaganda in International Affairs," *International Affairs (Royal Institute of International Affairs, 1931–1939)* 17, no. 6 (November–December 1938): 809–26; Nicholas Pronay and Philip M. Taylor, "An Improper Use of Broadcasting," 357–84.

28. Oron James Hale, "Nationalism in Press, Films, and Radio," *Annals of the American Academy of Political and Social Science*, vol. 175, "The Shadow of War"

(September 1934): 110–16; Special Committee Investigating the Munitions Industry, U.S. Senate, Pursuant to S. Res. 206, *Congressional Record* 75, no. 1, April 12, 1934; *Report of the Special Committee on the Investigation of the Munitions Industry*, U.S. Congress, Senate, 34th Cong., 2nd sess., February 24, 1936; this was the final report of the so-called Nye Committee, led by Senator Gerald Nye of North Dakota.

4. Dictators Conquer Their Media

1. See Gary S. Messinger, *British Propaganda and the State in the First World War* (Manchester: Manchester University Press, 1992), 249–56.

2. See, for example, Peter Kenez, *The Birth of the Propaganda State: Soviet Methods of Mass Mobilization, 1917–1929* (Cambridge: Cambridge University Press, 1985). Napoleonic France is sometimes called the "first propaganda state," because Napoleon sought to strengthen his rule by extensive, coordinated use of news reportage, censorship, espionage, mass pageantry, and visual propaganda such as paintings and images on coins. But communications technology was more industrialized by the early twentieth century, and theories on the use of media in politics were more detailed and self-conscious.

3. On Reed and Philips Price, see Phillip Knightley, *The First Casualty: From the Crimea to Vietnam; The War Correspondent as Hero, Propagandist, and Myth Maker* (New York: Harcourt Brace Jovanovich, 1975), 147–48.

4. Lippmann and Merz quoted in James Aronson, *The Press and the Cold War* (Indianapolis: Bobbs-Merrill, 1970), 25–28.

5. Robert W. Desmond, *Tides of War: World News Reporting, 1931–1945* (Iowa City: University of Iowa Press, 1984), 53–57; W. Vincent Arnold, *The Illusion of Victory: Fascist Propaganda and the Second World War* (New York: Peter Lang, 1998).

6. Edward R. Tannenbaum, *The Fascist Experience: Italian Society and Culture, 1922–1945* (New York: Basic Books, 1972), 211–48.

7. Desmond, *Tides of War*, 21–28.

8. The poster is reprinted in Tannenbaum, *Fascist Experience*, in the illustrations after page 210.

9. Quotations from Hitler and summary of *Mein Kampf* from Cedric Larson, "The German Press Chamber," *Public Opinion Quarterly* 1, no. 4 (October 1937): 53–70. A useful English-language edition of *Mein Kampf*, as originally translated by Ralph Manheim, and with a later introduction by Abraham Foxman, was published by Houghton Mifflin in 1999. For informative, detailed analyses of the Nazi takeover of Germany, including research on the Nazis' use of mass communication, see Richard J. Evans, *The Coming of the Third Reich* (New York: Penguin Books, 2003), and *The Third Reich in Power: 1933–1939* (New York: Penguin Books, 2006).

10. Oron J. Hale, *The Captive Press in the Third Reich* (Princeton: Princeton University Press, 1964); Anthony Smith, *The Newspaper: An International History* (London: Thames and Hudson, 1979), 177–78.

11. A moving account of two English intellectuals (Julian Bell and John Cornford) who participated in the war is Peter Stansky and William Abrahams, *Journey to the Frontier: Two Roads to the Spanish Civil War* (Boston: Atlantic Monthly Press/Little Brown, 1966).

12. Trevor Hoyle, *War Report: The War Correspondent's View of Battle from the Crimea to the Falklands* (London: Grafton Books, 1987), 15, cited in Philip M. Taylor, *Global Communications, International Affairs, and the Media since 1945* (London: Routledge, 1997), 121.

13. Information on Spanish media in the civil war is from Desmond, *Tides of War*, 36–45; and Anthony Beevor, *The Battle for Spain: The Spanish Civil War, 1936–1939*, rev. ed. (New York: Penguin Books, 2006), 239–50.

14. On Mao's approach to propaganda, see Frederick T. C. Yu, *Mass Persuasion in Communist China* (New York: Frederick A. Praeger, 1964).

15. For a detailed analysis of early-twentieth-century propaganda in China, see Marianne Bastide-Bruigueire, "Patterns of Propaganda Organization in the National-Revolutionary Movement in China in the 1920s," in *The Chinese Revolution in the 1920s: Between Triumph and Disaster*, ed. Mechtild Leutner, Roland Felber, M. L. Titarenko, and A. M. Grigoriev (London: Routledge/Curzon, 2002), 3–29. An expert summary by Rana Mitter of propaganda in China from ancient to modern times is available in Nicholas J. Cull, David Culbert, and David Welch, *Propaganda and Mass Persuasion: A Historical Encyclopedia, 1500 to the Present* (Santa Barbara: ABC-Clio, 2003), 73–77.

16. Smith, *The Newspaper*, 170; Desmond, *Tides of War*, 4–6, 10–11. On the development of the press in China, see Henrietta Harrison, "Newspapers and Nationalism in Rural China, 1890–1929," *Past and Present*, no. 166 (2006): 181–204; Barbara Mittler, *A Newspaper for China? Power, Identity, and Change in Shanghai's News Media, 1872–1912* (Cambridge: Harvard University Press, 2004); and Lin Yutang, *A History of the Press and Public Opinion in China* (Chicago: University of Chicago Press, 1936).

17. See Peter Rand, *China Hands: The Adventures and Ordeals of the American Journalists Who Joined Forces with the Great Chinese Revolution* (New York: Simon & Schuster, 1995). Also very informative is Baruch Hirson and Arthur J. Knodel, *Reporting the Chinese Revolution: The Letters of Rayna Prohme*, ed. with an introduction by Gregor Benton (London: Pluto Press, 2007).

18. See Andrew Sinclair, *Jack: A Biography of Jack London* (New York: Harper and Row, 1977), 104–7.

19. Images of the Nanking massacre were revived by U.S. propagandists in the Second World War, for example, by Frank Capra in his documentary film series *Why We Fight*. But then after the war, information about the horrors of the 1937 invasion of the city was again downplayed in the West, both by the U.S. government and by cooperative leaders of the media, out of fear of offending powerful political groups in Japan and losing Japan as an ally in the cold war. Thanks to disclosures by the historian Iris Chang in the 1990s, the truth about Nanking has become more widely known and is stimulating international debate. See Iris Chang, *The Rape of Nanking: The Forgotten Holocaust of World War II* (New York: Basic Books, 1997), esp. 143–58. Whether the events in Nanking, brutal as they were, were extensive enough to be described as a "holocaust" is discussed in Takashi Yoshida, *The Making of the "Rape of Nanking": History and Memory in Japan, China, and the United States* (New York: Oxford University Press, 2006). The Chinese communists' exploitation of memories of Nanking to sustain hatred against the Japanese is discussed in Ian Buruma, "Why They Hate Japan," *New York*

Review of Books, September 21, 2006, 78–82, a review of Yoshida's book. The problem of defining genocide is discussed in Allan A. Ryan Jr., "Genocide: What Do We Want It To Be?" *New England Journal of Public Policy* 19, no. 2 (Winter 2005): 111–10.

20. On Japanese media in the period covered by this chapter, see Desmond, *Tides of War,* 4–18 and 190–98; Smith, *The Newspaper,* 170–72; James Huffman, *Creating a Public: People and Press in Meiji Japan* (Honolulu: University of Hawaii Press, 1997); and Barak Kushner, *The Thought War: Japanese Imperial Propaganda* (Honolulu: University of Hawaii Press, 2006). An extensive collection of primary source material is Peter O'Connor, ed., *Japanese Propaganda: Selected Readings,* 10 vols. (Tokyo: Edition Synapse, 2003–4).

21. Dawson quotations from Richard Cockett, *Twilight of Truth: Chamberlain, Appeasement, and the Manipulation of the Press* (London: St. Martin's Press, 1989), 27 and 54. Additional information is in Desmond, *Tides of War,* 64–65, 67–69, 70–71; Anthony Adamthwaite, "The British Government and the Media, 1937–1938," *Journal of Contemporary History* 18, no. 2 (April 1983): 281–97; Frank McDonough, "*The Times,* Norman Ebbut and the Nazis, 1927–1937," *Journal of Contemporary History* 27, no. 3 (July 1992): 407–24. During the Munich crisis, in an attempt to mobilize German public opinion against Hitler's attempts to annex the Sudetenland, Chamberlain directed British espionage agents to broadcast the British point of view into Germany from the powerful radio transmitter that was available in Luxembourg. On this episode, see Nicholas Pronay and Philip M. Taylor, "'An Improper Use of Broadcasting . . .': The British Government and Clandestine Radio Propaganda Operations against Germany during the Munich Crisis and After," *Journal of Contemporary History* 19, no. 3 (July 1984): 357–84.

5. The Battle for the Mind Deepens

1. One study of propaganda directed at children in the First World War is Margaret R. Higgonet, *The Lion and the Unicorn* (Baltimore: Johns Hopkins University Press, 2007). Propaganda against children in the Second World War is discussed in Nicholas Stargardt, *Witnesses of War: Children's Lives under the Nazis* (New York: Vintage/Random House, 2005), esp. 28, 44, 51, 121, 142–43, 251; and in Judith K. Proud, *Children and Propaganda: Il était une fois . . . ; Fiction and Fairy Tale in Vichy France* (Oxford: Intellect Books, 1995). The effect of war propaganda on children is still not well understood. A valuable study of the effect of images of violence on children is Betsy McAlister Groves, *Children Who See Too Much: Lessons from the Child Witness to Violence Project* (Boston: Beacon Press, 2002). Also useful is Marsha Kinder, ed., *Kids' Media Culture* (Durham: Duke University Press, 1999).

2. Of the hundreds of books on Second World War propaganda in Germany, two especially informative works are David Welch, *The Third Reich: Politics and Propaganda,* 2nd ed. (London: Routledge, 2002); and Ian Kershaw, *The Hitler Myth: Image and Reality in the Third Reich* (Oxford: Oxford University Press, 1987). The vast extent of German propaganda organization is demonstrated in Richard J. Evans, *The Third Reich at War* (New York: Penguin Press, 2009), esp. 563–92. Italian propaganda is analyzed in W. Vincent Arnold, *The Illusion of Victory: Fascist Propaganda and the Second World War* (New York: Peter Lang, 1998).

3. For interesting descriptions of Albert Speer's use of mass rallies and newsreels to assure the German people that arms production was vigorous, see Adam Tooze, *The Wages of Destruction: The Making and Breaking of the Nazi Economy* (New York: Penguin Books, 2006), 554–56.

4. Quoted in Welch, *Third Reich*, 101.

5. Stargardt, *Witnesses of War*, 142.

6. Nigel Farndale, *Haw-Haw: The Tragedy of William and Margaret Joyce* (London: Macmillan, 2005); M. Williams Fuller, *Axis Sally* (Santa Barbara: Paradise West Publishing, 2003).

7. For opinion manipulation viewed in bio-behavioral terms, see Charles Cruickshank, *The Fourth Arm: Psychological Warfare, 1938–1945* (Oxford: Oxford University Press, 1981); William E. Daugherty and Morris Janowitz, *A Psychological Warfare Casebook* (Baltimore: Johns Hopkins University Press, 1958); and Charles Roetter, *Psychological Warfare* (London: B. T. Batsford, 1974).

8. William Sheridan Allen, *The Nazi Seizure of Power: The Experience of a Single German Town, 1922–1945* (New York: Franklin Watts, 1984), esp. 250–55, 301–2.

9. Information on news coverage in the USSR from 1939 to 1945 is from Robert W. Desmond, *Tides of War: World News Reporting, 1931–1945* (Iowa City: University of Iowa Press, 1984), 46–47, 161–80.

10. Denise J. Youngblood, *Russian War Films: On the Cinema Front* (Kansas City: University Press of Kansas, 2007).

11. On domestic propaganda in Soviet Russia, see Catherine Merridale, *Ivan's War: Life and Death in the Red Army, 1939–1945* (New York: Henry Holt, 2006); and David Brandenberger, *National Bolshevism: Stalinist Mass Culture and the Formation of the Modern Russian National Identity* (Cambridge: Harvard University Press, 2002).

12. On possible effects of propaganda on German army morale, see Edward Shils and Morris Janowitz, "Cohesion and Disintegration in the Wehrmacht in World War II," *Public Opinion Quarterly* 12 (1948): 280–315. Merridale, *Ivan's War*, 22, compares the German experience to that of the Soviet army.

13. Quotations from Japanese propaganda materials in Akira Iriye, *Cultural Internationalism and World Order* (Baltimore: Johns Hopkins University Press, 1997), 119–20, within his overall analysis at 119–35.

14. Masaya Duus, *Tokyo Rose: Orphan of the Pacific*, trans. Peter Duus (New York: Harper and Row for Kodansha International, 1983).

15. The fascinating history of cinema in Japan is traced in Donald Richie, *Japanese Cinema: An Introduction* (Hong Kong: Oxford University Press (China), 1990); and Joseph L. Anderson and Donald Richie, *The Japanese Film: Art and Industry* (Princeton: Princeton University Press, 1982), which includes a foreword by Akira Kurosawa.

16. The illustrated materials are reproduced in Barak Kushner, *The Thought War: Japanese Imperial Propaganda* (Honolulu: University of Hawaii Press, 2006), 124–27.

17. Japanese deficiencies in the propaganda war against China are discussed ibid., 117–55; for a more general discussion, see Philip M. Taylor, *Munitions of the Mind: A History of Propaganda from the Ancient World to the Present Day*, 3rd ed. (Manchester: Manchester University Press, 2003), 238–41. An extensive collection

of Japanese propaganda materials is Peter O'Connor, ed., *Japanese Propaganda: Selected Readings*, 10 vols. (Tokyo: Edition Synapse, 2003–4).

18. The racist elements in the U.S.–Japanese propaganda battle are analyzed in John W. Dower, *War without Mercy: Race and Power in the Pacific War* (New York: Pantheon Books, 1986).

19. Desmond, *Tides of War*, 181–90.

20. Churchill quoted in Alfred Havighurst, *Britain in Transition: The Twentieth Century*, 4th ed. (Chicago: University of Chicago Press, 1985), 298.

21. Churchill quoted in Asa Briggs, *A History of Broadcasting in the United Kingdom*, vol. 3, *The War of Words* (London: Oxford University Press, 1970), 4–5.

22. Quoted in Ian McLaine, *Ministry of Morale: Home Front Morale and the Ministry of Information in World War II* (London: George Allen and Unwin, 1979), 21.

23. Poster quotations and analysis from McLaine, *Ministry of Morale*, 21, 30, 54, 76, 183.

24. Priestley's radio broadcasts were transcribed in J. B. Priestley, *Postscripts* (London: W. Heinemann, 1941). For background see Sian Nicholas, *The Echo of War: Home Front Propaganda and the Wartime BBC, 1939–1945* (Manchester: Manchester University Press, 1996).

25. Quoted in Briggs, *War of Words*, 250.

26. Cartoon and caption reprinted in Briggs, *War of Words*, 254.

27. Angus Calder, *The People's War: Britain, 1939–45* (London: Jonathan Cape, 1969), 65–66, 360–62.

28. Quoted in Taylor, *Munitions of the Mind*, 221.

29. For overall discussion of British propaganda, see Taylor, *Munitions of the Mind*, 208–28; and for the general historical context see Havighurst, *Britain in Transition*, 288–366.

30. Nicholas J. Cull, David Culbert, and David Welch, *Propaganda and Mass Persuasion: A Historical Encyclopedia, 1500 to the Present* (Santa Barbara: ABC-Clio, 2003), 27, 60–61, 175.

31. Nicholas Cull, *Selling War: The British Propaganda Campaign against American "Neutrality" in World War II* (New York: Oxford University Press, 1995).

32. Quoted in Philip Seib, *Broadcasts from the Blitz: How Edward R. Murrow Helped Lead America into War* (Washington, D.C.: Potomac Books, 2006), 33.

33. Quotation from A. J. Liebling, "Notes from the Kidnap House," *New Yorker*, April 22, 1944, reprinted in *Reporting World War II*, pt. 2, *American Journalism, 1944–1946* (New York: Library of America, 1995), 89. Information on the Resistance from Liebling, "Notes," 80–89, and Olivier Wieviorka, "Between Propaganda and Telling the Truth: The Underground French Press during the Occupation (1940–1944)," in *France at War in the Twentieth Century: Propaganda, Myth and Metaphor*, ed. Valerie Holman and Debra Kelly (New York: Berghahn Books, 2000), 111–25.

34. Edwin Emery, *The Press and America: An Interpretative History of the Mass Media*, 3rd ed. (Englewood Cliffs, N.J.: Prentice Hall, 1972), 522–25.

35. John W. Dower, *Embracing Defeat: Japan in the Wake of World War II* (New York: W. W. Norton, 1999), 219–20.

36. Emery, *The Press and America*, 525– 527; John Morton Blum, *V Was for Victory: Politics and American Culture during World War II* (New York: Harcourt Brace Jovanovich, 1976), 21– 39.

37. On the famous photograph of Iwo Jima and its effects on the men it portrayed, see James Bradley and Ron Powers, *Flags of Our Fathers* (New York: Bantam, 2000). Richard Holmes, *World War II in Photographs* (London: Andrews McMeel Publishing, 2002); David Boyle, *World War II: A Photographic History* (New York: Metro Books, 2000); and Richard B. Stolley, ed., *LIFE: World War 2; History's Greatest Conflicts in Pictures* (New York: Bulfinch Press, 2001), are three of the hundreds of collections of Second World War photographs.

38. The Lucky Strike ad is reproduced in C. L. Sulzberger, *The American Heritage Picture History of World War II* (New York: McGraw Hill/American Heritage, 1966), 473.

39. S. J. Perelman, "Take Two Parts Sand, One Part Girl, and Stir," *New Yorker*, July 8, 1944, reprinted in *Reporting World War II*, pt. 2, 164–69.

40. Michael C. C. Adams, *The Best War Ever: America and World War II* (Baltimore: Johns Hopkins University Press, 1994), 17–18.

41. Harford Powel, "What the War Has Done to Advertising," *Public Opinion Quarterly* 6, no. 2 (Summer 1942): 195–203; Robert Griffith, "The Selling of America: The Advertising Council and American Politics, 1942–1960," *Business History Review* 57, no. 3 (Autumn 1983): 388–412.

42. See Colin Shindler, *Hollywood Goes to War: Films and American Society, 1939–1952* (London: Routledge and Kegan Paul, 1979); Clayton R. Koppes and Gregory D. Black, *Hollywood Goes to War: How Politics, Profits, and Propaganda Shaped World War II Movies* (New York: Free Press, 1987); Thomas P. Doherty, *Projections of War: Hollywood, American Culture, and World War II* (New York: Columbia University Press, 1993); and Larry Wayne Ward, *The Motion Picture Goes to War* (Ann Arbor: University of Michigan Press, 1985).

43. Taylor, *Munitions of the Mind*, 227.

44. Quoted in Taylor, *Munitions of the Mind*, 230. For background on the government's relationship to the film industry, see Clayton R. Koppes and Gregory Black, "What to Show the World: The Office of War Information and Hollywood, 1942–1945," *Journal of American History* 64, no. 1 (June 1977): 87–105.

45. Quoted in Doherty, *Projections of War*, 107.

46. Quoted in Taylor, *Munitions of the Mind*, 231.

47. James Agee, "So Proudly We Fail," in *Reporting World War II*, pt. 1, *American Journalism, 1938–1944* (New York: Library of America, 1995), 658–61.

48. Nicholas Reeves, *The Power of Film Propaganda: Myth or Reality?* (New York: Cassell, 1999); Shindler, *Hollywood Goes to War*, 23, 28, 31, 56, 67–70.

49. Daniel Todman, "'Sans peur et sans reproche': The Retirement, Death and Mourning of Sir Douglas Haig, 1918–1928, *Journal of Military History* 67, no. 4 (October 2003): 1083–1106.

50. The photo of Bacall and Truman is reproduced in Sulzberger, *American Heritage Picture History*, 474.

51. Phillip Knightley, *The First Casualty: From the Crimea to Vietnam; The War Correspondent as Hero, Propagandist, and Myth Maker* (New York: Harcourt Brace Jovanovich, 1975), 279–82, 298.

52. Stalin quotation from Merridale, *Ivan's War*, 96.

53. Kevin Starr, "Hollywood Canteen," in *Embattled Dreams: California in War and Peace, 1940–1950* (New York: Oxford University Press, 2002), 177.

54. Bradley and Powers, *Flags of Our Fathers;* George H. Roeder Jr., *The Censored War: American Visual Experience during World War Two* (New Haven: Yale University Press, 1993). The complaints of average soldiers about portrayals of their role are discussed in Paul Fussell, *Wartime: Understanding and Behavior in the Second World War* (New York: Oxford University Press, 1989).

55. Mauldin's cartoon is reprinted in Sulzberger, *American Heritage Picture History,* 433.

56. Knightley, *First Casualty,* 326–27.

57. Theodore H. White's experience is discussed briefly ibid., 277–78; and in greater detail in Peter Rand, *China Hands: The Adventures and Ordeals of the American Journalists Who Joined Forces with the Great Chinese Revolution* (New York: Simon & Schuster, 1995), 191–258. For self-censorship in print journalism generally, see the three-volume Library of America anthology *Reporting World War II: American Journalism, 1938–1946.*

58. E. B. White, "The Newspaper Reader Finds It Very Difficult to Get at the Truth," in *Reporting World War II,* pt. 1, 300–302.

59. Quotation and summary of Kennedy episode from Emery, *The Press and America,* 531.

60. Knightley, *First Casualty,* 326.

61. Quoted ibid., 328.

62. Quoted ibid., 300.

63. Information on the U.S. military's strategy for dissemination and control of information related to the bombings of Hiroshima and Nagasaki is in Richard Rhodes, *The Making of the Atomic Bomb* (New York: Simon & Schuster, 1986), 736–37. The reportage of Burchett and Laurence is discussed in Amy Goodman and David Goodman, "Hiroshima Cover-Up: How the War Department's Timesman Won a Pulitzer," August 10, 2004, www.commondreams.org; and in Knightley, *First Casualty,* 299–302. Portrayal of the bombings by the Japanese press and government is analyzed in Dower, *Embracing Defeat,* 414–19. Hersey's reportage is reprinted in John Hersey, *Hiroshima* (New York: Knopf, 1946). Allied censorship of reportage in Nagasaki is documented in George Weller, *First into Nagasaki: The Censored Eyewitness Dispatches on Post-Atomic Japan and Its Prisoners of War,* ed. Anthony Weller (New York: Crown Publishers, 2006). For an excellent analysis of the debate surrounding the decision to use the atomic bomb, see Ronald Takaki, *Hiroshima: Why America Dropped the Atomic Bomb* (New York: Little, Brown, 1995).

64. Deborah E. Lipstadt, *Beyond Belief: The American Press and the Coming of the Holocaust, 1933–1945* (New York: Free Press, 1986), esp. 1–10 and 240–78; Laurel Leff, *Buried by the Times: The Holocaust and America's Most Important Newspaper* (Cambridge: Cambridge University Press, 2005).

65. Quoted in Knightley, *First Casualty,* 329.

6. Symbolic War Takes Precedence

1. Robert W. Desmond, *Tides of War: World News Reporting, 1931–1945* (Iowa City: University of Iowa Press, 1984), 454–61.

2. Arch A. Mercey, "The U.N. Information Program: Some Recommendations of the Advisory Committee," *Public Opinion Quarterly* 12, no. 3 (Autumn

1948): 481–87; Benjamin Cohen, "The U.N.'s Department of Public Information," *Public Opinion Quarterly* 10, no. 2 (Summer 1946): 145–55.

3. Constitution of the United Nations Educational Scientific and Cultural Organization (1945), Preamble. The full constitution of UNESCO is reprinted in Walter H. C. Laves and Charles A. Thomson, *UNESCO: Purpose, Progress, Prospects* (Bloomington: Indiana University Press, 1957), 415–25. The organization's initial goals, as described by its first Director General, are in Julian Huxley, *UNESCO: Its Purpose and Its Philosophy* (Washington, D.C.: Public Affairs Press, 1947). An example of the sense of hope inspired by the creation of UNESCO is Charles A. Siepmann, "Propaganda and Information in International Affairs," *Yale Law Journal* 55, no. 5 (August 1946): 1258–80. For a critique, see "UNESCO's Program of Mass Communication: I," *Public Opinion Quarterly* 10, no. 4 (Winter 1946–47): 518–39. General surveys include Clare Wells, *The UN, UNESCO and the Politics of Knowledge* (London: Macmillan, 1987); and James Patrick Sewell, *UNESCO and World Politics: Engaging in International Relations* (Princeton: Princeton University Press, 1975). Reporting on the UN is discussed in Ronald Rubin, "The UN Correspondent," *Western Political Quarterly* 17, no. 4 (December 1964): 615–31.

4. Akira Iriye, *Cultural Internationalism and World Order* (Baltimore: Johns Hopkins University Press, 1997), 146–49, 157, 161, 172.

5. Philip M. Taylor, *Munitions of the Mind: A History of Propaganda from the Ancient World to the Present Day*, 3rd ed. (Manchester: Manchester University Press, 2003), 248. For the larger context of denazification, see Giles MacDonogh, *After the Reich: The Brutal History of the Allied Occupation* (New York: Perseus Books, 2007).

6. Anthony Smith, *The Newspaper: An International History* (London: Thames and Hudson, 1979), 172–73.

7. James Aronson, *The Press and the Cold War* (Indianapolis: Bobbs-Merrill, 1970), 32–38.

8. Truman quoted in Nicholas Cull, *The Cold War and the United States Information Agency: American Propaganda and Public Diplomacy, 1945–1989* (Cambridge: Cambridge University Press, 2008), 55. The aggressive approach to cold war propaganda during the Truman era is described in detail in Richard L. Brecker, "Truth as a Weapon of the Free World," *Annals of the American Academy of Political and Social Science*, vol. 278, *The Search for National Security* (November 1951): 1–11.

9. McCarthy quoted in Thomas Doherty, *Cold War, Cool Medium: Television, McCarthyism, and American Culture* (New York: Columbia University Press, 2003), 128.

10. Quotations in this paragraph from Doherty, *Cold War, Cool Medium*, 130–31.

11. Aronson, *The Press and the Cold War*, 21.

12. Truman quoted in Doherty, *Cold War, Cool Medium*, 171.

13. Extensive detail on Murrow's anti-McCarthy broadcasts is given in Doherty, *Cold War, Cool Medium*, 161–77.

14. Aronson, *The Press and the Cold War*, 127–52.

15. Paul M. A. Linebarger, "The Struggle for the Mind of Asia," *Annals of the American Academy of Political and Social Science*, vol. 278, 32–37; Francis F. Fuller,

"Mao Tse-tung: Military Thinker," *Military Affairs* 22, no. 3 (Autumn 1958): 139–45; Frederick T. C. Yu, *Mass Persuasion in Communist China* (New York: Frederick A. Prager, 1964).

16. A detailed analysis is Stephen Pease, *Psychological Warfare in Korea, 1950–1953* (Harrisburg, Penna.: Stackpole Books, 1992). A recent reinterpretation of the Korean War and the reporting that took place at the time is Bruce Cumings, *Korea's Place in the Sun: A Modern History* (New York: Norton, 1997). Reporting on Korea is discussed in Phillip Knightley, *The First Casualty: From the Crimea to Vietnam; The War Correspondent as Hero, Propagandist, and Myth Maker* (New York: Harcourt Brace Jovanovich, 1975), 336–55.

17. Richard H. Shultz and Roy Godson, *Dezinformatsia: The Strategy of Soviet Disinformation* (New York: Berkley Books, 1986), 118–19.

18. Aronson, *The Press and the Cold War*, 103–26.

19. For an example of criticism of the idea behind UNESCO, that wars originate in the minds of men and can be prevented there, see Frederick S. Dunn, *War and the Minds of Men* (New York: Harper & Brothers, 1950). An exploration of the same subject, voicing skepticism about broad attempts to influence large populations without regard to subcategories of their values, is Hans Speier, "International Political Communication: Elite vs. Mass," *World Politics* 4, no. 3 (April 1952): 305–17.

20. A description of cold war fears of brainwashing and the resemblance to Western psychology is Albert D. Biderman, "The Image of 'Brainwashing,'" *Public Opinion Quarterly* 26, no. 4 (Winter 1962): 547–63.

21. For Eisenhower's use of the media, see Kenneth Osgood, *Total Cold War: Eisenhower's Secret Propaganda Battle at Home and Abroad* (Kansas City: University Press of Kansas, 2006). A more general study spanning several presidencies is Leo Bogart, *Premises for Propaganda: The United States Information Agency's Operating Assumptions in the Cold War* (New York: Free Press, 1976). On the eccentric leadership of Charles Wick, President Reagan's USIA director, see Alvin A. Snyder, *Warriors of Disinformation: American Propaganda, Soviet Lies, and the Winning of the Cold War; An Insider's Account* (New York: Arcade Publishing, 1995).

22. See Victoria de Grazia, *Irresistible Empire: America's Advance through Twentieth-Century Europe* (Cambridge: Harvard University Press, 2005); and Andrew Yarrow, "Selling a New Vision of America to the World: Changing Messages in Early Cold War Propaganda," *Journal of Cold War Studies* 11, no. 4 (Fall 2009): 1–45.

23. Operations of the CIA, with particular reference to propaganda, are described in detail in John Prados, *Safe for Democracy: The Secret Wars of the CIA* (Chicago: Ivan R. Dee, 2006). Information regarding Hank Ketchum is from Marsha Kinder, ed., *Kids' Media Culture* (Durham: Duke University Press, 1999), 33–34.

24. Shultz and Godson, *Deszinformatsia*, 148–52.

25. Four excellent analyses of cold war cinema, all by Tony Shaw, are *British Cinema and the Cold War* (London: I. B. Tauris, 2001); *Hollywood's Cold War* (Amherst: University of Massachusetts Press, 2007); "Martyrs, Miracles, and Martians: Religion and Cold War Cinematic Propaganda in the 1950s," *Journal of Cold War Studies* 4, no. 2 (Spring 2002): 3–22; and, for broader context, "The Politics of Cold War Culture," *Journal of Cold War Studies* 3, no. 3 (Fall 2001): 59–76.

26. Isaiah Berlin, "Shostakovich at Oxford," *New York Review of Books*, July 16, 2009, 22.

27. Quotations from Edmund Wilson, "Doctor Life and His Guardian Angel," in *The Bit between My Teeth: A Literary Chronicle of 1950–1965* (New York: Noonday Press/Farrar, Straus and Giroux, 1967), 420–46.

28. An informative summary is David Caute, *The Dancer Defects: The Struggle for Cultural Supremacy during the Cold War* (New York: Oxford University Press, 2003).

29. Aronson, *The Press and the Cold War*, 153–69.

30. For the most authoritative account of Murrow and the Bay of Pigs disaster, see Cull, *Cold War and the United States Information Agency*, 190–91.

31. Aronson, *The Press and the Cold War*, 170–79.

32. Cull, *Cold War and the United States Information Agency*, 229–32.

33. See Margaret MacMillan, *Nixon and Mao: The Week That Changed the World* (New York: Random House, 2007).

34. See Deepti Hajela, "Media Had Wide Access in Vietnam War," Associated Press, June 27, 2006, reporting on an international reunion of war correspondents who were in Vietnam during the period from 1950 to 1975; Daniel C. Hallin, *The Uncensored War: The Media and Vietnam* (New York: Oxford University Press, 1986).

35. On JUSPAO, see Cull, *Cold War and the United States Information Agency*, 245–54, 267–78.

36. Michael J. Arlen, *Living Room War* (New York: Viking, 1966). On print journalism in the Vietnam War, see John Swain, *Rivers of Time* (New York: St. Martin's, 1989); Sandra Wittman, *Writing about Vietnam: A Bibliography of the Literature of the Vietnam Conflict* (Boston: G. K. Hall, 1989); and the excellent Library of America anthology compiled by Milton J. Bates and others, *Reporting Vietnam: American Journalism, 1959–1975* (New York: Library of America, 1998). For analysis of portrayals of the war, see William Hammond, *Reporting Vietnam: Media and Military at War* (Lawrence: University Press of Kansas, 1999). The Second World War could actually be called the world's first "living room war" because of the intimate use of radio by Roosevelt, Churchill, and commentators like Edward R. Murrow and J. B. Priestley; but television was a more influential presence because it combined sound and images.

37. For an eloquent, informative account of contesting media portrayals in the civil rights movement, see Gene Roberts and Hank Klibanoff, *The Race Beat: The Press, the Civil Rights Struggle, and the Awakening of a Nation* (New York: Alfred Knopf, 2006).

38. Todd Gitlin, *The Whole World Is Watching: Mass Media in the Making and Unmaking of the New Left* (Berkeley: University of California Press, 1980); Mark Kurlansky, *1968: The Year that Rocked the World* (New York: Ballantine Books, 2004).

39. Aronson, *The Press and the Cold War*, 21.

40. For a detailed analysis of the "Vietnam effect," see Philip M. Taylor, *Global Communications, International Affairs and the Media since 1945* (London: Routledge, 1997), 108–15.

41. Senator J. William Fulbright, *The Pentagon Propaganda Machine* (New York: Liveright Publishing Corporation, 1970).

42. Analyses of films about Vietnam include Linda Dittmar and Gene Michaud, eds., *From Hanoi to Hollywood: The Vietnam War in American Film* (New Brunswick: Rutgers University Press, 1990); Gilbert Adair, *Vietnam on Film: From "The Green Berets" to "Apocalypse Now"* (New York: Proteus Publishing Company, 1981); Christian G. Appy, *Working Class War* (Chapel Hill: University of North Carolina Press, 1993); Lawrence H. Suid, *Guts and Glory: The Making of the American Military Image in Film* (Louisville: University of Kentucky Press, 2002). See also Jonathan Schell, *The Real War: The Classic Reporting on the Vietnam War* (New York: Pantheon Books, 1968).

43. Marshall McLuhan and Quentin Fiore, *War and Peace and the Global Village* (New York: Bantam Books, 1968), 12, 98,132 .

44. Chomsky's writings are numerous and extensive. In the absence of any central text, three useful sources of additional information are James Peck, ed., *The Chomsky Reader* (New York: Pantheon, 1987); Noam Chomsky, *Manufacturing Consent: The Political Economy of the Mass Media* (New York: Pantheon, 1988); and Anthony Arnove, ed., *The Essential Chomsky* (New York: New Press, 2008).

45. Cull, *Cold War and the United States Information Agency*, 351–58.

46. Ibid., 381.

47. Robert Harris, *Gotcha! The Media, the Government, and the Falklands Crisis* (London: Faber and Faber, 1983).

48. Reagan and *Time* magazine quotations from Lou Cannon, *President Reagan: The Role of a Lifetime* (New York: Simon & Schuster, 1991), 655.

49. The centrality of image management in Reagan's approach to leadership, as well as the traits that made him a gifted politician, are explored in detail and with great intelligence in Cannon, *President Reagan*, esp. 458–92 and 137–39.

50. Melvyn P. Leffler, *For the Soul of Mankind: The United States, the Soviet Union, and the Cold War* (New York: Hill and Wang, 2007), 461.

51. On the Berlin airlift, see Andrei Cherny, *The Candy Bombers: The Untold Story of the Berlin Airlift and America's Finest Hour* (New York: Berkley Caliber, 2008).

52. On the Berlin Wall and the larger context of the Iron Curtain, see Ann Tusa, *The Last Division: A History of Berlin, 1945–1989* (Reading, Mass.: Addison-Wesley, 1997); and Frederick Taylor, *The Berlin Wall: A World Divided, 1961–1989* (New York: HarperCollins, 2006).

53. Tusa, *Last Division*, 63.

54. Margaret Thatcher, *The Downing Street Years* (London: Harper Collins, 1993), 459–63.

55. Imagery related to the atom bomb is discussed in Allan M. Winkler, *Life under A Cloud: American Anxiety about the Atom* (New York: Oxford University Press, 1993); and Spencer R. Weart, *Nuclear Fear: A History* (Cambridge: Harvard University Press, 1988).

56. Tusa, *Last Division*, 62.

57. On the dispersal of communications technologies to the developing world, see Taylor, *Global Communications, International Affairs and the Media*, esp. 27–57.

58. On the technological development of mass communication, see Daya Kishan Thussu, *International Communication: Continuity and Change* (London: Arnold/Hodder Headline Group, 2000). On China's increased sophistication in the use of

mass communication, see Joshua Kurlantzick, *Charm Offensive: How China's Soft Power Is Transforming the World* (New Haven: Yale University Press, 2007).

7. Mass Communication Becomes Multipolar

1. See Philip M. Taylor, *War and the Media: Propaganda and Persuasion in the Gulf War* (Manchester: Manchester University Press, 1992).

2. On the "CNN effect," see Philip M. Taylor, *Global Communications, International Affairs and the Media since 1945* (London: Routledge, 1997), esp. 83–98. For a general survey of the influence of the media on decision making, emphasizing print, see Ernest R. May, "The News Media and Diplomacy," in *The Diplomats, 1939–1979*, ed. Gordon A. Craig and Francis Loewenheim (Princeton: Princeton University Press, 1994), 665–700.

3. Warren P. Strobel, "The Media: Influencing Foreign Policy in the Information Age," *U.S. Foreign Policy Agenda* 5, no. 1 (March 2000): 37–39.

4. Michael Ignatieff, *Virtual War: Kosovo and Beyond* (New York: Picador, 2001).

5. Taylor, *Global Communications*, 188–92, 200, and 226–28.

6. On the rise and decline of the USIA, see Nicholas Cull, *The Cold War and the United States Information Agency: American Propaganda and Public Diplomacy, 1945–1989* (Cambridge: Cambridge University Press, 2008).

7. R. L. DiNardo and Daniel J. Hughes, "Some Cautionary Thoughts on Information Warfare," *Airpower Journal* (Winter 1995), www.airpower.maxwell.af .mil/airchronicles/apj/apj95/win95.htm; Col. John B. Alexander, *Future War: Nonlethal Weapons in Twenty-first-Century Warfare* (New York: Thomas Dunne Books/ St. Martin's Griffin, 2000).

8. The same themes were explored in Alvin and Heidi Toffler, *War and Anti-War: Survival at the Dawn of the 21st Century* (London: Little Brown, 1993).

9. For the most developed treatment, see Joseph S. Nye Jr., *Soft Power: The Means to Success in World Politics* (New York: Public Affairs Press, 2004). On the growing interest in "soft power" at the Pentagon, see Jim Mannon, "Led by the Military, War-Weary U.S. Awakens to 'Soft Power,'" Agence France Presse, December 13, 2007.

10. On the gradual dispersion of Western-dominated technologies of mass communication to the developing world, see Daya Kishan Thussu, *International Communication: Continuity and Change* (New York: Oxford University Press, 2000); and Jane Chapman, *Comparative Media History: An Introduction, 1789 to the Present* (Cambridge: Polity Press, 2005).

11. Rice and Rumsfeld quotations from John. B. Judis and Spencer Ackerman, "The Selling of the Iraq War: The First Casualty," *New Republic*, June 30, 2003, 14–25.

12. Powell quoted in Judis and Ackerman, "Selling of the Iraq War."

13. Informative accounts of the selling of the Iraq war are Michael Isikoff and David Corn, *Hubris: The Inside Story of Spin, Scandal, and the Selling of the Iraq War* (New York: Crown, 2006); and Laura Mille, "War Is Sell," *PR Watch* 9, no. 4, Center for Media and Democracy, www.prwatch.org/prissues/2002Q4/war.html.

14. Quoted in Jeff Gerth, "Military's Information War Is Vast and Often Secretive," *New York Times*, September 11, 2005.

15. See Jack G. Shaheen, *Reel Bad Arabs: How Hollywood Vilifies a People* (New York: Olive Branch Press, 2001).

16. See Frank Rich, "Don't Follow the Money," *New York Times*, June 12, 2005, a comparison of journalistic behavior in the time of Watergate and the early years of President George W. Bush; and Eric Boehlert, *Lapdogs: How the Press Rolled Over for Bush* (New York: Free Press, 2006).

17. On the belief that America won the Second World War by itself and the tendency of such a belief to cloud thinking about 9/11, see Nigel Hamilton, "We Were Allies Once: Lessons of D Day, 1944," *New England Journal of Public Policy* 19, no. 2 (Winter 2005): 57–70. Nostalgic views of the war are dissected in Michael C. C. Adams, *The Best War Ever: America and World War II* (Baltimore: Johns Hopkins University Press, 1994).

18. John Lippman, "The Politics of Oscar," *Wall Street Journal*, July 23, 2004.

19. Hendrik Hertzberg, "Floor War," *New Yorker*, December 5, 2005, 35–36; Frank Rich, "Dishonest, Reprehensible, Corrupt . . . ," *New York Times*, November 27, 2005.

20. Marcel Honore, "TV Station Backed by Chávez Goes on Air," Associated Press, October 31, 2005; Vanessa Arrington, "Countering U.S. Move, Cuba Mounts Attack via Billboard," Associated Press, December 18, 2004.

21. Robert Barr, "Report: Bush Talked of Bombing Al-Jazeera," Associated Press, December 22, 2005. Whether Bush actually made such statements was not confirmed, but evidence was available that the White House strongly pressured Qatar to discontinue allowing Al-Jazeera to operate out of that country. See Steven R. Weisman, "Under Pressure, Qatar May Sell Jazeera Station," *New York Times*, January 30, 2005.

22. Fareed Zakaria, "An Imperial Presidency: Bush's Travel Schedule Seems to Involve as Little Contact as Possible with the Country He Is In," *Newsweek*, December 19, 2005, msnbc.com.

23. Frank Rich, "It Takes a Potemkin Village," *New York Times*, December 11, 2005.

24. For a detailed analysis of U.S. recruitment strategies, see Timothy L. O'Brien, "Madison Avenue Wants You: How to Pitch the Military When a War Drags On?" *New York Times*, September 25, 2005.

25. Susan B. Glasser and Michael Grunwald, "DHS Undermined from Very Start," *Washington Post*, December 22, 2005.

26. Timothy L. O'Brien, "Spinning Frenzy: PR's Bad Press; A TV Host's Paid Pitch Is Roiling an Industry," *New York Times*, February 13, 2005.

27. Eleanor Clift, "Big Lies: Who Told the Worst Political Untruths of 2005?" December 22, 2005, msnbc.msn.com/id/10578257; Arlene Getz, "Where's the Outrage? Bush's Defense of his Phone-Spying Program Has Disturbing Echoes of Arguments Once Used by South Africa's Apartheid Regime," December 21, 2005, msnbc.msn.com/id/10562528.

28. Matea Gold, "Ex-Chair of Public Television Quits," *Los Angeles Times*, November 4, 2005.

29. Dana Priest, "CIA Holds Terror Suspects in Secret Prisons," *Washington Post*, November 2, 2005. Also see the related editorial and an article by Richard

Bernstein, "Skepticism Seems to Erode Europeans' Faith in Rice," *New York Times*, December 7, 2005.

30. Gerth, "Military's Information War Is Vast"; James Bamford, "The Man Who Sold the War," *Rolling Stone*, December 1, 2005, 53–62.

31. Stephen J. Hedges, "Media Use Backfires on U.S.," *Chicago Tribune*, December 11, 2005.

32. Quoted in Gerth, "Military's Information War Is Vast."

33. Gerth, "Military's Information War is Vast."

34. Matalin quoted in Gerth, "Military's Information War Is Vast."

35. Gerth, "Military's Information War Is Vast."

36. Eileen M. O'Connor and David Hoffman, "Made in Iraq: The Fallacy of Psy-Ops," *International Herald Tribune*, December 16, 2005.

37. Hedges, "Media Use Backfires on U.S."; Mark Mazzetti and Borzou Daragahi, "U.S. Military Covertly Pays to Run Stories in Iraqi Press," *Los Angeles Times*, November 30, 2005; Jeff Gerth and Scott Shane, "U.S. Is Said to Pay to Plant Articles in Iraq Papers," *New York Times*, December 1, 2005. For a defense of the practice of placing articles, written by a member of the U.S. military who was involved, see John R. Guardiano, "Reporting for Duty: The U.S. Military Tells Iraqis the Truth, and Some Call It a 'Scandal,'" *Wall Street Journal*, December 19, 2005.

38. Rumsfeld quoted in "Reporter Planted GI's Question for Rumsfeld," *CNN*, December 9, 2004.

39. Benedict Carey, "The Struggle to Gauge a War's Psychological Costs," *New York Times*, November 26, 2005. Recent research on the role of psychology in propaganda, interrogation, and torture is summarized in Drake Bennett, "The War in the Mind," *Boston Globe*, November 27, 2005. The medical consequences of images of war are discussed in Barry S. Levy and Victor W. Sidel, eds., *War and Public Health* (Washington, D.C.: American Public Health Association, 2000), esp. 168–85 and 323–35. For the Virtual Reality Medical Center in San Diego, see Carlos Bergfield, "War Vets Get a Dose of Virtual Reality," *Business Week*, July 26, 2006. Also very informative is Claire Hilton, "Media Triggers of Post-traumatic Stress Disorders 50 Years after the Second World War," *International Journal of Geriatric Psychiatry*, August 12, 1997, 862–67, and the comment in the issue of January 13, 1998, 64–65.

40. Douglas Jehl, "Spy Agencies Told to Bolster 'The Growth of Democracy,'" *New York Times*, October 27, 2005.

41. An example of one of the shadowy terrorist groups that focused on information warfare rather than physical aspects of war and terrorism was Hizb ut-Tahrir (the Party of Liberation), which used the Internet to disseminate radical concepts and literature. See Zeyno Baran, "Fighting the War of Ideas," *Foreign Affairs* (November–December 2005), 68–78. On use of the Internet by other al-Qaeda supporters, and attempts by the Saudi government to use the Internet and television programs to counter terrorist propaganda, see Hassan M. Fattah, "Good Jihad, Bad Jihad: Struggle for Arab Minds," *New York Times*, October 27, 2005; and Heba Kandil, "Arab TV Dramas Kindle Debate on Roots of Militancy," *Reuters*, November 2, 2005. For related discussions, see Steven R. Hurst, "Iraq Insurgents

Hit Back on the Net: Set Bounties on Top Leaders," Associated Press, September 13, 2005; Heather Robinson, "Insurgents Waging Media War," *Philadelphia Inquirer,* November 10, 2005; Scott Johnson, "How the U.S. Is Losing the PR War in Iraq," *Newsweek,* January 15, 2007; "The World through Their Eyes," *The Economist,* February 26, 2005, 23–25; "The Arab Media War," January 2, 2005, *New York Times Magazine,* 26–54; and Hugh Miles, *Al Jazeera: The Inside Story of the Arab News Channel That Is Challenging the West* (New York: Grove Press, 2005).

42. There were many echoes of the Abu Ghraib scandal. For example, in November 2005, a month before the Iraqi elections of December 15, there were media disclosures of a torture bunker in Baghdad being operated by the majority Shiites, who were cooperating with the United States in organizing the elections. See "Torture, Phosphorus Disclosures Hurt U.S.-Iraqi Image," Reuters, November 17, 2005. On Rumsfeld's secret offers of resignation, see "Defense Secretary Laments Abu Ghraib in Farewell," Associated Press, December 8, 2006.

43. For an informative discussion of the history and ethics of "leaking" by a veteran American reporter, see Max Frankel, "The Washington Back Channel," *New York Times Magazine,* March 25, 2007, 40–80.

44. By 2004, the Guantanamo prison was the subject of a hit play in London, and another play was in the works there accusing Secretary Rumsfeld of a cavalier attitude toward the suffering caused by the Iraq war. See John Daniszewski, "Stories of Guantanamo Detainees Brought to British Stage," *Los Angeles Times,* July 23, 2004.

45. Ana Marie Cox, "The YouTube War," *Time,* July 19, 2006. Use of the Internet tool Facebook as a means of fomenting revolution in Colombia and other Latin American countries was being studied by B. J. Fogg, director of the Persuasive Technology Lab at Stanford University. He asserts: "Mass inter-personal persuasion makes it possible for us to change the world in the next thirty years. . . . Social networking sites allow people to use inter-personal persuasions on their social groups. . . . It allows normal people to have a huge global impact." Brian Andrew, "Researcher Says Peace Possible through Facebook," *Stanford Daily,* February 7, 2008.

46. Bill Press, "We're Losing the Spin War," Chicago Tribune Media Services, January 18, 2002, www.cnn.com; Nancy Snow, *Information War: American Propaganda, Free Speech, and Opinion Control since 9/11* (New York: Seven Stories Press, 2003), 84–93.

47. Budget figures are in O'Connor and Hoffman, "Made in Iraq."

48. Gerth, "Military's Information War Is Vast."

49. "State Department to Audit Mideast TV Service," November 4, 2005, Associated Press; Guy Dinmore, "Troubled TV Network Draws Fire," *Financial Times,* November 7, 2005.

50. William J. Holstein, "Armchair M.B.A.: Erasing the Image of the Ugly American," *New York Times,* October 23, 2005; Bernd Debusmann, "Anti-Americanism Prompts Push for 'Citizen Diplomacy,'" *Reuters,* July 26, 2006. Activities of Business for Diplomatic Action are described in Brian Knowlton, "Letter from Washington: Combating the Image of the Ugly American," *International Herald Tribune,* August 17, 2006. The role of long-term cultural diplomacy in protecting America's overseas markets is noted in Alan Riding, "Rerun Our Cold War Cultural Diplomacy,"

October 27, 2005, *New York Times*. Also see Bronwen Maddox, "It Won't Suddenly Be Peace and Love When Bush Goes," *Times Online*, September 28, 2006, claiming that the reputation of President George W. Bush was, after six years in office, "toxic beyond repair in Europe."

51. David Barstow, "Courting Ex-Officers Tied to Military Contractors," *New York Times*, April 20, 2008; Michael D. Shear, "McClellan: Bush Misled U.S. on Iraq," *Washington Post*, May 28, 2008; Elisabeth Bumiller, "In Ex-Spokesman's Book, Harsh Words for Bush," *New York Times*, May 28, 2008.

52. For a summary of the two candidates' proposals for use of mass communication in foreign policy, see Amy Zalman, "Improving America's Reputation— McCain Would Lecture, Obama Would Listen," *Huffington Post*, December 5, 2008.

53. Michael Hirsh, "Washington: A Dysfunctional Democracy," *Newsweek*, January 25, 2007. For a dismissal of the importance of anti-American sentiment, see John Gibson, *Hating America: The New World Sport* (New York: Regan Books/ Harper Collins Publishers, 2004). Recommendations for conducting U.S. foreign policy without extensively consulting other countries are offered in David Frum and Richard Perle, *An End to Evil: How to Win the War on Terror* (New York: Random House, 2003); and Steven Rosefielde and D. Quinn Mills, *Masters of Illusion: American Leadership in the Media Age* (Cambridge: Cambridge University Press, 2007).

54. Howard LaFranchi, "Diplomacy Thriving, but without U.S.," *Christian Science Monitor*, June 3, 2008.

55. "Anti-Americanism: The View from Abroad," *The Economist*, February 19, 2005, 24–26.

56. David Brooks, "The Age of Skepticism," *New York Times*, December 1, 2005; Howard Gardner, "The Loss of Trust," *Boston Globe*, June 18, 2005. See also Bruce Morton, "A Strange Debate: Is America Really Arguing about Torture?" CNN News, www.cnn.com, November 15, 2005; and Fareed Zakaria, "Questions for the Interrogators," *Newsweek*, September 25, 2006, quoting Colin Powell's observation that the "moral posture" of the United States in the world was declining because of its lack of respect for the Geneva Conventions.

57. For example, see "Reservists Add Media Relations to Regimen," *Boston Globe*, December 27, 2005. In 2006 the Pentagon also expanded its public relations staff to include more Internet capacity and more coordinated efforts to reply to news stories quickly; see "Pentagon Ramping Up Public Relations Offensive," Associated Press, October 30, 2006.

58. Severe shortages of Arab-language capabilities at the Pentagon and the CIA are discussed in "Know Thine Enemy," *The Economist*, May 7, 2005. Programs funded by the Saudi Arabian government to increase English language competency among Saudi citizens are described in Joel Brinkley, "Scholarships Send Saudis to the U.S. as Students," *New York Times*, December 18, 2005. According to the article, the number of Saudis visiting the United States fell from 46,636 in 2001 to about 12,000 in 2005. For Pentagon and U.S. intelligence agency attempts to compensate for the shortage of language competency by developing machinery to translate spoken Arabic into written English, see Sheri Qualters, "BBN Technologies Gears Up for Largest Project to Date," *Boston Business Journal*, August

19–25, 2005. Also see Richard Pells, "Lost in Translation," *Chronicle of Higher Education*, October 14, 2005.

59. Pells, "Lost in Translation." On the potential for partnerships between the government and private-sector cultural organizations, see Riding, "Rerun Our Cold War Diplomacy." Riding emphasizes: "entrenched anti-Americanism will take years of persuasion—and, in some cases, policy changes by Washington—to be reversed." On the continuing importance of academic exchange programs, see H. D. S. Greenway, "An Education for Peace and Understanding," *Boston Globe*, June 6, 2008.

60. Keith Spicer, "Propaganda for Peace," *New York Times*, December 10, 1994, discusses ways that journalists might partner with the United Nations to promote peace. A call for greater awareness of ethical responsibility on the part of both the press and the government is Michael Socolow, "At War: Government and the Media," *Boston Globe*, December 13, 2005.

61. A description of changing attitudes toward journalistic objectivity is "The New Age of 'News,'" *Chicago Tribune*, February 26, 2005. See also Justin Lewis, Rod Brookes, Nick Mosdell, and Terry Threadgold, *Shoot First and Ask Questions Later: Media Coverage of the 2003 Iraq War* (New York: Peter Lang Publishing USA, 2005). A thoughtful analysis of press coverage of the Iraq war is Ian Fisher, "Reporting, and Surviving, Iraq's Dangers," *New York Times*, July 18, 2004. An excellent PBS symposium on journalistic ethics, titled *War Stories*, was televised in 2008 as part of a series on ethics in American life sponsored by the Fred W. Friendly Seminars at Columbia University Graduate School of Journalism. Participants were from ABC and CNN, the U.S. Senate, the Pentagon, the Washington, D.C., legal community, the *Washington Post*, and *Foreign Affairs* magazine. The discussion focused on issues such as whether to broadcast videotape of an atrocity and whether to prosecute those who leak classified information, and described nonconfrontational ways of sharing and disseminating news.

62. An example of excellence in dialogue between academia and the press is Stephen Klaidman and Tom L. Beauchamp, *The Virtuous Journalist* (New York: Oxford University Press, 1987). The difficulties that arise in dialogue between academia and the press are discussed in Rick Pearlstein, "If Journalists Listened to Media Scholars," *University of Chicago Magazine*, August 2004, 34–37.

63. Nancy Snow, *Propaganda, Inc.*, 2nd ed. (New York: Seven Stories Press, 2002), 37–38.

64. Bill Kovarik, "Journalism and Peace," www.radford.edu/wkovarik/peace .html. The article includes many valuable references. See also Monroe Price and Mark Thompson, eds., *Forging Peace: Intervention, Human Rights, and the Management of Media Space* (Bloomington: University of Indiana Press, 2002); and Gadi Wolfsfeld, *Media and the Path to Peace* (Cambridge: Cambridge University Press, 2004).

65. Elise Labott, "Google Earth Maps Out Darfur Atrocities," CNN.com, April 11, 2007.

66. Clive Thompson, "Saving the World, One Video Game at a Time," *New York Times*, July 23, 2006; "Video Game Designers Try to Help Save the World," Reuters, June 28, 2006; Allan Madrid, "Gaming the Poor," *Newsweek*, July 12, 2006; Hiawatha Bray, "Game On: Political Activism with a Flick of the Joystick," *Boston*

Globe, May 6, 2006; "Students Fight for Mideast Peace in Video Game," Associated Press, April 25, 2006; Ian MacKinnon, "Real-World Conflict Is a Moral Challenge for Gamers," *The Times*, October 24, 2006.

67. Joanna Chung, "'Social Bond' Will Benefit Emerging Free Press," *Financial Times*, May 3, 2006, www.ft.com.

68. Neil Katz and John W. Lawyer, "Communication and Conflict-Management Skills," in *A Peace Reader: Essential Readings on War, Justice, Non-violence and World Order*, ed. Joseph J. Fahey and Richard Armstrong (New York: Paulist Press, 1992), 258–66.

69. James Surowiecki, *The Wisdom of Crowds* (New York: Anchor Books/Random House, 2005). For examples of pioneering research, see Edward Shils and Morris Janowitz, "Cohesion and Disintegration in the Wehrmacht in World War II," *Public Opinion Quarterly* 12, no. 2 (Summer 1948): 280–315; Catherine Merridale, *Ivan's War: Life and Death in the Red Army, 1939–1945* (New York: Henry Holt, 2006); Nicholas Reeves, *Official British Film Propaganda during the First World War* (London: Croom Helm, 1986), and *The Power of Film Propaganda: Myth or Reality?* (London: Cassell, 1999). Pessimistic analyses of crowd behavior are given in Patrick Brantlinger, *Bread and Circuses: Theories of Mass Culture as Social Decay* (Ithaca: Cornell University Press, 1983); and Serge Moscovici, *The Age of the Crowd: A Historical Treatise on Mass Psychology*, trans. J. C. Whitehouse (Cambridge: Cambridge University Press, 1985). The importance of seeing receivers of messages as members of groups, not as isolated beings, was emphasized in a famous 1940 study, Paul F. Lazarsfeld, Bernard Berelson, and Hazel Gaudet, *The People's Choice: How the Voter Makes Up His Mind in a Presidential Campaign* (New York: Duell, Sloan and Pearce, 1944); and the elaboration of this "limited effects" model is discussed in Elihu Katz and Paul F. Lazarsfeld, *Personal Influence* (Glencoe, Ill.: Free Press, 1955). If access to primary, face-to-face groups is a bulwark against media manipulation, then one danger signal of loss of freedom is politicization of nonpolitical groups. Takeover of local, primary groups is one of the major themes of Richard J. Evans, *The Coming of the Third Reich* (New York: Penguin Books, 2003); and Richard J. Evans, *The Third Reich in Power: 1933–1939* (New York: Penguin Books, 2006). For a summary of social research on the influence of media, see Jennings Bryant and Susan Thompson, *Fundamentals of Media Effects* (New York: McGraw Hill, 2002).

70. Examples of analyses of strategies for eradicating hate speech include John B. Whitton and Arthur Larson, *Propaganda: Towards Disarmament in the War of Words* (Dobbs Ferry, N.Y.: Oceana Publications, 1963), published for the World Rule of Law Center, Duke University; and David Goldberg, "Transnational Communication and Defamatory Speech: A Case for Establishing Norms for the Twenty-first Century," *New York Law School Review* 50 (2005–6): 145–67. On organized efforts to eradicate hate speech and hate-inducing images from the Internet, see Christopher Wolf, "Online, the Shadow of Auschwitz," *International Herald Tribune*, October 25, 2006.

71. Salah Naswrawi, "Leaders Vow to Fight Extremist Ideology," Associated Press, December 8, 2005.

72. Elise Labott, "Saudi Arabia Promises to Revise Textbooks," CNN on-line, July 20, 2006.

73. Dina Temple-Raston, "Journalism and Genocide," *Columbia Journalism Review* 41, no. 3 (September–October 2002): 18–20. More recent efforts to use the media to promote reconciliation in Rwanda are described in Franziska von Scheven, "On Rwanda Radio Soap Opera, a Path to Healing," *International Herald Tribune*, January 8, 2008.

74. On problems of definition, see Allan A. Ryan Jr., "Genocide: What Do We Want It to Be?" *New England Journal of Public Policy* 19, no. 2 (Winter 2005): 111–30.

75. Caroline Elkins, *Imperial Reckoning: The Untold Story of Britain's Gulag in Kenya* (New York: Henry Holt, 2005); George Weller, *First into Nagasaki: The Censored Eyewitness Dispatches on Post-Atomic Japan and Its Prisoners of War*, ed. Anthony Weller (New York: Crown Publishers, 2006), 47–128 and 175–240; A. C. Grayling, *Among the Dead Cities: The History and Moral Legacy of the WWII Bombing of Civilians in Germany and Japan* (New York: Walker and Company, 2006).

76. Jan T. Gross, *Fear: Anti-Semitism in Poland after Auschwitz, an Essay in Historical Interpretation* (New York: Random House, 2006).

77. Samantha Power, *"A Problem from Hell": America and the Age of Genocide* (New York: Basic Books, 2002).

78. Helene Cooper, "Darfur Collides with Olympics, and China Yields," *New York Times*, April 13, 2007.

79. "Uncle Sam Wants Hollywood," CNN, November 9, 2001, www.cnn.com; "Hollywood Considers Role in War Effort," CNN, November 12, 2001, www.cnn .com. On a Hollywood attempt at cinematic interpretation of 9/11, see "Oliver Stone Shoots 9/11 Movie in N.Y.," Associated Press, November 3, 2005. An interesting example of attempts by independent filmmakers to address 9/11 and later events is Harbour Fraser Hodder, "Cinema Veritas," *Harvard Magazine* (November–December 2005), 35–43 and 102–3, which discusses films made by Harvard University students, faculty members, and graduates. A look at one independent film, in this case a left-wing film intended to counter the conservative influence of Fox News, is Robert S. Boynton, "How to Make a Guerrilla Documentary," *New York Times Magazine*, July 11, 2004, 20–23.

80. Gwladys Fouché, "Journalists Eligible for Nobel Peace Prize," MediaGuardian, October 6, 2006, www.guardian.co.uk/media.

Index

GARY MESSINGER grew up in Berkeley, California. He received a B.A. in history from Stanford University in 1965 and a Ph.D. in British history from Harvard University in 1971. He is the author of *Manchester in the Victorian Age* (1985) and *British Propaganda and the State in the First World War* (1992). For his book on Manchester he was awarded the Portico Prize, a major literary honor conferred in England for distinguished writing on local history and culture.

Messinger began his career in Washington, D.C., where he was the Congressional Relations Officer for the President's Advisory Council on Historic Preservation and a program officer at the National Endowment for the Humanities. He later served in academic administration at the University of Chicago and Boston College. He is now a member of the administrative staff at the University of Massachusetts Boston. Messinger and his wife, Cleo, live in Waltham, Massachusetts. Their son, Eric, is a graduate of Stanford and a journalist.